LINCOLN'S
ABOLITIONIST
GENERAL

LINCOLN'S ABOLITIONIST GENERAL

The Biography of David Hunter

Edward A. Miller, Jr.

University of South Carolina Press

Copyright © 1997 University of South Carolina

Published in Columbia, South Carolina, by the
University of South Carolina Press

Manufactured in the United States of America

01 00 99 98 97   5 4 3 2 1

Library of Congress Cataloging-in-Publication Data

Miller, Edward A., 1927–
    Lincoln's abolitionist general : the biography of David Hunter/
  Edward A. Miller Jr.
      p.   cm.
    Includes bibliographical references and index.
    ISBN 1–57003–110–X
    1. Hunter, David, 1802-1886. 2. Generals—United States—
  Biography. 3. United States. Army—Biography. 4. Abolitionists—
  United States—Biography. I. Title
  E467.1.H9M54 1997
  973.5'092—dc20
  [B]   95–50217

CONTENTS

PREFACE

When I entered the corps of cadets at the Virginia Military Institute it was considered necessary for Yankee freshmen to understand more of the history of the Confederacy and VMI's place in it than they were likely to know. Part of this knowledge concerned the battle of New Market to the winning of which the corps made an important contribution. One result of that fight—said to be in retaliation for the cadets' participation in it—was the destruction of the institute's main building by a Union army commanded by Maj. Gen. David Hunter. That was the extent of Hunter knowledge "rats" were expected to remember, and nothing further was said about Hunter's earlier and later careers. From those days I have been curious about General Hunter and was disappointed to find that his life had not attracted the attention of biographers. Indeed, historians who mentioned him or his deeds restricted themselves largely to critical observations of two of his early Civil War actions and, particularly, to what was seen as the heartless and unnecessary devastation he brought to the Shenandoah Valley in Virginia in 1864.

After the war and Hunter's retirement from the army, he was reported to be writing his memoirs, but the project was not accomplished. In correspondence with his former adjutant, who was a journalist and well-known contemporary author, Hunter spoke of the sort of records he had and from which, presumably, he would have drawn his story. These were official letter and order books of his wartime commands, and so any autobiography he might have written was likely to be based on them. Hunter also resented how he was treated by President Lincoln and more so by Secretary of War Stanton and army chief of staff Henry Halleck. Had Hunter written the promised memoir, it surely would have been justifications of wartime activities and discussions of why he thought himself right and his critics wrong. He probably would not have said much about his earlier life in the army.

When I began tracking down his army service, it was obvious that Hunter's Civil War accomplishments were only a small part of an unusually long time in the uniform of his country. It was experience beginning in 1822 with the army on the distant frontier which formed the man, and when sectional strife erupted into rebellion he was considerably older than most of his fellow general officers. Therefore, his background was unique and his service more diverse than that of others, which may partly explain why he was somewhat of an outsider in army circles and made friends with, for example, General Ulysses Grant during the war rather than before it.

Records of Hunter's West Point education and his fourteen years as a company officer in a tiny military establishment not long after the War of 1812 are not extensive and are largely restricted to routine monthly reports of posts and stations. Hunter's own writing of these times is limited to his response to court-martial charges brought against him by his first commanding officer. Fortunately, others described events of frontier army life and expeditions to the Indians in which Hunter participated, so something can be discovered of this time in Hunter's life.

Hunter left the army in 1836 to take advantage of commercial opportunities that his new wife's family were developing in the small village of Chicago, where Hunter had been stationed earlier. The annals of Chicago written by early settlers often mention Hunter, whose alliance with a leading family there made him prominent. The panic of 1837 and a decline in Hunter's fortunes in his wife's hometown led him to seek readmission to the army then engaged in the Second Seminole War. Recommissioned in 1841 as a major, Hunter was a member of the tiny paymaster corps. Although more complete records on the officer began to be kept again, Paymaster Hunter was out of the mainstream of the professional track followed by most army officers. His army service in Arkansas during the Mexican War and at Detroit and New York up to 1856 was routine. Then he was posted to Fort Leavenworth in the heart of "bleeding Kansas," where sectional violence over the issue of the expansion of slavery was being played out. From that time until the war, records and some memoirs of others show Hunter's development as one of the few abolitionists in the army officer corps.

His Civil War service is thoroughly described in the records that Hunter would have used to explain his accomplishments. How he became a friend of Lincoln, his role in the first battle of Bull Run (in which he was wounded, on his fifty-ninth birthday), and his appointment as one of the senior major generals of the army are fully chronicled. Hunter served in command positions in Missouri, Kansas, South Carolina, and Virginia, and he was sent on official inspection trips to Louisiana, Kentucky, and Tennessee. All these assignments are well documented, and they had the result of giving the general a broad view of the war. This exposure did not make Hunter a prominent strategist, but, then, his prewar paymaster background limited his professional development.

Upperclassmen at VMI did not mention Hunter's controversial activities while he commanded the Department of the South. He freed all the slaves in South Carolina, Georgia, and Florida and enlisted the first freed black men as soldiers in the Union army. Although repudiated, with considerable moderation, by the president, these acts earned Hunter a death sentence from a former army friend and colleague, Confederate President Jefferson Davis, and the rebel congress. Hunter was better remembered at VMI for depredations he allegedly committed in the Shenandoah Valley, of which the burning of the institute was only one. No one mentioned either that Hunter presided over the trial of those accused of Lincoln's assassination or that he lived to age eighty-two. Fortunately for the historian, some of Hunter's private correspondence has survived the years, and it adds details about what motivated the man.

Hunter was certainly dedicated to the proposition that the Union had to be restored as soon as possible and that moderation in war harmed attainment of the objective. To him the Civil War was not a conflict between belligerent nations. It was a rebellion against the United States, and its supporters—particularly former army officers—were traitors who should be brought to justice swiftly and summarily. In this Hunter was unyielding, and his vigor in declaring this principle may explain why he was passed over for some commands. Official policy was, after all, that conciliation might restore the South to the Union, a belief in moderation that lasted in the army until it waned in 1864. By then most agreed with Hunter that any means of ending the rebellion were necessary and moral, but Hunter was not credited with reaching the correct conclusion in advance of army leaders. He was somewhat tainted by also being ahead of his time with respect to the treatment of blacks, their freedom, their service as soldiers, and later their right to vote. Early advocacy of freedom for slaves had already tarnished Hunter in the eyes of the army. On this question he was in advance of Lincoln and most of the nation, and this position could not but have hurt his military ambitions. There is no evidence that Hunter was catering to the prejudices or political machinations of Radical Republicans and did not believe what he said and did. The staff officers who wrote of him thought Hunter incapable of self-serving objectives, and, since he was a straightforward person, it seems unlikely that he could have successfully concealed unworthy motives.

Hunter's life began at the start of the nineteenth century, and he died, still vigorous, close to its end. His forty-three years in the uniform of his nation covered the army's development as a small frontier force through the Mexican War, territorial expansion, and the Civil War. There is more to his story than excesses in the Shenandoah Valley. This book tells some of the rich life of an officer who did his duty faithfully, even without great distinction, in a critical period of American history.

Preface

This book was possible only with the outstanding professional assistance of the men and women who direct and staff the Library of Congress, particularly the Microform and Documents divisions; the National Archives; Fort Ward Museum and Historical Park, Alexandria, Virginia; the Lloyd House branch of the Alexandria Library; Preston Library, Virginia Military Institute; and the U.S. Army Military History Institute, Carlisle Barracks, Pennsylvania. Special thanks is due to Margaret M. Sherry, Princeton University Library; John H. Rhodehamel, Huntington Library; and Patricia Schmid, U.S. Senate Library. Valued and useful advice was supplied by the readers the University of South Carolina Press assigned to review the original manuscript, and, finally, I am grateful to my family for loving support.

LINCOLN'S
ABOLITIONIST
GENERAL

Chapter 1

THE START
OF A MILITARY LIFE

The old gentleman was in good health on the morning of 2 February 1886, and he had walked downtown on business from his nearby home at 1726 I Street NW in Washington, D.C. In the afternoon he came home complaining to his wife of chest pains and died twenty minutes later. Controversial in life, in death he was no less so among those who found his Civil War conduct as a major general in the Union army reprehensible and unworthy of a citizen of Virginia. Indeed, some supporters of the Confederacy were outraged that this villain should die a natural and peaceful death. As late as 1939, a claim was heard that General David Hunter did not die of the diagnosed heart failure but, rather, by his own hand with a pistol—presumably out of remorse for wartime atrocities.[1]

Contrary to what many have written about him, David Hunter was not a Virginian at all, but part of the reason he was criticized was that he was a traitor to his ancestral—if not native—state by remaining with the Union in 1861 and sticking to the colors for the rest of his life without apology or regret for the wartime actions he took in their defense. He was born in Princeton, New Jersey, on 21 July 1802, so he was not a young man when the Civil War began. He already had some familiarity with the military because his father, Pennsylvania-born Presbyterian preacher Andrew Hunter, was chaplain of the Third New Jersey Infantry Regiment from mid-1777 and was on duty at George Washington's Newburgh, New York, headquarters as a brigade chaplain at the end of the Revolution. Chaplain Hunter was praised for his heroic conduct at the battle of Monmouth, and he accompanied Maj. Gen. John Sullivan's excessively destructive campaign against Indians of the Six Nations in 1779. Andrew Hunter was in fact active before the war, opposing English policies applied to the colonies, and he and some other young men, dressed as Indians, burned the tea cargo of the ship *Grayhound* at Greenwich, New Jersey, in one of several colonial "parties" that followed the Boston Tea Party of 1774.[2]

David Hunter inherited a further rebellious and patriotic bent from his mother's side of the family. Mary Hunter, Andrew's second wife, was the daughter of Richard Stockton, a signer of the Declaration of Independence, who was imprisoned under harsh conditions at New York for treason to the Crown. Stockton died just after the Revolution—it is said from bad treatment while he was a prisoner of the English—and so David Hunter did not know him. The Hunter family may have lived at the Stockton family seat, "Morven," at Princeton, where the Reverend Hunter was associated with the governing of the college and a nearby academy and taught mathematics and astronomy until 1811, when he was appointed chaplain of the Washington Navy Yard.

David Hunter was one of three children, two boys and a girl. Unfortunately, nothing is known of the life that young David led in Princeton or in Washington, D.C., where the family lived on Capitol Hill. One can assume, however, that his father saw that he was prepared for higher education. Reverend Hunter, depending on navy pay, was not well-off, and he sought help to educate his children. He wrote from Washington to Secretary of War John C. Calhoun in March 1818, asking that his two sons, David and Lewis Boudinot, be accepted as cadets at the military academy at West Point. In those days the secretary made appointments based on whatever geographical, political, or other conditions he wished to apply. (It was not until some years later that appointment distribution was made by congressional district and, finally, upon nomination by members of Congress.) Hunter said: "David is about sixteen years old and Lewis about fourteen....They have been both well instructed in a classical school." He told Calhoun that the boys were New Jersey natives and could expect only modest inheritances of property in that state. He was concerned about being able to educate his sons because he was himself nearly seventy and without much means. He concluded, "In whatever situation they may be placed in life my ardent desire is that they may be conspicuously friendly to their country and to all mankind." The army selected David but not Lewis, who was too young. David accepted appointment in July 1818, writing to the secretary of war, "I accept with gratitude the appointment of a cadet in the service of the United States." He matriculated at the academy on 14 September 1818.[3]

His record at West Point was not particularly distinguished, and, regrettably, none of his classmates wrote impressions of him in those formative years. His grades and his conduct were neither outstanding nor deficient, and nothing in his academy record is unusual. David Hunter did well in natural philosophy and engineering, was fair at French and drawing and weak in chemistry. One of his classmates was a cousin, also named David Hunter, from the branch of the family which had moved sixty or seventy years before from Little York, Pennsylvania, to Martinsburg in the lower Shenandoah Valley of Virginia. Two David Hunters in the same class must have caused confusion, but fellow cadets simplified the matter by calling the New Jersey man "Little Dave" and his older Virginian cousin "Big Dave." The army's solution for the name duplication was to add *Jr.* and *Sr.* to their names in official records. The situation did not continue for the entire four years because the Virginia-born cadet resigned in late August 1820, for unrecorded reasons, although apparently not because of grades or conduct. David Hunter graduated on 1 July with the class of 1822, standing a modest twenty-fifth among forty-four. He and his classmates who successfully completed the course of study were appointed second lieutenants in the regular army—joining that service's 540 officers—and assigned to military posts across the nation. Most were sent to regiments on the frontier, which at that time did not extend much farther than the Mississippi River. David Hunter was posted to the Fifth Infantry—one of the army's seven regiments of that type—at Fort St. Anthony, Michigan Territory, a remote station on the edge of civilization near what is now St. Paul, Minnesota. It was the most northerly of a string of forts along the frontier. The location placed the post on the thoroughfare used by British fur traders who engaged in the sole commercial activity of the area.[4]

FRONTIER SERVICE

Lieutenant Hunter's trip to his first post took several months. After his arrival by riverboat at St. Louis, he made his way up the Mississippi to his regiment, occasionally riding on riverboats and sometimes traveling by sled. He camped or stayed in cabins of settlers along the way, reaching Fort St. Anthony in January 1823. His post was a substantial stone fort on a bluff at the junction of the St. Peter's and Mississippi Rivers. Behind it stretched nine or ten miles of flat prairie. Nearby were the falls of St. Anthony, a twenty-two-foot fall of water from which the fort got its name. The fort was diamond-shaped, surrounded by a ten-foot-high wall. Within it were two barracks buildings, one of them housing a single company and the other one housing two; officer accommodations consisting of twelve sets of two-room quarters (with kitchens in the basements); storehouses; and headquarters. Outside the walls were farms tended by soldiers on which crops were raised for support of the garrison. The fort was isolated, supplied when the water was high by barge—and occasionally by steamboat after 1823—from St. Louis. The closest settlement was well downriver, where the Wisconsin

River joined the Mississippi. Fort Crawford, an outpost of the Fifth Infantry, was located there at Prairie Du Chien, and Lieutenant Hunter was sent to join Company I at that post. He remained there until spring, when the post was deactivated.

Hunter returned to the regiment's Fort St. Anthony headquarters after a thirty-day leave and was on duty by June 1823. Because Company A's captain was on recruiting duty in the East, Hunter was appointed acting commanding officer. He remained in this responsible position for almost three years. Meanwhile, Fort St. Anthony was renamed (in January 1825) after the Fifth Regiment's colonel and Hunter's first commanding officer, Josiah Snelling, who was largely responsible for the fort's construction by soldiers of his Fifth Infantry. The colonel, an officer who had fought with gallantry at Tippecanoe in 1811, commanded the fort from 1820.[5]

The work of the garrison that varied from one hundred and fifty to three hundred soldiers was not primarily Indian fighting, as might be supposed but policing the line beyond which white men were not allowed without permission and a government license to trap and hunt. The line, which was firmly established by Congress in 1825, was the creation of James Monroe's secretary of war, John C. Calhoun. This western Monroe Doctrine was at the time thought to be as important as the one that opposed European influence in the Northern Hemisphere. Its purpose was not to protect Indians but to prevent U.S. strength from being dissipated by too-rapid expansion when much of the land east of the Mississippi had not yet been settled. The line itself ran from the Red River on the Mexican border, along the Arkansas Territory's and Missouri's western borders, eastward to the Mississippi and northward along the river to the Canadian border.[6]

The Fifth Infantry at Fort Snelling was called on from time to time to provide details and larger units for various purposes. In July 1823 Maj. Stephen H. Long took along an escort of the regiment's soldiers on one of his several exploratory expeditions, this one north along the Minnesota River, circling back to Green Bay on Lake Michigan. Three years later Colonel Snelling led three companies south to reoccupy previously abandoned Fort Crawford at Prairie du Chien on the Mississippi in response to a minor incident involving the Winnebago Indians. There was no fighting in the "Winnebago War," and the situation was rapidly calmed by the presence of the troops. The result was the reopening of Fort Crawford and the stationing of a garrison there. In 1824 Fort Dearborn, at present-day Chicago, Illinois, was also re-garrisoned, and Fort Winnebago, at the portage between the Fox and Wisconsin Rivers in central Wisconsin, was begun. The reconstitution of the northern frontier army's structure was to influence

Lieutenant Hunter's later military assignments, but he was not called on to provide support for any of these immediate activities, aside from two months spent at Fort Armstrong at Rock Island, Illinois, in late 1826. When he was not on leave, he supervised the frontier soldier's primary occupations—fort, road, and facilities construction and maintenance, woodcutting, and cultivating crops to support the garrison. Probably he also assisted Indian agents, army civilian employees, watching over their charges in the vicinity of the fort, protecting them from trader exploitation, preventing sale of liquor to them, and so on. An army inspector in 1826 found that he could not evaluate military activity on the post because training soldiers was "out of the question," given the regiment's extensive household tasks. The situation was improving because fort construction was by then almost completed, after six years of hard work. The inspector quoted Fifth Regiment officers who said, "our labours as farmers & builders are now comparatively closed," leaving more time for military training of the six companies then at Fort Snelling. Certainly, troop morale was poor, alcoholism high, and discipline and military spirit wanting. "Black Dave," as Hunter was now called by his fellow officers—because of his swarthy complexion, not his mood—must have been discouraged finding army service in the wilderness as harsh and unrefined as it was. It is doubtful that West Point had prepared him for the reality of army life, and its harshness may have made him short-tempered.[7]

Other than military and housekeeping work, there were few diversions for military personnel and the few families that were with them at Fort Snelling. The daughter of Maj. Nathan Clark wrote about her days growing up on the frontier; her playmate was Colonel Snelling's young son, Harry. She tells of the popular amateur winter theatricals, but Hunter does not seem to have been a part of this activity. Charlotte Clark described another less pleasant diversion. In June 1827 Colonel Snelling turned over several Sioux accused of murdering Chippewas to a band of the latter tribe in the fort. The garrison witnessed the execution of these unfortunates and the mutilation of the bodies. Young Clark had nightmares for a long time following this example of how Indian and soldier lives intermingled.[8]

Hunter's service at Fort St. Anthony Snelling was not uneventful. The lieutenant was on leave for six months, from April to November 1825, and he may have returned to the East to visit his family. Over his first two or three years with the Fifth, Hunter developed bad relations with the regimental commander, Colonel Snelling. Hunter told of an incident in late 1825 (Hunter said it was in September, but he was on leave then), when on an outing with friends he decided to return to the fort, loaning his horse to another. He was offered a ride in a carriage, not knowing it belonged to the colonel. Snelling, when he heard that Hunter had been in his carriage, said "he thought he had Lent his wagon for Gentlemen to ride in, and not for a 'Vile Assasin [*sic*],'" and he ordered his orderlies to cut up the body and seat of the conveyance. But the principal cause of Hunter's official difficulties appears to have been related to Snelling's orders concerning assignments of enlisted men to orderly duties and other matters of post discipline and housekeeping. One of the colonel's resented pronouncements was a threat to kill all the dogs on the post, perhaps because they were an annoyance. Colonel Snelling was a heavy drinker, unlike Hunter, and seems to have had an abrasive manner; he frequently told his subordinates that they could seek personal satisfaction from him if they wished to challenge his authority, decisions, or actions. Fighting duels over points of personal honor was common practice at the time, but it was as illegal in the army on the frontier as it was in civilized locales. The conflict between Snelling and Hunter came to a head on 31 July 1826, the lieutenant sending the colonel a written challenge. The letter said that Snelling was taking advantage of his official position to injure Company A, which Hunter temporarily commanded, and Hunter himself by arbitrarily assigning some of Hunter's men to other duty. It did not further specify the supposed offense to Hunter but justified the note, claiming:

> Your having Publickly offered to Give the Kind of Redress I wish to our Gray headed sutler when you had only Supposed you had injured him and Your having on Another occasion offered to meet any Officer who might be Offended at a Certain Order you threatened to give Concerning Dogs, All this induces me to Believe You will be Courteous enough to Comply with my Call as quick as Possible.[9]

Colonel Snelling's reaction was not to accept the challenge but, rather, to place Hunter under arrest, and he confined him to quarters while waiting to convene a general court-martial. Hunter later said that Snelling had denied him permission to go for his meals. "I was informed that if I came over the sill of my door a sentinel should be placed over me." After a few days Lieutenant Hunter was allowed more freedom on the post but in October was sent on duty—still under arrest—to Fort Armstrong at Rock Island, the outpost on the Mississippi. While he was away, brigade headquarters at Jefferson Barracks, Missouri, appointed a general court made up of officers from other military posts but was unable to convene it because Hunter did not return to Fort Snelling until that winter. By then one of the members of the court had been sent off on furlough, and one of Hunter's witnesses had been transferred. He immediately had another run-in with the colonel, a matter of Hunter paying too much (two bottles of whiskey instead of the usual one) to his men for a load of firewood. The conflict was not over the price paid but that Hunter accused Snelling of failing in his responsibility to furnish the wood at government expense. Once more Hunter was closely confined to quarters, and he said, "as I would not apply for an extension of my limits, . . . I Remained in confinement till the Month of June."[10]

An inspecting officer visited Fort Snelling in August 1826, the month during which Hunter challenged Snelling and was arrested. He observed that "the Officer in command & some of his junior Officers are at variance," but he did not comment further on the conditions that inspired this remark. He returned the following May, however, and then specifically reported his view of the conflict between Hunter and his colonel:

> I regret to state that dissensions still prevail between Colonel Snelling and some of his junior officers, even to a greater extent than was remarked upon in my last report. Lieutenant Hunter, who has been under arrest for some months, is now confined to his quarters for reasons best known to Colonel Snelling, of the propriety of which I will not venture a remark as it will doubtless shortly be passed upon by a court martial. I do not, however, commit myself in saying that each of the parties (Colonel Snelling and Lieutenant Hunter) believes himself to be correct. May it not, therefore, be that neither is morally wrong. Lieutenant Hunter is young and perhaps of a temper too warm and unyielding, and Colonel Snelling, sometimes irascible, may have in the moment of excitement, produced by some official anxiety, unguardedly expressed himself in language calculated to wound his feelings. Sympathy is expressed by most of the officers of the garrison, not, it may be, that he is believed to be unjustly arrested and confined, but because his confinement has been so long and may prove injurious to his health.[11]

By October 1827 Snelling, Hunter, and two potential witnesses were at Jefferson Barracks near St. Louis. Here a general court-martial consisting of thirteen members was named to hear whatever cases might be brought before it. All the court's officers were detailed from regiments other than the Fifth Infantry. The court met on 15 October to hear the charge against Hunter, and the convening authority, brigade commander Col. Henry Leavenworth, chose to sit as president. Snelling's accusation was simple. It read: "That the said 2nd Lieut. David Hunter, did at Fort Snelling on or about the Thirty first day of July 1826 send a Challenge to Colonel Josiah Snelling, his commanding officer to Fight a Duel in violation of the 25th Article of War."[12]

The trial itself lasted a couple of days, but very little evidence was presented, because Hunter did not deny that he had indeed challenged his colonel. Hunter expected to be convicted but asked for permission to point out details that might mitigate his offense. He was allowed to present a long written summary that constitutes almost half of the trial record. He began by telling the court that the article he was accused of violating, "if not considered Obsolete in the Army has at least Been so Considered in the 5th Regt. of Infantry." He said he did not have to prove further to the court that Snelling often issued the general invitation to his juniors—such as the sutler—to challenge him, since witnesses had earlier verified this. He was speaking out, although "it may appear to you useless that I should further trouble myself" because the court must inevitably find him guilty. He was, he said, speaking to "the Person whose duty the Law makes it to consumate [*sic*] or annul the Sentence"—the president of the United States—who "cannot be so well acquainted with the various Bearings of my Case as the Gentlemen composing this Court."[13]

Lieutenant Hunter's unusual presentation did not change the decision of the court-martial, which found him guilty of the charge and sentenced him to be dismissed from the army. He had made his point, however, because the court said, "From all the circumstances which have transpired during the trial the Court are induced unanimously to recommend Lieut Hunter in the strongest terms to the clemency of the President of the United States for a remission of the sentence which the Court have been bound to pass." Furthermore, the court denied Colonel Snelling's request to submit a rebuttal document. The matter was settled on 8 December 1827, when President John Quincy Adams signed a letter that approved the sentence but remitted "the penalty of cashiering." Neither the accuser nor the accused escaped without serious criticism, and the court itself was rebuked for allowing Hunter's letter to appear in the record and for denying Snelling the chance to refute the accusations. The colonel was found to be "in the habitual practice of obtrusively declaring his readiness to waive his rank and meet in private combat any of his inferior officers who might be dissatisfied with his conduct." This was found to be self-degrading and a "violation of the military character and duty" of the officer who made such statements. Hunter's accusations went too far, the president said, because self-defense "should not be suffered to be used as a cloak for slander."[14]

Hunter went on leave on 13 October 1827 and remained off duty until mid-April of the following year, but it is not known where he went during that time. Hunter then spent a month at dilapidated Fort Crawford at Prairie du Chien on the west bank of the Mississippi River, the Fifth Regiment's outpost, which was being rebuilt and regarrisoned in a "Winnebago War" realignment.

The assignment was brief, because in June the entire regiment was ordered to Jefferson Barracks, its Fort Snelling headquarters being taken over by the First Infantry. Hunter did not again encounter Snelling because the colonel was on leave in Washington, where he died on 20 August. Hunter seems to have suffered no serious damage to his career in the army as a result of his trial. But a certain consequence of it was that he had earned a reputation as a duelist, a label that would follow him throughout his years in the army. There is little evidence that he offered challenges to other officers or ever fought a duel. Perhaps the accusation had more to do with Hunter's volatile temper, which was likely to be aroused suddenly and which caused to him to take uncompromising and sometimes indefensible positions. Friends and enemies alike remarked on his impetuous nature, which might have been tolerated in a junior officer; unfortunately, it lasted all his life. Having reached a conclusion, no matter how faulty, Hunter seldom backed down.[15]

FORT DEARBORN

The court-martial did not prevent Hunter's promotion to first lieutenant, with date of rank 30 June 1828, exactly six years after his graduation from West Point. The regiment stayed at Jefferson Barracks until September, where Hunter was once again assigned as Company A's acting commanding officer. The regiment's records show Hunter's company "on the march" back to the northern frontier, all ten companies at or bound for Fort Howard at Green Bay. Companies A and I were redirected to Fort Dearborn, another abandoned installation that the Fifth Regiment reoccupied as a result of the Winnebago troubles. He remained at Fort Dearborn for about three years after his arrival on 3 October 1828. A visitor three years later described the fort as a "small stockaded enclosure with two block-houses, and it is garrisoned with two companies of infantry." Fort Dearborn was on the site of the future Chicago, south of the river (presently Wacker Drive and Michigan Avenue), but when Hunter arrived there it had decidedly fewer settlers—only fourteen taxpayers—and was mainly an Indian trading post. The same later visitor remarked, "The fort contained within its palisades by far the most enlightened residents, in the little knot of officers attached to the slender garrison." He took a broad view of these men:

> The officers of the United States Army have perhaps less opportunities
> of becoming refined than those of the Navy. They are often, from the
> time of receiving their commissions, after the termination of their
> Cadetship at West Point, and at an age when good society is of the

utmost consequence to the young and ardent, exiled for long years to
the posts on the Northern or Western frontier, far removed from
cultivated female society, and in daily contact with the refuse of the
human race.[16]

Lieutenant Hunter made the best of his situation and demonstrated sufficient refinement to attract the attentions of Maria Indiana, the daughter of John
Kinzie, a silversmith from Detroit, who had arrived in the future Chicago in
1804. Kinzie was an employee of John Jacob Astor's American Fur Company, but
he also engaged in trading activities on his own behalf. The family was rather
well self-educated and known as friends and protectors of the Indians. Kinzie
was the first white resident at the new settlement, and his daughter, born in 1807,
was one of its first native whites—her sister Ellen Marion, three years older, was
the first. John Kinzie died at the age of sixty-five, nine months before Hunter
reached Fort Dearborn, but Kinzie's three sons, John Harris, James, and Robert
Allen, carried on his work. The new first lieutenant and Maria Kinzie became
engaged to be married during Hunter's Dearborn posting, but the union was
delayed for several years, probably because of Hunter's military duties. Early on,
however, Hunter did develop close personal and commercial relations with Maria's
oldest brother, John H., who appears to have been the most entrepreneurial of
the Kinzie sons.[17]

In October 1829, a year after his arrival at Fort Dearborn, Hunter had a
curious encounter there with another officer. It was the start of a bond between
them which would be shattered by the Civil War. As Hunter described the incident:

> I saw a man on the north side of the River, opposite the Fort, a white
> man, and wondering where he could have come from, I got into a small
> wooden canoe, intended for only one person, and paddled over to
> interview him. He introduced himself as 2d-Lieut. Jefferson Davis, of the
> 1st Infantry, from Fort Winnebago, in pursuit of deserters. I invited him
> to lie down in my canoe, and I paddled him safely to the Fort. He was
> my guest until refreshed and ready to return to Fort Winnebego.[18]

Davis, future president of the Confederate States, was an 1828 West Point
graduate, assigned to recruiting duty at Fort Winnebego, a post located at the Fox
and Wisconsin Rivers near what is now Portage in Columbia County, central
Wisconsin (part of the Michigan Territory until 1836). Because of the scarcity of
potential recruits, Davis was sent off to round up deserters, of which there were

considerable numbers in those days of hard frontier duty. Davis, accompanied by a few men, had gotten lost and run out of rations. He said later that his party had gone ten days without food and three without water, so coming upon Fort Dearborn and receiving Hunter's hospitality was especially welcome. One might presume that Davis's enlisted men were similarly refreshed. In any case, Davis's biographer says that "for more that thirty years Davis retained a fondness for Hunter," a friendship that was strengthened by later duty together on another part of the western frontier and in Mexico.[19]

Chicago in 1830 had not changed much since Hunter's assignment there in 1828. John H. Kinzie's new wife, Juliette, described it that year. She said that the Kinzie family "mansion" was on the north bank of the river, "a long, low building, with a piazza extending along its front, a range of four or five rooms." A collection of log buildings near it included the Indian agency and quarters for its employees, most of them Canadians and half-breeds. The Kinzies rented their home, and Maria, her sister, a brother (James?), and mother lived in the agency buildings. The fort south of the river was a palisade structure with whitewashed buildings within. As Juliette described it, Chicago at that time had only a few whites besides soldiers, the Kinzies, a Mr. and Mrs. Forbes, a doctor (Alexander Wolcott, who married Ellen Kinzie?), the schoolteacher, and a sutler and two lieutenants at the fort. One of the latter was Hunter, temporarily in command in the absence of Maj. John Fowle and Capt. Martin Scott.[20]

In all, Chicago had about fifty people and thirty buildings. The town was platted, and in 1831 Cook County was formed from part of Peoria County (in 1833 Chicago was incorporated as a town). In May 1831 Hunter and his Company A were transferred from the growing town to the regiment's headquarters post at Fort Howard two hundred miles north at Green Bay, another American Fur Company station. Fort Dearborn was closed. These actions were part of a redeployment of America's few frontier soldiers, a result of new threats of trouble with the Indians. Hunter had been engaging in commerce with his future brother-in-law, but John H. Kinzie had taken on the job of Indian agent at Fort Winnebago, arriving there in 1830. Hunter's transfer and perhaps John Kinzie's absence from Chicago were causes for Hunter to sell his real estate for what seemed a handsome sum of twenty thousand dollars. The new owner shortly afterward sold the same properties for a hundred thousand, a matter that certainly did not escape Hunter's attention. That such princely sums were to be had in speculation in the newly booming frontier town likely caused him to consider whether life in the army was what he should pursue. It took a few more years of frontier hardship before David Hunter made a decision about this, but, after only a month at Fort Howard, he asked for and was granted a sixty-day leave, which he had extended for a year, "through the Spring of 1832." This time he went back to Fort Dearborn, joining his fiancé and engaging in further business.[21]

Conditions on the seemingly tranquil northwest frontier were about to change. The cause of unrest was a dissatisfied branch of the Sac Indian tribe in Illinois. The group of about 2,000, including 450 warriors led by Black Hawk, objected to the state's plan to sell Indian farmland to white settlers in violation of a treaty. Black Hawk's opposition caused the Illinois governor to call up the militia, and federal troops in the West and even from East Coast units were positioned for action. Black Hawk headed for what is now Wisconsin, where he had a tentative alliance with the Winnebagoes, and two battles were fought, the first in July 1832 with militia and the second a month later with a regular army-militia mix. Calling these skirmishes a war stretches the definition, because they resulted in only six whites being killed against the eventual near extermination of Black Hawk's band.[22]

Lieutenant Hunter returned to Fort Howard from leave in June 1832, two months before the Black Hawk uprising, but he did not participate in the military campaign against the Indians. He was assigned once again to command Company A, which with Company I was one of two companies left at Fort Howard. Regimental headquarters and the other companies had relocated at Fort Winnebago in December 1831. Regular units from Atlantic states, the lower Mississippi, and the Great Lakes were called up, and they were distributed among army posts in the Northwest. The arrival of these troops put a strain on army facilities, and, because of widespread illness, existing posts were burdened with many newcomers unable to participate in the campaign. Hunter's duties in this period are not known, but, despite the Indian unrest, he obtained another leave in August 1832 and once again returned to Chicago. He and Maria Kinzie were married by a magistrate on 18 September. Perhaps the couple had planned to wed while Hunter was on his earlier yearlong leave, but, as he explained it, there had been a complication: it would have been necessary "to send a soldier one hundred miles, on foot, to Peoria [Fort Clark] for a license." That Hunter trusted a soldier with this mission is curious because of the very low standard of discipline in the army. A visitor to Fort Armstrong at Rock Island told of officers regularly riding a hundred miles to get their mail: "The officers must go themselves, as the soldiers if permitted to go would desert the service."[23]

It is uncertain if the couple returned by wagon or sailing vessel to Hunter's permanent station at Green Bay. Given the uncertainties of the time, Maria may not have chosen to join her husband that winter. His company was assigned in October to the more remote Fort Brady on Lake Superior, but the newlywed Lieutenant Hunter was not required to transfer there. He was appointed assistant chief of staff and assistant quartermaster at the regimental headquarters, once again located at Fort Howard. This was a temporary assignment, and in November Hunter was made commanding officer of Company H at the Green Bay post. On 1 February 1833 Hunter began a sixty-day leave, probably so that he could return to Chicago and accompany Maria back to his permanent station at Fort Howard when lake traffic resumed in early spring.[24]

Juliette Kinzie wrote that, in early February 1833, "my husband and Lieut. Hunter, in company with one or two others, set off [from Fort Winnebago] on a journey to Chicago." The purpose of the trip was so that John Kinzie could divide up and sell what was known as the Kinzie claim, or "Kinzie's Addition," one hundred and two acres in what would become the center of the city. Land values were growing rapidly, the town becoming a trade center as agriculture developed in Wisconsin and on the prairie southwest of Chicago. Another visitor reported his impressions of the town a few months after Hunter and Kinzie arrived in 1833. The population was about 140, and building was an active business. "The lots [laid out on both sides of the river], many of them, are improved with temporary buildings, some not more than ten foot square, and they are scattered about like cattle on the prairie"; one hundred structures were built that year. The visitor said of the bustling Sunday traffic on the south bank: "I saw men on the streets as the New England people would be on a week day, and I saw some Indians drunk. They had been fighting and were covered with blood." It was obvious to Hunter and Kinzie that there was money to be made in the booming, primitive town, but Hunter was not yet ready to take on a business career. He had been offered an opportunity for advancement in the army, a promotion to captain in a new regiment. He returned to Fort Howard in April to clean up his affairs, with transfer orders dated 6 March 1833 in his pocket.[25]

CAPTAIN OF DRAGOONS

The effect of the Black Hawk affair on the army was important because it showed the difficulty with employing just infantry (and artillery) against Indians, but another example of the failure of this type of unit was also illustrated by 1829 operations mounted from the new Fort Leavenworth, near Independence, Missouri, along the Santa Fe Trail. The army's leaders had wished that cavalry be added to the military establishment ever since the elimination of that arm in 1821. They succeeded in the spring of 1832—before confrontations with Black Hawk—in obtaining legislation that would allow for this expansion. In the belief, not shared by the regular army, that the militia system should be followed, a compromise cavalry organization was established. It was a battalion of mounted rangers—six companies of one hundred and ten men each, not counting officers. As for the latter, in deference to army wishes, the president was to appoint them subject to Senate confirmation. The troopers, each one to serve for one year, were required to equip and arm themselves and to provide their own horses. Pay was one dollar a day. Appointed to command the Battalion of Mounted Rangers was Col. Henry Dodge, a former Wisconsin lead miner with military experience as a Missouri and Michigan volunteer officer.[26]

It did not take a year for the army to conclude that the rangers, who had fought no battles and shed no blood, were not up to the job to be done. The secretary of war asked Congress to replace the rangers with a regular army unit, to be called a regiment of dragoons—soldiers trained as riflemen and cavalry. The House of Representatives committee report on this request accepted the argument that a regular regiment, better sized for the job "on the inland frontier in contact with Indians," would cost less than the rangers. The report said of the rangers that they were "but little superior to . . . ordinary militia" and could not be kept ready for operations because of year-to-year enlistments. Consequently, the second session of the Twenty-second Congress, the first session of which had authorized the rangers, voted to dissolve them and create the dragoons.[27]

Because Hunter's reputation as an officer was good, he was selected for promotion to captain in the new regiment, effective 4 March 1833, and ordered to Jefferson Barracks. He left Fort Howard on 18 April but did not join the new regiment at once. He was told to proceed to Cincinnati to recruit a company of dragoons. Colonel Dodge, temporarily acting as commanding officer of both units, assembled the first of his new officers—among them 1st Lt. Jefferson Davis—and began organizing the regiment. The post at Jefferson Barracks, ten miles from growing St. Louis, was a pleasant one, consisting of stone buildings in a quadrangle, one side open to a terrace along a bluff overlooking the Mississippi River. It was a good center for support of the army to the north and south but less suited for operations westward on the open plains. Dodge preferred Fort Leavenworth, a forward position at the junction of the Little Platte and Missouri Rivers, two hundred and fifty miles west, for the dragoons' home base. Later the regiment did make its home station at Leavenworth, closer to the Indian country, and Hunter was to serve out the last of his time as a company officer at the Kansas post. But for now the dragoons continued organizing at Jefferson Barracks.[28]

It is not clear whether Maria Hunter accompanied her husband to St. Louis, where he took up his new assignment commanding Company D, having arrived on 3 August 1833, "with his company," seventy-one recruits he had signed on in Cincinnati and brought by riverboat to St. Louis. She later was to accompany

Hunter wherever the army would order him for most of the rest of his career in uniform but, for now, probably remained in Chicago, because the Regiment of Dragoons was scheduled for field service. A captain's pay (just over fourteen hundred dollars yearly with allowances) could not have bought many luxuries, and she was learning that army life on the frontier meant long separations. Meanwhile, the regiment had to be raised, the officers had to learn now-forgotten cavalry tactics and mounted drill, and the dragoons had to be trained and equipped. Dodge was certain that he wanted a new type of soldier for this special duty. A traveler who encountered thirty dragoon recruits near Prairie du Chien said that they were unlike the "rag-tag-and-bob-tail" of regular army men and particularly the mounted rangers. They were, he said, "picked, athletic young men of decent character and breeding. They were all Americans, whereas, the ordinary recruits consist either of the scum of the population of the older States, or of the worthless German, English, or Irish emigrants." These particular men had already had an arduous journey from the Atlantic states, moving through Detroit, Lake Huron, Green Bay, and Fox River into the Wisconsin River. From Prairie du Chien they had to go by barge six hundred miles down the Mississippi in cold weather, a nine-day trip, and no settlements would be encountered until a hundred miles from the Missouri River at St. Louis.[29]

The dragoons were indeed a special unit, made up of native citizens, twenty to thirty-five years old. It was clear to one of their officers that the old "'sweepings of the cities,' &c." would not do; dragoons had to be special men. He said that men like these could "easily obtain at home double or treble the wages of dragoons. . . . It was discovered, that the main, if not the sole inducements to those enlisted, were a craving for excitement, and romantic notions of the far West, &c, operating on enterprising, roving inclinations." Indeed, the officer—who had left the army because of boredom with frontier infantry service a year or two earlier—had felt the same attraction. He said he "was among the hearty sons of West Tennessee, seeking to infuse an ardor for service in a new regiment of Cavalry, one destined, we believed, to explore far and wide the Western Territory, and bear the arms of the Union into the country of many Indian tribes."[30]

A soldier who enlisted in the regiment at Philadelphia in August 1833 wrote that conditions at Jefferson Barracks were poor, not because the buildings were insufficient to house the regiment but because uniforms and arms were not available or were of poor quality. The new troops had to purchase many of their comforts and necessities themselves, such as kitchen utensils for the mess and bunks for the barracks. In addition, they were put to work renovating stables for the regiment's horses, which arrived in October. The clothing situation was acute by early fall that year since recruits had given theirs away on the trip from their homes to Jefferson Barracks based on promises that they would be issued complete uniforms on arrival. Not only was this promise not kept, but the rifles issued were "condemned pieces that had lain in the arsenal since the war [of 1812, probably]." Desertions were common because of these disappointments; 12 men out of 380 deserted in September. The soldier wrote of the unkept promises, "I only mention these things to show how superior a band of young men could have been induced to enlist themselves as common soldiers in the illiberal army of America, where the very fact of a man's being a soldier seems to imply that he is fit for no other employment."[31]

PAWNEE PICT EXPEDITION

Still without uniforms but well mounted and with only half of the regiment ready, in November Colonel Dodge ordered preparation for a march into Indian country. Clothing was whatever could be found at Jefferson Barracks, all colors and styles. Rifles only arrived that same month, and not much training had been accomplished. A lieutenant in the regiment thought it incredible that Dodge wanted to take the field as winter approached, short five companies of the authorized ten and without equipment. "In what," he asked, "originated this march? Was an important public end to be attained? Was it to repel an invading foe? Was it to make a sudden and important attack upon a foreign enemy?" He continued: "To these questions there is but one answer—No! There has been assigned, as the only and great motive, *that the corps having been raised for the defense of the frontier, would be disbanded if it remained inactive so far in the interior as Jefferson Barracks.*"[32]

Colonel Dodge, whom a soldier described as "a thorough backwoodsman," may have considered his dragoons tough enough for a winter march. The same soldier thought his commanding officer "on the whole a clever man, but not much of a soldier." It is not recorded how he was viewed by Hunter and the other officers of the regiment, but the five companies of dragoons, about three hundred and fifty men, left Jefferson Barracks on 20 November 1833, bound southwest for Fort Gibson on the Arkansas River (across the river from present-day Muskogee, Oklahoma). Hunter's Company D, about seventy men, was assigned "advance, flank and rear guard" duties and was also put in charge of prisoners, mostly apprehended deserters. These eighteen men were in handcuffs and chains, some with a cannonball, weighing about forty-two pounds, attached to a leg. Such shackling and newly reinstituted flogging were common punishments for apprehended army deserters, who still had to complete their enlistments—but without further pay.[33]

The expedition was overtaken by a severe snowfall three days out from

Jefferson Barracks and had generally cold weather the whole four hundred and fifty miles to the stockaded Fort Gibson, arriving there on 17 December. At the camp the dragoons were welcomed by the four hundred men of the Seventh Infantry. There was no room for the dragoons in the fort, and no corn was available for the now badly spent horses. Dodge's troopers camped on a nearby sandbar and were put to work building Camp Jackson, which would consist of leaky barracks covered with oak shingles. The horses were turned loose to forage for themselves "on cane in an Arkansas bottom," and army food—pork, flour, and beans with coffee—was not much more abundant for the men. The winter was very bad, a temperature of eight degrees below zero once being recorded, and clothing, sabres, and pistols did not reach the regiment until February, salvaged after the steamboat carrying them foundered on the way. Meanwhile, recruiting and training of the remaining five companies and replacements for the companies at Camp Jackson continued at Jefferson Barracks.[34]

Dodge became upset with some of his officers, a situation no doubt exacerbated by harsh conditions. Contributing as well was a busy regimental routine. Reveille was at sunrise, muster at 7:30 a.m., breakfast at 8:00, and guard mount at 9:00. The day was filled with horse and foot tactics and target shooting, ending with tattoo at 9:00 in the evening. Dodge wrote about his officers' unrest: "I find more treachery and deception practiced in the army than I ever expected to find with a body of men who call themselves gentlemen. . . . Davis, who I appointed my adjt [adjutant] was among the first to take a stand against me. Major [Richard B.] Mason and Davis are now two of my most inveterate enemies. The desire of these gentlemen appears to be to harass me in small matters. They don't want to fight." He did not write whether Hunter was another officer with whom he was then dissatisfied, but in later years he praised his captain. Supplies were getting through, however, and so were some visitors. One of the latter was artist George Catlin, who had the secretary of war's permission to go with the dragoons on a field expedition. He went to Fort Gibson by steamboat from New Orleans up the Mississippi and Arkansas Rivers, arriving in April. Also joining was Brig. Gen. Henry Leavenworth, who commanded the Southwestern Department. Catlin wrote his impression of the improving dragoons: "Each company of horses has been selected of one entire color. There is a company of bays, a company of blacks, one of whites, one of sorrels, one of grays, [and later] one of cream color." He thought the dragoons would "be a credit to themselves and honor to the country—as far as honors can be gained and laurels plucked from their wild stems in a savage country." Leavenworth, who also reached Fort Gibson and Camp Jackson in April, made a more professional evaluation and, in an order to the regiment, said that he was impressed with the soldiers' appearance and their uniforms. He ordered Dodge to prepare to march and assumed command of the expedition. He noted, however, that he had heard that "there are some desertions and asks a stop to it." One soldier claimed that there were "over one hundred" deserters from the dragoon companies in the field, but there were actually less than half that—still a good percentage of the regiment.[35]

The last five companies of the regiment, Companies F through K (there is no Company J in army nomenclature because of possible confusion with I), left Jefferson Barracks in May and arrived on the Arkansas in June. By now the weather, which had been too cold for the first dragoon march, was growing too hot for the next. In June temperatures on the plains of 103 to 107 degrees Fahrenheit were recorded; it was probably two months too late for an expedition such as Leavenworth and Dodge had planned. The purpose of the proposed march was to meet the Pawnee Picts and Comanches—the two remaining Plains Indian tribes that had not signed a treaty with the United States—and to induce them to come to terms. The first tribe was said to be located along the Arkansas River and the Comanches on the Red River, which marked the border with Mexico. The trip to the Red River was to be about two hundred miles over somewhat unknown terrain. The move from Camp Jackson began on 15 June, nine companies of dragoons making up the party of about five hundred men. (Company A had left in May to accompany a group of traders to Santa Fe and to see if cavalry were indeed better than infantry in this role.)[36]

General Leavenworth had left Camp Jackson and Fort Gibson early, taking some dragoons and infantrymen ahead to prepare the path for the regiment. In addition, other infantry units were also scattered westward, most of them engaged in constructing stockades, nearly all of which proved temporary. The reason for such preparation as Leavenworth directed was reliance on wagons to carry the regiment's baggage. These needed cleared paths through brush and some woods, and fords over rivers and streams had to be located and marked. The dragoons and seventy head of cattle set out on the trail on 21 June, and already twenty-three men were found unfit and were sent to Fort Gibson. Crossing the north fork of the Canadian River (near Holdenville) was difficult, each wagon needing the help of thirty or forty men to ascend the steep banks of the stream. Going in the early days was relatively easy, over open prairie alternating with timber. The dragoons caught up with General Leavenworth's party a week on the march, and all reached the Washita River about ten miles above its mouth at the beginning of July, only a few days after encountering the first buffalo. After another difficult crossing, Leavenworth decided to make a camp for the numerous sick and to send Dodge and the main body on to the Pawnee country. Leavenworth and more than a hundred officers and men were left behind, and the reorganized dragoons set out for the Indian nations on 8 July. Artist Catlin noted that the expedition was reduced to half its original size and reported that Leavenworth looked "very feeble now." A few days later the depleted dragoons were divided into three columns, Captain Hunter commanding the center, Companies D and E.[37]

After passing through the Cross Timbers, an area characterized by interlaced ravines, scrub bush, and trees, the party of about two hundred and fifty men, many of them ill, entered the Great Plains, encountering a group of Indian warriors, Comanches, on 14 July. Dodge told the Indians, through a Spaniard among them, "that the President, the great American captain, had sent him to shake hands with them; that he wished to establish peace between them and their red brethren around them, to send traders among them, and to be forever friends." Many dragoons were impressed with the mostly naked Indians. "A Comanche fully equipped on horseback, with his lance and quiver and shield by his side, is beautifully classic," said one. Yet another soldier saw things differently: "Those Commanch Indians are the most homely featured being very large & corpulent in size . . . of a heavy square and inelegant proportion." Continuing on in company with the party of Indians, the dragoons reached an encampment of Comanches and arrived at the main objective, a large Pawnee village, on the twenty-first. Only 183 men were fit for duty; 75 more had been left behind in a makeshift fort. A few days later Comanches and Pawnees met with Dodge and his officers and were invited to accompany the dragoons east and to go to Washington to see the president. The Indians, however, were reluctant to accept the invitation; they thought that the timbered country between the plains and the white man's settlements was too difficult for them to pass through. A few eventually decided to march with the dragoons, and the party set out to the east on 25 July.[38]

The return trip was as arduous as the one out. The weather remained excessively hot, water was sometimes scarce, terrain was often rough, and food for horses and men was hard to come by. Fortunately, there were few flies and mosquitoes. Sick were gathered up as their camps were passed, but nothing was heard from Leavenworth at the Washita bivouac. Dodge was concerned. The plan had been for the dragoons to return to their intended home station at Fort Leavenworth, rather than Fort Gibson. He was following an easterly path that crossed the Washita near present Chickasha and the Canadian River near Norman, ninety miles north of the outward bound crossings where he had left the general. On 4 August Dodge decided that Fort Leavenworth was not a possible goal (it was four hundred miles farther) because the horses were in bad shape, and he decided to proceed to Fort Gibson. The following day he was notified by a messenger of General Leavenworth's death, and he sent an order for the men at the Washita camp (possibly at Ardmore, Oklahoma) to meet him at Fort Gibson. He and his men finally reached Fort Gibson by mid-August. As Hunter described them, "our men present a sorry figure, but one that looks like service; many of them literally half naked." The sick soldiers from the Washita, led by Lt. Col. Stephen W. Kearney, arrived in comparable condition a few days later.[39]

FORT LEAVENWORTH

The Regiment of Dragoons was in poor shape following its two months on the trail. A lieutenant said of the trip, "Nature would seem to have conspired with an imbecile military administration for the destruction of the regiment." Dodge wrote of the expedition, "Perhaps their [*sic*] never has been in America a campaign that operated More Severely on Men & Horses. The excessive Heat of the Sun exceeded anything I ever experienced." He went on to say that he had less than half the regiment fit for duty upon reaching the Pawnee village and had lost at least a hundred horses. The Indians who had agreed to return with Dodge had mostly dropped off along the way, and Dodge apparently failed to convince any of them to go to Washington. Consequently, in September he called for a meeting at Fort Gibson of seven or eight Indian tribes to discuss peace.[40]

The council, which was held over the first four days of September, was thought by Dodge to be a success; he extracted promises of peace between the Indians. The battered regiment, for the moment scattered among several locations in and around Fort Gibson, prepared to move on to its next assignment. The plan called for dispersal of the dragoons, four companies destined for Fort Leavenworth, three for the new Fort Des Moines (under Lieutenant Colonel Kearney), and three to remain temporarily eighty miles up the Arkansas River from Fort Gibson (under Major Mason). It was likely thought that the better climates found in these places would help the regiment recover from the effects of the month on the plains. The regimental history says that "Captain Hunter marched from Fort Gibson on the 14th September and arrived at Fort Leavenworth the Head Qrs of the Regiment on the 29th Sept."[41]

Pawnee expedition losses of 89 dead and 118 deserted were made up with new recruits—and apprehended deserters—and the Regiment of Dragoons was ready for new activities in the spring of 1835. It began that year's work with what would be routine for many years to follow, showing United States presence in Indian territory and awing the Indians with the disciplined appearance of the soldiers. Dodge took three companies of dragoons west to the valley of the Platte in the shadow of the Rocky Mountains, leaving on 28 May for what would be a sixteen-hundred-mile ride. Other companies received other orders, and all of them were on the move by June. Hunter, however, was given a separate mission. He left Fort Leavenworth a day earlier than Dodge, moving south with his Company D toward an Osage Indian band reported to be along the Neosho River. Another dragoon company, probably one from Arkansas, was to join him at the Indians' village. He proceeded as ordered, but the second company did not appear. Further, Hunter later reported, many of the Osage were absent from the Neosho, and, he said, they "were not expected to return or be troublesome." Therefore, after a few days' halt, he went slowly toward Fort Gibson because the horses were breaking down. Arriving at the post on 21 June with thirty-five men, he decided to return to Fort Leavenworth. He started out on 3 July and was back at his station on the eighteenth, half his company and the surgeon ill and the horses in poor condition. Since Dodge did not return to Leavenworth until September and no officers senior to him were on post, Hunter was commanding officer of the fort and its two hundred men for almost two months. Hunter said in his report to the adjutant general in Washington that he was prepared to take up the Osage mission again anytime but thought that travel on the prairie would be risky until October. He added as well that he had been asking for some time to be granted a four-month leave because he had to take care of "private affairs in the East."[42]

The private affairs were, of course, his business interests in Chicago. In addition, his wife, Maria, was recovering from a severe attack of "fever and ague," a traveler having remarked on the "sunken eyes and ashy cheeks" of the many sufferers at Leavenworth. Maria was tired of the desolate post and eager to return home. An officer of the regiment wrote that Leavenworth was "a 'fort' by courtesy, or rather by order; it was in reality but a struggling cantonment, but on an admirable site." The town of Independence some miles away and across the river in Missouri consisted of a few log huts or frame houses, "two or three so-called hotels, alias grogshops, a few stores, a bank, printing office, and a barn-looking church."[43]

The rest of the dragoons returned in September, and it is possible that Hunter made another trip that month to the Osage villages. He returned in October even more anxious to get his leave approved. Finally, on 5 November he wrote to the secretary of war complaining that his request had been pending for over a year and that the delay had already cost him ten thousand dollars, because of business affairs that he had been unable to attend to. In this application he said that, if his leave were not approved, he would resign from the army effective a year after the date of his letter. Hunter's four-month leave was authorized effective 20 January 1836, and he was expected to return to Fort Leavenworth in May.

By then Hunter had resigned his commission in the dragoons, and he was discharged on 30 July. Coincidentally, Colonel Dodge also resigned his position that same month, and he went on to be appointed the first governor of Wisconsin and later a U.S. senator.[44]

Hunter did not return to Fort Leavenworth; he asked for and received his discharge while he was still in Chicago. He was at his wife's home in mid-1836, where he was well-known and where he was already deeply involved in the civilian business world. Chicago had, meanwhile, become a boomtown in which fortunes could be made—and lost.[45]

NOTES

1. William Couper, *One Hundred Years at V.M.I.,* 4 vols. (Richmond: Garrett and Massie, 1939), 4:41 n.

2. Andrew Hunter's Record, roll 621, Record Group 93, Compiled Service Records of Soldiers Who Served in the American Army during the Revolutionary War, National Archives (NA), Washington, D.C.; Francis Bernard Heitman, *Historical Register of Officers of the Continental Army during the War of the Revolution, April, 1775, to December, 1783,* rev. ed. (Washington, D.C.: Rare Book Shop Publishing Co., 1914), 43, 310; Parker C. Thompson, *The United States Army Chaplaincy: From Its European Antecedents to 1791* (Washington, D.C.: Office of the Chief of Chaplains, U.S. Army, 1978), 1:87, 182, 186; John C. Miller, *Origins of the American Revolution* (Boston: Little, Brown and Co., 1943), 350.

3. *National Cyclopaedia of American Biography* (New York: James T. White and Co., 1904), s.v. "Richard Stockton"; Dumas Malone, ed., *Dictionary of American Biography* (New York: Charles Schribner's Sons, 1927), s.v. "Andrew Hunter"; William B. Skelton, *An American Profession of Arms: The Army Officers Corps, 1784–1861* (Lawrence: University of Kansas Press, 1992), 139; Statement of the military service of David Hunter, late of the United States Army, 20 March 1886, Letters Received by the Appointment, Commission, and Personal Branch, Adjutant General's Office (hereafter Statement of Service, 1886, NA) and letters, 18 March and 25 July 1818, U.S. Military Academy Application Papers, 1805–66, all RG 94, Records of the Adjutant General's Office, 1780–1917, NA; J. E. Norris, *History of the Lower Shenandoah Valley* (1890; reprint, Perryville: Virginia Book Co., 1972), 581–82. Andrew Hunter died in 1823; Lewis Hunter became a physician, was commissioned as a navy surgeon in 1828, retired in October 1866, and died in Philadelphia in 1887 (*General Register of the United States Navy and Marine Corps* [Washington, D.C.: Thomas H. S. Hamersly, 1882], 372; Thomas

Coates Stockton, *The Stockton Family of New Jersey and Other Stocktons* [Washington, D.C.: Carnahan Press, 1911], 81).

4. *Register of Graduates of the United States Military Academy* (West Point: West Point Alumni Foundation, 1970), 212–13; Norris, *History of Lower Shenandoah Valley,* 581–82; Cecil D. Eby, Jr., *A Virginia Yankee in the Civil War: The Diaries of David Hunter Strother* (Chapel Hill: University of North Carolina Press, 1961), 191; Register of Cadets, 1803–65, Reports of the Conduct of Cadets, 1820–22, Monthly Reports of Conduct, 1820–25, Merit Rolls, 1818–66, Consolidated Weekly Grade Reports, 1819–23, U.S. Military Academy, West Point, all RG 94, NA. Big David Hunter was a sergeant in the Second Virginia Cavalry in Confederate service in the Civil War.

5. Robert C. Schenck, "Major-General David Hunter," *Magazine of American History* 27 (February 1887): 129–30; Philip St. George Cooke, *Scenes and Adventures in the Army* (Philadelphia: Lindsay and Blakison, 1859), 32; Fifth Infantry Returns, January 1823–April 1826, Returns for Regular Army Infantry Regiments, June 1821–December 1916, rolls 53–54, M665, RG 94, NA (hereafter Fifth Infantry Returns, NA); Francis Paul Prucha, *The Sword of the Republic: The United States Army on the Frontier, 1783–1846* (Toronto: Macmillan Co., 1969), 147–48, 177; Francis Paul Prucha, *Broadax and Bayonet: The Role of the United States Army in the Development of the Northwest, 1815–1860* (Madison: State Historical Society of Wisconsin, 1953), 126–30; Marcus Lee Hansen, *Old Fort Snelling, 1819–1858* (Iowa City: State Historical Society of Iowa, 1918), 30, 73–75, 86.

6. Dale Van Every, *The Final Challenge: The American Frontier, 1804–1845* (New York: Mentor Books, 1964), 172–73, 313–14; Frederick Merk, *History of the Westward Movement* (New York: Alfred A. Knopf, 1978), 166.

7. Inspector's report, August 1826, vol. 2, Records of the Inspector General, 1814–42, RG 159, Records of the Office of the Inspector General, NA (hereafter Inspection Records, NA); Prucha, *Sword of the Republic,* 162–70; R. Carlyle Buley, *The Old Northwest: Pioneer Period, 1815–1840,* 2 vols. (1950; reprint, Bloomington: Indiana University Press, 1962), 2:57–58.

8. Citing Charlotte Ouisconsin (Clark) Van Cleve, "*Three Score and Ten,*" *Life-Long Memories of Fort Snelling, Minnesota, and Other Parts of the West* (Minneapolis: Harrison and Smith, 1888), 79; Edward M. Coffman, *The Old Army: A Portrait of the American Army in Peacetime, 1784–1898* (New York: Oxford University Press, 1986), 132–33.

9. George W. Cullum, *Biographical Register of the Officers and Graduates of the U.S. Military Academy From 1802 to 1867* (New York: James Miller, Publisher, 1879), 1:232; Fifth Infantry Returns, May 1826–November 1826, NA; Court-Martial Record, I-39, Court-Martial Case Files, 1809–94, box 17, RG 153,

Records of the Office of the Judge Advocate General, NA (hereafter Court-Martial File, NA).

10. Court-Martial File, NA; Post Return of Troops, Fort Snelling, July 1827, Returns from United States Military Posts, 1800–1916, RG 94, NA (hereafter Post Return, Fort ——, date, NA) shows Hunter "Present in arrest" in June; Fifth Infantry Returns, September–December 1826, NA; enlisted men were paid extra for labor details—fifteen cents a day for fort construction, for example (Hansen, *Old Fort Snelling,* 27).

11. Reports, August 1826 and May 1827, vol. 2, Inspection Records, NA; the May report is also in George Croghan, *Army Life on the Western Frontier: Selections from the Official Reports Made between 1826 and 1845 by Colonel George Croghan* (Norman: University of Oklahoma Press, 1958), 154–55.

12. Court Martial File, NA; Post Return, Fort Snelling, September–October 1827, NA.

13. Court Martial File, NA.

14. Letter, signed "J. Q. Adams," Washington, D.C., 8 December 1827, ibid.

15. Cullum, *Biographical Register,* 232; Statement of Military Service, 1886, NA; Post Return, Fort Snelling, April 1828, NA; Fifth Infantry Returns for January–September 1828, NA; Hansen, *Old Fort Snelling,* 58, 178; for example, Henry Algerton Du Pont, *The Campaign of 1864 in the Valley of Virginia and the Expedition to Lynchburg* (New York: National American Society, 1925), 37–38. How many duels army officers fought is uncertain, one authority recording only eleven from 1827 to 1861, but it is likely not many of them were reported (Skelton, *An American Profession of Arms,* 1992, 195).

16. Milo Milton Quaife, *Chicago and the Old Northwest, 1767–1835* (Chicago: University of Chicago Press, 1913), 321–32; Post Return, Fort Dearborn, October 1828, NA; Fifth Infantry Returns, July–December 1828, NA; Charles Joseph Latrobe, *The Rambler in North America,* 2 vols. (New York: Harper and Bros., 1835), 2:150–52; Alfred Theodore Andreas, *History of Chicago,* 3 vols. (1884–85; reprint, New York: Arno Press, 1975), 1:99; Buley, *Old Northwest,* 2:54.

17. Buley, *Old Northwest,* 2:54; J. Seymour Currey, *The Story of Old Fort Dearborn* (Chicago: A. C. McClung and Co., 1912), 30–31; Andreas, *History of Chicago,* 1:73, 76; John Wentworth, *Early Chicago,* vol. 7 of Fergus' History Series (lecture delivered 7 May 1876; Chicago: Fergus Publishing Co., 1876), 17.

18. Hunter letter, 18 May 1881, John Wentworth, *Early Chicago: Fort Dearborn* (Chicago: Fergus Publishing Co., 1881), 28.

19. Abstract, Company Muster Roll, Fort Winnebego, Michigan Territory, 31 October 1829, Haskell M. Monroe, Jr., and James T. McIntosh, eds., *The Papers*

of Jefferson Davis, 8 vols. (Baton Rouge: Louisiana State University Press, 1991–95) 1:126; Post Return, Fort Winnebego, September 1829, NA; William C. Davis, *Jefferson Davis: The Man and His Hour* (New York: HarperCollins, 1991), 42.

20. Juliette Kinzie, *Wau-Bun: The "Early Day" in the Northwest* (1856; reprint, Urbana: University of Illinois Press, 1992), 100–102.

21. Post Return, Fort Dearborn, December 1830, April–May 1831, NA; Fifth Infantry Returns, December 1830–June 1832, NA; Henry Putney Beers, *The Western Military Frontier, 1815–1846* (1935; reprint, Philadelphia: Porcupine Press, 1975), 83; Kinzie, *Wau-Bun,* 138; Quaife, *Chicago and the Old Northwest,* 322; Buley, *Old Northwest,* 2:55; Wentworth, *Early Chicago,* 30; Andreas, *History of Chicago,* 1:131.

22. Emory Upton, *The Military Policy of the United States* (Washington, D.C.: Government Printing Office, 1911), 159–60; Merk, *History of the Westward Movement,* 169–72.

23. Upton, *Military Policy of the United States,* 160; Statement of Military Service, 1886, NA; Maria Hunter's Pension Record, Civil War and Later Survivors' Certificates, Civil War and Later Pension Files, RG 15, Records of the Veterans Administration, NA; Post Return, Fort Howard, October 1832–March 1833, NA; Fifth Infantry Returns, December 1831–October 1832, NA; Hunter letter, Andreas, *History of Chicago,* 1:99; Caleb Atwater, *Remarks Made on a Tour to Prairie du Chien, Thence to Washington City, in 1829* (1831; reprint, New York: Arno Press, 1975), 176–77.

24. The first steam-driven vessel, the *Sheldon Thompson,* did not reach Chicago until July 1832, bringing Winfield Scott and regular soldiers for the Black Hawk buildup (John Wentworth, *Early Chicago,* vol. 8 of Fergus' History Series [lecture delivered 11 April 1875; Chicago: Fergus Publishing Co., 1876], 27); Fifth Infantry Returns, October 1832–February 1833, NA. A Chicago historian says Maria accompanied Hunter to Green Bay after their marriage but errs in claiming the couple married and moved to Fort Howard in 1831 (Andras, *History of Chicago,* 1:99).

25. Kinzie, *Wau-Bun,* 255; Colbee Chamberlain Benton, *A Visitor to Chicago in Indian Days: "Journal to the 'Faroff West,'"* ed. Paul M. Angle and James R. Getz (Chicago: Claxton Club, 1957), 68–76; Fifth Infantry Returns, March–April 1833, NA.

26. Cooke, *Scenes and Adventures in the Army,* 40; Louis Pelzer, *Marches of the Dragoons in the Mississippi Valley* (Iowa City: State Historical Society of Iowa, 1917), 8–10; Ray Allen Billington, *The Far Western Frontier, 1830–1860* (New York: Harper and Row, 1956), 37–38; Upton, *Military Policy of the United States,* 160; "Army Register," 1833, *American State Papers, Documents, Legislative and Ex-*

ecutive, of the Congress of the United States (Washington, D.C.: Government Printing Office, 1860), 5:141; Francis Bernard Heitman, *Official Army Register of the Regular and Volunteer Forces of the United States Army,* 2 vols. (Washington, D.C.: Government Printing Office, 1903), 1:235.

27. Report, 28 December 1832, House Committee on Military Affairs, *American State Papers,* 5:18.

28. "Army Register," 1834, *American State Papers,* 5:280. The Indian threat did not begin until Council Grove, 150 miles beyond Leavenworth (Billington, *Far West Frontier,* 29); Louis Pelzer, *Henry Dodge* (Iowa City: State Historical Society of Iowa, 1911), 81, 90.

29. Post Return, Jefferson Barracks, August 1833, NA; Returns, Regiment of Dragoons, August 1833, Returns from Regular Army Cavalry Regiments, 1832–1916, M744, roll 1, RG 94, NA (hereafter Dragoons Return, NA); Latrobe, *Rambler in North America,* 2:229–32; Hunter's pay as a captain (including mileage and per diem for the Cincinnati trip, $114.06) was $1,253.20 for nine months in 1833; in 1834 he drew a $750 salary, $292 for subsistence, $232 for forage for a horse, $188.50 for servant allowances (pay, subsistence, and clothing), and $88.08 for forage in kind—"Items of all accounts and Claims for Pay and Allowances of Every Kind which were Paid in 1833 and 1834 to Officers of the Army" (Audit Reports, Department of War, 1836, *American State Papers,* 6:245).

30. Cooke, *Scenes and Adventures in the Army,* 197, 219, 221.

31. Dragoons Return, September 1833, NA; James Hildreth, *Dragoon Campaigns to the Rocky Mountains* (New York: Wiley and Long, 1836), 37, 42, 44–47.

32. Cooke, *Scenes and Adventures in the Army,* 220.

33. Post Return, Jefferson Barracks, November 1833, NA; Hildreth, *Dragoon Campaigns,* 42–43, 59; Hamilton Gardner, "The March of the First Dragoons from Jefferson Barracks to Fort Gibson in 1833–1834," *Chronicles of Oklahoma* 31 (Spring 1953): 28–29.

34. Cooke, *Scenes and Adventures in the Army,* 220, 224; Pelzer, *Marches of the Dragoons,* 23–27; Gardner, "March of Dragoons," *Chronicles of Oklahoma* 31 (Spring 1953): 30; Fred S. Perrine, ed., "The Journal of Hugh Evans, Covering the First and Second Campaigns of the United States Dragoon Regiment in 1834 and 1835," *Chronicles of Oklahoma* 3 (September 1925): 180; Raymond Bradford Agnew, *Fort Gibson: Terminal on the Trail of Tears* (Norman: University of Oklahoma Press, 1980), 118.

35. Dodge letter, 18 April 1834 (original in Historical Department, Des Moines), in Pelzer, *Marches of the Dragoons,* 28; and William Salter, ed., "Letters of Henry Dodge to Gen. George W. Jones," *Annals of Iowa,* 3d ser., 3 (October 1897): 221–22; George Catlin, *Letters and Notes on the North American Indians,* ed.

Michael MacDonald Mooney (1841; reprint, New York: Clarkson N. Potter, 1975),
273–74; Orders, Headquarters, Left Wing, Western Department, 20 and 23 April
and 1 May 1834, quoted in Hildreth, *Dragoon Campaigns,* 101–9; Dragoons Return, summary for 1835, NA.

36. Pelzer, *Henry Dodge,* 93; Cooke, *Scenes and Adventures in the Army,* 225;
Hildreth, *Dragoon Campaigns,* 119; Catlin, *Letters and Notes,* 274; T. B. Wheelock,
"Journal of Colonel Dodge's Expedition from Fort Gibson to the Pawnee Pict
Village," 26 August 1834, in Report of the Secretary of War, 1834, *American State
Papers,* 5:373.

37. Wheelock, "Journal," *American State Papers,* 5:374–75; Catlin, *Letters and
Notes,* 281.

38. Wheelock, "Journal," *American State Papers,* 5:375–80; Perrine, "Journal of
Hugh Evans," 188.

39. Perrine, "Journal of Hugh Evans," 381–82.

40. Cooke, *Scenes and Adventures,* 225; Dodge letter, 1 October 1834 (original in Historical Department, Des Moines), in Pelzer, *Marches of the Dragoons,* 47;
and in Salter, "Letters of Henry Dodge," 221–22; Catlin, *Letters and Notes,* 299.

41. Dodge's Report of 1834, 11 February 1835, and Dragoons Return, August–September 1834, NA; Post Return, Fort Leavenworth, September–October 1834, NA; Perrine, "Journal of Hugh Evans," 215.

42. Dragoons Return, June–July 1835, NA; Dodge report, 28 May 1835,
Hunter report, 29 July 1835, documents 113 and 0082, M567, RG 94, Letters
Received by the Office of the Adjutant General, 1812–88, NA (hereafter AGO
Letters Received, NA); Post Return, Fort Leavenworth, July, August, and Sep-
tember 1835, and Fort Gibson, June 1835, NA; David Lavender, *Bent's Fort* (Gar-
den City, N.Y.: Doubleday and Co., 1954), 159–63.

43. Quoting a traveler, 3 September 1835, Louise Barry, *The Beginning of the
West: Annals of the Kansas Gateway to the American West, 1540–1854* (Topeka:
Kansas State Historical Society, 1972), 295; Cooke, *Scenes and Adventures,* 93; quoting
a traveler, Billington, *Far Western Frontier,* 28.

44. Post Return, Fort Leavenworth, September–October 1835, January–
July 1836, NA; Hunter letter, 5 November 1835, document 0279, M567, AGO
Letters Received, NA.

45. Post Return, Fort Leavenworth, July 1836.

Chapter 2

CIVILIAN LIFE
AND RETURN TO THE ARMY

The reason that Hunter was anxious to reach Chicago in late 1835 was that he was engaged in business enterprises he hoped would be lucrative. He was not the only officer in the army who saw riches in Chicago. A Fort Dearborn officer wrote to his brother in June 1835, "There is an opportunity here of making something such as few Officers have, and I feel it would be wrong to neglect it." Hunter's was a project that, it was hoped, would take advantage of the excellent economic condition of the city. With John H. Kinzie and a number of other prominent Chicagoans, Hunter invested in the construction of a new hotel to accommodate visitors to the town. It was the Lake House at Rush and North Water Streets, a brick structure, three stories tall, which cost one hundred thousand dollars to construct. Chicago had three other hotels, but Lake House was to be the best.[1]

Chicago was very different from the crude frontier town it had been when Hunter left in mid-1833 for his assignment with the dragoons. It was still crude but growing at a breathtaking rate, fueled by a number of factors and events. Part of the growth was stimulated by reaction to the Black Hawk War. Following the conflict, lands in northern Illinois and Wisconsin became well-known, perhaps because of tales of soldiers returning from the chase. Furthermore, for the first time settlers were appearing to occupy those lands that as late as 1830 had been populated only by Indians. At a gathering of six to eight thousand Indians at Chicago in 1833, the natives were persuaded—by gifts, promises of land west of the Mississippi, and not a little fraud—to give up their property west of Lake Michigan between the Rock and Milwaukee Rivers. A resident of the town wrote a few years later about the "great Indian payment . . . , at which some of the inhabitants distinguished themselves by their dexterity in basely stealing blankets from the ignorant and besotten Indians." A year later the Winnebagoes were likewise induced to migrate. Green Bay became an important town, growing from its fur trade beginnings, and it was the center of a boom in land sales for eastern and central Wisconsin territories. These activities, along with increased lead mining in Illinois and Iowa, meant good times for the people of well-situated Chicago.[2]

The town of Chicago was struggling to meet the demands of explosive growth—perhaps the main reason for Hunter's involvement in the hotel—but it was not doing a very good job. A traveler said in 1833 that the town of about a thousand residents living in rough plank buildings was "one chaos of mud, rubbish, and confusion." "Emigrants and land speculators [are] as numerous as the sand," he said, and the town was populated by "sharpers of every degree; pedlers, grog-sellers; Indian agents and Indian traders." Furthermore, the town was noisy day and night, the Indians contributing much of the late-night disturbance. In a year or two Chicagoans' attempts to get control over the situation took the form of ordinances limiting the running of horses in the town's precincts, banning free-ranging pigs without rings in their noses, and so on. Communication with the outside world was becoming regularized, not depending as it formerly did on casual suppliers. By 1834 there was weekly steamboat service to St. Joseph, Michigan, schooners sailed Lake Michigan, and a stage ran east twice weekly.[3]

When Hunter arrived in his wife's native Chicago, a land boom was in full swing, properties appreciating 100 percent or more in weeks or months, a situation aggravated in 1836 by a canal bill passed by the Illinois legislature. That legislation alone is said to have resulted in $3.5 million in lot sales that year. An 1836 visitor had "never seen a busier place than Chicago" and noted, particularly, the rushing speculators. To her "it seemed as if some prevalent mania infected the whole people." Streets were being laid out and water supplies being worked on, but labor and sometimes food were in short supply. The town had about thirty-three hundred residents, three times as many as in the year Hunter went to Missouri, and it was on its way to doubling again in three years. Of course, the speculative atmosphere was not restricted to Chicago and Illinois; the entire nation was optimistic that good times would continue, and public land entries increased ten times in the six years ending in 1836. Hunter opened a business on North Water Street near Rush, with John Kinzie, engaged as "forwarding, commission merchants" and, one assumes, in land sales, perhaps with James Kinzie, who was a real estate agent. Lake House construction continued in 1836, and the Hunters lived near it on Illinois Street.[4]

The bubble burst in 1837 with a nationwide panic caused primarily by the reckless speculation, although the full effects of the resulting depression did not reach Chicago until 1839. Nonetheless, Chicago business began its decline in the year of the panic, particularly the real estate market, which depended on now-failed banks. An observer of the 1837 Chicago scene said that speculation "gave color and direction to most business transactions" so that, when the bubble burst, "many of her most business and enterprising citizens were insolvent." The West did not recover from the shock until 1842 and later, and, although there are no records to show it, Hunter's fortunes surely declined. The city's growth was likewise damaged and, until the coming of the railroad in 1842, did not significantly recover its earlier momentum. The hotels suffered from slower business, and it is likely that the panic of 1837 was the primary reason for the later failure of Hunter and Kinzie's relatively luxurious Lake House. There was still no bridge across the Chicago River (the town depending on a rope ferry), streets remained unpaved, and water system installation was halted. The crisis had political fallout as well, seriously damaging the incumbent Democratic Party nationally and leading to the rise of Whig Party opportunities in northern Illinois and elsewhere.[5]

Further east along the frontier bordering Canada, unrest erupted in late 1837. It was connected with an armed dispute between Upper and Lower Canada, and Americans south of the line took sides in the controversy. American sympathizers formed irregular military units, and some of them entered Canada on raids supporting the rebellion. The consequences of these activities and of unwise British acts soon inflamed Americans west of the New York border, where the confrontation was most serious, and led to the raising of volunteer troops for protection of the nation against the danger of war. The army successfully prevented incidents, and the threatened hostilities had died down by mid-1838. Formation of Chicago's first militia unit was inspired by this possible clash. The organization was raised in late February 1838, and David Hunter, possibly the only trained and experienced soldier in the city, was elected captain of the company. The militia does not seem to have been very active, but it was called out in July 1840 to attend the hanging of a criminal. Hunter commanded his company of sixty men, yet his authority was limited because two Illinois militia colonels were also on the scene.[6]

Hunter, certainly now an important citizen of the town, showed his temper in reaction to an article in the 30 November 1839 *Chicago Democrat* which castigated unnamed Chicagoans with responsibilities concerning Indian claims. Hunter took the editorial as an attack on his (and John Kinzie's?) business practices, "came into the office of the *Democrat,* and then and there demanded satisfaction from John Wentworth, the editor, and laying two pistols upon the table, offered him his choice of weapons." Wentworth calmed Hunter by promising a printed apology, which Hunter accepted in the form of an advertisement in the paper. The incident surely added to Hunter's reputation as a duelist, but he explained in mitigation that the pistols offered were at the time not loaded.[7]

Chicago had changed since Hunter's return from the army in 1836. His old post, Fort Dearborn, was occupied by a single caretaker. Lake House remained the best hotel, and a narrow slate pavement—the only one in town—surrounded it. The fashionable citizens, some of whom had substantial houses, lived north of the river, still linked by the rope ferry. Brick-fronted stores had replaced many of the earlier plank buildings, but life remained rough. The town's nature as a commercial center was changing, however, from trading to other commerce, and it was a transportation hub, served by a canal connecting the city with the Illinois River and the Mississippi and by lake vessels.

The national election of 1840 was different from those that had preceded it. Campaign practices of Martin Van Buren's Democrats and William Henry Harrison's Whigs were noted for misrepresentations and other irrelevant abuses and distortions. The new Liberty Party—which was to hold the balance of power in later elections—was against slavery and in favor of its formal abolition. This movement was only a reflection of an important other one that had been dormant after the 1820 Missouri Compromise but which had arisen in Congress three years before the election. The status of slavery was not an important campaign issue, but it would shortly dominate U.S. politics. Hunter's interest in the question is not apparent at this early date; his only known comment on slaves was this remark to the officers on his court-martial in 1827: "You Gentlemen will know how to forgive me when you know that I have Suffered particularly from that Man [Colonel Snelling] what would make the Blood of a Slave boil." This was hardly a political statement and put him in neither the abolitionist nor antislavery camp. Yet the election that returned Harrison and his vice presidential running mate, John Tyler, did offer Hunter a personal opportunity that required his political allegiance to the Whigs and would lead him to the slavery issue.[8]

PAYMASTER MAJOR

Because his economic success in Chicago was disappointing, Hunter sought to provide better for his wife and himself. He was able to leave his local business affairs in the hands of brother-in-law John Kinzie, so he sought to reenter the army. The line of the army was very small, and, since he had surrendered his position on the seniority list, he was unable just then to secure a commission with the dragoons or an infantry regiment. Instead, he requested appointment in the paymaster corps, which, like all the army and particularly its supporting bureaus, was heavily influenced by patronage. The army at the time readily accepted untrained men into low and high officer grades, part of the emphasis held over from Jacksonian attitudes. No West Pointers were found among the army's thirty-seven generals who served from 1802 until the beginning of the Civil War. In fact, twenty-three of them had little or no military experience when they were appointed. Consequently, political activity—at least to further a military career—did not seem out of line for army officers, and many of them actively engaged in it.[9]

An army reorganization act in 1838 motivated by requirements of the Seminole Wars in Florida—still another failure of the militia system—gave Hunter his opening back to the army. In addition to increasing generally staff positions that were earlier filled by officers from already shorthanded regiments, an increase in support department officers was authorized. One section of the law authorized the president to appoint what were called "additional paymasters" on the basis of one for each two militia or volunteer regiments on active service. These temporary officers were to continue in service only as long as the nonregular forces were serving in the army. The rest of the army—all its regular soldiers—continued to be paid by the fifteen existing paymasters.[10]

Hunter began his attempts to return to uniform in early 1839, but he did not seek the paymaster route at once. He may have considered it his duty to reenter the army because of the British threat, which seemed genuine on the frontier. He obtained a letter of recommendation from his last commanding officer, Henry Dodge, then governor of the Wisconsin Territory. Dodge wrote that Hunter's "attention to his duties was unremitted in taking care of his sick men and the preservation of his horses" on the Pawnee Pict expedition. In general, he concluded that Hunter was a "brave, talented, high-minded, efficient Officer" and should be appointed to some position so that he would be available to be promoted to colonel "in the event of a war with England." No action was taken on Dodge's recommendation, and Hunter's attempts to rejoin the army were delayed until a better political atmosphere existed.

The successful 1840 campaign of Harrison and Tyler, which overturned Democratic Party control of the national government, provided that change. Following the election Hunter got a recommendation from "active commercial precincts" in Chicago, signed by four prominent businessmen, all of them Whigs. They were William Loomis Newberry, a banker, merchant, and philanthropist; John Gage, a former Chicago mayor; William Butler Ogdon, Chicago's first mayor (1837) and a future railroad president; and Benjamin Wright Raymond, a merchant and another former mayor (1839). Their letter was addressed to President-Elect Harrison, showing the importance of the change of administration to Hunter's ambitions. A few months later—and just before the new administration took office—Hunter's cause was furthered by still more prominent men, among them U.S. senator Augustus Seymour Porter, a Michigan Whig; John Todd Stuart, an Illinois Whig congressman and Abraham Lincoln's law partner; and other Chicago and state politicians. James Duane Doty, Wisconsin delegate to the U.S. Congress, also responded. They wrote to the incoming secretary of war, John Bell, one remarking that Hunter should be appointed a paymaster so that in case of an emergency he would be able "to exchange his position for Rank in the Line of the Army."[11]

Hunter did neglect other army contacts who might have furthered his appointment, but not many of them would have been that useful in what was a political contest. The records of the army's paymaster general contain numerous contemporaneous letters from other office seekers, but none of them showed political power comparable to Hunter's. Hunter asked War of 1812 hero Winfield Scott, then commanding the army's Eastern Division from Elizabethtown, New Jersey, for support. Scott wrote to the paymaster general Nathan Towson that Hunter was "late one of the very best Captains in the Army." He saw that it would be useful to appoint Hunter a paymaster, a position "he would be eager to exchange for rank in a marching Regiment" in case of army expansion. Hunter called on relatives also. Capt. Robert Field Stockton, a naval officer, wrote to secretary of state designate Daniel Webster that he should support Hunter's petition: "He is my cousin and I can say that he has the very highest & most influential recommendations." Stockton, the current owner of his grandfather's Princeton home, "Morven," was at the time commanding the *Ohio,* its home port in Philadelphia. Being more politically active than most naval officers, he had campaigned vigorously for Harrison in his native New Jersey during the 1840 race, and he was to gain national attention during the war with Mexico.[12]

The candidate did not wait, however, for matters to take their course, and he went to Washington before or just after inauguration day, 4 March 1841. Hunter saw Daniel Webster (or he was sent Webster's letter of recommendation) and managed to call on the new secretary of war on 11 March to present Webster's letter. The following day he wrote to Bell stressing the standing of his supporters, among them, Webster, three former Chicago mayors, the president of "our Tippicanoe Club," Senator Porter, and others. The campaign was successful: Hunter was appointed an additional paymaster effective 13 November 1841 and was assigned to Tallahassee, Florida.[13]

Hunter's duty was to travel in Florida and Georgia, paying soldiers as he went. In the summer of 1841 the governor of the latter state had called up some of his militia without an army request. An officer was sent by the general-in-chief in Washington to look into the need for these units, and he reported that "there has not existed the slightest necessity for calling these militia companies into the service." Nonetheless, political reasons called for federal recognition and activation of the Georgia units in November 1841 and their immediate deactivation. This short incident provided justification for Additional Paymaster Hunter's assignment. The war, however, had by then degenerated to minor skirmishes among settlers and the small number of scattered Indian warriors, but the campaign, while not officially ended until August, was over by early spring 1842.[14]

By that time Hunter had succeeded in converting his additional paymaster status to paymaster with the rank of major in the regular service. The four-year appointment was effective in mid-March 1842, and he was ordered to Washington the following month. Major Hunter was soon posted to Fort Smith, Arkansas, and he arrived at his new station in June. An early Indian frontier post, Fort Smith had been abandoned later, its functions taken over in part by nearby Fort Gibson, only sixty miles further up the Arkansas River. Fort Gibson was controversial, however, because Arkansas residents considered it too far from their settlements to defend them satisfactorily, so Fort Smith was reactivated in 1838. An army inspector general who visited the post two years after Hunter's arrival there had not much good to say about the facility. It is clear that living conditions for soldiers and their dependents were poor. He thought that quarters were "rapidly approaching dilapidation" and that all buildings were in poor shape. He described them as "put together in the Canadian manner, short logs let into grooved uprights and with no seeming regard to strength and durability.... They all stand on wooden posts two or three feet high, which rotting of course cause the superstructure to settle." Soldiers were doing repairs, and, were the old facilities to be replaced, soldiers would do the work. The inspector said of this: "I am not at all disposed to order them to waste their time and strength upon such as can never be of any public benefit and which are required only at the call of some political aspirant merely to advance his own private ends." He thought that Fort Smith "will stand as a lasting monument to the folly of the administration," which had approved the fort's unnecessary reopening because of "the earnest and repeated declarations and prayers of Arkansas." Nevertheless, it was a good location for a paymaster, who could reach other military posts such as Fort Gibson, Fort Towson on the Texas border, and the newly opened Fort Washita further west on the Red River in Indian country. Hunter and his wife spent the next four years at Fort Smith, the small garrison adjacent to a growing village.[15]

Fort Smith was headquarters of the Second Military Department, then commanded by Bvt. Brig. Gen. Zachery Taylor; his staff was only four officers. Also on the post were two companies of the Sixth Infantry, which contributed a few more officers. In all, Fort Smith averaged less than a hundred officers and men.

Hunter's main responsibility was not their pay alone; he also had to go on the road about once every two months to pay troops in the field at Fort Gibson and posts along the Red River. Pay, which was supposed to be disbursed every two months, was further delayed by the difficulties Hunter had on the remote frontier exchanging pay orders for cash, traveling over unimproved trails and unbridged rivers and streams, and communicating with his Washington headquarters.

Hunter explained some of his problems in a letter to the paymaster general. A paymaster had to estimate his funding requirements each month and wait for Washington to respond with a pay order. This process, he said, took at least forty days because of poor communications. When the order was received, the paymaster had to convert it into specie, preferably gold, but silver was sometimes acceptable. Because Fort Smith had few commercial businesses, specie was in short supply. In fact, very little of it could be found in Arkansas. Therefore, Hunter found it necessary to travel frequently to New Orleans for his cash. Reaching that city was in itself a complicated matter. He had the choice of going by land, something over 850 miles, or by boat, about 1,200 miles. The first was difficult because of the terrain and the risk of highwaymen in an undeveloped country. Travel by steamer was sometimes impossible because of low water on the Arkansas and Mississippi Rivers. On the other hand, high water was frequently encountered, blocking all travel. On one specie trip returning from New Orleans, Hunter's ship, the *Republic,* sank a few days into the voyage, but he saved the cash, losing all his personal baggage. That trip required passage on two other vessels before reaching Fort Smith on the Arkansas.[16]

Even if he could convert treasury orders to specie, Hunter still had to visit the posts for which he was responsible. If he covered all three posts on one circle, the trip was 540 miles. He went by wagon through, he said, "Indian country," accompanied by his clerk, servant, and "a small guard" supplied by General Taylor. Hostile Indians do not seem to have been a cause for concern, though Hunter once reported Cherokee unrest over a tribal election which caused violence, mostly against Indians. The dispute also was responsible for the lynching of an officer's "servant [slave?]" at Fort Gibson. The way between posts was "through a rough mountainous country, over as bad a road as there is in the United States. This journey will take another month, should I not be detained by high water, or the breaking down of my wagon. . . . At most of the rivers & creeks there are neither bridges or ferries; and in case of high water I am obliged to raft the streams, or encamp on their banks until they may run down." For these reasons, Hunter explained, the time from estimate to payment of the soldier was three months, not the desired two.[17]

On 20 December 1844 Hunter reported his return to Fort Smith from Fort

Gibson, where he paid some of the First Dragoons. One of the soldiers wrote of his encounter with the major: "I was at Fort Gibson, when the time arrived, and on the 11th of December 1844, punctual to the day a full statement of my accounts with the government, having been drawn out and audited, I was discharged. The paymaster happening to be at the fort at the time, I was fortunate in that, as he cashed the duplicates in full, so I was not compelled to submit to a discount, which I should have had to do, had he not been there." Had Hunter not been at Fort Gibson, the private would have been charged a fee by the post sutler to cash pay vouchers, a common problem when soldiers' enlistments at remote stations had expired.[18]

By 1846 Major Hunter and most of the regular soldiers in the West were called to a new conflict; major redeployments of the small regular army were begun the year before. The army had not been ordered to begin preparation and troop movements when war was first anticipated eight years earlier. In 1835 Texas, then a Mexican state, declared its independence, an important issue in that decision being the importation of slaves, which Anglo-American Texans supported but Mexico barred. The new nation called at once for recognition by the United States and hoped for eventual annexation. President Andrew Jackson granted the first request in 1837, but the problem of slavery delayed the second. President John Tyler accomplished annexation by a legislative maneuver in February 1845, at the end of his term in office. Mexico broke diplomatic relations with the United States, but the catalyst for war was a boundary dispute. Texas claimed its southern border was the Rio Grande, while the Nueces River had been the recognized boundary of the Mexican state of Texas. The new president, James K. Polk, accepted the Texas claim and alerted troops headed by Gen. Zachary Taylor, then commanding the First Military Department from Fort Jesup, Louisiana.

Taylor had assembled what regulars he could gather at Fort Jesup, and he arrived with them in New Orleans on 10 July 1845. A day short of two weeks later the army (two regiments of infantry and some artillery) embarked aboard sailing vessels for Corpus Christi, Texas. Taylor ordered other troops concentrated at San Antonio, from which they could proceed overland and support operations. The first of these movements to affect Hunter was the deployment of three companies of dragoons from Fort Washita to Austin, Texas. He traveled to the Red River post in mid-September to pay the troops before they departed their home station. Two months later he wrote to the paymaster general that he was anxious to leave Fort Smith and would like an assignment in Texas. It appears that he made arrangements to switch places with Paymaster Daniel Randall, who was assigned to Taylor's Army of Occupation at Corpus Christi. Soon, however, he said, "But now that the prospect of active service in Texas, or in Mexico, has ceased, I can see nothing to be gained by a change into Texas, and I should therefore greatly prefer remaining here, until the casualties of severe service shall enable the Paymaster General to give me a little status [a promotion]." Taylor's army "at the big camp on the Nueces" was, in the words of an army historian, spending its time in "drilling, horsebreaking, and parades, interspersed with boredom and dissipation." This seemingly placid situation was to change in a few months, and Hunter's routine duties at Fort Smith would be disturbed.[19]

WAR IN MEXICO

Hunter was reappointed a paymaster in March 1845, the normal procedure for such officials. Paymaster commissions expired every four years but were always renewed. Hunter's reappointment came just three years after his original commission, but it was customary to anticipate the expiration date so that there would be no suspension of paymaster coverage in the field. He was required to take the oath of office again and to provide a new bond for his performance in handling the government's money. Hunter used the assets of his mother in Princeton for the purpose and said that his sister Mary Stockton, also in New Jersey, would see to the bond's execution. A month later Hunter told the paymaster general that he had just heard of his mother's death (she died on 18 March 1846) and that this was probably the reason his bond was delayed. He suggested that the Washington officials contact Mary, adding that his friend and relative in Princeton, Richard V. Field, Esq., might be of assistance. The matter was soon resolved without further correspondence.[20]

As directed by Polk, Taylor's small army left Corpus Christi and entered the disputed territory in March 1846, and, when Mexico reacted in May, Polk convinced Congress that a state of war existed. A greatly outnumbered U.S. Army was immediately successful against the Mexican army, and the North Americans advanced south of the Rio Grande. By this time the army on the frontier was almost entirely committed to the buildup in Texas. Hunter had left on one of his specie runs to New Orleans on 5 May, three days before the fighting began along the Rio Grande. He was no doubt concerned about the situation in Mexico and was anxious to return to Fort Smith so that he could pay the few remaining regulars before they took the field. Unfortunately, it was then that Hunter's ship sunk on the Mississippi, and it was late June by the time he reached Fort Smith, where he found companies under orders for Texas.[21]

Hunter had a continuing duty to pay troops at Fort Smith, Fort Gibson, Fort Washita, and Fort Towson, although soldiers at these posts were being drawn off rapidly to meet war requirements. In addition, state units were appearing at Fort

Smith, the first ones Arkansas volunteers who required payments. By early July Hunter returned to Fort Smith from a trip to Fort Gibson, and he reported to Washington that there were only two companies of regulars remaining in the department. It was clear that routine paymaster duties were ending at Fort Smith, and Hunter suggested how the army in the field might be paid. He was interested in the troops—among them only a few regulars, most of these dragoons from Fort Washita—assembling at San Antonio under the command of Brig. Gen. John E. Wool, General Taylor's subordinate. Hunter assumed that Wool was going to move into Mexico, and he recommended that pay requirements be met from New Orleans, landing the cash on the Texas coast, rather than proceeding overland from Fort Smith or elsewhere. Hunter said that British sovereigns should be the currency supplied, and not silver coins, because gold was more likely to be acceptable in Mexico. The paymaster general by then decided to assign Hunter to be the senior paymaster with General Wool's column, and he ordered the major to San Antonio on 6 July.[22]

Orders reached Hunter a few weeks later, and he prepared to proceed to New Orleans for transport to the Texas coast. He remarked that since 24 June he had traveled six hundred miles overland, paying troops, and he was concerned that volunteer cavalry regiments from Kentucky and Tennessee had not yet passed through Arkansas as expected, but he thought they could be paid later. He left Fort Smith on 10 August by steamer, and probably Maria went downriver with him to New Orleans. Hunter left the Louisiana city on 26 August with troops from the Sixth Infantry, bound for Lavaca, Texas, on the coast about a hundred and fifty miles from San Antonio. Arriving on the last day of August, he was carrying one hundred thousand dollars, most of it in gold. Hunter started for San Antonio the next day, accompanied by an escort of seventy-five soldiers and the newly commissioned additional paymaster John B. Butler. The party arrived at Wool's headquarters on 9 September, finding a Texas regiment, whose short enlistment had expired, seeking its final pay. This unexpected requirement nearly exhausted Hunter's funds, and he recommended that the Texans be serviced from Fort Towson so that he would have some money left for the advance into Mexico.[23]

While Hunter was thus engaged in Texas, his cousin Capt. Robert F. Stockton, of the frigate *Congress,* took command of U.S. naval forces then off the coast of the Mexican state of Northern California. Stockton arrived after his predecessor had supported the revolt of the resident Americans, but he went further and, on 17 August, declared the annexation of the territory. He also appointed Capt. John Charles Frémont, an American army officer who happened to be in California, as one of the military commanders. The situation remained unstable for some time because the Mexicans revolted against U.S. authority. The new territory was not finally pacified until January 1847, after fighting with the Mexicans and intrigue among the Americans. Hunter did not record his views of Stockton's accomplishments, and he would not have heard of them for some time because of the lack of communications between the West Coast and American territory east of the Rocky Mountains. Stockton was not universally praised for his actions in California, and Frémont was convicted by a court-martial for exceeding his authority there. Frémont resigned from the army but returned to it at the start of the Civil War. Hunter was to cross paths with him early in that conflict.[24]

On 16 September Hunter told the paymaster general that he expected Wool to begin his march soon, and ten days later the first units of Wool's twenty-six hundred largely volunteer troops left San Antonio. Wool and his staff, including Major Hunter, departed the Texas town on the twenty-ninth with an escort of two companies of the First Dragoons, the same regiment that Hunter had joined as a captain in 1833. Two more detachments followed, on 2 and 9 October, Major Butler accompanying the latter group as paymaster. The columns were bound for the Rio Grande near present-day Eagle Pass—a distance of one hundred and eighty miles. The plan was to continue westward to the commercial center of Chihuahua. The health of the soldiers was poor, and the force moved slowly. A soldier wrote that the country between the Nueces and Rio Grande Rivers "is divided into sandy deserts and marshy chapparals, almost as difficult of access as the jungles of India. It will be the haunt only of savages and wild beasts for many generations, if not forever." The first detachment and Wool's column crossed the Rio Grande together on 8 October and reached Monclova, one hundred and fifty miles farther on, at the end of the month. Taylor told Wool to make camp there, giving Wool three weeks to train the raw and poorly disciplined volunteers, scout the roads to Chihuahua, and allow his stragglers to catch up. The march continued in late November, Wool arriving eleven days and another hundred and fifty miles later at Parras, on 5 December.[25]

While Wool was on the march, General Taylor had taken Monterrey in heavy fighting and occupied Saltillo, the latter town about a hundred miles southwest of Parras. His Army of Occupation needed to rebuild after the hard fighting at Monterrey, and Taylor was unable to continue his advance. By the middle of December, however, Taylor received intelligence that a large force under Mexican general Antonio Lopez de Santa Anna was advancing on his army from San Luis Potosi, one hundred and eighty-five miles south on the road to Mexico City. The result was that Taylor canceled Wool's campaign to Chihuahua and, on 17 December, ordered the general from Parras to Saltillo, Wool's army reaching the town on the twenty-first.[26]

Hunter had been out of touch with the paymaster general during the two-month march from San Antonio—or at least none of his dispatches from that period reached Washington. He summed up the trip and the military situation in a letter four days after arriving at Parras. The march had not been too difficult, particularly because the roads were in good condition, and the column had encountered no rain since San Antonio. Hunter thought Parras a good location, and he said, "The place is well supplied with drinkables," specifically, wines and brandies. Rations were good because Wool had captured a large amount of flour being sent to Santa Anna at San Luis Potosi. Hunter thought that Santa Anna was retreating to the capital, but this was to prove wrong. The paymaster still had his duties to perform, and Hunter sent Additional Paymaster Butler on the long trip to New Orleans to obtain two hundred and eighty thousand dollars to pay the soldiers. Hunter accompanied Wool's army from Parras to Saltillo late in December.[27]

Taylor's victory at Monterrey earned him a promotion to brevet major general, but President Polk decided that continuing the central Mexico campaign was unlikely to end the conflict. The inconclusive war situation caused Polk to accept the plan of Maj. Gen. Winfield Scott, who proposed landing at Veracruz and marching on Mexico City. When this plan was implemented in late December, Taylor gave up half his troops to Scott and was ordered to evacuate Saltillo. Taylor, however, ignored the evacuation order and, with his seven thousand remaining men, made plans to consolidate his positions. Because of Taylor's new deployments, Hunter was ordered from Wool's force at Saltillo to Monterrey, where he became the senior paymaster for Taylor's Army of Occupation. He had several additional paymasters working under his direction, and he reported directly to the paymaster major Thomas Jefferson Leslie, West Point class of 1813, at New Orleans. Maj. Edmund Kirby was the senior paymaster in Mexico, but he was with Scott's army en route to Veracruz and thus was not in touch with Hunter. Hunter told the paymaster general that Taylor expected an attack by Santa Anna but thought that Saltillo was not a defensible position. Taylor planned to protect Saltillo and the road to Monterrey from a hill to the west of the town. Hunter said that the matter would be decided by 20 January, according to what he was told were Wool's and Taylor's forecasts.[28]

By that time Taylor was convinced that Santa Anna was not going to attack him, so he made some further changes of his Army of Occupation's positions. More than half his force was sent under General Wool to Agua Nueva, eighteen miles beyond Saltillo. Taylor seems to have soon discounted the threat from Santa Anna and was, instead, preparing for a mid-March advance on San Luis Potosi. A paymaster with Wool wrote to Hunter at Monterrey that Taylor was saying "he will take it or they shall whip him." Another reason to move the troops from the town was that the almost entirely volunteer force was sadly lacking in discipline, and Taylor hoped to correct this in the camps at Agua Nueva outside the corrupting influences of Mexican towns. He had no opportunity to do so, however, because Santa Anna unexpectedly advanced on his positions with a force of about fifteen thousand, almost three times the number of Taylor's troops forward of Saltillo.[29]

Because he had warning, Taylor withdrew from the Agua Nueva positions to better ones at Buena Vista closer to Saltillo. The North Americans occupied a narrow mountain defile, La Angostura, which provided a fair natural defense, a position most historians say was chosen by Wool. One of Hunter's admirers later claimed that "it was well understood in army circles that it was at Hunter's suggestion that the ground was selected on which the battle of Buena Vista was fought." This seems unlikely, because Hunter was not on the battlefield; he was still in Monterrey, seventy-five miles north of the scene of conflict. A lieutenant who was present recorded later that Wool personally chose the positions to be defended; he did not mention any paymaster's contribution. Hunter wrote to Washington on the first day of the fight, concerned with the defense of Monterrey and reporting that Taylor had fallen back on Saltillo and was preparing to defend the town on the hill to the west. Taylor rejoined Wool south of Saltillo, won the hard-fought battle at Buena Vista on the following day, and Santa Anna withdrew his shattered force. The decisive victory at Buena Vista ended Taylor's part in the war, and the action shifted to the march on Mexico City. General Scott landed at Veracruz in early March 1847 and a month later headed inland to avoid yellow fever. After much hardship and a few hard-won victories, he entered Mexico City in September. A military government was established to run the city. Major fighting was over, and Scott's army remained in the capital and along a continually threatened supply line to the coast until the final peace, which came late in the following spring. Major Hunter remained with the depleted northern army as chief paymaster; he never reached Mexico City.[30]

Hunter and the other paymasters with Taylor were needed in Mexico to pay demobilizing volunteers and the few regular troops deployed from Monterrey to the Rio Grande. Taylor's Army of Occupation heard very little from Scott during his advance, and the main concern seems to have been getting the soldiers home. Although by June Hunter thought that Taylor's army was too small to advance south, the general was planning such a move two months later. Nothing came of these plans, and Hunter's work was arduous because of a War Department decision calling for demobilizing troops to be paid in Mexico, rather than at New Orleans. He complained about this, but only because two of his additional paymasters, Alfred Holt Colquitt and Nathan Watson, Jr., requested home leave and discharge at this critical time. Hunter recommended disapproval, but the men left their posts anyway. He wanted them detained and court-martialed, but Taylor refused to take any action. To his annoyance the only thing Hunter could do was to ask that more paymasters be sent to him.[31]

The city of Monterrey was thought quite pleasant, with commerce, shops, and other amenities of civilized life. Hunter may have asked his wife, Maria, to join him there. She was with him in Mexico, but it is not certain when. Major Hunter was apparently doing his job well. An officer recorded, "As the troops were regularly paid, and with these almighty dollars whose talismanic influence is acknowledged in all quarters of the globe, it was within their power to obtain many little comforts."[32]

Hunter's funds had to be brought overland from the Rio Grande at Camargo, a town almost a hundred miles from the mouth of the river and the port for New Orleans at Port Isabel. The road was "much infected with robbers," and money shipments required strong escorts. As the forces were reduced, there seemed less reason for Taylor to remain at Monterrey, and he moved his headquarters to Matamoras at the beginning of November, making Hunter's payroll security problem easier. Hunter, of course, went along with the general and continued his activities from the more accessible town on the south bank of the Rio Grande, near where the river joined the Gulf of Mexico. Maria may have remained at Matamoras, but conditions there could not have been sufficiently civilized, and she may have returned to New Orleans to wait for her husband.[33]

On the other hand, it is possible that David Hunter and Maria found Matamoras comfortable, because in February 1848 the paymaster told Lt. Col. Benjamin Franklin Larned, the deputy paymaster general then at New Orleans, that he was happy in the Mexican town but thought that in a few months he would like a chance "of going to the other line." The reference was to opportunities with the line of the army, some of which were the result of a reorganization a year earlier. Then Congress authorized a new regiment of dragoons and nine of infantry. Although these regiments were to serve only during the war, a peace treaty was not yet ratified, and positions might be available for officers with Hunter's experience. Hunter did not get this chance for command of troops, probably because of army reduction following final withdrawal of U.S. forces from Mexico.[34]

POSTWAR PAYMASTER

Hunter was among the last soldiers to leave the theater of war, arriving at New Orleans on 10 July 1848. Winding down the war mobilization was the responsibility of the New Orleans headquarters, and occupation troops, many of them by now regulars in the regiments raised for the war, had to be processed and sent on to their homes or to new posts. Hunter's duties seem to have been routine at New Orleans, and he made the usual trips to places supported by his post—Pascagoula, Mississippi, and probably Fort Jesup. Judging from correspondence in the files, there was uncertainty among paymaster ranks because of competition among the officers for the reduced number of peacetime positions. The thirty-one paymasters in service were to be cut to twenty-five (plus the paymaster general and two deputies). Hunter was particularly senior, but he may have felt threatened by fellow paymaster majors who received brevet promotions during the war while he did not. In January 1849 he showed some discontent with his situation, for this cause or another, and asked the paymaster general for permission to travel to Washington with "a part of Genl. Taylor[']s family," for the purpose, he said, of reviewing his accounts. Taylor had been elected president in November, resigned from the army at the end of January, and planned a leisurely trip up the Mississippi and Ohio Rivers, arriving in Washington prior to his 5 March inauguration day. Mrs. Taylor preferred to travel directly to the capital, and she was accompanied by her son-in-law, Col. William W. S. Bliss, who was Taylor's aide, and her daughter, Betty. Hunter and his wife were socially involved with Taylor's wife and daughter in the small military community at New Orleans, and perhaps the paymaster saw a way of going further in the army through the Taylor connection. It would not have been the first nor would it be the last time that David Hunter thought it useful to be in Washington on inauguration day.[35]

Although it is not certain, David and Maria Hunter probably did reach Washington with the Taylor family before the president-elect arrived on 23 February. The Taylors stayed at Willard's Hotel, and perhaps the Hunters did as well. The army records say only that Hunter's New Orleans assignment officially ended in March 1849 and that he went to the capital, but he did not remain in the city and was not rewarded by Taylor. He was instead assigned to Detroit, still as a paymaster major. Hunter's three years at this post were not unusual. His circuit was Fort Gratiot, Michigan, on Lake Huron; the Detroit arsenal; Forts Brady and Mackinac in northern Michigan; and Hunter's old post, Fort Howard, at Green Bay. Generally, he was at each post once every two months. This routine was interrupted in early June 1851, when Hunter asked permission to go to Princeton to look in on his sister, Mary Stockton, whom, he said, "is very sick." The visit could not have taken long because he reported paying troops at all his posts later that month. He was quite busy the last six months of 1851, his last year at Detroit. His itinerary included two trips to Fort Gratiot and trips to Dearbornville, Howard, Mackinac, Brady, and the arsenal, all in July. From late August to early September he returned to Brady, Mackinac, and Howard, and late in September and early

October paid at Gratiot and the arsenal. In November he went only to the arsenal. Hunter made one more long trip, Green Bay and return, in late December, and that seems to have ended his work at Detroit. In February he was offered a change of station to New York City, and he telegraphed the postmaster general, saying, "I should like the New York State very much."[36]

Paymaster Hunter left Detroit on 23 March and reported at New York on 29 April 1852, relieving the paymaster major, Thomas J. Leslie, who had been his superior in Mexico. A year later Acting Paymaster General Larned must have concluded that posts in New England could better be served were Hunter to operate from Boston. In March 1853 Hunter paid the garrisons at Eastport, Augusta, and Portland, Maine; Portsmouth, New Hampshire; and Newport, Rhode Island, but he said, although it went satisfactorily, he preferred to remain based in New York. Hunter may have been allowed to stay because the headquarters of the army was also in New York, General Scott preferring that city to Washington. Hunter was considering a move to Baltimore, however, a post that was likely to open up when the paymaster position at Norfolk was closed and another at Philadelphia moved. This did not work out, and Hunter was soon complaining that he was having trouble handling the paperwork of the New York post. He could manage the travel but said that he needed another clerk. Although he was permitted to hire one, the new man resigned almost at once. The work was no doubt tedious—and the clerks underpaid.[37]

Posts for officers of the paymaster corps changed, as did the army, following the Mexican War because of the need to cover the huge new territories that resulted from it. While the postwar army was much the same size as before the conflict, its responsibilities were increased by Indian activities, as white Americans traversed and increasingly took over tribal lands. In August 1854 paymasters were spread thinly across the nation, and most of them followed troop deployments in the West. The Department of the East was reduced to Hunter's post at New York (he had with him Maj. Benjamin Walker) and to others at Detroit; Washington City; Fort Moultrie, South Carolina; Tampa Bay, Florida; and New Orleans Barracks. The Department of the West had just four paymasters, one at department headquarters in St. Louis and the others at Forts Snelling, Leavenworth, and Gibson. The expansion was apparent in departments of Texas (paymasters at four places), New Mexico (also four, but one of them, Fort Bliss, was at El Paso, Texas), and the Pacific (five). By 1855 Congress recognized that the army's coverage of its responsibilities was marginal and authorized the addition of two new regiments of cavalry and two of infantry. Hunter did not this time consider applying for a line assignment; he was content as paymaster.[38]

After four years at the New York City paymaster's office, Hunter was transferred again, this time to Fort Leavenworth, a post he had not seen since his dragoon days twenty years before. His orders arrived the first day of May 1856, and Hunter planned to leave the city for St. Louis in the middle of the month. On 14 June Hunter reported his arrival at Leavenworth two weeks earlier, so he did not take leave at Chicago en route. The paymaster at Leavenworth was responsible to pay Forts Riley and Kearney, but the work was increasing steadily. When Hunter was last at the fort, it had been the only white settlement in Kansas, but now the army was just a military detachment in the center of growing civilian communities. The town of Leavenworth had been founded only two years before Hunter's 1856 arrival, then boasting of a population of two hundred. By 1856 it had fifteen hundred residents occupying a rough settlement of prefabricated frame buildings brought up the Missouri River and less professional structures. In the midst of a speculative boom, the town must have been very much as Chicago had been when Hunter was there after his resignation from the dragoons.[39]

KANSAS BEFORE THE CIVIL WAR

Fort Leavenworth in 1856 was still a dragoon home station, and the soldiers were performing the same sort of duties symbolizing the strength of the United States to the Indians which Colonel Dodge had first set them on more than two decades earlier. The Leavenworth garrison included 8 officers and 212 men. Settlement westward was increasing, but there was not much before the Columbia River except Forts Laramie and Kearney on the Platte. The frontier, however, was very different, and intense national political controversy had reached the western territories. From the 1840s sectionalism drove national politics, and slavery was causing a well-defined division between North and South. The new territories acquired in the Mexican war and the older ones that were growing to a size justifying entry as states had to be entered into the Union in a way that maintained a political balance primarily on the critical slavery issue. The Compromise of 1850 admitted California as a free state and left the rest of the Mexican cession, Utah and New Mexico Territories, without restrictions concerning slavery. The first provision upset the equal balance between free and slave states in the Senate, and the second was to lead to the doctrine of popular sovereignty, allowing each territory to decide for itself if it would allow bondage within its borders. The compromise had other effects as well. It caused the 1852 breakdown of the Whig Party's North and South alliance, and it did not defuse the festering slavery question.[40]

Illinois senator Stephen A. Douglas's Kansas-Nebraska Act, approved in 1854, changed the status of slavery in the two territories, allowing popular sovereignty where slavery had been excluded since 1820. The immediate place of conflict was Kansas, just west of Missouri and on the most important existing route to the Pacific. Popular sovereignty—soon named squatter sovereignty—was fought out in lawless Kansas between settlers from the Old Northwest, some New Englanders, and others recruited by abolitionists and proslavery advocates from Missouri and other slave states. Eventually, Kansas had two territorial governments, each accusing the other of illegitimacy. Hunter arrived in the territory just when the confrontation had its most serious results. "Border ruffians" from Missouri terrorized Free-Soil settlers, and some of the latter, "Jayhawkers," did the same to their opponents. In the spring that Hunter arrived in Kansas open warfare had broken out, election unrest in the new town of Leavenworth had led to several deaths, and in September the commanding officers at Forts Leavenworth and Riley were ordered to assist the territorial governor to bring order to Kansas, a difficult task, which was largely accomplished by the end of 1856. One of Hunter's aides wrote after the Civil War that Hunter had been a tolerator or even a supporter of slavery when he came to Kansas but was "there converted to the anti-slavery faith by witnessing the atrocities of the Border Ruffians" and others. The aide concluded—no doubt with exaggeration—that Hunter and Capt. Nathanial Lyon (then at Fort Riley), a New Englander and 1844 West Point graduate, "were about the only avowed anti-slavery officers in the army previous to the breaking out of the late rebellion."[41]

"Bleeding Kansas" was the 1856 national election theme. The new Republican Party, which had replaced the northern Whigs, nominated John C. Frémont, the former army officer known for explorations and a strong antislavery position, and the Democrats a passive James Buchanan. Had Frémont been elected, the South might have then left the Union, but the Republicans were narrowly defeated. Kansas statehood, free or slave, was not settled for four more years, and the slavery debate consumed the nation. It is not surprising that army officers on the frontier in Kansas should have had opinions on the question. The army's officer corps was not unified politically, and officers' sentiments evolved over late 1850s sectional crises. Many appear to have preferred the Democrats, the party that seemed to them the more moderate, but this alignment may have been a holdover from the fact that most of the regulars serving then had been appointed to West Point over the long period of Democratic domination of Congress. As recipients of Democratic patronage, they may have reflected their fathers' political bias or may have felt an obligation to their sponsors. Some officers, such as Zachary Taylor and Winfield Scott, previously Democrats, became new Whigs;

Hunter was also one since his Chicago days. To be a Whig or later a Republican did not make one an abolitionist, however, and most Whig/Republican officers did not share Hunter's antislavery views. Those who did, did not advocate force to bring about freedom for blacks, nor for that matter did army officers preferring secession to compromise on the slavery issue advocate defending their position with violence.[42]

The question of expansion of slavery into the territories became entwined with Mormon Utah's singular "peculiar institution," polygamy, and one result was an increase in paymaster work at Leavenworth. In late May 1857 President Buchanan ordered military units from the Kansas post to move toward Salt Lake City to enforce respect for U.S. institutions, laws, and officials in the territory. In July and August fifteen hundred troops accompanied by a like number of teamsters and others moved west toward Utah's borders. The Mormons under Governor Brigham Young's direction attacked the wagon trains, burned some of them, and captured more than half of the approaching army's two thousand head of cattle. The harassment caused the force's commander, Col. Albert Sidney Johnston, to order a halt for the winter near Fort Bridger in what is now Wyoming. Although the Mormons were careful not to kill U.S. troops, this cautious approach was marred in September by the Mountain Meadows Massacre, in which Indians and Mormons slaughtered one hundred and forty men, women, and children in southern Utah—migrants who were on their way to California. The situation was calmed by April, when Young accepted a Washington-appointed governor, Buchanan granted the Mormons amnesty, and only a part of the troops earlier sent West peacefully entered Utah's Salt Lake Valley in June. The federal troops remained at Camp Floyd, forty miles from Salt Lake City, until the Civil War. The Utah Expedition resulted in no battles or casualties, but the situation was thought to be serious enough for Congress to authorize enlistment of two volunteer regiments "for the purpose of quelling disturbances in the Territory of Utah, for the protection of supply and emigrant trains, and the suppression of Indian hostilities on the frontier."[43]

Hunter reported paying Utah-bound troops in May 1858, and he doubtless did the same from mid-1857. His work was growing, and he asked the paymaster general to transfer Major Walker's clerk in New York, J. L. Bradley, to assist him at Leavenworth. The transfer was approved, possibly because Walker was ill and could no longer employ Bradley. In July Hunter went up the Missouri to Fort Randall, a post on the border between Nebraska and Dakota Territories. In the following month, however, Hunter got an assignment that he did not want.[44]

Hunter had applied for a permanent change of station to Jefferson Barracks, probably because life near St. Louis was better than at Fort Leavenworth. He discovered, however, that the opportunity there was only temporary, to fill in for a paymaster on six months' leave, so he declined the offered appointment. By then, however, it was too late to change army plans, and a new paymaster was sent out to replace him in Kansas. The replacement was Maj. James Longstreet, an 1838 military academy graduate who transferred from the line to the paymaster corps in mid-July 1848. Longstreet did not reach Fort Leavenworth to take Hunter's place until mid-August, and Hunter sent him off to Fort Randall, a trip to take thirty days. Hunter told Washington that he heard that Capt. Barnard E. Bee, Tenth Infantry, was on the road back from Utah with volunteer troops, but he had no way of estimating pay requirements. In addition, ten companies of the First Dragoons were due to arrive at Fort Riley from Utah, and they needed fifty thousand dollars.[45]

Hunter went downriver to St. Louis in September to obtain funds, and he was back in Kansas at the end of the month, before Bee's party arrived. Longstreet was still on a trip to Fort Riley, where Hunter had sent him after Fort Randall. He had a hundred thousand dollars to turn over to Longstreet, and he left for the new and temporary St. Louis assignment, arriving on 11 October. At once he protested the plan to return him to Fort Leavenworth after six months, and, characteristically, he sought political support for his petition. U.S. senator John R. Thompson of New Jersey wrote from Princeton in November:

> My friend Major Hunter, Pay Master in the Army, for whose wife & family I feel a deep interest, is very much concerned for fear he is about to be removed from his present post at St Louis. When he left the Station at New York, he left a considerable amount of furniture for which he has not recovered and probably never will receive much—if any thing. When he left Leavenworth, unable to take he had to give away what he had there, and now, having just established himself in his present post, to be compelled to remove, and make another sacrifice, seems to be a very great hardship & if it is not absolutely necessary for the service I hope my dear Sir, that you will take these matters into consideration, and suffer him to remain the usual length of time in his present position.[46]

Senator Thompson's intervention and Hunter's requests had no effect on the army, and Hunter was ordered to return to Leavenworth, arriving there on 8 April 1859, after a four-day trip from St. Louis. Longstreet showed irritation with Hunter, who was, he said, supposed to bring funds with him from St. Louis so that Longstreet could pay the Fort Randall garrison, but Hunter came with none. Longstreet wrote, "There seems to have been some misunderstanding on his part." Hunter took over from Longstreet (who was transferred to New Mexico) in early August and was once again the paymaster at Fort Leavenworth.[47]

Although very little is recorded about the Hunters' time in Kansas, an important event in their lives took place in 1858. Some years before, Maria Hunter's youngest brother, Robert A. Kinzie, had moved his family from Chicago to Kansas, to Independence or Leavenworth, to engage in trade, probably to supply the army's Mormon campaign in what was called the "contractors' war." Kinzie's daughter, named Maria after her aunt, met a young officer of dragoons, Capt. George Hume Steuart, an 1848 graduate of West Point, eldest son of a prominent and wealthy Baltimore family. The young man and woman were married in 1858, lived at Fort Leavenworth, and became very close to their Hunter relatives. The Hunters' attachment to their Chicago niece was important to the childless couple, and their interest in the youthful Maria helped her to cope with the constant separations from her husband, whose field service kept them apart for months at a time. It is likely that Maria remained at Leavenworth even when her husband's company was temporarily stationed at more primitive frontier posts.[48]

Major Hunter's duties over the next two years were not unusual. He reported some of his trips to pay soldiers at Forts Riley, Randall, and Larned, but he was not very active, since he had another paymaster, Benjamin William Brice, to assist him. Fort Leavenworth remained an important post because it was still central to the routes west to Santa Fe, California, and Oregon. Teamster activity supporting the Utah Expedition had contributed to eastern Kansas's prosperity, and the discovery of gold on the territory's far western edge did even more for Leavenworth's merchants. Freighting and stagecoach service to the new city of Denver, aided by army contracts to supply frontier forts and mail subsidies, boomed at least for a time.

Other than possible involvement in his brother-in-law's business, Hunter was not directly concerned with this commercial activity, and his remaining time at Fort Leavenworth did not go beyond the routine. His monthly reports from December 1859 to December 1860 note nothing unusual, except a month's leave to Princeton from mid-August 1860. One speculates that when he was at home he discussed the political situation with his cousin Comdr. Robert Stockton, who had been a Democratic U.S. senator from New Jersey seven years earlier and who subsequently supported the nativist American Party. Stockton forecast the end of slavery but believed in noninterference with it. Where he and Hunter might have agreed was in Stockton's belief that free blacks deserved to have the franchise, not a common position even in New Jersey. Hunter's opinion on this question is documented later in his life, a view that he advocated even when it was out of fashion in Washington to do so.[49]

Hunter's ties to Illinois gave him more reason to be interested in the dispute over slavery, particularly when the election of 1860 paired two Illinoisans, popular sovereignty author Stephen Douglas against Abraham Lincoln. Hunter was one of few army officers to support Lincoln, and his antislavery, if not abolitionist, sentiments were well-known to his fellow officers. A historian suggests that Hunter's views were important and that he "was influential in arousing southern emotions against the Lincoln administration," but, more likely, his opinions merely widened the sectional breach between the officers with whom he served. One of his fellow officers wrote in a tribute to Hunter about his "outspoken loyalty and support of Mr. Lincoln," evidence that he took sides openly and frankly.[50]

A FRIEND OF LINCOLN

Before the 1860 election Hunter wrote to Lincoln in Springfield, the first communication between the men. These contacts soon developed into mutual respect and friendship that would last throughout the Civil War. Hunter said:

> On a recent visit to the east, I met a lady of high character, who had been spending part of the summer among her friends and relatives in Virginia. She informed me that a number of young men in Virginia had bound themselves, by oaths most solemn, to cause your assassination, should you be elected. Now Sir, you may laugh at this story, and really it does appear too absurd to repeat, but I beg you to recollect, that "on the institution" these good people are most certainly demented and being crazy, they should be taken care of, to prevent their doing harm to themselves or to others.[51]

Lincoln responded a week later to Hunter's warning, but he did not accept Hunter's advice that he should ask Buchanan's secretary of war to insure his safety if elected. Lincoln said that he had heard from another source that officers at Fort Kearney, Nebraska Territory, were threatening to go south with arms to resist the government, but he thought there were "many chances to one that this is a hum-bug." Nonetheless, he said he appreciated Hunter's warning and, since the threat might be real, "if it would not be unprofessional, or dishonorable . . . I shall be much obliged if you will apprize me" of developments. Hunter responded immediately, promising to send any evidence of treason which he might run across to Lincoln and agreeing with the candidate that the Fort Kearney information is "as you suppose, a mere hum bug."[52]

After Lincoln's election (and just two days prior to South Carolina's secession from the Union) Hunter wrote again, providing more information on yet another plot against the president-elect. He reminded Lincoln that before the 1856 election Governor Henry A. Wise of Virginia had sent a "circular to all the Southern Governors, requesting their co-operation, and stating that he had twenty thousand men ready, in case of Frémont's election, to march to Washington and prevent his inauguration." He also said that some army officers were in favor of a similar action with respect to Lincoln. Hunter was more specific later, identifying these officers as those of the Leavenworth garrison, many of whom "were of Southern origin and sympathies, and they freely discussed the political question then agitating the country." It is difficult to determine which Leavenworth-based officers Hunter thought were a danger. Of the twenty besides Hunter assigned to the post at election time, only six later joined the Confederate army. The most senior among them was Bvt. Lt. Col. John B. Magruder, First Artillery, who became a major general—but he was in the East on leave from October 1860 on. The other future rebels were one captain (who did not rise above that same rank in the Confederate artillery) and four lieutenants, all of the latter later colonels. Hunter wrote, "Believing then, as I do now, the substantial truth of these representations," it was his duty to inform Lincoln. At the time he also gave Lincoln advice about what countermeasures to take. "Would it not be well, to have a hundred thousand Wide Awakes [members of Republican clubs], wend their ways to Washington, during the first three days of March [inauguration day was 4 March], taking with them their capes and caps[?] By a coup-de-main we could arm them in Washington." Nothing came of this rather overwhelming scheme, for Lincoln had decided to take a small group of loyal officers and others with him to Washington, and Hunter was one of them. He left on leave from Fort Leavenworth on 4 February; Maria probably stayed behind to await developments.[53]

Lincoln planned to take about two weeks on his trip from Illinois to Washington for the inauguration, visiting cities along the way. Already the seven states of the lower South had seceded, and the national mood was tense. Lincoln was provided with a special train to carry his party, an American 4-4-0 engine of the Wabash Railroad, a yellow-painted baggage car and a coach. He left Springfield before 8 a.m., 11 February 1861, a Monday, planning overnight stops at Indianapolis, Cincinnati, Columbus, Pittsburgh, Cleveland, Buffalo, Albany, New York, Philadelphia, and Harrisburg. His military escort was Elmer E. Ellsworth, a former Lincoln law student dressed in the colorful uniform of colonel of the U.S. Zouave Cadets, a ceremonial and unofficial drill team with which he had toured the North a year or two earlier. Another in uniform, one he had designed himself, was Lincoln's friend, Col. Ward H. Lamon, whose military connection was that he was an aide to Illinois governor Richard Yates. Four regular officers of the army—none of them authorized for this detail by the army's general-in-chief, Bvt. Lt. Gen. Winfield Scott—joined the train en route. Two of them, Major Hunter and Colonel Sumner, who commanded Fort Leavenworth when the army was keeping the peace as best it could during Bleeding Kansas days, traveling together from St. Louis, were on approved leave from their military organizations. They boarded the train at State Line on the Illinois-Indiana border after midnight on 11 February. Two other officers joined at Indianapolis: Capt. George W. Hazzard, who was on sick leave, and Capt. John Pope, then on detached service with the Lighthouse Board. (Technically, Pope was absent without leave, and President Buchanan ordered him cited for court-martial, though no action was taken.)[54]

After huge, enthusiastic receptions at several cities the train arrived at Buffalo on 17 February, where Lincoln was met in the Central Depot by former president Millard Fillmore. The crowd there was very large, and, trying to get around in the surging mass of people seeking to get near Lincoln and Fillmore, Hunter suffered a dislocated collarbone. Consequently, he was left behind for treatment but caught up with Lincoln a few days afterward. The injury bothered him for some months. Hunter was more than fifty-eight years old and was almost thirty-eight years past his graduation from West Point. The once young infantry and cavalry officer, toughened by rough frontier service, was still healthy and strong but was showing signs of age, which he sought to disguise by dyeing his full mustache and wearing a matching dark-brown wig. An aide described "Black David" as the product of good habits of a lifetime. His "still white and perfect teeth give evidence of a stomach never disarranged by strong potations, a mouth never misused as a receptacle for tobacco or its fumes." Hunter was five feet eight inches tall, "his shoulders are broad and powerful, his chest deep, and his limbs still sinewy and active. Swarthy and Indian-like both in complexion and feature, his gray eyes dilate into blackness and brilliancy under excitement." The same officer recognized, however, Hunter's major defect—that he was "liable to sudden fits of rage," which would be demonstrated during his Civil War service.[55]

At Harrisburg, after Hunter caught up to Lincoln, information was received that the president-elect was to be assassinated on the next leg of the trip. Advised by detective Allen Pinkerton and with trusted friend Lamon, Lincoln left the rest of his escort behind and arrived secretly via Philadelphia in Washington. Colonel Sumner and Major Hunter were said to have felt hurt that they were left out of the arrangements for Lincoln's safety, but they were soon to be concerned with other security problems.[56]

Lincoln's inaugural address described the national crisis, and he spoke particularly of slavery, remarking that he did not propose to alter its status in any state in which it then existed. Hunter's position at this time may not have been much different than Lincoln's, but he was to be far ahead of the administration with respect to the continuation of slavery in slave states, slaves as legal property, and even arming slaves for war. His primary concern—as it was Lincoln's—was preservation of the Union, although Hunter, unlike Lincoln, saw secessionists as traitors. He may not, for example, have approved of allowing officers to resign their commissions to return to Southern states and from there to oppose the flag to which they had earlier sworn allegiance. That to Hunter was a treasonable act, but the War (and Navy) Department let such officers (but not enlisted men) go without concern. Of course, senators and representatives of seceding states freely joined the new Confederacy, and the departure of these Democrats further so-lidified Republican control of the new Congress. Improvement of Republican strength in the Senate in the new Thirty-seventh Congress helped Lincoln to confirm in the July 1861 special session the actions he had taken to counter the rebellion.[57]

Hunter wrote to Lincoln on inauguration day: "I am anxious to command in this city [Washington], under Gen. Scott, to preserve it, if possible, from being desecrated by traitors." The major saw how this could be accomplished because of recent vacancy among the army's brigadiers. Brig. Gen. David E. Twiggs, in command in Texas, had surrendered the federal installations in the state and had been dismissed on 1 March. Hunter told Lincoln that he thought he should have the appointment. He had heard that Colonel Sumner was a candidate, but, Hunter said, "I am as old if not a better soldier than Col. Sumner." Furthermore, Sumner had advanced to his present grade "by subserviency to Democratic rulers, while I have been kept down. He was a Douglas Democrat, up to the day of your election, while I was persecuted on account of my love for Freedom and the Whig and Republican parties." Hunter was well aware that political influence could be useful to him, and he called for support from Illinois politicians. Two recommendations sent to Lincoln seem to have been sponsored by Chicago congressman Isaac N. Arnold, a friend of Hunter and the president. His first petition simply asked that Hunter be appointed to the dismissed officer's post and concluded, "His well known qualifications for the office make it unnecessary to make particular mention of them." Arnold followed up with more justifica-tion soon after, stressing the political aspect of the request: "We believe the ap-pointment would give general satisfaction to all persons who are in favor of the Union and the maintenance of the law, and would be particularly gratifying to his numerous friends who feel his past chances for promotion have hitherto been overlooked on account of his devotion to the Whig and Republican party." Of course, until just then, Hunter had had no opportunities for promotion, not because of his politics but because he was in the paymaster corps, in which the senior rank, except for three, was the one he held. Yet the efforts were to no avail, and Sumner got the post a few days later. Hunter would have to wait to be promoted beyond his grade of paymaster major.[58]

While continuing to campaign for an improved position for himself in the army, Hunter did not neglect friends and relatives. Ellsworth also wanted a commission, and he seemed well placed to secure it. Not only was Lincoln fond of the young man, but Ellsworth was nationally known for the drill team of youths dressed as Zouaves which he had toured with. Ellsworth went to see Secretary of War Simon Cameron, suggesting that he be appointed to a new job to be called inspector general of militia affairs, in which he would be responsible for coordinating the employment of state troops. On Cameron's advice or on his own initiative, Ellsworth visited Lincoln in the White House. He brought along Pope and David Hunter to help argue his case. Hunter suggested how Ellsworth's goal might be attained. Ellsworth wrote: "Major Hunter then explained that Mr. Lincoln could appoint me to the Pay Department and then make me Chief of a Bureau of Militia." Nothing came of this, possibly because the army bureaucracy did not like it, and Ellsworth found his military position in his home state of New York, colonel of the Fire Zouaves, a colorful regiment largely made up of city firemen. Hunter was more successful advancing the case of his wife's brother Robert in Kansas. Hunter visited Lincoln concerning this matter, and Lincoln soon after wrote to Cameron, "For the sake of my friend, Major Hunter, I especially wish Robert A. Kinzie to be appointed a Pay-Master. This is not a formality, but an earnest reality." Kinzie was appointed an additional paymaster on 1 June and served through the war and until his death in 1873. Lincoln was deluged by politicians and other prominent men seeking favors in the new administration. Hunter's access shows the high regard in which the president held the very ordinary, low-ranking military officer.[59]

GUARDING THE PRESIDENT'S MANSION

The situation in Washington following the inauguration was uncertain. The Confederacy was organized and had elected as president Jefferson Davis, Hunter's now former friend and fellow officer from dragoon days (and Mexico, where Davis had commanded a regiment of Mississippi volunteers in Taylor's army). The new government had seized federal forts and arsenals throughout the South, and South Carolina had prevented reinforcement of U.S. troops still occupying Fort Sumter in Charleston harbor. President Buchanan had done little in face of these events, but Lincoln decided in early April to supply Sumter. On 12 April Confederate batteries fired on the fort, which surrendered the following day. The incident electrified the North, and Lincoln requested seventy-five thousand three-month volunteers. Virginia, which had not yet joined the Confederacy, took Lincoln's call as a threat to invade the South, and the state seceded on 17 April (Arkansas, Tennessee, and North Carolina followed later). Virginia's action put Washington under immediate threat of capture and caused panic in the city. Anticipating the need to defend the District of Columbia, the city's inspector general had recommended in early January using armed volunteer companies to defend public buildings, since there was little federal armed force available. His deployment proposal was considered premature at the time, but he was encouraged by General Scott to drill companies for future employment. On 8 April four companies were mustered in, another four as the Sumter crisis deepened, and finally thirty units were put in service. Some of these new companies had disloyal members, and it was only with difficulty that they were weeded out. The militia units were scattered throughout the city, including on the grounds of the White House. The interior of that building, except for a basement detachment, was left to another force.[60]

The South was not able to capture Washington immediately, for, like the North, it was unprepared for war. The threat did not seem less real to the citizens of the city, and the coals of panic were certainly fanned by information from the South. Reacting to Lincoln's call for volunteers, a Richmond newspaper claimed that "there is one wild shout to capture Washington City at all and every human hazard" to stop the flight South "of Abolition harpies" and "their brutal warfare." The journal concluded:

> Great cleansing and purification are needed and will be given to that festering sink of iniquity, that wallow of Lincoln and Scott [who was a Virginian]—the desecrated city of Washington; and many indeed will be the carcasses of dogs and caitiffs that will blacken the air upon the gallows, before the great work is accomplished. So be it.[61]

Willard's Hotel, adjacent to the White House, became a center for those who believed it would soon be necessary to head off the coming invasion from Virginia. One would imagine that thirty companies of raw militia were enough, but the emergency seemed to be immediately pressing and requiring action. Furthermore, some believed that "not much reliance could be placed on" the nearly two thousand volunteers so far enrolled. Meanwhile, Hunter had been assigned by General Scott "to the President's Mansion" to be on hand "in case of alarm," but without specified duties. He probably coordinated his activities with Capt. Lockwood Todd, Mrs. Mary Lincoln's cousin and an officer of the regular army then residing at the White House. Two groups of loyal citizens, a hundred men in all, were assembled at the hotel and offered to the president to protect his dwelling and person. On 18 April they were put under Major Hunter's orders. He brought one company to the President's Mansion and left the other at Willard's as a reserve and to patrol the streets at night. The latter was led by Cassius M. Clay, a senator from Kentucky, and the other by James H. Lane, senator-elect from the new state of Kansas. Both companies (although Clay's styled itself a battalion) contained several prominent men, a great many of them Jayhawkers from the earlier Kansas troubles but also a few Easterners and a sprinkling of exotic for-eigners.[62]

Major Hunter appointed Lane his second in command and gave him a new sword as his badge of office. Lane and his Frontier Guards were sworn to defend the Union, were installed in the East Room at the White House, and were issued muskets and ammunition. Tension was particularly high, because 18 April was the day on which news of Virginia's ordinance of secession was received. Lane was a curious person, given to violence but with cunning and ambition. He was an Indianan and had commanded a regiment of that state's infantry in Taylor's army in Mexico. Hunter surely knew him then, but it cannot be determined if the two were acquainted during the Bleeding Kansas days, when Lane led the Jayhawker reaction to Missouri border ruffians and committed atrocities in his own right. Although he was a senator-elect from Kansas, the new Thirty-seventh Congress did not convene until a special session in July, which allowed Lane freedom to use his power to control patronage appointments and to secure an army com-mand for himself. In any event he accepted his role under Hunter's command, John Hay, one of Lincoln's secretaries, writing, "Jim Lane walked proudly up and down the ranks with a new sword that the Major had given him." That night an officer inspecting the earlier militiamen deployed on the White House grounds said that he "was surprised to see a bright light in the East room." Inquiring about it, he was told that "many gentlemen had entered the house at a late hour, but they had come in boldly, no objection had been made from within, but on the contrary Captain Todd had told them that all was right." In the East Room "I found more than fifty men. . . . All were armed with muskets which they were generally examining, and it was the ringing of many rammers in the musket barrels which had caused the noise I had heard." Tiring of their exertions, the company bedded down on the velvet carpet, a few guards posted to give the alarm. [63]

Hunter appointed Hay his aide-de-camp, but the secretary was somewhat unclear about his duties; he wrote, "I labored under some uncertainty, as to whether I should speak to privates or not." The major was being politically aware, however, because Hay had the responsibility for overseeing the protection of the president and the mansion. The next morning, 19 April, Hay "consulted with Major Hunter as to measures proper to be made in the matter of guarding the House," and Hunter said that he would carry out whatever was asked. There was a sense of real anxiety, because rumors were constant about suspected plots to raid Washington and kill or carry off the president. That afternoon, adding to the anxiety, news came of the capture of the federal arsenal at Harper's Ferry. Rather than being concerned about the loss, "It delighted the Major, regarding it as a deadly blow at the prosperity of the recusant Virginia." At about midnight Hay toured the White House: "Hunter and the Italian exile, Vivaldi, were quietly sleeping on the floor of the East Room, and a young and careless guard loafed around the furnace fires in the basement. Good-looking and energetic young fellows, too good to be food for gunpowder,—if anything is." Not all of Lincoln's secretaries were so pleased with the intruders. William Stoddard, looking on them more realistically, remarked that the "full battalion of those very patriots who crowded the White House" earlier were now its defenders. He suggested that they had bivouacked there "so that they would be there in the morning, first thing, ahead of everyone else, with their muskets stacked around them, and with better chances for interviews with Lincoln."[64]

David Hunter said later that for six weeks "I spent every night in the East Room" with "gentlemen from all parts of the Union." It is certain, however, that the unofficial unit was no longer needed just a few days after its formation, and it was put on Potomac bridge guard duty. Volunteer troops initially from Pennsylvania, Massachusetts, and New York had arrived to defend the capital. Lane's Frontier Guards were disbanded on 3 May and Clay's men at about the same time. Hunter himself may have remained in the White House, but it is more likely that he lived elsewhere in the town while he was awaiting a new military assignment. The East Room was unoccupied by irregular or other troops in late May when the body of Colonel Ellsworth, the first senior officer killed in the war, was brought there for the funeral, which Lincoln and other high officials attended. The young man had been shot after tearing down a rebel flag during the occupation of Alexandria, Virginia. That occupation had meaning for Hunter because Union forces could now deploy all along the Potomac River south of the District of Columbia, and new regiments were constantly arriving from the North. They would need brigade and division commanders. On 14 May Major Hunter was appointed colonel of the Third Cavalry, a regular regiment organized at Pittsburgh ten days before, but he did not report to it. Instead, he was ordered to Arlington Heights opposite Georgetown in the District as commander of the Aquaduct Brigade, the unit named after the canal crossing the Potomac near there.[65]

By this time Mrs. Hunter had joined the new colonel in Washington, accompanied by Maria Steuart and a young Steuart daughter. Captain Steuart, who had commanded an honor guard of dragoons at Lincoln's inaugural, shared his elderly father's view of where his loyalties should be. George H. Steuart, Sr., a major general commanding the Maryland militia, was too old for war service, but he left his estates in Baltimore behind and went south to the Confederacy. Following this example, Captain Steuart resigned his United States commission on 22 April and accepted a captaincy in the regular Confederate service, his first assignment being at Harper's Ferry. Hunter did not record what he thought of this action, but David and Maria Hunter welcomed their now-homeless niece and cared for her the rest of the war and later.[66]

NOTES

1. Major Lafayette Wilcox, quoted in Francis Paul Prucha, *Broadax and Bayonet: The Role of the United States Army in the Development of the Northwest, 1815–1860* (Madison: State Historical Society of Wisconsin, 1953), 215; John Wentworth, *Early Chicago: Fort Dearborn* (Chicago: Fergus Publishing Co., 1881), 93; Alfred Theodore Andreas, *History of Chicago,* 3 vols. (1884–85; reprint, New York: Arno Press, 1975), 1:634; R. Carlyle Buley, *The Old Northwest: Pioneer Period, 1815–1840,* 2 vols. (Bloomington: Indiana University Press, 1962), 2:111.

2. Buley, *Old Northwest,* 2:99, 121–32; William Cronon, *Nature's Metropolis: Chicago and the Great West* (New York: W. W. Norton and Co., 1991), 26–29; Andreas, *History of Chicago,* 1:122–24; Joseph N. Balestier, *The Annals of Chicago* (lecture delivered 21 January 1840; Chicago: Fergus Publishing Co., 1876), 28.

3. Charles Joseph Latrobe, *The Rambler in North America,* 2 vols. (New York: Harper and Bros., 1835), 2:152–53; Buley, *Old Northwest,* 2:109.

4. Cronon, *Nature's Metropolis,* 29; Buley, *Old Northwest,* 2:109–11, 147; Harriet Martineau, *Chicago in 1836* (Chicago: Fergus Publishing Co., 1876), 37; *Fergus' Directory of the City of Chicago, 1839,* comp. Robert Fergus (Chicago: Fergus Publishing Co., 1876), 19, 21.

5. Cronon, *Nature's Metropolis,* 30; "Historical Sketches Compiled for Chicago Directory of 1843," *Fergus' Directory, 1839,* 61–62; Burley, *Old Northwest,* 230–34.

6. Francis Paul Prucha, *The Sword of the Republic: The United States Army on the Frontier, 1783–1846* (Toronto: Macmillan Co., 1969), 311–18; Andreas, *History of Chicago,* 1:634.

7. Andreas, *History of Chicago,* 1:151–52.

8. Henry Putman Beers, *The Western Military Frontier, 1815–1846* (Philadelphia: Porcupine Press, 1975), 130; Court-Martial Record, I-39, Court-Martial Case Files, 1809–94, box 17, Record Group 153, Records of the Office of the Judge Advocate General, National Archives, Washington, D.C.

9. Samuel P. Huntington, *The Soldier and the State: The Theory and Politics of Civil-Military Relations* (Cambridge: Belknap Press, 1957), 206–8, 247. Because there were few line major positions available, appointment as a paymaster was the best way for a captain to become a major (William B. Skelton, *An American Profession of Arms: The Army Officer Corps, 1784–1861* [Lawrence: University of Kansas Press, 1992], 151, 198).

10. Emory Upton, *The Military Policy of the United States,* 3d ed. (Washington, D.C.: Government Printing Office, 1911), 182.

11. Letters, Dodge to Secretary Poinsett, 24 April 1839; four Chicago political figures to Bell, 2 November 1840; Doty, to Bell, 13 February 1841; A. S. Porru(?) to Bell, 15 February 1841, Letters Received, Paymaster General, box 219, RG 99, Records of the Office of the Paymaster General, NA (hereafter Paymaster Letters Received, NA).

12. Letters, Scott to Towson, 16 February; and Stockton to Webster, 5 March 1841, ibid. Hunter probably met Webster when the latter visited Chicago in June 1837 and was entertained at the Lake House (Andreas, *History of Chicago,* 1:150); Dumas Malone, ed., *Dictionary of American Biography* (New York: Charles Schribner's Sons, 1927), s.v. "Robert Field Stockton."

13. Letter, Hunter to Bell, 11 March 1841, Paymaster Letters Received, NA, Webster and Porter letters not found; Statement of the Military Service of David Hunter, late of the United States Army, 20 March 1886, Letters Received by the Appointment, Commission, and Personal Branch, Adjutant General's Office, RG 94, Records of the Office of the Adjutant General, 1780–1917, NA (hereafter Record of Service, 1886, NA).

14. Captain Bliss's report to the adjutant general, Upton, *Military Policy of the United States,* 188–89; Prucha, *Sword of the Republic,* 300.

15. Statement of Service, 1886, NA; Prucha, *Sword of the Republic,* 358–60; 27 June 1844, report, George Croghan, *Army Life on the Frontier: Selections from the Official Reports Made between 1826 and 1845 by Colonel George Croghan* (Norman: University of Oklahoma Press, 1958), 31–32, 52. Forts Gibson and Smith watched over the Cherokees, Creeks, and Seminoles displaced from the Southeast; Towson,

the Chickasaws and Choctaws; and Washita, the Comanches and Pawnees.

16. Hunter's reports and letters, 31 January, 10 April, 2 May 1842; 20 May, 14 February, 3 June 1843; 1 November, 2 April, 7 May, 20 June, 26 March 1844; 5 May 1845; 22 June 1846, box 223, Paymaster Letters Received, NA.

17. Hunter's letters, 23 and 30 August and 12 February 1843; 1 November 1844, ibid.

18. Hunter letter, 20 December 1844, ibid.; John Fynn, "Reminiscences of Some Incidents in the Career of an United States Dragoon between the Years 1839 and 1844" (MS, Miscellaneous Collection, U.S. Army Military History Institute, Carlisle Barracks, Pa.).

19. John S. D. Eisenhower, *So Far from God: The U.S. War with Mexico, 1846–1848* (New York: Anchor Books, 1989), 32–33; Ethan Allen Hitchcock, *Fifty Years in Camp and Field: Diary of Major-General Ethan Allen Hitchcock* (1909; reprint, Freeport, N.Y.: Books for Libraries Press, 1971), 193; letters, Hunter to paymaster general, 14 September and 17 December, Randall to paymaster general, 17 November 1845, Paymaster Letters Received, NA; Maurice Matloff, ed., *American Military History,* Army Historical Series (Washington, D.C.: Government Printing Office, 1969), 163.

20. Report of the Paymaster General in *Report of the Secretary of War, 1844,* Senate Document, 28th Cong., 2d sess., 2 December 1844, 1:149–50; letters, Hunter to paymaster general, 14 March and 15 April 1846, Paymaster Letters Received, NA; oath of office, 14 March 1846, document 102, 1846, Letters Received, Adjutant General's Office, RG 94, NA (hereafter AGO Letters Received, NA). Mary had married her cousin navy Lt. Samuel Witham Stockton and had two children. Widowed, in 1852 she was married to the Reverend Charles Hodge, a Princeton College teacher (Thomas Coates Stockton, *The Stockton Family of New Jersey and Other Stocktons* [Washington, D.C.: Carnahan Press, 1911], 80–81, 129).

21. Letter, Hunter to paymaster general, 22 June 1846, Paymaster Letters Received, NA.

22. Letters, Hunter to paymaster general, 4 July and 1 August 1846, ibid.

23. Letters, Hunter to paymaster general, 1, 8, and 31 August, 16 September 1846, ibid.; report, Lt. L. Wetmore, Sixth Infantry, 25 August 1846, AGO Letters Received, NA.

24. Eisenhower, *So Far from God,* 212–32.

25. Letters, Hunter to paymaster general, 16 September, 9 December 1846, box 228, Paymaster Letters Received, NA; Wool's 14 October 1846, report and unidentified soldier's description, *The Mexican War and Its Heroes: Being a Complete History of the Mexican War* (Philadelphia: Lippincott, Grambo and Co., 1848),

136–44; Eisenhower, *So Far from God,* 156–57.

26. *Mexican War and Its Heroes,* 138.

27. Letter, Hunter to paymaster general, 9 December 1846, box 228, Paymaster Letters Received, NA.

28. Letter, Hunter to paymaster general, 18 January 1847, Paymaster Letters Received, NA.

29. Letter, Additional Paymaster A. S. Dix to Hunter, 8 February 1847, ibid.

30. Eisenhower, *So Far from God,* 181; Maurice Matloff, ed., *American Military History,* Army Historical Series (Washington, D.C.: Office of the Chief of Military History, 1969), 171; Robert C. Schenck, "Major-General David Hunter," *Magazine of American History* 27 (February 1887): 140; Aurora Hunt, *Major General James Henry Carleton, 1814–1873, Western Frontier Dragoon* (Glendale: Arthur H. Clark Co., 1958), 100; letters, Hunter to paymaster general, 9 and 22 February 1847, Paymaster Letters Received, NA. Taylor's battle report, 6 March 1847, praises Wool's and his own staff officers by name for their help at Buena Vista but does not mention Hunter (*Report of the Secretary of War, 1847,* Senate Exec. Doc. No. 1, 30th Cong., 1st sess., 2 December 1847, 132–41).

31. Letters, Hunter to paymaster general, 8 May, 3, 12, and 30 June, 4 August, 3 September 1847, box 876, Consolidated Correspondence Files, 1794–1856, RG 92, Records of the Quartermaster General, NA (hereafter QMG Correspondence, NA). These records belong in the paymaster's files but are maintained in error with quartermaster correspondence.

32. [Luther Giddings], *Sketches of the Campaign in Northern Mexico: In Eighteen Hundred Forty-six and Seven* (New York: G. P. Putnam and Co., 1853), 230, 236–40.

33. Letters, Hunter to paymaster general, 3 September, 1 November 1847, QMG Correspondence, NA.

34. Letters, Hunter to Larned, 28 January, 24 February 1848, ibid.; Upton, *Military Policy of the United States,* 206; letter, Hunter to paymaster general, 2 July 1848, box 230, Paymaster Letters Received, NA.

35. Letter, Paymaster Daniel Randall to paymaster general, 13 July 1848, box 231, December 1848; telegram, Hunter to paymaster general, 12 January 1849, box 232, Paymaster Letters Received, NA; Brainerd Dyer, *Zachery Taylor* (New York: Barnes and Noble, 1946), 302–4. All additional paymasters were to be kept in uniform until March 1849, to support troops being moved and released (Paymaster General's report in *Report of the Secretary of War, 1848,* House Exec. Doc. No. 1, 30th Cong., 2d sess., 10 December 1848, 245–46).

36. Record of Service, 1886, NA; letters, Hunter to paymaster general, 1 July 1851, 2 and 31 January and 6 November 1852, QMG Correspondence,

NA; letters, Hunter to paymaster general, 3 June 1851, 18 February 1852, telegram, 12 February 1852, Paymaster Letters Received, NA.

37. Letter, 29 April 1852, and box 236, letters, 9 August, 19 October, 1 December 1854, Paymaster Letters Received, NA; letter, Hunter to paymaster general, 17 March 1853, QMG Correspondence, NA. Clerks were paid seven hundred dollars annually.

38. Special Orders No. 143, Adjutant General's Office, 22 August 1854, box 235, Paymaster Letters Received, NA. Paymaster General Towson died on 20 July of that year and was replaced by Larned (General Orders No. 11, Adjutant General's Office, 20 July 1854, ibid.; Upton, *Military Policy of the United States,* 223–24).

39. Letters, 1 and 13 May, 14 June 1856, QMG Correspondence, NA; Elvid Hunt, *History of Fort Leavenworth, 1827–1927* (Fort Leavenworth: General Service Schools Press, 1926), 101; Eugene Bandel, *Frontier Life in the Army, 1854–1861* (Glendale, Ill.: Arthur H. Clark Co., 1932), 115–16.

40. George T. Ness, Jr., *The Regular Army on the Eve of the Civil War* (Baltimore: Toomey Press, 1990), 104–5.

41. William B. Skelton, *An American Profession of Arms: The Army Officer Corps, 1784–1861* (Lawrence: University of Kansas Press, 1992), 352; Charles Graham Halpine [Private Miles O'Reilly], *Baked Meats of the Funeral* (New York: Carleton, 1866), 329. Future Confederate general James Longstreet wrote that there were fewer than a dozen, "if so many, officers in the army who were Abolitionists" (qtd. in Edward M. Coffman, *The Old Army: A Portrait of the American Army in Peacetime, 1784–1998* [New York: Oxford University Press, 1986], 92).

42. Coffman, *Old Army,* 90–92.

43. Leonard J. Arrington, *Brigham Young: American Moses* (New York: Alfred E. Knopf, 1985), 252–63, 274; report, Colonel E. B. Alexander to secretary of war, 9 October 1857, *Report of the Secretary of War, 1857,* Senate Exec. Doc. No. 11, 35th Cong., 2d sess., 5 December 1857, 29–31. Secretary John B. Floyd wrote (23–24) that the Mormons "have filled their ranks and harems chiefly from the lowest classes of foreigners," with a few Americans. In his 1859 report he remarked on the "murders and robberies of the most atrocious character . . . perpetrated" on emigrants transiting Utah. The extent of Mormon participation was not then fully understood, but Floyd was convinced "that these murders are the work of the Mormon people themselves, sanctioned . . . by the authority of the Mormon church." His uncertainty was only whether those authorities directed the atrocities (*Report of the Secretary of War, 1859,* Senate Exec. Doc. No. 2, 36th Cong., 2d sess., 1 December 1859, 2:14–15); act approved 7 April 1858; Upton, *Military Policy of the United States,* 224.

44. Letters, Hunter to paymaster general, 31 July 1857, 26 January and 26 July 1858, Paymaster Letters Received, NA. Records for 1847 are missing.

45. Letters, Hunter and Longstreet to paymaster general, 11, 12, and 23 August 1848, Paymaster Letters Received, NA.

46. Letters, Hunter and Thompson to paymaster general, 25 September, 11 October, and (box 238) 16 November 1848, ibid.

47. Letters, Hunter and Longstreet to paymaster general, 5 May (with Special Orders No. 3, Adjutant General's Office, 6 January 1859), 18 April and 3 August 1859, ibid.; Post Return, Fort Leavenworth, April 1859, Post Returns of Troops for United States Military Posts, 1800–1916, roll 611, RG 94, NA.

48. Steuart's obituary, *Baltimore Sun,* 23 November 1903.

49. Hunter's reports, 31 December 1859–31 December 1860, box 241, Paymaster Letters Received, NA; Post Returns, Fort Leavenworth, June–July 1859 and September 1860, NA; Samuel John Bayard, *A Sketch from the Life of Com. Robert F. Stockton* (New York: Derby and Jackson, 1856), 205–10, app. E, 72–73.

50. Maj. Gen. (ret.) James B. Ricketts, in *Seventeenth Annual Reunion of the Association of the Graduates of the United States Military Academy at West Point, New York, June 10, 1886* (East Saginaw, Mich.: Evening News, 1886), 76; William Hanchett, *The Lincoln Murder Conspiracies* (Urbana: University of Illinois Press, 1983), 21.

51. Letter, Hunter to Lincoln, 20 October 1860, document no. 4074, Abraham Lincoln Papers, Documents Division, Library of Congress (LOC), Washington, D.C.

52. Letter, Lincoln to Hunter, 26 October 1860, Roy P. Basler, ed., *The Collected Works of Abraham Lincoln,* 9 vols. (New Brunswick, N.J.: Rutgers University Press, 1953), 4:132; letter, Hunter to Lincoln, 1 November 1860, document no. 7759, Lincoln Papers, LOC.

53. Letter, Hunter to Lincoln, 18 December 1860, document no. 5163, Lincoln Papers, LOC; David Hunter, *Report of the Military Services of Gen. David Hunter during the War of the Rebellion, Made to the War Department, 1873* (1873; reprint, New York: Van Nostrand, 1892), 7; and Hunter's April 1873 report to the adjutant general, U.S. Army Generals' Reports of Civil War Service, 1864–87, microfilm M1098, roll 5, RG 94, NA, 9: 645–6; Francis Bernard Heitman, *Official Army Register of the Regular and Volunteer Forces of the United States Army,* 2 vols. (Washington, D.C.: Government Printing Office, 1903), vol. 1; Post Returns, Fort Leavenworth, November 1860, February–March 1861, NA. Hunter's invitation came through Col. Edwin Vose Sumner, commanding Department of the West at Jefferson Barracks, who was a dragoon captain with Hunter on the Pawnee Pict expedition.

54. Request for sixty days' leave, Hunter to adjutant general, 18 December 1860, AGO Letters Received, NA; Victor Searcher, *Lincoln's Journey to Greatness: A Factual Account of the Twelve-Day Inaugural Trip* (Philadelphia: John C. Winston Co., 1960), 1–13; Earl Schenck Miers, ed., *Lincoln Day by Day: A Chronology,* 3 vols. (Washington, D.C.: Lincoln Sesquicentennial Commission, 1960), 3:10.

55. Searcher, *Lincoln's Journey,* 121; Halpine, *Baked Meats,* 330–31.

56. Searcher, *Lincoln's Journey,* 252. Sumner, the more aggressive officer, wanted to fight Lincoln's way through Baltimore (Ward Hill Lamon, *Recollections of Abraham Lincoln, 1847–1865,* ed. Dorothy Lamon Teillard [Washington, D.C.: by the editor, 1911], 41).

57. Upton, *Military Policy of the United States,* 235–41.

58. Letter, Hunter to Lincoln, 4 March 1861, document no. 7759, Lincoln Papers, LOC; petitions signed by Arnold and six other influential Illinois citizens, n.d., but in early March 1861 file no. 697 CB 1863, Letters Received by the Commission Branch of the Adjutant General's Office, 1863–70, RG 94, NA (hereafter Commission Branch Letters, NA).

59. Quoting Ellsworth, Carl Sandburg, *Abraham Lincoln: The War Years,* 4 vols. (New York: Charles Schribner's Sons, 1939), 1:168; letter, Lincoln to Cameron, 16 April 1861, Basler, *Works of Lincoln,* 4:335; Personal History of Paymasters, 1848–89, and Register of Paymasters, USA, 1815–68, RG 99, Records of the Office of the Paymaster General, NA; letter, Kinzie to paymaster general, 10 June 1861, accepting appointment, Paymaster Letters Received, NA; John H. Kinzie was appointed as additional paymaster from 1 June 1861; he served until his death in Chicago on 22 June 1865, but it is not known if Hunter had anything to do with the appointment of his former Chicago partner, (Register of Paymasters, RG 99, NA).

60. Charles P. Stone, "Washington on the Eve of the War," in *Battles and Leaders of the Civil War,* ed. Robert Underwood Johnson and Clarence Clough Buel, 4 vols. (1887; reprint, Secaucus, N.J.: Castle, 1989), 1:7–25; Upton, *Military Policy of the United States,* 226; Charles P. Stone, "Washington in March and April, 1861," *Magazine of American History* 14 (July 1885): 3, 6; Edward Davis Townsend, *Anecdotes of the Civil War in the United States* (New York: D. Appleton and Co., 1884), 11; Margaret Leech, *Reveille in Washington, 1860–1865* (New York: Harper and Bros., 1941), 55–57.

61. *Richmond Examiner,* 23 April 1861.

62. Henry Villard, *Memoirs of Henry Villard,* 2 vols. (1902; reprint, New York: De Capo Press, 1969), 1:168; attachment, n.d., to General Orders No. 4, 26 April 1861, Office of the Adjutant General, confirming earlier informal assignments, U.S. War Department, *The War of the Rebellion: A Compila-*

tion of the *Official Records of the Union and Confederate Armies* (Washington, D.C.: Government Printing Office, 1880–1902), ser. 1, 3:602–3.

63. Diary entry, 18 April 1861, John Hay, *Lincoln and the Civil War in the Diaries and Letters of John Hay* (1939; reprint, Westport, Conn.: Negro Universities Press, 1972), 1; Stone, "Washington in March and April," 8.

64. Diary entry, 19 April 1861, Hay, *Diaries and Letters,* 3; William Osborn Stoddard, *Lincoln's Third Secretary: The Memoirs of William O. Stoddard,* ed. William O. Stoddard, Jr. (New York: Exposition Press, 1955), 70. Lincoln's other secretary had little to say of the bivouac, only that "Lane's improvised Frontier Guards were drilling and sleeping in the East Room" (Helen Nicolay, *Lincoln's Secretary: A Biography of John G. Nicolay* [New York: Longmans, Green and Co., 1949], 96).

65. Hunter, *Report of Military Services,* 8; Albert Castel, *A Frontier State at War: Kansas, 1861–1865* (1958; reprint, Westport, Conn.: Greenwood Press, 1979), 34; Heitman, *Official Army Register,* 1:72; List of Army Promotions, n.d., submitted to Senate, 31 July 1861. Hunter is on the list, which Lincoln said is made up of "officers I wish to remember" (Basler, *Works of Lincoln,* 4:418); letter, Hunter to adjutant general, 27 May 1861, accepting appointment, AGO Letters Received, NA.

66. Ezra Warner, Jr., *Generals in Gray: Lives of the Confederate Commanders* (Baton Rouge: Louisiana State University Press, 1959), 290–91; Steuart's obituary, *Baltimore Sun,* 23 November 1903. Steuart was soon commissioned lieutenant colonel of the First Maryland Infantry Battalion.

Chapter 3

MILITARY AND POLITICAL CONFLICTS

Col. David Hunter's orders read that, "having reported for duty in compliance with orders from the War Department, [he] is assigned to the command of the brigade to consist of the Fifth, Twenty-eighth, and Sixty-ninth New York Regiments," then camped at Arlington Heights. The regiments, lately arrived in the Washington area, were digging trenches and fortifications—later named Fort Corcoran and then Fort Lincoln—when the new commanding officer arrived on 28 May. Two days later Hunter was welcomed at a brigade review. A reporter present wrote:

> The Sixty-ninth New York regiment, having transplanted their flag from Georgetown College to their new camp on Arlington Heights, celebrated the raising of the Stars and Stripes. Near sunset, Col. [Michael] Corcoran having assembled all the troops, numbering over thirteen hundred, not on duty, he introduced Col. Hunter, of the Third Cavalry U.S. Army, who has just been assigned the command of the brigade of the aqueduct. . . . Col. Hunter was received with great enthusiasm, and Col. Corcoran made some patriotic allusions to the Flag, and was loudly cheered.[1]

Hunter's assigned aide, Charles Graham Halpine, who was to serve with him for much of the war, was an acting second lieutenant in the Sixty-ninth, a regiment made up mostly of immigrants from Ireland, and was himself a native of that land. Halpine was a New York reform politician of some note and a newspaperman and publicist. He had been a private secretary to Stephen Douglas and possibly met Hunter through that Illinois politician's efforts. His impression of Hunter was that he was a "very elegant and courtly gentleman," strict but polite with the officers of the brigade. Hunter told stories of Indian fighting and days on the frontier, and this must have seemed exotic to his young listeners. Hunter's wife, Maria, lived in Washington, and Hunter and Halpine often rode into the city for early breakfast. The thirty-two-year-old officer wrote of Hunter, "He has taken a strange affection for me, having no son himself; and I feel towards him the most sincere affection." Halpine even had a room in the Hunter home. David and Maria Hunter had no natural daughter either; Halpine's presence must have pleased them. Mrs. Steuart made up for the lack of a child, and Halpine supposes that Maria Steuart was adopted by the Hunters. Although no legal action to accomplish this may have occurred, the lady resided in the Hunter home and was certainly treated like a daughter. She moved with the general's wife wherever the old soldier was stationed. Meanwhile, her husband was assigned to the Army of the Shenandoah under Brig. Gen. Joseph E. Johnston. He would soon be in action opposing the Union force in which Colonel Hunter was serving. The divided loyalties that Mrs. Steuart undoubtedly had were common at the time, and she was not aware that her husband and her adoptive parent would be facing each other soon on a field of battle.[2]

BATTLE OF BULL RUN

Hunter's stay with the brigade lasted just a month, when he was given another assignment, commanding the Second Division of the rapidly growing Union army at the capital led by Brig. Gen. Irvin McDowell. Hunter was relieved by Col. William Tecumseh Sherman, a former army officer just returned to uniform and, like Hunter, given command of a new regular regiment. The reason for Hunter's elevation to command of one of the five existing divisions was because plans were under way to take the offensive against growing Confederate forces at Manassas, south of Washington, the larger part of them under McDowell's West Point classmate, Brig. Gen. Pierre Beauregard, conqueror of Fort Sumter. McDowell—and his superior, Winfield Scott—thought it premature to send the green, newly arrived volunteer regiments into battle, but a number of factors argued against delay. First, there was the political need to counter the Manassas buildup and to show the nation activity in defense of the capital. Perhaps more to the point, however, was that the three-month enlistments under which many of the volunteer regiments entered federal service were about to expire. In face of the expected loss of so many men, McDowell's five divisions were prepared for an early July march against Beauregard's positions.[3]

Planning for the advance began in June, and on the twenty-ninth McDowell met with his officers at Hunter's headquarters to outline assignments and describe the plan of attack. The operation was ambitious for an inexperienced army because it called for coordinated attacks by several columns and an envelopment of General Beauregard's right flank. The officers present—Hunter; Colonel Sherman, representing the First Division; and Col. Samuel P. Heitzelman and William B. Franklin, both of the Third Division—all of them regular officers, did not object to the plan. (Since the Fourth and Fifth Divisions were to be a reserve force, their commanders' comments were not solicited.) Many delays caused by building up arms, provisions, and ammunition for the thirty thousand–man force postponed departure until 16 July, McDowell marching with Hunter the first day.[4]

The destination was Centreville, twenty-two miles from Arlington, to be reached in two days. An officer who witnessed the departure wrote: "It was a glorious spectacle. The various regiments were brilliantly uniformed according to the aesthetic taste of peace, and the silken banners they flung to the breeze were unsoiled and untorn." Hunter's division—two brigades commanded by Cols. Andrew Porter and Ambrose E. Burnside—left the fortifications at Arlington "in light marching order," as directed, and proceeded down Columbia Pike to Bailey's Crossroads, where the command stopped for a supper of two loaves of bread and a pound of salt pork for each man. The division continued into the evening, reaching its assigned bivouac at Annandale at 10:00 p.m. After a late start the next morning Hunter's division (marching on the Little River Turnpike) reached Fairfax Court House, where the "enemy in force" was expected but from which all inhabitants had fled and no rebels were seen. Since discipline was marginal to begin with, the troops thoroughly looted the village. They were bedded down for the night and completed the last six miles to Centreville on the morning of 18 July. Beauregard was deployed roughly northeast to southwest along Bull Run two miles south of Centreville. Because of improvident maneuvers by Brig. Gen. Daniel Tyler, commanding the First Division, the original plan to envelop the Confederate right was seen as unsound, and the proceedings were delayed to scout alternatives, prepare new plans, and resupply the men, who had eaten their three-day ration in two.[5]

As McDowell saw the situation, attacks on the middle of the Confederate position—which were protected by woods, Bull Run's steep banks, and limited fords—were too much for inexperienced troops. He therefore decided to circle around Beauregard's left, crossing the run at Sudley's Ford which had been found usable and clear of rebels by his engineers. The Union troops would then roll up Beauregard's flank and allow the remaining federal regiments to cross Bull Run and finish the destruction. The plan was still complex, but McDowell depended on his heavily regular army commanders to keep the matter coordinated. Hunter's 2,485-man division—followed by Heintzelman with his four brigades of 8,000 soldiers—was designated to lead the envelopment on 21 July. Hunter's orders read:

> The Second Division (Hunter's) will move from its camp at 2 a.m. precisely, and, led by Captain [Daniel P.] Woodbury, of the Engineers, will, after passing Cub Run [about a half-mile below Centreville], turn to the right and pass the Bull Run stream above the lower ford at Sudley Springs, and then, turning down to the left, descend the stream and clear away the enemy who might be guarding the lower ford and bridge. It will then bear off to the right, to make room for the succeeding division [Heitzelman's].

The march was expected to take several hours, but the route turned out to cover twelve miles instead of the expected six, so Hunter was two and a half hours late reaching Bull Run. This delay was not as important as the two-day delay that McDowell had called for ration resupply, a move that allowed Beauregard to receive reinforcements from the Shenandoah Valley which proved critical in the coming battle.[6]

Burnside's lead brigade, accompanied by Hunter, turned left after the ford and moved on the Confederate flank, but the maneuver was detected by Col. Nathan G. Evans commanding the brigade on the rebel left. Evans, without orders and on his own initiative, turned his troops to face Hunter's advance and attacked. The sudden shock stopped the Union forces, and Hunter, "while endeavoring to induce my advanced guard to charge the enemy with the bayonet," was wounded in the left cheek and neck. Hunter, fifty-nine years of age that day, was injured severely enough that he had to turn the division over to Colonel Porter, his senior brigade commander, and he left the field with a small escort. Hunter was the first Union division commander wounded in the Civil War, and it turned out to be a positive factor in his future career. It gave him standing as a fighting officer, but it also took him from the field at Bull Run, which meant that none of the blame for the Union defeat and disorderly retreat that followed was assigned to him. In fact, he was somewhat of a hero on a day when there were very few. Hunter's report of his part in the battle was understandably brief, but he did find room in it to commend a "volunteer aide, Congressman Isaac N. Arnold, of Illinois who worked with the wounded," and his own aide-de-camp, Lt. Samuel Whitham Stockton, a regular officer in Hunter's old regiment, the First Dragoons (soon to be renamed the First Cavalry), and the son of his sister Mary in Princeton. He said of Stockton, who was on Hunter's staff for much of the war, "his conduct on the field was perfectly beautiful."[7]

The next day the defeated Union army found itself back in Washington instead of in Richmond, the objective of the 21 July advance. It returned in a day over the distance that had taken three on the way to the battlefield. Hunter's arrival in the city was in an army wagon accompanied by a few aides, "his face wrapped in a bloody handkerchief." McDowell's time in this command was over, and he was replaced at once by Maj. Gen. George B. McClellan, who had had some early successes in western Virginia. Before he had gone on to other assignments McDowell complimented Hunter in his report of the engagement as one of those who "did the most effective service and behaved in the most gallant manner." Although McDowell appears to have included every senior officer in his list, Hunter's reputation was nevertheless high, at least with Lincoln and particularly Illinois politicians. Lincoln visited the recuperating colonel twice at his Washington home before 31 July. The next day Hunter wrote to Halpine—in the first letter he had written since the battle—describing the president's visit: "Yesterday he informed me that the Illinois Delegation had unanimously recommended me as Major General for the Illinois forces, that I have been recommended by Gen. McClellan as well, for a Brigadiership, as they were in immediate want of Brigadiers, but that any acceptance of this would not interfere with the other." That being the case, Hunter accepted the brigadier appointment backdated to 17 May. The ambitious Hunter was not satisfied with this promotion, which merely confirmed the grade he should have held at Manassas; he also expected a new and important assignment beyond his current divisional command. He told Halpine what a proper assignment might be, asking the journalist, then in New York, to help promote the idea. While it cannot be certain Hunter was dissatisfied with the potential of commanding Illinois's regiments in the war, he may have hoped for an even larger role. His suggestion was to set up a training camp for one hundred thousand men near Baltimore, a location that Hunter thought central to oppose any Confederate threat to the capital, Maryland, and Kentucky; in his opinion the place allowed troops to be moved by sea to the coasts of Virginia, the Carolinas, and Georgia. Hunter recognized, however, that there were political realities involved: "every politician wishes a Camp and money expended in his own State, but I think all will admit, that the great interests of the Country have suffered quite enough from the selfishness of our politicians." Hunter told Halpine that he had spoken to Lincoln about the concept, "and he appeared to think very highly of the plan, but he may forget it, unless the press take it up." While Hunter did not say so, he must have seen a place for himself in charge of the camp and grand army to be formed there, but training was not consolidated as he had wished.[8]

The army reorganization act, approved on 29 July—the same legislation that created new positions allowing Hunter's elevation to brigadier general—also redesignated the two regiments of dragoons, the regiment of mounted rifles, and two regiments of cavalry as numbered regiments of cavalry; a sixth regiment was also added. This reorganization was cause for Hunter's permanent appointment in the regular army, as colonel of the Third Cavalry, to be changed to colonel commanding the Sixth, a position he continued to hold throughout the war and until his retirement.[9]

ASSIGNMENT IN THE WEST

Hunter did not have the brigadier general rank for long due to Representative Arnold's campaign for his further advancement, which Lincoln had told Hunter about on 31 July. The effort took the form of a petition similar to the pre–Bull Run one asking that Twiggs's vacated brigadiership be given to him. This one was signed by every senator and congressman in the Illinois delegation except one. In the forwarding letter Arnold said, "I express the sentiments of all Northern Illinois where he is known in urging his appt." He was able to go beyond this, calling on his observation of Hunter at Bull Run: "An experienced soldier of tried bravery, he has earned a reputation which will make his appointment one which will inspire confidence in our soldiers & citizens." The members of Congress aimed to see Hunter appointed major general of Illinois volunteers so that he could lead the citizens of the state in the war, and this appeal from his home state was not lost on Lincoln, the practical politician.[10]

The president's response was to write to Secretary of War Cameron on 13 August: "Let *now* Brigadier Genl. David Hunter be a Major General of Volunteers to be assigned a Division of Illinois Volunteers." The appointment was made (and accepted) the same day, Hunter being one of the four additional major generals authorized by the 29 July act. All four men were politically important, but only Hunter had any substantial military background. John A. Dix had been a captain in the War of 1812 but was now prominent in New Hampshire politics and a former speaker of the House of Representatives. Nathanial P. Banks and Benjamin F. Butler were both Massachusetts politicians without pre–Civil War military connections. It cannot be said that Hunter was chosen to join this group for his military experience; it was as much for how his appointment would be seen in Illinois. Lincoln went to see the new major general at Hunter's house on the morning of 22 August and told Hunter that he wanted him to go to Illinois as soon as he was physically able. Hunter's health was not good; he was then suffering from a severe attack of fever, probably a result of the Bull Run wound. Hunter wrote to Halpine just after Lincoln left him and said that the president had instructed him to make up "a list of the gentlemen I wished on my Staff. I took the liberty of suggesting that you might be appointed one of my Aids-de-Camp, with the rank and pay of Major." The reference to pay may have been a suggestion that Halpine, then in New York, might find a way out of his financial difficulties by army service.[11]

Formal orders sending Hunter to his adopted state followed immediately; later on 22 August Hunter was directed, "as soon as his health will permit," to "repair to Illinois to take command of troops from that State, and . . . report to Major-General [John C.] Frémont, commanding Western Department." The deficiency in those orders was that there were no state troops suitable for Hunter's command, and Frémont, who had not taken up his assignment at St. Louis until 25 July, had very little need for or interest in another general. Hunter, accompanied by his wife and Maria Steuart, reached Chicago early in September. The ladies were no doubt pleased to be able to visit relations in the city, and newly commissioned Major Kinzie, young Maria's father, was also in town, having been assigned to Hunter's thus far nonexistent Illinois troops command. Hunter wrote to Frémont's headquarters, saying that his "health was not entirely restored," possibly to avoid reporting to what must have seemed to him a dead-end job. He was soon called back to Washington, there to hear from Lincoln, who had a problem that Hunter might solve.[12]

The problem was Frémont, but in a broader sense it was the deteriorating situation in Missouri, along the Mississippi River, and to a lesser extent in Kansas, where the dividing line between Union and Confederate remained uncertain and conditions violent. Frémont saw the military situation as hazardous, and, indeed, Missouri was narrowly saved for the Union by earlier actions of Brig. Gen. Nathaniel Lyon, the outspoken antislavery regular army captain commanding the Union force in the southwestern part of the state. On his arrival at St. Louis, Frémont thought Lyon's activities should be left to the young officer's discretion, but Lyon was soon facing a Confederate force almost two times larger than his own at Wilson's Creek south of Springfield. In a 10 August battle Lyon was killed and his force defeated, but the ill-organized and poorly trained and equipped Confederate force was unable to follow up immediately. Frémont was thus given time to organize his defense of St. Louis and the railhead southwest at Rolla. The battle was seen in the East as another humiliation like Bull Run, and the reaction to it was a good part of the reason Frémont looked for new ways to prevent the slip of Missouri into the enemy's camp. He blamed the critical situation on "the untoward and obstructing conduct of the people of Missouri," and he decided on a countermeasure. "Accordingly, on the 30th of August, I issued a proclamation affixing penalties to rebellion and extending martial law over the State of Missouri. By this proclamation the property of persons in rebellion against the United States was held confiscated, and their slaves were declared free. As a war measure this, in my opinion was equal to winning a deciding battle." Lincoln's reaction to the proclamation was one of disapproval, given his concern about Kentucky's then ambivalent war position. He asked Frémont to rescind the declaration, but the general refused, inviting the president to do so himself. Not in the least recognizing his own insubordination, Frémont said later that this incident was the cause of the administration's loss of confidence in him, but there was more.[13]

Frémont also had a reputation of being unapproachable. Francis P. Blair, Jr., the leader of Union men in Missouri since 1860, wrote on 1 September from St. Louis to his brother, Montgomery, Lincoln's postmaster general, that "men coming here are not allowed to approach Frémont, and go away in disgust." Blair concluded that Frémont should be relieved. This and other reports and also allegations of improper contracting were quickly acted upon. General Scott explained to Lincoln the problem and the suggested solution: "If . . . Hunter could be brought in close relations with . . . Frémont some rash measures might be staved off & good ones accepted by insinuation." The difficulty was, however, that Hunter's new rank of major general did not allow his appointment as Frémont's chief of staff, the ideal position from which to influence actions. Thus, Lincoln appealed to Hunter:

> Gen. Frémont needs assistance which it is difficult to give him. He is losing the support of men near him whose support any man now in his position must have to be successful. His cardinal mistake is that he isolated himself, & allows nobody to see him; and by which he does not know what is going on in the very matter he is dealing with. Will you not, for now, take that place? Your rank is one grade too high to be ordered to it; but will you not serve the country and oblige me, by taking it voluntarily?[14]

Hunter immediately accepted because he could see the opportunity the assignment offered and also because he likely was promised Frémont's post if his moderating influence were not effective. He arrived in St. Louis on 13 September, and Frémont appointed him to the command of the First Division, then at the Rolla railhead, with orders to march north to Jefferson City on the Missouri.

Hunter wrote that he had asked Frémont to let him take all available forces by rail from St. Louis to Sedalia and from there to Warrensburg, thirty-five miles south of Lexington, where intelligence had indicated that a large rebel force was located. "I suppose it was considered a great piece of presumption on my part, to make suggestions, when the Gen. was surrounded with such *distinguished* Hungarians," the latter a reference to Frémont's staff, on which a number of colorful and quite unofficial foreign officers served. Hunter's request for an active campaign was refused, and he found himself "banished" three days later to "this miserable place Rolla." He was not pleased with his division because it was made up mostly of poor-quality state troops and had no regular units to provide a professional example. Arriving at Jefferson City a week later, he wrote to Halpine, who would soon be rejoining his staff, and described his banishment as well as the insignificance of his command, which was supposed to be a division but had only two unready regiments at hand. The rest of his troops were "scattered pretty much all over the State, indeed I understand that two of the Regiments are in Kansas, at Fort Leavenworth," and "all the Regular Artillery, Infantry and Cavalry, I believe to be with Gen. Frémont." He told Halpine to take his time coming from New York because nothing much was happening, and Lieutenant Stockton was apparently filling in as assistant adjutant general. Mrs. Hunter and Mrs. Steuart were comfortably settled at the Planter's House hotel in St. Louis, although Maria had "stolen up" to Jefferson City for a few days. Hunter was hoping "something may turn up to enable me to act," but it was clear to him that he was being "entirely ignored by our present Commanding General, and I shall remain a zero, until we get another commander." Hunter did not mention that he was in line for that job. [15]

Frémont was, of course, aware of Hunter's possible threat to his position, and that his department was being investigated by political and military officials. He explained that he was suffering from "the intrigues of men who were in confidential relations with the President . . . who urge[d] misrepresentations." Furthermore, he was plagued by "high officers" looking into the conduct of the Department of the West and by "leading journals," presumably not antislavery ones. All these, he claimed, "weakened my authority." He did not know that on 12 October Hunter was questioned at Tipton, Missouri, by Secretary of War Cameron, one of the "high officers" who was then in Missouri with Adj. Gen. Lorenzo Thomas investigating procurement scandals. Hunter "expressed to the Secretary of War his decided opinion that Gen. Frémont was incompetent and unfit for his extensive and important command. This opinion he gave very reluctantly, owing to his position as second in command."

Frémont's position was further weakened when Maj. Gen. Sterling Price, a former governor of the state and now leading the ragged army that had been victorious over Lyon at Wilson's Creek, turned up before Lexington on the Missouri River, laid siege to the town, and forced the surrender, on 20 September, of the three-thousand-man Union garrison. It was clear to Frémont, who had refused Hunter's request to attack Price earlier and who thought himself unable to assist the force at Lexington, that it was time to counter Price, who was calling for Missourians to join his victorious army. Toward this end Frémont ordered his troops to concentrate at Springfield for a campaign against Price which he planned would not end until he reached Memphis—or even New Orleans. At the end of October, convinced that Price had decided to offer battle, Frémont considered conditions auspicious for an attack from Springfield with his twenty-one thousand men. Before this happened, however, Frémont took a rather unusual action; he opened negotiations with General Price. An agreement was made between them on 1 November that provided, Frémont wrote, "1st, for an exchange of prisoners, hitherto refused by our Government; 2d, that guerrilla fighting should be suppressed, and the war confined to the organized army in the field; 3d, that there should be no arrests for opinion." The agreement was immediately seen as overstepping his authority and giving de facto recognition of rebels as ordinary combatants. It became one more count against Frémont.[16]

Lincoln had already decided that Frémont must go, and Hunter was his replacement. He did not directly notify either one of them but chose another route, because he did not want to relieve a general on the eve of battle. A 24 October order was sent to St. Louis, addressed to Brig. Gen. Samuel Curtis, directing him to present it to Frémont if he thought Frémont was not about to fight a battle or if he had already won one. In the belief that no attack was going to occur, Curtis had the order delivered to Frémont, who turned over command to Hunter on 2 November. Hunter was in possession of an unusual letter, which had been hand-carried to him by the Blair brothers. In it were suggestions from Lincoln about how Hunter should conduct the campaign in the West. Hunter's later comment about the Lincoln guidance was that it showed "the soundness of Mr. Lincoln's judgment even in military affairs," although he added that what Lincoln advised against "was so absurd that I should not have thought of it for a moment, even if I had not had the good advice of Mr. Lincoln." Written on 24 October, a week before Frémont's planned offensive against Price, it said that Price was in full retreat from Missouri, a fact not accepted by Frémont. Lincoln also said that it was unlikely that Price could be caught and engaged by Union forces. The president recommended that Hunter give up pursuit and withdraw to cover the railheads at Rolla and Sedalia, from which "it would be so easy to concentrate and repel any army of the enemy returning on Missouri from the

Southweast," and that such an advance was unlikely before spring. Lincoln said, of course, that he was leaving Hunter "a considerable margin for the exercise of your judgment and discretion."[17]

There is some reason to suspect that General Scott was responsible for the letter, or perhaps it was General McClellan, who took the ailing Scott's post of general-in-chief of all the armies of the United States on the day that Frémont was relieved. Frémont went quietly, departing the command for Washington on 7 November, about a hundred days since his appointment. It was suggested that before he left he challenged Hunter to a duel, but the story may have been made up, fueled by Hunter's earlier reputation. A newspaper took Hunter's measure and concluded that he would not stand for the confusion that had dominated Frémont's headquarters. "Gen. HUNTER is not the sort of man it would be safe to trifle with."[18]

And what was Hunter's view of Frémont, under whom he had served just a few weeks? Less than a year later he told a friend: "I admire his anti-slavery and his proclamation. That was well, but his military operations were ridiculous and he came near losing us Missouri." To set some of this right, one of Hunter's first actions was to cancel the agreement that Frémont had made with Price. He saw much wrong with it, that it would make enforcement of martial law in Missouri impossible, would give liberty to "propagandists of treason," would seriously hinder the use of militia, and so on. But the action that stirred many was Hunter's retreat from Springfield and redistribution of the five divisions of the Department of the West to covering positions, thereby opening up southwestern Missouri to Confederate reconquest and abandoning loyal citizens. Brig. Gen. Franz Sigel, whose own reputation for falling back in the face of the enemy was yet to be fully earned, called the retreat "a deplorable military blunder, but also a political mistake." A reporter who saw the withdrawal wrote that it was "one of the most stupendous and miserable farces ever exhibited to this or any other public." It might very well have been that such criticism of Hunter's uncritical obedience of the "suggestions" he had received, as well as McClellan's apprehension that superseding Frémont might have raised jealousy or dissatisfaction in the army, contributed to what happened next.[19]

THE GREAT JAYHAWK EXPEDITION

On 9 November Hunter was relieved of command of the Department of the West, the department was abolished, and a new division of responsibility in the West was instituted. Frémont's defenders saw justice in Hunter's weeklong tenure in their champion's position, because they believed that he had orchestrated Frémont's dismissal—as indeed he may have done. Under the new organization, the Department of the Ohio, under Brig. Gen. Don Carlos Buell, was responsible for operations in Kentucky and Tennessee, and Maj. Gen. Henry W. Halleck was assigned to St. Louis, heading the Department of Missouri but with supervision over a broader area, nearly the entire Mississippi River basin north of Mississippi. Hunter was given the Department of Kansas, and he assumed command on 20 November. He was then at St. Louis but soon moved to his headquarters at Leavenworth, his department to encompass Kansas, Indian Territory west of Arkansas, and the territories of Nebraska, Colorado, and the Dakotas. Halpine, commissioned as a major in early September, was appointed his assistant adjutant general, and his nephew, Lt. Samuel W. Stockton, remained one of his aides. Another nephew, 2d Lt. Arthur Magill Kinzie, from Chicago, was also appointed as an aide, as was Lt. Charles Edward Hay, newly commissioned in the regular Third Cavalry. Hay was a brother of John Hay, Lincoln's secretary. The new posting was certainly a backwater when it came to immediate, important action, and it was, accordingly, supplied with minimum Union forces. It was not peaceful, however, because Lincoln still entertained the idea of using Kansas as a place from which to launch attacks against Arkansas, reaching the Mississippi near Memphis. The proposal was similar to the operation Frémont had planned, but this one was brought to the president by Senator James Lane, Hunter's subordinate during the White House occupation at the start of the war.[20]

Lane had kept busy in Kansas in the late summer of 1861 and into the early fall. He had obtained a commission of colonel from the governor of Indiana, perhaps as a way of avoiding legal difficulties from holding two public offices in Kansas, the state he represented in the U.S. Senate. When Lyon was defeated at Wilson Creek in early August, Lane found himself at Fort Scott on the Kansas side of the border with Missouri in command of troops he had raised in Kansas. With his army, which was little better than rabble, he followed the Confederate forces northward on their march to Lexington. He did not overtake them, however, but, rather, engaged in a private war against slave owners and Missourians generally. On 22 August his force sacked and burned Oceola, shot some of its citizens, and generally ravished the countryside. Lane was proud of this destruction and pillage, saying that it was a good way to stamp out treason.

Frémont had tried to rein in Lane, who was under his command, but his control was imperfect, and Lane continued his private war, although without fighting any engagements. Lane, believing that Kansas was threatened—although it was not—supported the reorganization that created the Department of Kansas, and he was disappointed that he was not chosen over Hunter to lead it. Lane was still at large in Missouri when Hunter took over the department, and the new commander attempted to bring Lane under his control, because, in addition to military reasons, the destruction was helping Confederate recruiting, not strengthening the Union. A newspaper reporter wrote from St. Louis on 17 November: "The indiscriminate depredations of LANE's men upon the inhabitants drew upon the head of that philanthropic warrior a malediction from Gen. HUNTER, less complimentary than deserved. He expressed a strongly-worded doubt of LANE's honesty, and when that gentleman undertook explanations, he (HUNTER) was not less reserved in informing him that he doubted his veracity—both remarks comprising, in substance, the terms thief, liar." Hunter, the old soldier, was probably less annoyed at Lane personally than he was appalled by the lawless Jayhawk brigade, which he said was "in a state of demoralization," ignorant of the most basic principles of soldiering—drill, paperwork, and discipline.[21]

Halpine explained the conditions that the new commander faced:

Nothing could exceed the demoralized condition in which General Hunter found the Third and Fourth Kansas Infantry and the Fifth and Sixth Kansas Cavalry, formerly known as "Lane's Brigade." The regimental and company officers knew nothing of their duties and apparently had never made returns or reports of any kind. The regiments appeared in worse condition than they could possibly have been in during the first week of their enlistment, their camps being little better than pig-pens, officers and men sleeping and messing together; furloughs in immense numbers being granted, or, where not granted, taken; drill having been abandoned almost wholly, and the men constituting a mere ragged, half-armed, diseased and mutinous rabble, taking votes as to whether a troublesome or distasteful order should be obeyed or defied.

I would state that it was General Hunter's opinion, and that of all the experienced regular officers at the post [Leavenworth] that until the more objectionable Kansas regiments can be reofficered to a great extent and removed from local influences they can never assume a respectful position in the service of their country.[22]

Hunter was further discontent from the start in Kansas because he thought he had been unfairly passed over for more responsible positions. From Leavenworth seven days after he took command Hunter asked Washington for permission to "muster into the service a Brigade of Kansas Indians to assist the Creeks, Seminoles & Chickasaws in adhering to their loyalty." Confederates were simultaneously seducing Indians into their ranks, and Hunter intended to head this off. He saw in the Indians a resource available to augment his minuscule number (only three thousand) of available men. He planned at once to hold a tribal conference at Leavenworth and sought to bring in Brig. Gen. James W. Denver to manage the effort. The officer was well-known to Hunter from paymaster days; Denver had been President Buchanan's commissioner of Indian affairs and was a former governor of the Kansas Territory. Nothing was to come of Hunter's Indian proposal because of objections from a new secretary of war, and Denver's appointment was effectively blocked by Lane, who controlled Kansas patronage. The two had clashed in years past. Approval of Indian enlistment, while it might have helped Hunter's command, was not going to be enough to satisfy his concern that he was in exile without a significant military force. Never one to be concerned with military channels, he wrote to U.S. senator Lyman Trumbull of Illinois, the letter expressing well his disappointment and ambition:

> On application of my Illinois friends I was appointed a Major General to command the Illinois troops, but contrary to the intentions and wishes of the President I was sent to Missouri, and now find myself in Kansas, without a man from Illinois under my command. . . . I am here without a suitable command, not having a full Brigade, while most of the Brigadiers have full Divisions. I think I have a right to complain. . . .
> I am anxious to be placed in command of the Illinois troops, and to advance with them into Kentucky. . . . We have wasted time enough. It is time slavery had its quietus, we have been trifling long enough. With Buell's command in Kentucky, which my rank entitles me to, I would advance south, proclaiming the negro free and arming him as I go. The Great God of the Universe has determined that this is the only way in which this war is to be ended, and the sooner it is done the better. If I am the instrument, I shall not stop short of the Gulf of Mexico, unless laid low by His Almighty hand.[23]

The letter is important because it shows Hunter's attitude toward slavery, how he proposed to end the rebellion, and his frustration—beyond his personal situation—with the conduct of the war. Hunter was in that group of Americans who favored declaring at once that the central issue was whether slavery would survive or triumph and that there was no good in compromise and accommodation. He, unlike Lincoln, did not have to be concerned with keeping the border states in the Union, or at least "neutral," and he surely had an unrealistic view of what it would take to defeat the South and of the contribution to expect from armed black men once they were freed from bondage. Yet Hunter was not the only officer with grand vision and belief in the efficacy of columns of Union soldiers penetrating the South. For example, McClellan, the general-in-chief, who did not to Lincoln's frustration think he was ready to make much use of the

Army of the Potomac under his direct command, had no difficulty approving daring operations in the West. He told General Halleck in St. Louis that he was going to send Hunter some troops "to enable him to move into the Indian Territory west of Arkansas and upon Northern Texas. That movement will relieve you very materially." McClellan's position reflected James Lane's lobbying in Washington.[24]

Hunter had received an early warning of McClellan's intentions in late November, when Adjutant General Thomas told him that the general-in-chief "thinks an expedition might be made to advantage for your department west of Arkansas against Northeastern Texas." Thomas asked Hunter for suggestions on how he would bring this operation about, and, after a few days, Hunter gave him an answer:

> I think the expedition proposed by the General-in-Chief altogether impractible [*sic*]. We have a hostile Indian force, estimated at 10,000, on our west and north. To cope with this force we have only about 3,000 effective men, scattered over an extended frontier. So far as from being able to make a successful expedition into the enemy's country, I think we shall be very fortunate if we prevent his having possession of the whole of Kansas.

For good measure Hunter added, "In my humble opinion the division of the Western Department was not for the good of the service." Thomas reported Hunter's comments to McClellan, who wrote that Hunter's reply "surprised me greatly." He told Hunter to do as he was asked—that is, send to Washington his requirements for a southern expedition. He also said that he had already dispatched three regiments of Wisconsin infantry to Kansas and that more would follow.[25]

Lane was in the capital in late November, anticipating the opening of the second session of Congress on 2 December and actively pressing the administration to approve his military agenda. He still had the problem of choosing between a military role or his seat in the Senate, yet, until he had been sworn in to the former, his seat was safe—to the dismay of his opponents. Lane's plan was what he called the "Southern Expedition"; others labeled it the "Great Jayhawk Expedition." The proposal called for use of a force of Indians, Kansas troops, and regiments and artillery batteries from elsewhere. Lane intended to lead this force from Kansas to Texas, meeting another expedition from the Gulf. He took this proposition to Lincoln, who, while not authorizing it in detail, endorsed it in principle. Lincoln apparently thought the entire matter had been approved by

Hunter, his commander of the department, but it had not. On the contrary, Lane seems to have encouraged Lincoln's erroneous conclusion. While it might be thought that Hunter would have approved an expedition not much different than the one he had in mind, he saw much wrong with Lane's plan when he finally heard about it. Lane's first communication with Hunter about the plan seems to have been at the beginning of January. He announced that the expedition had been approved and added that the government wanted Lane to work with Hunter "for an active winter's campaign." Lane had done a good job of securing resources; he told Hunter: "They have ordered to report to you eight regiments cavalry, three of infantry, and three batteries, in addition to your present force. They have also authorized you, in conjunction with the Indian Department, to organize 4,000 Indians." Finally, he said, he would be on his way to Leavenworth soon. McClellan was aware that Hunter, as the department commander, felt that he was being ignored as well as that the operation would be impractical because of poor roads and the predictable failure of resupply. He may also have objected to the marauding and atrocities that Lane had allowed his men to engage in a few months earlier.[26]

Lane was mistaken about the status of Hunter's request to raise a brigade of Indians for the expedition. McClellan had brought the matter to the attention of the president, and the cabinet considered it—as well as the practicality of the entire operation—on 10 December. As was perhaps usual with unstructured cabinet meetings, the question of the Jayhawk expedition itself and the difficulty of coordinating and supplying simultaneous offensives to western Texas from Kansas and the Gulf was not seriously discussed. A decision was reached, however, concerning the enlistment of Indians—not on the basis of the practicality of the idea but on technical grounds. President Lincoln concluded that he could not authorize the Indian brigade because he had already reached the ceiling for enlistments which Congress had voted. Therefore, the matter was dropped.[27]

At the end of December Hunter had complained directly to Lincoln about his situation, his discontent very likely exacerbated by what rumbles were reaching him about Lane's activities. His complaint did not mention Lane but, instead, had to do with his supposed exile to a command he thought was too small and unimportant for his rank and prestige. "I am deeply mortified, humiliated, insulted and disgraced" to have been placed "in banishment" at Fort Leavenworth. He said it was wrong to give General Buell a hundred thousand men for Kentucky operations. Buell was, after all, nineteen years Hunter's junior and a brigadier as well. "You owe it to my honor and to my Friends in Illinois, to place me in a different position" rather than in "a wilderness with three thousand [men]." Lincoln's reply was prompt, and he started by saying, "I am constrained to say it is difficult to answer so ugly a letter in good temper." Lincoln continued:

> I am, as you intimate, losing much of the great confidence I placed in you, not from any act or omission of yours touching the public service up to the time you were sent to Leavenworth, but from the flood of grumbling dispatches I have seen from you since. . . . [I have not], up to this day, heard an intimation that you have been wronged coming from anyone but yourself. . . . The position assigned to you is as responsible and as honorable as that assigned to Buell. . . . The idea that a command in Kentucky was very desirable, and one farther west very undesirable, never occurred to me. You constantly speak of being placed in command of only 3,000. Now tell me, is not this mere impatience? Have you not known all the while that you are to command four or five times that many? I have been, and am, sincerely your friend; and if, as such, I dare to make a suggestion I would say you are adopting the best possible way to ruin yourself. . . . He who does something at the head of one regiment will eclipse him who does nothing at the head of a hundred.[28]

Hunter also wrote to Secretary of War Cameron, but that letter was not confined to the same complaints he had made to Lincoln. Instead, he apparently described his plan for freeing and arming blacks as he proceeded on military operations in the South. "Your views upon the slavery question as connected to this war," Cameron answered, "must . . . meet the approval of all men who are not controlled by the magical powers of the slave interests. I believe that the war can be only successfully terminated by carrying out the policy which is indicated in your letter." Cameron had spoken to Lane the day before and was informed for the first time of the Jayhawk expedition plans. Cameron said that Lane was to be entirely under Hunter's control and that thirty thousand troops were being prepared to send west. The question arises about Hunter's sincerity in raising the slavery issue. Some have speculated that he only did so to ingratiate himself with the Radical Republicans in Congress, but there is no evidence either way. It is likely that he was indeed committed to seeing slavery ended—with the use of armed blacks, if it came to that—and to punishing those who rebelled against the Union. That was his position at the beginning of the war, and it remained so throughout. He was never accused of deceit, and not one of the officers closely associated with him accused him of duplicity in this or any other matter.[29]

Lane does not seem to have been the subject of any of Hunter's protests to Washington, possibly because the expedition promised to increase Hunter's responsibility. Question still remained, however, about Lane's veracity and especially his claim that he had discussed everything with Hunter. This representation was good enough for Lincoln (and perhaps McClellan) to tell Cameron: "Since you spoke to me yesterday about General J. H. Lane of Kansas, I have been reflecting on the subject, and have concluded that we need the services of such a man out there at once; that we better appoint him a brigadier-general of volunteers to-day, and send him off with such authority to raise a force . . . as you think will get him into actual work quickest." Lincoln's final words to Cameron lead one to conclude that the president's irritation with Hunter's complaining was acute and that Hunter's attitude may have been the key factor in the president's having approved Lane's commission and charge. "Tell him when he starts to put it through. Not be writing or telegraphing back here, but put it through." That same day Halleck, in St. Louis, gave his opinion of the expedition—but not of its advocate, Lane—to General McClellan. "Such a project, if it be contemplated, is contrary to every military rule." The column would have to go hundreds of miles, being moved and supplied at a huge cost. Halleck concluded: "It is certainly not a military operation. It may, however, be intended to gratify some political partisan." A few days later General Thomas told Hunter more about the Lane plan, listing, as Lane had done, the forces being sent to him but also adding a bit of new information. Thomas made it clear that Hunter was in charge, and he even said that Hunter could personally lead the Jayhawkers south if he wished.[30]

In mid-January General and Mrs. Hunter (and Mrs. Steuart) had an official visitor at Leavenworth, and he and his wife, who came west with him, dined in Hunter's quarters. He was Maj. Absalom Baird, lately appointed an assistant inspector general, based in Washington. Baird was a 1849 West Point graduate, and the major and the old soldier apparently got along well, sharing similar abolitionist stands. When he got back to his headquarters Baird wrote Hunter a long letter describing the situation there with respect to Lane and Hunter's prospects for the future. He began with the results of a meeting he had had with General McClellan, "who has the general command of any body in these parts." Baird described conditions in Hunter's department, but the general-in-chief explained that he had no control over Lane's expedition, "it having been determined upon by the President." All the same, it was clear that nothing was to be done without Hunter's approval. "I understood that Lane had told the President that the movement which he proposed was the result of an understanding with you, and I have no doubt that he has used your name with the President to accomplish his ends." He continued:

> Gen Thomas [the adjutant general] remarked that Lane had not a
> particle of Authority to do any thing but to report to you and do what

you may direct. He has been sent to you with a view to carrying out a plan which he has persuaded the President will be very useful & feasible. . . . As this is to be done with your command, I should have thought that you were the proper person to advise with regarding it. It seems however that things are managed differently now-days. I have felt it my duty my dear General to give you this information that you may not be deceived as to Lane[']s status when he reaches Leavenworth.

When he [Lane] left here he had not accepted the appointment of Brig. General, but said he would do so after he had reached Kansas and had resigned his senatorship to the Governor. Should you refuse to recognize him until he presents proper evidence of his appointment, . . . you might perhaps force an understanding that would be a benefit to all parties.

Hunter was to take the advice on how to control Lane by strict application of army procedures, and this move served to neutralize the Kansas politician. Baird said that a leave request that Hunter had sent to headquarters was not being approved because McClellan thought Hunter should stay at Leavenworth "to watch over" the distrusted Lane. Yet, Baird added, Hunter should apply again and return to Washington "before Congress adjourns" so that he could improve his political position.

Baird also met with the president's secretary, John Hay, who told him that Lincoln had thought Hunter "had been treated badly & felt distressed about it." Hay did not think Lincoln had made a very good job of the letter to his general. As for Congress, however, Baird heard that Hunter "had two thirds of the Senate devoted to you, but that from your supposed views on the slavery question, the administration could not appoint you to Ky. or to S.C. at present, but that things were not yet sufficiently advanced." The problem was, the major offered, that "the administrative department of the Govt. whose object is to restore things to their old condition, [was] either ignoring the slavery question or determined to put aside every one whom they choose to style anti slavery." Baird had not been able to see the president to point out to him "the absurdity of placing a man of your [Hunter's] rank in what they call an important command with no troops. I shall however spare no occasion that occurs of placing it in its proper light. There are too few honest republicans in the Army to permit of them being laid on the shelf."[31]

Secretary of War Cameron became a victim of poor administration of his department and his own cleverness, when Lincoln unexpectedly appointed him minister to Russia. His replacement in mid-January was Edwin M. Stanton, who had been the department's legal advisor. Hunter quickly congratulated Stanton on his appointment, and he offered to communicate "with the political Chief of the Army" as he had with Cameron. He took the occasion to establish his own position:

> In the expedition about to go South from this Department, I beg that I may have a large discretion, that I may be allowed to strike wherever I can do the most harm. Selfishness might dictate a different request, but I do not fear responsibility if I can injure our enemy. Please let me have my own way on the subject of slavery. The Administration will not be responsible. I alone will bear the blame; you can censure me, arrest me, dismiss me, hang me if you will, but permit me to make my mark in such a way as to be remembered by friend and foe.[32]

Hunter did not wait for Stanton's permission to contact him with matters of concern, and three days later he complained about Lane, who had just arrived at Fort Leavenworth. The problem was that Lane was showing reluctance in accepting a subordinate role, and a few days afterward Hunter wrote a similar letter to Lincoln, additionally complaining that he heard that Lane was talking badly of him to Lincoln. Lincoln more or less settled this to-and-fro argument by deciding that both generals were needed and declaring that they would have to work together; Hunter's seniority would override Lane when coordination did not work out. As the president put it, "if they cannot come to an amicable understanding, General Lane must report to General Hunter for duty, . . . or decline the service." On 13 February Hunter sent Lane a directive for the expedition. He said that Lane's job was to "secure the Indian Territory west of Arkansas, as well as to make a descent on Northern Texas, in connection with me to strike at Western Texas from the Gulf." By this time, however, Lane was wavering on the question of soldiering. Hunter explained in an exchange of letters with Halleck that regiments were arriving at Leavenworth for "Lane's great Southern expedition," but Lane had so far not officially reported in nor taken the oath as a brigadier general. In fact, he told Hunter at their single meeting that he was just a visitor in the headquarters, there as a senator and "'a member of the Military Committee of the Senate of the United States.'" Hunter was surprised that those in Washington believed there was a "Damon and Pythias affection between that gentleman and myself. The Kansas Senator would seem to have effectually 'jayhawked' out of the minds of the War Department any knowledge or remembrance of the general commanding this department." Halleck was sympathetic, and he told Hunter he had tried to head off some of the troops designated for Lane's expedition. He complained that Washington was also paying no attention to him on the question and that his protests to McClellan and Thomas had not been answered. He put this down to reluctance by the War Department to address the question "without exposing the plans of the great jayhawker."[33]

Not only the army's senior generals saw problems with Lane. His reputation was not very good among many junior officers either—at least those opposing excess and with a sense of ethics. A lieutenant colonel in a Missouri regiment wrote to his father, "I do not think that the fact that God Almighty makes use of wicked men like Lane and his coadjusters to accomplish his own good purposes, should be any reason for us to praise him or imitate their example." The officer did not believe "in doing evil that good might come."[34]

As it developed, Lane himself solved the difficulty that the generals in the field and others were having over being forced to support a military adventure with little chance of success. It was clear that, despite his maneuverings on the matter, he would have to give up his Senate seat if he accepted the commission. It also looked as though he would not have the independent command he had lobbied for, so he decided to remain a politician. The great Jayhawking expedition was never mounted.

While Lane was the major difficulty that Hunter had beyond his own standing in the army, another problem was caused by requests from other departments for some of Hunter's already limited troops. Ulysses S. Grant, one of Halleck's brigadiers, needed help for operations beginning against Confederate forts along the Cumberland and Tennessee Rivers. Hunter had no choice but to send the support, but he did not do it with good spirit. Halleck smoothed it over with a 19 February note to Hunter: "To you . . . we are indebted for our success at Fort Donelson. In my strait for troops to reinforce Gen. Grant, I appealed to you. You nobly and generously placed your forces at my disposition. This enabled us to win the victory." Surely, Hunter's contribution was not as decisive as Halleck declared it to be, but the compliment softened Hunter's resentment somewhat about his department being little more than a source for helping the campaigns of others. On what he claimed was his own initiative, Hunter sent his First Colorado Volunteer Regiment by forced marches from Denver to Fort Union, New Mexico Territory, outside of his department. Led by Col. John P. Slough, the regiment's late March action at the "battle" of Glorieta destroyed the Confederate invading column's supplies and led to the permanent evacuation of rebel forces from the territory. Hunter took more satisfaction from this use of his soldiers, perhaps because the Colorado regiment's activity was decisive while the help to Grant was not. Hunter also had to deal with problems partly resulting from Lane's demise as a military figure in Kansas. One was the plight of the

Indians, whom the Kansan and Hunter had planned to enlist in the army, at least for the expedition south. Stanton, unlike Cameron, did not agree to use of the Indians, and Indians fleeing Confederate forces in Indian Territory, and others, were left without the promised paid federal service. This led to very poor conditions for them during a harsh winter, and Hunter did what little he could to send them food and medical assistance.[35]

As it happened, Hunter's command, the Department of Kansas—the one that, since the beginning, he had said was unimportant—was ordered combined with the victorious Halleck's Department of Missouri. Halleck also inherited that part of Buell's forces and responsibilities west of Knoxville. The new, greatly enlarged command was renamed the Department of the Mississippi (Frémont was given the Mountain Department [West Virginia], and McClellan, no longer general-in-chief, took over the Army of the Potomac at the same time). Hunter's four months at Leavenworth did not give him any opportunities to demonstrate effective military leadership, although his attempts to give the Kansas volunteers a military polish may have been significant had those troops been in an active theater of war. They were not, however, because they still could not be trusted to interact with Missouri soldiers without conflict, a legacy of Bleeding Kansas days and Lane's marauding in Missouri the previous summer. It is understandable that Hunter's clash with Lane and his subsequent neutralization of the adventurous Kansan enhanced Hunter's reputation in the army for defending that institution's professional prerogatives, but why Hunter's constant appeals out of army channels to the president, secretaries of war, and other politicians seem to have done his reputation little damage cannot be so easily explained. It certainly could not have been his abolitionist stand, advocacy of arming blacks, and belief that the South should pay for its treason. Those positions had little support in the army, and they ran counter to Lincoln's moderate approach, driven by his border state worries. The president's loyalty to one of the few officers—one identified with Illinois as well—who had early showed devotion to the Republican Party and Lincoln personally may be the reason that Hunter was allowed latitude that might not have been permitted to others.[36]

David Hunter could not be left in the new Department of the Mississippi because, as Adj. Gen. Thomas pointed out to Halleck, his "date is senior to yours." There is no evidence that Hunter was asked to place himself under the command of a lower-ranking major general, but likely he would not have agreed to it. Instead, a small expeditionary force was elevated to a new department, and Hunter was sent to command it, his orders arriving at Leavenworth just four days after the Department of Kansas was dissolved.[37]

NOTES

1. General Orders No. 1, 28 May 1861, Headquarters, Department of Northeast Virginia, Alexandria, U.S. War Department, *The War of the Rebellion: A Compilation of the Official Records of the Union and Confederate Armies* (Washington, D.C.: Government Printing Office, 1880–1902) (hereafter *ORA* and ser. 1, unless otherwise indicated), 41, pt. 1, 399; *Daily National Intelligencer* (Washington, D.C.), 1 June 1861.

2. William Hanchett, *Irish: Charles G. Halpine in Civil War America* (Syracuse: Syracuse University Press, 1970), 34–37; Jon L. Wakelyn, *Biographical Dictionary of the Confederacy* (Westport, Conn.: Greenwood Press, 1977), 399–400; Ezra J. Warner, *Generals in Gray: Lives of the Confederate Commanders* (Baton Rouge: Louisiana State University Press, 1959), 290–91.

3. Special Orders No. 16, 30 June 1861, Department of Northeast Virginia, *ORA*, 41, pt. 1, 408. Halpine was not with Hunter because his ninety-day enlistment expired in mid-July (Hanchett, *Irish,* 37). Halpine's military status was questionable because his regiment had no vacancy for him, and he was not mustered in as a lieutenant (Halpine's compiled service record, Records of Volunteer Union Soldiers Who Served during the Civil War, Record Group 94, Records of the Office of the Adjutant General, 1780–1917, National Archives). He was properly commissioned later.

4. William C. Davis, *Battle at Bull Run: A History of the First Major Campaign of the Civil War* (Garden City, N.Y.: Doubleday and Co., 1977), 75–77, 92; James B. Fry, "McDowell's Advance to Bull Run," in *Battles and Leaders of the Civil War,* ed. Robert Underwood Johnson and Clarence Clough Buel, 4 vols. (1887; reprint, New York: Castle, 1989), 1:175.

5. Fry, "McDowell's Advance," 1:176–79; Davis, *Battle at Bull Run,* 92–97; General Orders No. 17, 16 July 1861, Headquarters, Department of Northeast Virginia, Arlington, *ORA*, 2:303–4.

6. Fry, " McDowell's Advance," 1:184; Davis, *Battle at Bull Run,* 155–56, 168; Abstract of Returns of the Department of Northeast Virginia, 16 and 17 July 1861, and General Orders No. 22, 20 July 1861, Headquarters, Department of Northeast Virginia, Centreville, *ORA*, ser. 2, 2:309, 326.

7. Fry, "McDowell's Advance," 1:185; David Hunter, *Report of the Military Services of Gen. David Hunter during the War of the Rebellion, Made to the War Department, 1873* (1873; reprint, New York: Van Nostrand, 1892), 9; Hunter's report, August 1861, *ORA*, 2:382–83. Colonel Steuart did not reach the battlefield until 4 p.m., long after Hunter had left it; his division's (and another's) arrival from the Shenandoah caused the Union retreat. Old General Steuart, accompanying

Beauregard's force as an observer, hearing false news that his son was wounded, went to the front line and was captured; he was soon released as a noncombatant (Steuart's obituary, *Baltimore American,* 24 November 1903).

8. Margaret Leech, *Reveille in Washington, 1860–1865* (New York: Harper and Bros., 1941), 102; McDowell's report, 4 August 1861, *ORA,* ser. 2, 2:323. After the battle Hunter thought McDowell was incompetent and a coward (MS, n.d., probably late 1862, letter, Hunter to Halpine, 1 August 1864, Hunter MSS, Huntington Library, San Marino, Calif).

9. Emory Upton, *Military Policy of the United States* (Washington, D.C.: Government Printing Office, 1911), 252.

10. Letter, Arnold to Lincoln, 30 July, resolution signed by nine of ten congressmen, file no. H693 CB 1863, Letters Received by the Commission Branch of the Adjutant General's Office, 1863–70, RG 94, NA. The men were Senators Lyman Trumbull and Orville H. Browning (who replaced the late Stephen Douglas on 4 July) and Representatives William A. Richardson, John A. McClernard; Arnold, William Kellogg, Philip B. Fouke, Owen Lovejoy, and Elihu B. Washburne, but not John A. Logan of southern Illinois, a former slave catcher.

11. Letter, Lincoln to Cameron, 13 August 1861, Roy P. Basler, ed., *The Collected Works of Abraham Lincoln,* 7 vols. (New Brunswick, N.J.: Rutgers University Press, 1953), 4:483; Upton, *Military Policy of the United States,* 252; letter Hunter to Halpine, 22 August 1861, Hunter MSS, Huntington Library.

12. Special Orders No. 139, Adjutant General's Office, 22 August 1861, letter, Hunter (in Washington) to adjutant general, accepting promotion to major general, 13 August 1861, letter, Hunter to assistant adjutant general, Western Department, 5 September 1861, Hunter's file, General's Papers, box 12, RG 94, NA; General Officers, U.S. Volunteers, Francis B. Heithman, *Historical Register and Dictionary of the United States Army, from Its Organization, September 29, 1789, to March 2, 1903,* 2 vols. (1903; reprint, Urbana: University of Illinois Press, 1965), 1:28.

13. John C. Frémont, "In Command in Missouri," in Johnson and Buel, *Battles and Leaders,* 1:282, 286; Frémont's proclamation, Western Department, 30 August, letters, Lincoln to Frémont, 2 September, Frémont to Lincoln, 8 September, Lincoln to Frémont, 11 September 1861, *ORA,* 3:466–67, 469–70, 477–78, 485–86. Frémont did not give up, printing and distributing two hundred copies of his 30 August proclamation on 23 September (ibid., 543).

14. Letters, Francis P. Blair, Jr., to Montgomery Blair, 1 September, Scott to Lincoln, 5 September 1861, Basler, *Works of Lincoln,* 4:513; Lincoln to Hunter, 9 September 1861, document no. 11569, Abraham Lincoln Papers, Documents Division, Library of Congress (LOC).

15. Letters, Hunter to Halpine, 21 and 28 September 1861, Hunter MSS,

Huntington Library; letter, R. A. Kinzie to paymaster general, 19 September 1861, in which Kinzie asks what is to become of him in Chicago: "Gen. Hunter has been ordered from here by Gen. Frémont to Missouri. How will this affect me who was ordered to report to him here, which I did?" (Letters Received, Paymaster General, RG 99, Records of the Office of the Paymaster General, NA).

16. Letter, Frémont to Hunter, 22 September, Thomas's trip report, 21 October, documents on negotiations with Price, 1 November 1861, *ORA,* 3:503, 540–49, 562–65; Frémont, "In Command in Missouri," 1:286–87.

17. General Orders No. 18, 24 October 1861, Adjutant General's Office, General Orders No. 28, 2 November, Headquarters, Western Department, letter, Lincoln to Curtis, 24 October 1861, *ORA,* 3:553, 559; Basler, *Works of Lincoln,* 4:513, 516 n; Robert C. Schenck, "Major-General David Hunter," *Magazine of American History* 27 (February 1887): 142–43; letter, Lincoln to Hunter, 24 October 1861, document no. 12630, Lincoln Papers, LOC.

18. Jay Monaghan, *Civil War on the Western Border* (New York: Bonanza Books, 1955), 206; *New York Times,* 11 November 1861.

19. Letter, 24 June 1862, Rupert Sargent Holland, ed., *Letters and Diary of Laura M. Towne Written from the Sea Islands of South Carolina* (1912; reprint, New York: Negro Universities Press, 1969), 71; letters, Hunter to Thomas and Price, 7 November 1861, *ORA,* 3:561–62, 565; Franz Sigel, "The Pea Ridge Campaign," in Johnson and Buel, *Battles and Leaders,* 1:314–15; *New York Times,* 22 November 1861; Schenck, "General Hunter," 143.

20. General Orders No. 97, Adjutant General's Office, 9 November 1861, General Orders No. 1, Headquarters, Department of Kansas, 20 November 1861, *ORA,* 3:567, 8:370. Hays's father erroneously thought Charles's appointment to Hunter's staff was "an honor never conferred on so young a man ... since Alexander Hamilton was made aide to Gen. Washington" (letter, n.d., William Roscoe Taylor, *The Life and Letters of John Hay,* 2 vols. [Boston: Houghton Mifflin Co., 1908], 1:153). Volunteer major generals were allowed three aides-de-camp of their own choice (Upton, *Military Policy of the United States,* 252).

21. Monaghan, *Civil War on the Western Border,* 195–97; John McElroy, *The Struggle for Missouri* (Washington, D.C.: National Tribune Co., 1909), 272–75. Although Lane's newspaper, the *Leavenworth Daily Conservative,* 13 November 1861, praised Hunter's appointment, it was not to Lane's liking (Albert Castel, *A Frontier State at War, Kansas, 1861–1865* [1958; reprint, Westport: Greenwood Press, 1979], 78); *New York Times,* 22 November 1861; Annie Heloise Abel, *The American Indian in the Civil War, 1862–1865* (1919; reprint, Lincoln: University of Nebraska Press, 1992), 43, 54–57; Wendall Holmes Stephenson, *The Political Career of James H. Lane* (Topeka: Kansas State Printing Plant, 1930), 3:113–14.

22. Letter, Halpine to Halleck, 14 March 1862, *ORA*, 8:615–17.

23. Telegram, Hunter to Adjutant General Thomas, 27 November 1861, document no. 13123, Lincoln Papers, LOC; letter, Hunter to Trumbull, 9 December 1861, microfilm roll 12, vol. 44, Lyman Trumbull Papers, LOC.

24. Letter, McClellan to Halleck, 10 December 1861, Stephen W. Sears, ed., *The Civil War Papers of George B. McClellan: Selected Correspondence, 1860–1865* (New York: Ticknor and Fields, 1989), 144.

25. Letters, Thomas to Hunter, 26 November, Hunter to Thomas, 11 December, and McClellan to Hunter, 11 December 1861, *ORA*, 8:379, 428–29.

26. McElroy, *Struggle for Missouri*, 276–77; Abel, *American Indian in the Civil War*, 73–76; letter, Lane to Hunter, 3 January 1862, *ORA*, 8:482.

27. Diary entry, 10 December 1861, David Herbert Donald, ed., *Inside Lincoln's Cabinet: The Civil War Diaries of Salmon P. Chase* (New York: Longmans, Green and Co., 1954), 50.

28. Letter, Hunter to Lincoln, document no. 13531, 23 December, 1861, Lincoln Papers, LOC; letter, Lincoln to Hunter, 31 December 1861, *ORA*, 53:511.

29. Letter, Cameron to Hunter, 3 January 1862, answering Hunter's 19 December (which was not located), *ORA*, 53:512–13.

30. Letters, Lincoln to Cameron, 20 January, Halleck to McClellan, 20 January, Thomas to Hunter, 24 January 1862, *ORA*, ser. 3, 2:280–81, 508–11, 525–26.

31. Letter, Baird to Hunter, 26 January 1862, General Manuscripts (Misc.), Box Baa-Bai, Special Collections, Princeton University Libraries, Princeton, N.J. Baird left the desk for a brigade command in Kentucky in the spring of 1862 and finished the war a major general; in 1896 he was awarded a Medal of Honor (Dumas Malone, ed., *Dictionary of American Biography*, 9 vols. [New York: Charles Scribner's Sons, 1927], s.v. "Absalom Baird").

32. Letter, Hunter to Stanton, 29 January 1862, document no. 50521, Edwin M. Stanton Papers, LOC.

33. Letters, Hunter to Stanton, 1 February 1862, document no. 14331, Hunter to Lincoln, 4 February 1862, document no. 14375, Lincoln to Hunter and Lane, 10 February 1862, document no. 14461, Hunter to Lane, 13 February 1862, document no. 14499, Lincoln Papers, LOC; letter, Hunter to Trumbull, 21 February 1862, Trumbull Papers, LOC; letters, Hunter to Halleck, 8 February, and Halleck to Hunter, 13 February 1882, *ORA*, 8:829–31, 554–55.

34. Letter, Eugene A. Carr, to father, 28 January 1862, Carr Papers, U.S. Army Military History Institute, Carlisle Barracks, Pa.

35. Letter, Halleck to Hunter, 19 February 1862, Schenck, "General Hunter," 143; Hunter, *Report of the Military Services*, 15; Abel, *American Indian in the Civil War*, 76, 80–96.

36. President's War Order No. 3, 11 March 1862, *ORA*, 8:554–55.
37. Letter, Thomas to Halleck, 12 March 1861, ibid., 8:606.

Chapter 4

COMMAND AND ABOLITION

On 19 April 1861, in the same eventful week that Fort Sumter was surrendered to the Confederacy, the president called on the states for three-year volunteers, Virginia seceded from the Union, and Lincoln proclaimed a blockade of the Southern coast. The proclamation seemed more ambitious than practical at the time, because the Union navy did not have sufficient ships to sustain a blockade. As a way of reducing blockading fleet shortages, the navy planned to seize bases on Southern coasts. The plan recognized that a blockade from within a harbor could be maintained by a few ships, while one off enemy-controlled and fortified seaports required a large number and could not be as effective. A number of small operations were undertaken to capture strategic harbors, and the lessons learned were applied to a more ambitious project to help block Confederate use of the critical coast between Savannah and Charleston.

The officer who designed the blockade, Flag Officer Samuel Francis Du Pont, was put in command of the expedition, and he was assigned Brig. Gen. Thomas W. Sherman, who was told to organize a twelve thousand–man army component to support Du Pont's fleet. Du Pont's preferred objective was the large natural harbor of Port Royal, a fine anchorage that could have easily hosted the entire navy. It was not an important rebel port, however, yet it was defended by forts on each side of the harbor mouth. The Union fleet appeared off Hilton Head on 4 November and was ready to attack three days later. Naval bombardment forced abandonment of the fortifications, and Sherman's army troops occupied them, and other important points, without fighting. The Union not only had the fine harbor it sought but also held the towns of Port Royal and Beaufort, commercial centers for the important long-staple cotton so prized in European markets. With the harbor, towns, and plantations of South Carolina's Sea Islands, Sherman's occupying troops also had to deal with the mass of black slaves left behind by their fleeing masters.[1]

General Sherman was concerned about the low number of whites among the Sea Islands population because, without that class, there was little hope of using the blacks as laborers. He issued a proclamation immediately, declaring that he had "no desire to . . . interfere with any of your [white Sea Islanders'] lawful rights or your social institutions." This can be taken to mean that, as far as he was concerned, property in the form of slaves would be protected, the price of getting the blacks to work. Sherman complained that "the wealthy islands of Saint Helena, Ladies, and most of Port Royal are abandoned by the whites, and the beautiful estates of the planters, with their immense property, left to the pillage of hordes of apparently disaffected blacks." There was some immediate unrest of the sort feared by Sherman, but the real difficulty was making the blacks at least self-sufficient and perhaps producing some profit for the treasury.[2]

Sherman had received instructions before the expedition departed the North which allowed him to use the black population for labor service in support of his and Du Pont's bases. The authority was to prove valuable later to Sherman's successor because it appeared to give the commander wide discretion. The instruction cautioned Sherman to "avoid all interference with the social systems of local institutions of any State" and said:

> You will . . . in general avail yourself of the services of any persons, whether fugitives from labor or not, who may offer themselves to the National Government. You will employ such persons in such services as they may be fitted for—either as ordinary employes [sic], or, if special circumstances seem to require it, in any capacity, with such organization (in squads, companies, or otherwise) as you may deem beneficial to the service; this, however, not being a general arming of them for military service.[3]

Sherman wrote to the adjutant general in mid-December expressing his dissatisfaction with the blacks on the Sea Islands. He complained that he had been able to find only a few more than three hundred willing to work for the army, "most of them women and children; only 60 able-bodied males." In general, he thought that the blacks "appear to be so overjoyed with the change of their condition that their minds are unsettled to any plan. . . . Their present ease and comfort on the plantations, as long as their provisions will last, will induce them to remain there until compelled to seek our lines for subsistence." He recognized that the plan to use black laborers was a failure because, in his view, "they are disinclined to labor, and will evidently not work to our satisfaction without those aids to which they have ever been accustomed, viz, the driver and the lash." He concluded that the sudden change "from servitude to apparent freedom is more than their intellects can understand," and he concluded that "this circumstance alone renders it a very serious question what is to be done with the negroes who will hereafter be found on conquered soil." Sherman had no long-term solution, but he recommended that teachers be sent to him at once to instruct the blacks in "the necessary rudiments of civilization" and to supervise work on the plantations.[4]

Sherman's plea for help was not immediately responded to by the War Department, partly because the Treasury Department had some responsibilities for the occupied territory—specifically, collection of the war tax that Congress had imposed on the states in rebellion. It could only be collected where Union forces were in occupation, so the Treasury Department's interest was strong in the Port Royal territories. Treasury agents, many of them army officers working for secretary of the treasury Salmon P. Chase, were confiscating what could be found in the Sea Islands, principally cotton but also furniture and other items of value. It was important to get the blacks to produce new crops so further taxes could be satisfied. A few army officers, but more Northern abolitionists and others who wished to uplift the black race, were attracted to Port Royal, which was seen as a testing ground for the rehabilitation of freed slaves. The confluence of General Sherman's need to relieve the army of responsibility for feeding blacks, Chase's war tax requirements, and the perhaps more noble objectives of missionaries led to the "Port Royal Experiment," which was to be the model for the future.[5]

As 1862 began, Sherman was growing more concerned about the condition of the black population within Union lines. Some treasury agents and missionaries arrived in January, but none of this helped feed the nine thousand starving blacks Sherman had counted. In February he expressed again his beliefs regarding the ability of his charges. To him they were "hordes of totally uneducated, ignorant, and improvident blacks [who] have all been abandoned by their constitutional guardians, not only to all the future chances of anarchy and starvation, but in such a state of abject ignorance and mutual stolidity as to preclude all possibility of self-government and self-maintenance." Consequently, he ordered superintendents to be appointed in the districts under his command with the responsibility to "enroll and organize the willing blacks into working parties." The army took the responsibility of transporting the missionaries from Boston, New York, and Philadelphia and providing them protection and rations. Thus was set up the structure that until war's end was to govern the society of former slaves in that corner of South Carolina.[6]

Of course, Sherman had responsibilities other than the civil administration of the Port Royal area. He had under way the difficult task of investing Fort Pulaski on a nearly unapproachable island in the Savannah River. The activity called for the placement of artillery batteries on mud flats and islands near the installation, a task that occupied several regiments beginning in December 1861. By early April preparations for the bombardment were completed. The engineer of the operation was the acting brigadier general, Quincy A. Gillmore.[7]

DEPARTMENT OF THE SOUTH

General Orders No. 26, 15 March 1862, was the War Department's direction for the reorganization of the Expeditionary Force. It read: "The States of South Carolina, Georgia and Florida, with the expedition and forces now under Brig. Gen. T. W. Sherman, will constitute a military department, to be called the Department of the South, to be commanded by Major-General Hunter." David Hunter was in Washington when the orders were published; he had come east on advance notice that he would be given this new command when the Department of Kansas was eliminated. Hunter had earlier complained about Brigadier General Sherman commanding the Expeditionary Force, which looked like a department and had more troops than Hunter commanded from Fort Leavenworth, so perhaps his new assignment was a result of that complaint. The War Department told Hunter what was expected of him:

> You will co-operate with Commodore Du Pont in the taking of Fort Pulaski and Savannah. You will be held strictly responsible that you attack and beat the enemy whenever and wherever an opportunity offers. . . . In regard to Contrabands, or persons heretofore held to involuntary service by rebel masters, you will observe instructions hithertofore given by the President to Brigadier General Sherman.[8]

Hunter might have gone with his wife to Princeton for a few days before proceeding by ship to Hilton Head. Apparently, he was thinking over the briefings and assurances he had received in Washington from Stanton, because he wrote to the secretary on 27 March from the steamship *Adelaide,* then in Baltimore before the vessel sailed for Fort Monroe. "I have to state that my continued reflection convinces me that for an efficient action it is indispensable that more troops be sent immediately to South Carolina. I know as well now as I can possibly know when I shall have reached there that from 20,000 to 25,000 additional troops should be sent." Hunter promised that he "would almost guarantee to have our flag waving over Fort Sumter by the anniversary of its capture," that is, 13 April. Hunter asked the secretary to telegraph him at Fort Monroe with a decision on whether he would receive the troops he thought necessary. That the nearly immediate result he forecast could only be obtained by delivering to Hunter at once double the number of soldiers then in the entire Department of the South might have made Stanton think Hunter unbalanced, and no response was made to the request. Not finding the answer he expected at Fort Monroe, Hunter wrote again from the steamer *Atlantic,* anchored off that post, telling Stanton he had just heard that rebels were in strength at Savannah and Charleston and, consequently, he needed reinforcements immediately. Hunter had regularly made such troop requests from Kansas, and he was to continue to make them from the Department of the South. Manpower shortages in his widespread command, which were constantly on his mind, needed to be offset, and Hunter sought ways to do this. His innovative and preemptive actions meant to accomplish this were to cause problems for him in Washington.[9]

Although Hunter's new command was indeed spread thin, the situation he found on arrival at Hilton Head on 31 March was good. General Sherman told him that the Union controlled the entire coast from Edisto Island north of Port Royal to Saint Augustine, to Key West, and nearly all of western Florida. Only a few places had Confederate forces in sufficient strength to challenge Union activities, and the most important of them, Fort Pulaski, was ready to be bombarded. Hunter assumed command the day he arrived and named his personal staff. It included Major Halpine as assistant adjutant general and Lts. Samuel W. Stockton and Arthur M. Kinzie. The general stayed in Hilton Head for a few days before inspecting the Fort Pulaski operation. Before he left he sent Stanton another letter emphasizing that his command was "entirely much too scattered and subject to be cut off in detail." He said again that he needed more soldiers or else would have to abandon Jacksonville, where he had fourteen hundred troops concentrated. He did not think Stanton would object to the new request since, he said, "on my leaving Washington you had the kindness to promise me whatever force I might ask." Hunter did not stop with playing that card, however, and asked for fifty thousand muskets with two hundred rounds of ammunition for each, "with authority to arm such loyal men as I can find in the country." He obviously meant that he intended to arm blacks but did not say so directly. He may have confused the matter somewhat by adding, "It is important that I should be able to know and distinguish these men at once, and for this purpose I respectfully request that 50,000 pairs of scarlet pantaloons may be sent to me; and this is all the clothing I shall require for these people." Whether Hunter had spoken in Washington to Stanton about black troops is not known, but it seems likely considering Hunter's previous correspondence on the subject. In any event,

Stanton did not react to the fact that Hunter's weapons and trousers request was the general's poorly camouflaged attempt to force a change of national policy clearly at odds with President Lincoln's cautious approach on matters pertaining to blacks.[10]

Commodore Du Pont, the senior naval officer at Port Royal, met Hunter the day he took command. Du Pont was sorry, however, that General Sherman had been relieved and thought it unjust. He did not have a strong opinion of Hunter at their first meeting and wrote to his wife that night, "*mon impression n'est pas très haute.*" This view would soon change, but relations between the services were sometimes strained. Sherman told Hunter that he had been ordered by General McClellan in January to stop a planned attack to capture Savannah "for want of the promised co-operation on the part of the Navy." Meanwhile, the attack on Fort Pulaski, to protect that city, was ready, so Hunter proceeded down the coast aboard the steamer *McClellan* to inspect the arrangements. Hunter sent a flag of truce to the fort's commander just after sunrise on 10 April and ordered the bombardment to begin as the rebels declined a request to surrender. By midday on 11 April the Confederate forces struck their colors, and Hunter's representative on the scene, Brig. Gen. Henry W. Benham, sent Major Halpine to the fort to offer terms and to accept the capitulation on his behalf. Casualties in the engagement were one Union soldier killed (by accident) and three Confederates wounded. Nevertheless, the accomplishment was important because it stopped Savannah's use as a port for blockade runners, and it completed Union control of the East Coast south of Charleston.[11]

While the capture of Pulaski allowed Hunter to redeploy some of his limited number of troops elsewhere in the command, he was still facing what he thought were overwhelming numerical odds just to hold his positions, which was all that his instructions required of him. Perhaps so as not to contribute to rebel army strength, he refused to parole the Pulaski garrison and sent all the men to New York aboard the *Atlantic* as prisoners of war—the trip supervised by Lieutenant Stockton, who was thereby given a chance to visit his family in New Jersey. Whether for ideological reasons or because he somehow saw the action as a way to improve his manpower shortage, on 13 April, just two days after the surrender, Hunter declared all slaves found in Fort Pulaski or on its surrounding island free and said that they "shall hereafter receive the fruits of their own labor." The declaration drew little or no notice in the North, probably because it affected few blacks and was not recognized to be the important assumption of authority which it was. The question of slaves and their status in free states, the Confederacy, and the Union army was not yet decided, but Hunter was about to make the issue prominent.[12]

General Hunter continued to be worried about the status of the department, and on 22 April he wrote to Stanton yet again, this time requesting an unspecified number of new regiments to offset the sixty-five thousand troops his intelligence had reported were aligned against him, thirty thousand at Savannah, twenty-five thousand at Charleston, and ten thousand at Augusta. "With proper re-inforcements," he said, "I confidently hope to report to you in a few weeks the fall of Sumter, Charleston, and Savannah." Otherwise, his own force of sixteen thousand did not seem sufficient even to hold off the numbers he had estimated. That the Confederates actually had a force (about nineteen thousand in South Carolina and Georgia) much equal to his own was not known to him, and Hunter, like McClellan and other Union generals, consistently overestimated the opposition—often by many times. Stanton did not answer, distracted possibly by results of the recent battle of Shiloh in the West, the fall of New Orleans to the Union navy, and General McClellan's move of the Army of the Potomac to the peninsula between the James and York Rivers in Virginia. It was perhaps these same events that convinced Hunter that he could not depend on Washington and that he had to find his own solutions.[13]

FREEDOM AND ARMED BLACK MEN

The first such solution was expressed in an order published on 9 May 1862. Declaring that Georgia, Florida, and South Carolina had "declared themselves no longer under the protection of the United States," had taken up arms against it, they were now consequently under martial law as "a military necessity." "Slavery and martial law in a free country are altogether incompatible; the persons in these three States, . . . heretofore held as slaves, are therefore declared free." The declaration went beyond Frémont's proclamation, which had been limited to slaves whose owners were in rebellion, and the president continued to protect the slave property of loyal masters—at least until such owners could be compensated, as authorized in April for the District of Columbia. Hunter did not, however, limit his actions to the declaration of freedom but decided, instead, to take firm action to induce or even force the black men he liberated to fight in a Union uniform in defense of their new status. As logical as this policy may seem, it was not understood by the blacks and, in fact, was opposed. General Sherman had been asked by the adjutant general to hire and send to Key West for labor duties three to four hundred black men, but Sherman said such a number could only be obtained over some time so as not to cause a panic. He said that "many of them surmise that they will ultimately be sent to Cuba and sold," an outcome, their masters had said, which would surely follow Union occupation.[14]

Hunter expected the blacks to enlist voluntarily, and he directed his district commanders to sign up willing applicants to be "paid, fed, and clothed, as well as drilled, in the same manner with our other troops." From the first he expected to enlist two regiments—about a thousand men each—the regiments to be led by white officers selected from qualified noncommissioned officers among the troops in the command. To Hunter's surprise hardly any black men came forward, and within a few days he decided that the need for new troops was serious enough to call for more drastic action. Halpine explained what happened: "General Hunter one fine morning, with twirling glasses, puckered lips, and dilated nostrils—(he had just received another 'don't-bother-us-for-reinforcements' dispatch from Washington)—announced his intention of 'forming negro regiments' and compelling 'every able-bodied black man in the department to fight for the freedom which could not but be the issue of the war.'" Without consulting his subordinate generals and without discussions with the treasury employees overseeing black workers on the plantations, on 9 May, the same day as the freedom order, Hunter directed a roundup of black men between the ages of eighteen and forty-five in the Port Royal area. The order said to "send immediately, to this headquarters, under a guard, all the able-bodied negroes capable of bearing arms." It took a few days to coordinate the effort, and the plan was put into motion on 11 May, a Sunday. It took the form of a circular from the Second Brigade commanded by Brig. Gen. Isaac I. Stevens at Beaufort, which asked all agents and overseers of plantations on Ladies, Saint Helena, and Coosaw Islands to send the able-bodied black men to Beaufort in the morning. Agent Edward L. Pierce, the senior treasury official—who was required to accept military orders—asked his subordinates to obey the directive. He did not, however, think Hunter's initiative wise and, after consulting with General Stevens, protested in writing. He said that the War Department had appointed him "general superintendent and director of the negroes" with responsibility for caring for the blacks and putting them to work raising food and cotton crops on the plantations abandoned by the white masters. Hunter's impressment of the black men, however, would put an end to cultivation at the height of the season and would cancel the "social experiment which it was deemed important to make." Furthermore, Pierce feared for the effect on the "ignorant, suspicious, and sensitive" blacks, who "have not so far recovered the manhood which two centuries of bondage have rooted out." It will take time to convince them "they have a country to fight for" and time to overcome "their indisposition to become soldiers."[15]

The following morning about five hundred black men were gathered up by the civilian superintendents aided by details of white soldiers. The former slaves were loaded aboard the *Mattano* at Beaufort and were transported to Hilton

Head. Pierce wrote to Hunter again, this time describing the scenes at several places where blacks were taken from the fields and hurried away without being allowed to go to their houses for coats or other articles. Some ran off into the woods and had to be chased down. Another agent said that his charges "sighed . . . for the 'old fetters' as being better than the new liberty," and yet another concluded his description of the affair with the remark: "The plea of military necessity has been stretched to cover up many a mistake and some acts of criminal injustice, but never, in my judgment, did [a] major-general fall into a sadder blunder and rarely has humanity been outraged by an act of more unfeeling barbarity." Laura Towne, a Northern schoolteacher on Ladies Island, called 11 May "the black day," and said that the "Negroes feared 'Hilty-Head'" because "it is the shipping-off point, and they have great fears of Cuba."[16]

Pierce discussed the situation with Hunter at the Hilton Head department headquarters, and the general agreed that he would not keep any of the blacks against their will and would direct General Stevens to give the former slaves who did not voluntarily choose military service certificates of freedom and transportation back to their homes. Pierce wrote to his superior, Secretary Chase, that General Hunter had evidently been acting in this matter "upon certain notions of his own which he has been revolving in his mind, rather than upon any observation of his own or the testimony of others." Chase, however, no doubt distracted by more pressing matters, passed the entire package of letters and orders received from Pierce on to Secretary Stanton, remarking, "All the papers are worth reading and are important to a correct view of the state of things on the island." He did not, however, make a recommendation, and so Stanton took no immediate action, and he did not comment on what must have appeared to be a typically impulsive action by Hunter.[17]

Hunter's actions did not equally escape attention in the press. The *New York Times* early on thought that arming blacks was "laden with possible dangers to humanity," reflecting the current belief that blacks were savages who would seek revenge against whites. Word of Hunter's emancipation decree reached the North by the middle of May and was noticed more than was the black soldier initiative. Newspapers were almost uniformly against his action, which one of them called a "sudden and unwarranted assumption of power by a subordinate officer of the Government." Others recognized that the Lincoln administration was "at sea on the subject" and had no solid policy, yet "this action of General Hunter is by far the most arbitrary exercise of power by any public official, either civil or military." A Philadelphia daily viewed Hunter's move as lacking wisdom and justice, the *New York Daily Herald* correctly noted that Hunter had not distinguished between slaves of loyal and rebel masters, but another New York journal said simply that "paper projectiles of the longest range will hardly prove efficient." Lincoln was forced to deal with Hunter's freedom order just as he had with Frémont's less far-reaching 1861 proclamation.[18]

THE ADMINISTRATION REACTS

Lincoln responded by proclamation on 19 May and without coordinating with his entire cabinet. Stanton helped with the wording, but Chase, who later wrote to newspaper editor Horace Greeley that he thought Hunter's order "should be allowed to stand," did not. Lincoln began by distancing the administration from Hunter's order, claiming that he had only read of it in the public press:

> I, Abraham Lincoln, president of the United States, proclaim and declare, that the government of the United States, had no knowledge, informa- tion, or belief, of an intention on the part of General Hunter to issue such a proclamation; nor has it any authentic information that the document is genuine. And, further, that neither General Hunter, nor any other commander, or person, has been authorized by the Government of the United States, to make proclamations declaring the slaves of any State free; and that the supposed proclamation, now in question, whether genuine or false, is altogether void.

Lincoln continued that only he as commander-in-chief had the authority, and, furthermore, that his policy was to give pecuniary aid to states that may adopt voluntary and gradual abolishment of slavery.[19]

Curiously, neither Lincoln nor Stanton made any attempt to ask Hunter to verify his order, and, other than the language in Lincoln's proclamation, Hunter never received official censure. Hunter himself acknowledged that "Lincoln re- pudiated, *in the newspapers,* my orders freeing the slaves" but did not otherwise act. He said, "I believe he rejoiced in my action," but politics had made it impossible for the president to support his general openly. Hunter said much the same thing to Du Pont, who went to see him at Hilton Head to sympathize about Lincoln's rebuke. General McClellan, then commanding the Peninsula campaign against Richmond, wrote to his wife: "I am very glad that the President has come out as he did about Hunter's order—I feared he would not have the moral courage to do so. I can't think how Hunter could have done such a thing without authority from someone." An admirer thought Hunter had been "the brave exponent of ideas and wishes timidly entertained at headquarters" and that, in later years, others got the credit he deserved. Hunter's emancipation fallout died down quickly, although Lincoln made reference to it in early July as he continued to struggle with the problem. He wrote: "Gen. Hunter is an honest man. He was, and I hope, still is my friend. I valued him none the less for his agreeing with me in the general wish that all men everywhere, could be free." He explained that he had had to repudiate Hunter's order because Hunter "expected more good, and less harm, from the measure, than I could believe would follow." Lincoln recognized that he caused dissatisfaction among many whose support he needed, but "this is not the end of it. The pressure is still upon me and is increasing." As for Hunter, the old soldier had little more involvement in the matter, but he apparently supplied emancipation arguments to others. One was a response to "disloyal dough-faces at the north" who were arguing that newly freed blacks "will flock north" and compete with white laborers for work. Hunter countered this fear: "So great is the loyal attachment of the negro to the south, ... very few of them will leave." His proof was that less than a dozen of them, although free to do so, sought to go to the North from Port Royal. While no longer making news on the slavery issue, Hunter was nevertheless about to make national headlines again—this time over the enlistment of blacks in the army.[20]

Hunter's position in the Department of the South required that he keep on good terms with Commodore Du Pont. By mid-May the naval officer's opinion of the general had changed from the negative first impression he had on 31 March. Du Pont wrote to his wife: "General Hunter is a man of the finest bearing, tone, and address; silent, but not like most silent men, he is uncommonly gracious and benign in his intercourse. He is easy in his private means, and very independent in thought and action, has no fear of responsibility, yet very devoid of pretension." Two weeks later Du Pont went up to Beaufort to greet Maria Hunter, who had just arrived from the North. (Mrs. Steuart was not along; she may have been staying with Chicago or Washington relatives.) "I said ... it strikes me as very absurd for the General to have encouraged if not ordered the departure of the other officers' wives and then bring out his own. [Comdr. C. R. P.] Rodgers quietly observed, 'Perhaps he has not the say in these matters.' I believe Mrs. Hunter is a fine woman and, having no children, Army officer fashion has followed her husband." On the other hand, although he seemed to have been charmed by the couple, Du Pont was more cautious regarding the general's professional accomplishments. "All I see of him I like, yet I do not know him and I think all that has been done since he came here with Benham, if viewed through any medium but one of strong predisposition, would show apathy and blundering—for Pulaski, I consider, was taken in one sense before they came."[21]

Du Pont grew more fond of Hunter as they met aboard ship or at department headquarters at Hilton Head. Soon the commodore found Hunter "a most estimable person," and he invited the general and his lady to Episcopal church services aboard the *Wabash*. He told his wife that Maria Hunter was "much more of a lady than any other person we have sent out here. She has followed her husband everywhere, having no children, and has been a great deal in Washington." A few days later Hunter entertained schoolteacher Towne at Hilton Head. She wrote of Hunter: "He says he shall burn Charleston if he ever has the chance to take it," evidence of his desire to make the South pay for rebellion. "He is a generous but too impulsive man," she continued, "kind to a fault to his soldiers, and more anti-slavery than I expected. He wore a loose undress coat made of white cassimir and a straw hat, when walking on the piazza. His manner is very quick and decided, and to his wife attentive and as if he were very much attached to her. He told me how she went out with him on all his campaigns and how it was impossible for him to do without her." Towne did not write whether she discussed the use of blacks from the plantations for army service, but the matter certainly had Hunter's attention at the time.[22]

The reason for the matter's prominence was not the result of Hunter's requests for permission to enroll blacks; these were not answered by the War Department. The catalyst was a question raised in the U.S. House of Representatives by Congressman Charles Anderson Wickliffe from Kentucky, who had read something that disturbed him in the *New York Tribune*. On 9 June a resolution was passed directing Stanton to inform the House if General Hunter had organized a regiment "of black men (fugitive slaves) and appointed the colonel and other officers to command them." The secretary was further asked if Hunter had authority to muster "fugitive or captive slaves" as U.S. soldiers and if he had furnished clothing and uniforms for the force and arms "to be placed in the hands of these slaves." Stanton answered in much the same language that Lincoln used in his proclamation canceling Hunter's emancipation order. He said that the War Department had no official information that Hunter had set up a regiment but had asked him about it. In fact, Stanton knew of Hunter's actions, and he allowed them, his biographers say, "without Lincoln's knowledge and with his own implied consent." Hunter also had received clothing and arms without specifying how the items might be used, but no arms were supplied specially for use by slaves. Stanton asked Hunter to make an immediate report to him on the situation. Two days later he also told Hunter that Brig. Gen. Rufus Saxton was ready to be assigned under him in the special job of taking charge of the Sea Island plantations. On 31 March Saxton had left the Department of the South, where he had been a captain and chief quartermaster under General Sherman. He had much impressed War Department officials and had been jumped to general's rank. (Returning to South Carolina in mid-May, he was shipwrecked, went back to Washington, and was diverted to command the defense of Harper's Ferry against Stonewall Jackson, an engagement that led to his being awarded a Medal of Honor some years later.) Saxton's experience in supply and logistics was just the talent needed to care for black farmworkers. Before Saxton's arrival Hunter had perfected the organization of the regiment—not the two that he had earlier ambitiously hoped to form.[23]

By 8 May Hunter had appointed his nephew and aide Lt. Arthur M. Kinzie colonel and regimental commander, a bit of nepotism that Major Halpine justified by noting that Hunter "asked nothing of others which he was not willing that one of his own flesh and blood should not be engaged in." Kinzie, however, became ill sometime in June and was replaced by another of Hunter's aides, the politically important Capt. James D. Fessenden, son of a U.S. senator from Maine. Hunter initially called the unit the First Contraband Regiment but soon changed the name to the First South Carolina Volunteer Infantry. Hunter had trouble in the beginning obtaining enlisted men to apply for officer positions in the black regiment. Perhaps some were put off by the unofficial nature of the unit, but more were deterred by the supposed stigma of serving with blacks. Hunter said: "Never mind, the fools or bigots who refuse are punished by their refusal. Before two years," he accurately forecast, "they will be competing eagerly for the commissions they now reject." The regiment's perhaps four to five hundred recruits—some of them originally impressed and others newly enlisted—were equipped with uniforms and began basic training at Hilton Head. The unit, however, was not welcomed by its white comrades in uniform, but the real problem was that the black soldiers were unpaid, while other former slaves employed by the army as civilians earned a wage.[24]

Halpine described how Hunter received the request from Stanton to answer the congressional resolution originated by Representative Wickliffe. "The fool, that old fool has just given me the very chance I was growing sick for! The War Department has refused to notice my black regiment; but now, in reply to the resolution, I can lay the matter before the country, and force the authorities either to adopt my negroes or disband them." Hunter and Halpine worked all night on the answer so as to catch the mail going north on the *Arago*, the three-times-a-month steamer departing the next morning. His reply to accusations that he had exceeded his authority did not include humility and might even be termed arrogant. Stanton had the letter in a few days, and he sent it to the House on 2 July. He did not edit it nor make any comment except that he was enclosing Hunter's reply. Hunter took the questions as asked. He denied he had formed a regiment of "fugitive slaves" but said, "There is, however, a fine regiment of persons whose late masters are 'fugitive rebels,' men who everywhere fly before the appearance of the national flag, leaving their servants behind them to shift as best they can for themselves." As to his authority for raising the unit, Hunter said General Sherman's 14 October instructions from the War Department provided sufficient justification, without restriction as to race and civil or military employment. Hunter said that he was authorized to enroll fugitive slaves but added once again that none had been found in his department. "In the absence of any 'fugitive master law,' the deserted slaves would be wholly without remedy, had not the crime of treason given them the right to pursue, capture, and bring back those persons of whose protection they had been suddenly bereft." Finally, he admitted that he had no specific authority to issue government-owned equipment to any particular class of person, the government trusting him to use supplies as military exigencies might require. In conclusion, because McClellan's Peninsula campaign meant that he could not expect reinforcement of his department, Hunter said that he hoped to raise forty-eight to fifty thousand "of these hardy and devoted soldiers" to make up his shortages.[25]

Major Halpine was delighted with Hunter's answer—which he termed a "politico-military champagne cocktail"—but Congressman Wickliffe and others were not. Kentucky Union Democrat Robert Mallory was particularly upset with the reaction of the House when Hunter's letter was read. "The scene was one of which I think this House should forever be ashamed." "A spectator in the gallery," he continued, "would have supposed we were witnessing here the performance of a buffoon or of a low farce actor upon the stage." The reading "was received with loud applause and boisterous manifestations of approbation by the Republican members of the House. . . . It was a scene, in my opinion, disgraceful to the American Congress." Hunter described, with some delight, the letter's reception: "The moment it was received and read in the War Department, it was hurried down to the House, and delivered, *ore rotundo,* from the Clerk's desk. Here its effect was magical. The clerk could scarcely read it with decorum; nor could half his words be heard amidst the universal peals of laughter." Hunter's defiance of the Kentucky congressman, formerly an antislavery Whig, and his Democratic supporters doubtless made the general a hero to the Radical wing of the Republican Party which wished to punish the South, but it also may have moved the Lincoln administration closer to openly advocating the use of black troops to meet real and imagined manpower shortages.[26]

OPERATIONS AND TROOP SHORTAGES

While Hunter was dealing with Washington's rejection and ignoring of the initiatives he thought were needed in his command, he was not neglecting offensive action against Confederate forces, as his instructions directed. Two events helped the planning of where the strike should be made. One was the bringing out of a barge from Charleston harbor by some slaves and the other the abduction of the armed Confederate steamer *Planter* by a particularly daring and well-informed black man, Robert Smalls, and his associates. These self-liberated slaves had information of interest to the army, particularly data on weaknesses in recent redeployments of the rebel defenses of Charleston. Hunter's second in command, Brigadier General Benham, began planning an operation early in May, when the barge crew was interrogated, and refined the attack orders with Smalls's more detailed information in mid-month. On 20 May Du Pont acted on what Smalls had informed him about, the removal of Confederate guns from Cole's Island, and he sent gunboats up the now-uncovered Stono River. This action secured an important base for Benham's army operations, which called for landings by Union troops on James Island to be followed up by an advance inland to outflank Charleston's defenses. Hunter directed that preparations be made, and the landing was successfully accomplished on 2 June. Hunter felt that his forces were not yet of sufficient size to accomplish the objective, however, and he ordered Benham, the commander on the scene, not to make offensive moves on the rebels' positions. Du Pont thought that Hunter would not on his own have launched the operation, "but Benham persuaded him to go up, then to occupy James Island, and so on, while it would have been better not to have threatened any movement until we were entirely ready." Undoubtedly, Hunter was hoping that Stanton would send him the reinforcements he had several times requested before the Confederate forces reacted strongly to the initiative.[27]

He made yet another request to Stanton on the last day of May, again offering a count of the troops he thought opposed him—the same sixty thousand against his sixteen thousand—as an argument for reinforcements. He asked for only a "few thousand additional troops" and felt that with them he could secure Charleston, Georgetown, Brunswick, Savannah, St. Mary's, and Jacksonville to be rallying points. He said, "Slaves would flock to our posts," fleeing from their masters. He suggested that this would particularly hurt slave-owning rebels: "according to my experience they would rather lose one of their children than a good negro." It only took a little more than a week for Washington to refuse the request. No regiments could be made available because McClellan was sustaining heavy casualties before Richmond. That Peninsula campaign was about to have another impact on the forces that Hunter would have available for his wide responsibilities.[28]

Hunter had not escaped from all the consequences of his impetuousness demonstrated by the freedom order and using slaves as soldiers, and there was talk that he would be relieved of his command on the ground that he was too controversial. It was also conjectured that Hunter himself might be so frustrated as to ask for a reassignment. A former New York congressman serving as Benham's aide wrote to Salmon Chase: "Regarding Hunter's position I apprehend that the President will not supersede him; but he may ask to be relieved, I hope he will not, and I would desire to suggest that you write to him not to leave. He has the entire confidence and personal regard of Gen Benham and the other officers of the command and all would be sorry to see him leave." Hunter was not that well liked by all his subordinates, and he was about to make Benham very angry at him indeed. Brig. Gen. Isaac I. Stevens wrote what he really thought on 1 June, "I have two commanders, Hunter and Benham, who are imbecile, vacillating, and utterly unfit to command."[29]

Benham tested his own competence on 16 June, attacking Confederate positions in what is known as the battle of Secessionville. Hunter said that he had given clear orders to Benham not to advance until he received "further explicit orders from this headquarters." Although Hunter later acknowledged that his restriction was clear, it was not seen as such by Benham. The attack resulted in "a disastrous repulse," over five hundred Union casualties, and a retreat from James Island. Two of Du Pont's captains considered Hunter's withdrawal order premature and felt that the time had never been better to take Charleston. The captain of the armed steamer *Pocahontas* went farther, stating that, in his view, "Hunter must be either mad or a traitor." Hunter, however, blamed the failure on Benham and wrote that "General Benham endeavors to evade the responsibility for having violated his instructions by terming his attack upon the enemy's works a 'reconnaissance in force,' but such a plea is too puerile to deserve consideration." Therefore, he said, Benham was being sent north under arrest and with a recommendation that he be dismissed from the service. Yet Hunter did not escape criticism for the failure. Stanton claimed that Hunter was not authorized to operate against Charleston but had been instructed, rather, to maintain purely defensive positions. As he told Hunter, "It could not have been expected that a general of your experience would undertake at his own discretion, without orders and without notice to the Department, a hazardous expedition 'with fears of failure' for want of adequate transportation." Stanton was also irritated with Hunter's repeated manpower requests; he had clearly rejected the request of 30 April and could not understand why Hunter had sent yet another one just over a month later.[30]

In July the news from Washington did not get any better. On the third Hunter was directed to send ten thousand infantry to the hard-pressed McClellan, who was then on the James River outside Richmond. Stanton qualified the order by adding that the requested number should be sent only if the troops "can be spared." In any event, Stanton at least inferred that Hunter's first concern should be the safety of his command. Hunter, above all a good soldier, sent six regiments by 12 July (commanded by General Stevens) and the seventh five days later. Hunter ordered the evacuation of Edisto Island, moving the former slave plantation workers to Beaufort, and he withdrew all Union forces from Daufuskie Island north of Fort Pulaski. The Department of the South's forces were thus reduced to about ten thousand in South Carolina, a thousand at Fort Pulaski, and about five thousand in several Florida positions, with the largest concentration at Pensacola in West Florida. General Hunter wrote to Stanton: "It is in my judgment extremely important that [Edisto and Daufuskie Islands] should be reoccupied, and also that strong posts should be established at Georgetown, Brunswick, and Saint Simon's Island. I have, therefore, to request that reinforcements may be sent to this department as soon as possible, not only with a view to future operations, but also for the further security of our present positions and depots."[31]

Brig. Gen. Horacio Wright left the department at the end of July, reporting to Washington for reassignment, and Stanton asked him for his opinion of the troop situation. Wright was matter-of-fact in his reply: "The force remaining in the Department of the South is not only sufficient to hold the posts now occupied, with the aid afforded by the Navy, but may in my judgment be still further reduced without endangering the safety of any of the positions." He recommended as well that four more regiments be withdrawn and that the First Massachusetts Cavalry, Hunter's only mounted unit, also be sent to assist the army in Virginia.

Hunter apparently did not know what his former subordinate was saying in Washington, but his interest in increasing forces in the department went beyond requesting Stanton to send him troops from the North. He also continued to seek War Department approval for his regiment of black men, although it could be said that the House of Representative's 5 July vote not to pursue further Congressman Wickliffe's resolution concerning black soldiers in the Department of the South had indirectly supported Hunter's actions. He still did not have the specific authority he wanted from Washington, and so he wrote again to Stanton on 11 July, complaining that sending troops to McClellan was about to threaten the security of the command. Hunter asked the secretary to give him "full authority to muster into the service of the United States, as infantry, all loyal men to be found in my department, and that I be authorized to appoint all the officers." The request did not mention race. The only answer Hunter received was a telegram from the adjutant general: "Your orders only required you to send to Fort

Monroe such troops as you could spare without endangering your command. You will retain such forces as will secure the safety of your positions." Nothing was said about arming "loyal men" to make up shortages.[32]

Possibly because he thought he was not making himself clear, Hunter tried again to get Stanton's attention on the black soldier question. This time he addressed the real issue, pay for the remaining members of the one regiment he had recruited. "Not satisfied that I shall be furnished with the means of making compensation to these loyal men for their services, and for the reason that their officers hold an anomalous position as men without commissions discharging the duties of commissioned officers, I desire earnestly to have a speedy and favorable decision upon the organization of the regiment." He said he had stopped active recruiting but was ready to put six regiments in the field in two months. Of course, the single unauthorized regiment was reported as "organized, . . . uniformed, and [drawing] its rations. The uniform consists of a dark blue coat, blue [red?] trousers, conical broad-brimmed black hats and black haversack—no stripes or trimmings of any sort and no bright buttons." The regiment did not often appear under arms and was generally confined to labor service on the docks at Hilton Head. As before, Stanton declined to answer the request, and Hunter showed his frustration in a 10 August letter to Stanton, "Failing to receive authority to muster the First South Carolina Volunteers into the service of the United States, I have disbanded them."[33]

What Hunter may not have known was that the climate was changing in Washington regarding the black soldier, and Lincoln was modifying his position regarding the abolition of slavery. Stanton had brought Hunter's "all loyal men" letter to a 21 July cabinet meeting, stressing that the general anticipated problems caused by the McClellan levies. Treasury secretary Salmon Chase noted that the proposed enlistments were to be made "without reference to complection [sic]." Stanton recommended that Hunter's black soldier initiative be approved, and Chase and William Seward, the secretary of state, agreed. Yet the president was reluctant to arm blacks, and the matter was deferred without decision until the following day. On the twenty-second the president was still unwilling to take the step many of his advisors recommended, because, Chase said, he "thought that the organization, equipment and arming of negroes, like other soldiers, would be productive of more evil than good." Lincoln usually kept his own counsel about slavery and arming blacks, but on 13 July he had uncharacteristically discussed these issues with navy secretary Gideon Welles and Seward. He did not fully reveal his thoughts, however, but did acknowledge that "the slaves, if not armed and disciplined, were in the service of those who were," remarks that could have been taken as uncertainty in Lincoln's mind. So, although the 21 and 22 July

meetings did not give Hunter what he wanted just then, other events were leading Lincoln toward a less ambiguous policy regarding blacks.[34]

One of the new influences on Lincoln was legislation that he approved in
mid-July, two laws called the Militia Act and the Confiscation Act. Neither was
revolutionary, and both did little more than confirm the already-existing power
of the president to use freed slaves in any way he considered would aid the war
effort. The legislation did, however, liberalize the treatment of black men similar
to Hunter's earlier procedure of giving men in the First South Carolina certificates of freedom. The Militia Act authorized the president to receive into the
service of the United States "for the purpose of constructing intrenchments, or
performing camp duty, or any other labor, or any military or naval service . . .
persons of African descent." It provided that such men (or boys) previously held
in bondage by persons now in rebellion—along with their wives, children, and
mothers—"shall forever thereafter be free." The Confiscation Act freed all slaves
whose masters were rebels without requiring the blacks to perform military
service. On the same day of the cabinet meeting that declined to allow Hunter to
arm blacks, Lincoln ordered his military commanders to employ blacks "as laborers, . . . giving them reasonable wages for their labor." He directed further that
accurate records be kept so that compensation might be paid—presumably to
loyal slave owners whose slaves were employed by the government. The legislation and order were silent about arming blacks, so that question remained open.[35]

As might be expected, Washington refused Hunter's 31 July request for more
troops. The letter with this news, dated 13 August, reminded Hunter of the new
chain of command. General Halleck had been recalled from the West and was
made the general-in-chief effective 11 July, although it took another two weeks
before he reached Washington. None of Hunter's aides recorded his reaction to
the circumstances that forced him to dissolve the black regiment, but one may
assume that the subject irritated him considerably. Blacks in uniform were not
well accepted among the troops under his command. A captain of General Stevens's
command, in a letter to the *Rochester Union and Advertiser,* showed his resentment,
which was shared by many uniformed whites: "They have the Silby tent and
Enfield rifles, and their clothing is far better than worn by our men." Another
newspaper blamed the fact that several hundred of the blacks "skedadled" because "the white troops have annoyed and irritated the black soldiers whenever
they came in their reach"; the writer did not mention lack of pay. Another,
reporting from Port Royal, said that scarlet trousers were everywhere, as black
soldiers sought transportation home after the regiment broke up. He too saw
little good in the experiment: "The negroes, before insolent and supercilious,
became more so as they were elevated." These reports clearly expressed the feel-

ings of many of the Northern civilian and military whites on the Sea Islands. Hunter reacted to a complaint raised by two missionaries over black soldiers quartered in their garden. Laura Towne wrote, "General Hunter, who has always suspected the superintendents of preventing enlistments and frowning on negro soldiers, became so exasperated by them that he threatened to send them home in irons if they oppose the negro regiment any more." Hunter also took official action against those whose activities or omissions with respect to former slaves were cruel or contemptuous. In a general order he said: "It is with deep regret that the general commanding the department has received several reports against officers for returning fugitive slaves in direct violation of a law of Congress [act approved 13 March 1862]. It will hardly be believed when it is announced that a New England colonel is to-day, in the second year of the rebellion, in arrest for having been engaged in the manly task of turning over a young woman, whose skin was almost as white as his own, to the cruel lash of her rebel master." He also remarked that "numerous acts of pilfering from the negroes have taken place in the neighborhood of Beaufort, committed by men wearing the uniform of the United States. I cannot and will not call them soldiers [and shall assign troops to police the plantations]."[36]

Hunter's patience was tried again when he received a telegram ordering his single cavalry unit out of the department, the order possibly based on General Wright's report ten days before. Hunter wrote immediately to Stanton (who referred the matter to Halleck without comment), protesting that the loss of his mounted troops was going to make it necessary "to leave Saint Helena, Ladies, Port Royal, Paris, and Spring islands, . . . all under a fine state of cultivation." He thought that the "beautiful town of Beaufort, so necessary to our hospital purposes," would also have to be given up. "Abandoning these fine islands to the enemy after having them planted and promising the negroes protection," he said, "is a very sad termination to our exertions in this department." It was a measure of Hunter's despair over the situation in South Carolina that the following day he wrote to Stanton: "You recollect that when you sent me down here, you promised me something to do. I am well aware of the exigencies of the service, which have prevented you from fulfilling your promise. And, as there can be no chance for active service here, I beg you will give me a chance in some other direction."[37]

Although Hunter had thus given up, the issue of black soldiers was still important to him and, he believed, to the Department of the South, but the matter was to be left in the hands of General Saxton, the officer picked by Washington to oversee the black population and the missionaries. On 9 August the two generals met with Du Pont (recently promoted to rear admiral) at Hunter's

Hilton Head headquarters and were unexpectedly joined by the Reverend Mansfield French, the missionary leader, accompanied by Robert Smalls, the slave who had escaped from Charleston in the *Planter* and was by now a national celebrity. French was seeking support of the Port Royal experiment and planned to take Smalls to the North for some fund-raising. Du Pont had not approved of this, since he felt he needed Smalls's piloting skills, but the officers decided that a trip to Washington might also help military needs. French was to take a letter to Stanton which made another appeal for black regiments, and he might also lobby other cabinet members.

The letter was craftily designed to take into account the changed climate regarding the issue and recent legislation and implementing orders. It was not known, however, that Stanton had just asked the army judge advocate general to determine how the Confiscation Act applied to full military use of black troops and had received a preliminary opinion that the unqualified use of blacks appeared authorized. The letter from Hilton Head, to be signed by Saxton, emphasized that the department was requesting authority to enroll five thousand laborers for use by the quartermaster department in South Carolina, "the men to be uniformed, armed, and officered by men detailed from the Army." That was the only mention of weapons in the letter, but the rest of the text was obviously designed to illustrate that armed blacks were necessary. It told of the fear of a Confederate attack among blacks along the coast and how removing that threat would cause many more slaves to flee to Union lines, crippling agriculture in rebel-held areas. Saxton made a particular point of describing the situation on Saint Simon's Island, Georgia, where—he did not mention—the single remaining, unauthorized company of the First South Carolina Regiment had been sent. Finally, Saxton argued, organized and disciplined blacks would get along better with white troops, and "a happy reciprocal influence upon the soldiers and ready helpers would almost necessarily be the result." French and Smalls departed Port Royal harbor on 16 August aboard the *Massachusetts* and met with Stanton in Washington on the twentieth. It cannot be said with certainty that this visit was the catalyst for what followed, but it may have been.[38]

Stanton replied to Saxton on 25 August, the answer an enclosure to a letter from Halleck to Brig. Gen. John M. Brannan, the next senior department officer, who had just taken over from General Hunter. Apparently, Hunter's request for reassignment had had the desired result, although he was not permanently ordered elsewhere but was given a sixty-day leave, effective 22 August. Hunter was still at Hilton Head but was preparing to take his wife to Washington, where he hoped to find more rewarding work. He was not expected to return. Stanton gave Saxton more than he had asked for, allowing him "to arm, uniform, equip, and receive into the service of the United States such number of volunteers of African descent as you may deem expedient, not exceeding 5,000." His order also agreed to pay these men and to permit the detail of officers to command them. Stanton claimed that the permission was justified by the need to protect "the plantations and settlements occupied by the United States from invasion and protect the inhabitants from captivity and murder by the enemy." He continued, "You are therefore authorized by every means within your power to withdraw from the enemy their laboring force and population, and to spare no effort consistent with civilized warfare to weaken, harass, and annoy them." Finally, Halleck gave the department permission to retain its cavalry regiment to support these objectives. Thus, Hunter's goal regarding black troops was entirely satisfied, although they were intended to have a more limited mission than what he sought. Full soldier status for blacks was still five months off.[39]

David and Maria Hunter and some of his staff (Halpine had gone ahead and was in Washington by 21 August) left Hilton Head on 7 September aboard the steamer *McClellan,* bound for New York. Also aboard were General Saxton, the Reverend French, and Robert Smalls, the latter accompanied by his wife and young son. (French and Smalls were going to New York to raise money and support for the Port Royal experiment.) Admiral Du Pont saw to it that the navy gave Hunter an appropriate send-off, a fifteen-gun salute and men manning the yards of his flagship. That night Du Pont told his wife about the departure and said: "I *like* General Hunter. He is manly, frank, brave, cordial, and a Christian man to boot—makes it a point as a military man, that his Bible and prayer book shall be on his table in his sitting room." The local newspaper said:

> The salvoes of artillery which last evening awakened the echoes in Port Royal Harbor, as they burst from the grim sides of the *Wabash* and the grassy slopes of Fort Welles [on Hilton Head Island], were given in honor of General Hunter. . . . Gen. Hunter goes home on leave, but there is little probability of his returning. . . . It is likely . . . that Gen. Hunter will be called to an active command as soon as he reaches Washington. During his administration of this department his course on some questions, particularly that of forming a negro regiment, made him many enemies, but even those most bitterly opposed to his political views, respect him for his sincerity, courage and firmness of purpose.[40]

Hunter was to return to the Department of the South, but in August 1862 he had no particular prospects for future employment in another position of leadership in the army. There is no doubt that he had been ahead of the nation and the administration when it came to the issues of freedom and military service for blacks, but now his views were seen as less radical than before.

NOTES

1. Daniel Ammen, "Du Pont and the Port Royal Expedition," in *Battles and Leaders of the Civil War,* ed. Robert Underwood Johnson and Clarence Clough Buel, 4 vols. (1887; reprint, Secaucus, N.J.: Castle, 1989), 1:671–91.

2. Reports, Sherman to Adjutant General's Office, 8 (with proclamation) and 11 November 1861, U.S. War Department, *The War of the Rebellion: A Compilation of the Official Records of the Union and Confederate Armies* (Washington, D.C.: Government Printing Office, 1880–1902) (hereafter *ORA* and ser. 1, unless otherwise indicated), 6:3–6.

3. Letter, Acting Secretary of War Thomas A. Scott to Sherman, 14 October 1861, *ORA,* 6:176–77.

4. Letters, Sherman to Adj. Gen. Lorenzo Thomas, 14 and 15 December 1861, ibid., 6:201–2, 205.

5. Willie Lee Nichols Rose, *Rehearsal for Reconstruction: The Port Royal Experiment* (Indianapolis: Bobbs-Merrill Co., 1964), 11–20.

6. Letter, Sherman to adjutant general, 9 February 1862, with enclosure, General Order No. 9, Headquarters, Expeditionary Force, 6 February 1862, letters, Edwin M. Stanton to Sherman and to assistant quartermaster general, New York, 18 February 1862, *ORA,* 6:222–23.

7. Quincy A. Gillmore, "Siege and Capture of Fort Pulaski," in Johnson and Buel, *Battles and Leaders,* 2:2–6.

8. General Orders No. 26, Adjutant General's Office, 15 March 1862, *ORA,* 6:248; instructions, adjutant general to Hunter, 15 March, David Hunter file, General's Papers, box 26, Record Group 94, Records of the Adjutant General's Office, 1780–1917, National Archives (NA), Washington, D.C. The *New York Times,* 21 March 1862, welcomed Hunter's appointment and expressed satisfaction that he was not an abolitionist.

9. Letter, Hunter to Stanton, 27 March 1862, *ORA,* ser. 1, 6:254; letter, Hunter to Stanton, 28 March 1861, document no. 51026, Edwin M. Stanton Papers, Documents Division, Library of Congress (LOC).

10. General Orders no. 1, 31 March 1862, Department of the South, General Orders, Department of the South, RG 293, U.S. Army Continental Commands, 1821–1920, NA (hereafter RG 293, NA); letters, Sherman to Stanton and Hunter, 27 and 31 March 1862, Hunter to Stanton, 3 April 1862, *ORA,* 6:254–58, 263–64.

11. Letter, Du Pont to his wife, 31 March 1861, John D. Hayes, ed., *Samuel Francis Du Pont: A Selection from His Civil War Letters,* 3 vols. (Ithaca: Cornell University Press, 1969), 1:396; Gillmore, "Siege and Capture of Fort Pulaski," 2:7–10; reports, Hunter and Benham to adjutant general, 12 and 13 April 1862, *ORA,* 6:132–34, 137.

12. Special Orders No. 45, 18 April; General Orders No. 7, 13 April 1862, the last issued at Fort Pulaski, Headquarters, Department of the South, RG 293, NA.

13. Letter, Hunter to Stanton, 22 April 1862, *ORA,* ser. 1, 14:337; G. T. Beauregard, "The Defense of Charleston," in Johnson and Buel, *Battles and Leaders,* 4:3–4.

14. General Orders No. 11, 9 May 1862, Department of the South, RG 293, NA; letters, adjutant general to Sherman and Sherman to adjutant general, 12 February, 8 March 1862, *ORA,* 6:224, 240.

15. Charles Graham Halpine, *Baked Meats of the Funeral* (New York: Carleton, 1866), 174; letters, Benham to Pierce, 6 May, Hunter to Stevens, 8 May, order from Department of the South to Benham, 9 May, circular, 11 May, letter, Stevens to agents and Pierce, 11 May 1862, *ORA,* ser. 3, 2:29–30, 54–56.

16. Letters, Pierce to Hunter, G. M. Welles and L. D. Phillips (both Saint Helena Island agents) to Pierce, 13 May 1861, *ORA,* ser. 3, 2:57–60; Rupert Sargent Holland, ed., *Letters and Diary of Laura M. Towne Written from the Sea Islands of South Carolina* (1912; reprint, New York: Negro Universities Press, 1969), 41, 53.

17. Letters, Pierce to Chase, 12 May, and Chase to Stanton, 21 May 1862, *ORA,* ser. 3, 2:53, 50.

18. *New York Times,* 6 May 1862, 16; *Daily National Intelligencer* (Washington, D.C.), 16 May (quoting *New York Evening Post,* 15 May), 17 May editorial, 19 May 19 1862 (quoting *New York Commercial Advertiser,* 16 May; *Newark Daily Advertiser,* 16 May; *Newark Daily Mercury,* 16 May; *Philadelphia Inquirer,* 17 May; *New York World,* 16 May; and *Philadelphia North American,* 17 May).

19. Benjamin P. Thomas and Harold M. Hyman, *Stanton: The Life and Times of Lincoln's Secretary of War* (New York: Alfred A. Knopf, 1962), 236; letter, Chase to Maj. Gen. Benjamin Butler, 24 June 1862, *ORA,* ser. 3, 2:173–74; Chase letter, 21 May 1861, quoted in Frederick J. Blue, *Salmon P. Chase: A Life in Politics* (Kent, Ohio: Kent State University Press, 1987), 182–83; Lincoln's proclamation, 19 May 1962, Abraham Lincoln, *Speeches and Writings, 1859–1865: Speeches, Letters, and Miscellaneous Writings, Presidential Papers and Proclamations* (New York: Library of America, 1989), 318–19.

20. David Hunter, *Report of the Military Services of Gen. David Hunter during the War of the Rebellion Made to the War Department, 1873* (1873; reprint, New York:

Van Nostrand, 1892), 17; Hunter's 1873 MS report, U.S.Army General's Reports of Civil War Service, 1864–87, vol. 9, RG 94, NA (hereafter Hunter's 1873 MS report, NA), 659; letter, Du Pont to his wife, 30 May 1862, Hayes, *Du Pont,* 2:79– 80; letter, 22 May 1862, Stephen W. Sears, ed., *The Civil War Papers of George B. McClellan: Selected Correspondence, 1860–1865* (New York: Ticknor and Fields, 1889), 274; Robert C. Schenck, "Major-General David Hunter," *Magazine of American History* 27 (February 1887): 144; "Appeal to Border-States Representatives for Compensated Emancipation," 12 July 1862, Lincoln, *Speeches and Writings,* 341; document in Hunter's hand, n.d., probably June 1862, Hunter MSS, Huntington Library, San Marino, Calif.

21. Letters, Du Pont to his wife, 11 May and 3 June 1862, Hayes, *Du Pont,* 2:45, 98. Hunter had indeed ordered officers' wives home at the beginning of April, and Du Pont thought "he did it with a good deal of *tact"* (letter, Du Pont to his wife, 4 April 1862, ibid., 1:400).

22. Letter, Du Pont to his wife, 16 June 1862, ibid., 2:118; diary entry, 24 June 1862, Holland, *Towne Letters and Diary,* 71.

23. *Congressional Globe,* 37th Cong., 2d sess., 2587, 5 June, 2620–21, 9 June, 2762, 17 June 1862; letters, Stanton to speaker of the House of Representatives, 14 June, and Stanton to Hunter, 16 June 1862, *ORA,* ser. 3, 2:147–48, 152; Thomas and Hyman, *Stanton,* 234.

24. Halpine, *Baked Meats,* 175–76; Special Orders No. 73, 8 May 1862, Headquarters, Department of the South, RG 293, NA.

25. Halpine, *Baked Meats,* 181; letters, Stanton to Speaker, 2 July, and Hunter to Stanton, 23 June 1862, *ORA,* ser. 3, 2:196–98; *Congressional Globe,* 37th Cong., 2d sess., 2 and 8 July 1862, 3087, 3120–21.

26. Quoted in William Hanchett, *Irish: Charles G. Halpine in Civil War America* (Syracuse: Syracuse University Press, 1970), 52; *Congressional Globe,* 37th Cong., 2d sess., 3 and 8 July 1862, 3102, 3109, 3127–28; Hunter, *Report of the Military Services,* 26. Hunter's description of the House's reaction is not included in the actual report he made to the adjutant general in April 1873 but was added to the published *Report* (Hunter's 1873 MS report, NA, 643–98).

27. Edward A. Miller, Jr., *Gullah Statesman: Robert Smalls from Slavery to Congress, 1839–1915* (Columbia: University of South Carolina Press, 1994), 1–7; Benham's plan, 17 May 1862, *ORA,* 14:983–86; letter, Du Pont to his wife, 4 July 1862, Hayes, *Du Pont,* 2:149.

28. Letters, Hunter to Stanton, May 31, Stanton to Hunter, 9 June 1862, *ORA,* 14:347–48, 350.

29. Letter, Captain Alfred B. Ely, to Chase, 20 May 1862, document no. 7357, Salmon Chase Papers, Documents Division, LOC; letter, Stevens to his wife, 11

June 1862, Hazard Stevens, *The Life of Isaac Ingalls Stevens, by His Son,* vol. 2 (Boston: Houghton, Mifflin and Co., 1900), 393. Stevens may have been irritated with Hunter for sending Mrs. Stevens north, the first officer's wife ordered home (letter, Du Pont to his wife, 4 April 1862, Hayes, *Du Pont,* 1:400). The *New York Times,* 21 May 1862, reported that Hunter would not be recalled, but that Lincoln would send for him to have a face-to-face talk.

30. Letter, Lt. John P. Bankhead, gunboat *Pembina,* to Fox, 29 June 1862, quoting Lt. Percival Drayton, Gustavus Vasa Fox, *Confidential Correspondence of Gustavus V. Fox,* 2 vols. (New York: Naval History Society, 1920), 2:317–20; Hunter's report, 23 June 1862, letter, Stanton to Hunter, 19 June 1862, *ORA,* 14:42–104, 354–55. Benham was later returned to duty, the dispute attributed to a misunderstanding (*ORA,* 14:979).

31. Letter, Stanton to Hunter, 3 July 1862, ORA., 11, pt. 3, 290; Abstract return of troops, letter, Hunter to Stanton, both 31 July 1862, ibid., 14:366–67.

32. Letter, Wright to Stanton, 5 August, Hunter to Stanton, 11 July, telegram, Thomas to Hunter, 23 July 1862, ibid., 14:368–69, 362–63, 365; *Congressional Globe,* 37th Cong., 2d sess., 8 July 1862, 3127–28.

33. Letters, Hunter to Stanton, 4 and 10 August 1862, *ORA,* ser. 3, 2:346, 292; *Daily National Intelligencer,* 28 June 1862. Perhaps as a reward, Hunter sent Acting Colonel Fessenden to New York in charge of prisoners on the same day that he dissolved the regiment (Special Orders No. 258, Headquarters, Department of the South, 10 August 1862, RG 293, NA).

34. Diary entries, 21 and 22 July 1862, David Herbert Donald, ed., *Inside Lincoln's Cabinet: The Civil War Diaries of Salmon P. Chase* (Longmans, Green and Co., 1954), 96, 99–100; diary entry, 13 July 1862, Gideon Welles, *Diary of Gideon Welles,* ed. Howard K. Beale, 3 vols. (New York: W. W. Norton and Co., 1960), 1:70–71.

35. "Pay and rations now allowed by law to soldiers" were authorized, but blacks received $3.00 to $6.50 less monthly than whites (summary of legislation pertaining to black soldiers, Report of the Provost Marshal General to the Secretary of War, 17 March 1866, *ORA,* ser. 3, 5:654–56).

36. *Daily National Intelligencer,* 13, 16, and 18 August 1862; *Washington Evening Star,* 19 August 1861; letter, 13 August 1862, Holland, *Towne Diary and Letters,* 83; General Orders No. 27, 17 August 1862, Department of the South, RG 293, NA.

37. Letter, Hunter to Stanton, 14 August 1862, *ORA,* 14:374; letter, Hunter to Stanton, 15 August 1862, document no. 51826, Stanton Papers, LOC.

38. Hayes, *Du Pont,* 2:190; Benjamin P. Thomas and Harold M. Hyman, *Stanton: The Life and Times of Lincoln's Secretary of War* (New York: Alfred A. Knopf, 1962), 234; Saxton to Stanton, 16 August 1862, *ORA,* 14:374–75, document no. 51836,

Stanton Papers, LOC; Smalls's speech, 30 July 1886, *Congressional Record,* 49th Cong., 1st sess., app., 319–20.

39. Special Orders No. 202, Adjutant General's Office, 22 August 1862, letter, Halleck to Brannan, with enclosure Stanton to Saxton, both 26 August 1862, *ORA,* 14:376–78. Halpine suggested that Hunter had been relieved "on the motion of certain prominent speculators in marine transportation, with whose 'big things' in Port Royal harbor . . . the General had seen fit to interfere," but he gives no evidence (Halpine, *Baked Meats,* 192).

40. No longer authorized an adjutant, Hunter tried to get Halpine a good position, asking Stanton to appoint the major an "additional aide-de-camp" with rank of colonel to newly installed General-in-Chief Halleck—but to be assigned to Hunter. The adjutant general turned down the request because a new law did not allow such appointments (letter, Hunter to Stanton, 29 July, and endorsement, 8 August 1862, Miscellaneous Correspondence, Halpine Papers, Huntington Library); letter, Du Pont to his wife, 7 September 1862, Hayes, *Du Pont,* 2:216–17; "Departure of General Hunter," *New South* (Port Royal), 8 September 1862.

Chapter 5

COMMAND AND
CONTROVERSY

Hunter was officially on leave—in New York, Princeton, and Washington—until 23 September 1862, when he reported at Washington for duty. He was not returned to the Department of the South but, instead, was appointed senior officer of a temporary board to consider whatever matters might be brought before it, an assignment that cut his authorized sixty-day vacation to two weeks. The first investigation he was called to preside over concerned the conduct of Brig. Gen. Julius White, an inexperienced political general from Illinois, in the 15 September fall of Harper's Ferry to the Confederate army. Following his defeat by Lee at the second battle of Manassas during the last days of August, Maj. Gen. John Pope, commanding the Army of Virginia (soon to be combined with the Army of the Potomac), fell back to cover Washington. General McClellan superseded Pope, and he moved to head off Lee, who appeared to be poised for an invasion of Maryland and Pennsylvania. These maneuvers by the opposing armies immediately endangered the Union position at Harper's Ferry, which controlled the fords across the upper Potomac. White, falling back from Martinsburg, in the lower Shenandoah Valley with twenty-five hundred men, placed his forces under the Harper's Ferry commander Col. Dixon S. Miles. The post was soon surrounded by a superior force commanded by Maj. Gen. Thomas J. Jackson. Miles appointed White commissioner to negotiate surrender of the almost thirteen thousand–man federal garrison, a procedure that was carried out immediately. The rapid surrender, which, some alleged, allowed Lee's forces to be concentrated on the Antietam battlefield over the next few days, was severely criticized, leading to Hunter's investigation.[1]

The commission convened shortly after its appointment and took a month to announce its findings. They were that White "appears from the evidence to have acted with decided capability and courage" but that Miles—who was mortally wounded shortly after making White his commissioner—also deserved censure. Others received blame as well for what was seen as a major cause of the Antietam battle going badly, but no serious action was taken against any officer involved. In general, the inquiry appears to have been conducted in a leisurely fashion, leaving Hunter time to pursue future assignments.[2]

SUPPORTING BLACK FREEDOM

Hunter was still provisionally commanding the Department of the South, temporarily assigned to special duties in Washington. The *New York Times* reported that Hunter was likely to be returned at once to South Carolina now that his policy regarding the use of blacks in the army appeared to have been adopted by Lincoln. Hunter did not think the administration's approval of the black South Carolina troops was enough—or he believed it was too late to have maximum effect on the Confederacy. He told Secretary of the Treasury Chase, a supporter of Hunter's emancipation proclamation and black troops initiative, at dinner in mid-September that, had the orders not been revoked, "he would have had the whole coast lined with disciplined Southern men—black, to be sure, but good soldiers and true." Others believed that Hunter would not return to Hilton Head, but he himself planned to do so. He was looking for a well-qualified brigadier to take the place of Benham, although there were officers of that rank still in the department. In late September Brig. Gen. James Garfield, the future president, had discussions with Hunter and was offered a position at Port Royal, second in command for an assault on Charleston. Garfield said little more about the offer but did record that "General Hunter thinks the Government is bound to neglect that or any other place where negroes are to be treated as men." This comment showed that Hunter's enthusiasm over returning to South Carolina may have been somewhat diminished because he thought that Lincoln's policy toward blacks was not forward enough and created a limit on military options.[3]

On the matter of freedom for the slaves, the administration was abandoning the policy of appeasing border slave states in favor of one that included partial abolition as necessary to preserve the Union. At a special cabinet meeting on 22 September, Lincoln discussed the matter again with his advisors, this time reading a proclamation he considered timely in light of the dubious victory General McClellan had won at Antietam. Although he had been prepared earlier to free some slaves, he was dissuaded from doing so by the likelihood that it would be taken in Europe and elsewhere as a sign of weakness, a substitute for military defeat of the South. The preliminary emancipation proclamation—issued on 22 September 1862—in some respects did not go as far as did Hunter's, but, like the general's, would not have freed many blacks beyond some who were under Union control. Lincoln's proclamation, the final version of which was issued and effective on 1 January 1863, freed no slaves in loyal states and even excluded those in areas of Virginia and Louisiana occupied by Union troops. It was received with praise and condemnation and not a little cynicism, the *New York Times,* for one, editorializing that not much good would come of it but hoped no harm either. The paper linked Lincoln's action with Hunter's: "This proclamation with regard to the contingent emancipation of slaves in the insurgent States not being self-enforcing any more than the proclamation of Gen. Hunter in regard to the immediate emancipation of slaves in the States of South Carolina, Georgia, and Florida, the only difference between the two resides in the signatures respectively attached to them." Although Lincoln's proclamation proposed gradual and compensated emancipation, which abolitionists such as Hunter considered too cautious, the measure changed the nature of the war and is not now remembered as having such limits. The announced purpose of the proclamation, "military necessity," has been overwhelmed—perhaps as Lincoln intended all along—by its cumulative impact.[4]

Hunter had not left behind the controversy over his actions concerning black soldiers. That he had enlisted them in the service of the United States outraged Confederate leaders, to whom blacks should never be entrusted with guns. He personally was given by the rebels the credit and the blame for allowing such inferior beings to oppose Southern troops. Jefferson Davis wrote to General Lee about Hunter's black regiment, asking his general to inquire of the Union army about the matter. Davis outlined the danger: "The newspapers received from the enemy country announce as a fact that Major-General Hunter has armed slaves for the murder of their masters and has done all in his power to inaugurate a servile war which is worse than that of the savage, insomuch as it superadds other horrors to the indiscriminate slaughter of all ages, sexes and conditions." The following day Lee sent a letter with identical language to the "General Commanding U.S. Army" and, understandably, received no answer. The rebel reaction to this silence was issuance of a general order by the Confederate war department which said:

> Whereas, Major-General Hunter, recently in command of the enemy's forces on the coast of South Carolina, and Brigadier General [John Wolcott] Phelps a military commander of the enemy in the State of Louisiana, have organized and armed negro slaves for military service

against their masters, citizens of the Confederacy. And Whereas, the Government of the United States has refused to answer an enquiry whether said conduct of its officers meets its sanction, and has thus left this Government no other means of repressing said crimes and outrages than the adoption of such measures of retaliation as shall serve to prevent their repetition. *Ordered* that Major-General Hunter and Brigadier-General Phelps be no longer held and treated as public enemies of the Confederate States, but as outlaws; and in the event of the capture of either of them, or that of any other officer employed in drilling and organizing slaves, with a view to their armed service in this war, shall not be regarded as a prisoner of War, but held in close confinement for execution as a felon, at such time and place as the President shall order.[5]

Phelps's offense was that he had raised some black troops at Camp Parapet outside New Orleans. When this was disavowed by Washington, he resigned his commission, coincidentally on the day of the Confederate order. Therefore, nothing more was heard of Phelps's transgression, but Hunter continued to be the target of rebel venom. A Savannah newspaper linked the entire matter to the perversity of President Lincoln: "The cold-blooded abolition miscreant who, from his headquarters at Hilton Head, is engaged in executing the bloody and savage bequests of the imperial gorilla who, from his throne of human bones at Washington, rules, reigns, and riots over the destinies of the brutish and degraded North." Hunter was outraged by the transfer of such denunciations into legal actions by the Confederate government. His adjutant (then working temporarily for General Halleck in Washington), Major Halpine, suggested that he take the question up with Secretary of War Stanton, calling on him to demand revocation of the order—or to announce that Hunter's former South Carolina policy was adopted by the Union army. These options were not then implemented, and the government never challenged Davis's remarkable initiative. In fact, in a few months, Davis called on his congress for further action against those who would arm black men.[6]

Hunter, however, who may have heard of the Confederate general order before he left Hilton Head in early September, wrote a long letter from Washington later that month to his old comrade Jefferson Davis. Halpine says that the letter was "subsequently suppressed and never sent, owing to influences which the writer of this article does not feel himself as yet at liberty to reveal—further than to say that Mr. Stanton knew nothing of the matter." In his letter addressed to Davis as "Titular President of the so-called Confederate States," Hunter said that the campaigns and "social relations" between the two men dating from prewar army service allowed them "to understand each other thoroughly." For this reason Hunter believed that Davis was capable of carrying out the threat, and the president of the "pretended government" of the Confederacy could be assured that Hunter would accept martyrdom for the principles he believed in. Hunter then offered his own threat. If Davis failed to repeal the order in a month, Hunter would "reciprocate it by hanging every rebel officer who is now, or may hereafter be taken, prisoner by troops of the command to which I am about to return." It was likely this statement that caused Hunter's letter to be suppressed (probably by President Lincoln).

The rest of the communication outlines in detail how Hunter viewed the war and those disloyal to the Union. He said that treason was "the sum of all felonies and crimes, . . . The most wicked, enormous, and deliberately-planned conspiracy against human liberty and for the triumph of treason and slavery." On the other hand, Hunter wrote, some in the North thought the rebels but mis-guided patriots. He was aware that his view was not "the language in which the prevailing etiquette of the army is in the habit of addressing" Davis's conspiracy. He took the opposite position that the South's objectives were "the plunder of the black race . . . and further degradation of ninety per cent of the white popu-lation of the South in favor of its ten percent aristocracy." If this be true, as Hunter believed, the federal government should have "hung every man taken in arms against the United States" from the very beginning of hostilities.

Reviewing his experiences "during a lifetime of active service," Hunter had seen "the seeds of this conspiracy planted in the rank soil of slavery." As he saw it, "Had we at an earlier time commenced to call things by their right names, and to look at the hideous features of slavery with our common eyesight and common sense, instead of the rose-colored glasses of supposed political expediency, there would be three hundred thousand more men alive to-day on American soil." Hunter concluded by observing that "the South has already tried one hanging experiment, but not with a success—one would think—to encourage its repeti-tion." He was referring to John Brown—"who was well known to me in Kansas [where Brown murdered five citizens in 1856]"—and his hanging after the Harpers Ferry incident in 1859. To Hunter Brown was a hero, and he thought that a million Union soldiers shared this view. Therefore, "to ascend the scaffold made sacred by the blood of this martyr" would be an honor, and Hunter would wel-come the opportunity to die with his officers at Davis's order—a sure way to hasten the end of the conflict. Finally, he said, he was pleased with Davis's action because he would now "be able to treat rebellion as it deserves, and give to the felony of treason a felon's death."[7]

During October, while Hunter was primarily occupied with the Julius White inquiry, he dined several times at the home of treasury secretary Chase. He was there on 10 October with General McDowell, Major Halpine, General Garfield (who was Chase's houseguest), and others. The following night Hunter and Halpine again joined Garfield at Chase's home. Chase asked Hunter, whom he greatly admired, for his opinion of President Lincoln and recorded Hunter's answer: "A man irresolute but of honest intentions—born a poor white in a Slave State, and, of course, among aristocrats—kind in spirit and not envious, but anxious for approval, especially of those to whom he has been accustomed to look up—hence solicitous of support of the Slaveholders in the Border States, and unwilling to offend them—without the large mind necessary to grasp great questions—uncertain of himself, and in many things ready to lean too much on others."[8]

Hunter also gave his opinion of Stanton: "Know little of him. Have seen him but once [before leaving for South Carolina], and was then so treated that I never desire to see him again. Think from facts that have come to my knowledge that he is not sincere. He wears two faces; but has energy and ability, though not steady power." Hunter told Chase that he wanted "to retire from the army, and have some position in New-York which will enable him to resume his special vocation as a writer for the Press. He says he has written some leaders for the '*Republican,*' and has *aided* the Proprietor of '*Wilkes' Spirit of the Times.*'" No such contributions to journalism have been found to support Hunter's claim, and he published nothing under his name for the rest of his life. His talk at the dinner may have been just idle embellishment expressing ambition, not accomplishment.[9]

The Hunters had taken only temporary lodgings in Washington, and Maria was reportedly seeking better accommodations. She spoke, for example, to the socially prominent Elizabeth Blair Lee about putting furniture in a house Mrs. Lee was offering for rent but was unsuccessful. Mrs. Steuart was not with the Hunters, because her husband had been badly wounded at the battle of Cross Keys in May 1862. A brigadier general in Jackson's army in the Shenandoah Valley, Steuart had broken a shoulder bone, which refused to knit. After three months commanding at Winchester, Steuart took a ninety-day leave to Savannah to recuperate. The lady appears to have gone south to join her husband in Georgia; the frontier between Confederate and Union was porous, and travel of noncombatants and traders was common. General Garfield wrote on 12 October 1862 that Mrs. Steuart (he spells the name Stuart) "got a letter through to General Hunter [he says from Atlanta] a few days ago complaining of her being shut off from all her Union friends." The separation from the Hunter household was not permanent, however, because Mrs. Steuart later returned, possibly with the help of Maj. Gen. John A. Dix, who was commanding the Department of Virginia at Fort Monroe, sometime after her husband had healed, about a year after the injury. Indirect evidence suggests that Dix provided the needed pass for Mrs. Steuart to leave the North and/or to return, Hunter writing of his fellow officer, "I shall not forget his kindness on behalf" of the lady.[10]

In early November, without duties now that the White investigation was completed, Hunter talked further with the likewise unemployed Garfield about the two going together to the Department of the South. Garfield wrote to his wife that he was planning to be Hunter's second in command and that the two officers had "laid plans for making a speedy and thunderous attack on Charleston and Sumter." Yet the proposed operation was delayed by information from Port Royal that "the yellow fever was raging and that no more troops should be sent till the black frosts set in." Indeed, there was a serious epidemic of the disease in South Carolina; it even killed the department commander, who had taken Hunter's place in early September.[11]

Maj. Gen. Ormsby M. Mitchel arrived at Hilton Head on 15 September 1862. A 1829 West Point graduate who had left the service after one year, he had almost no military experience when he was commissioned a brigadier general of volunteers in 1861. Earlier he had been an engineer and world-renowned astronomer. His first campaigns were under Buell, but he had been relieved at his own request under somewhat of a cloud in July. It cannot be determined if Mitchel—who seems to have been as quarrelsome as Hunter—was meant to be assigned permanently to Hilton Head. Probably, his posting was intended to be temporary if Hunter returned and permanent if Hunter found the more active employment he once sought. Mitchel just happened to be available when Hunter left South Carolina, and the army staff probably thought it best to have a major general on the scene where the navy commander was a rear admiral. Additionally, Du Pont was planning an assault on Charleston, and a senior general had to be there to coordinate army efforts.[12]

Mitchel, whose command was elevated to an army corps (the Tenth), began at once to plan operations and to establish a working relationship with Du Pont. He must have appeared to have been no change over Hunter because his first letters to General Halleck and Secretary Stanton were as much as anything else requests for reinforcements. He asked both men to send him the division he had commanded under Buell because, he was convinced, those men were devoted to him. He said, "While a soldier may enlist through motives of patriotism he fights for his general." His opinion of Saxton's black soldiers was not favorable: "I find a feeling prevailing among the officers and soldiers of prejudice against the blacks, founded on an opinion that in some ways the negroes have been more favored by the Government and more privileges granted to them than to the volunteer soldier." To correct this, he sought to place General Saxton and all his officers under his direct control. Mitchel's promises to thus disturb the structure Hunter and Saxton had pioneered came to nothing because the new general died on 30 October. General Brannon took over once again.[13]

Temporary work was soon found for Garfield and Hunter; they were detailed to join other officers in a politically prominent general court-martial proceeding. Garfield saw this as a temporary delay to the pair's assignment to South Carolina, at least until the "fever may be fully abated." They were appointed in late November as members of the trial of Maj. Gen. Fitz John Porter, accused by General Pope of disobedience at the second battle of Bull Run. Being the senior officer, Hunter was president of the court, which met for the first time on 27 November. A reporter remarked that the trial added color to Washington in the winter of 1862–63, the armies in Virginia settling down in winter quarters after the slaughter at Fredericksburg.[14]

Porter's conduct had been investigated without result by two other panels in November—perhaps by Hunter's military commission. The court-martial was a new proceeding, and it heard testimony from a large number of officers. In a verdict announced on 10 January the panel found Porter guilty of disobedience of orders, and he was sentenced to "be cashiered and forever disqualified from holding any office of trust or profit under the Government of the United States." The record of the trial tells nothing about Hunter's participation apart from his presiding role. As usual in such military proceedings, the court sat as a jury and decided little except the verdict. One of Porter's defense attorneys was Reverdy Johnson, one of the nation's most prominent lawyers, a former attorney general, and a U.S. senator-elect from Maryland. It is said that Hunter developed a dislike for Johnson at this trial, and this would have a bearing on a much more important proceeding that Hunter would head a few years later. Perhaps Johnson was too vigorous in his defense, and Hunter found it unseemly and wasting time.[15]

Garfield vividly described Hunter's appearance and manner at court: "He is a man of about sixty years of age, wears no other wiskers [sic] than a moustache, which together with his somewhat thin hair is dyed black. He has keen gray eyes, a long nose, slightly aquiline, a large mouth with corners slightly depressed and the whole shut with a sharp decisiveness. He has a habit of swaying his head from side to side when he speaks and seems to sling his quick decisive words right and left." This is a portrait of a no-nonsense (and somewhat vain) officer who could be expected to encourage rapid proceedings and have little tolerance for delay.[16]

Porter had friends in the army, one of them General McClellan, who wrote to him in mid-December 1862, discussing the officers then sitting in judgment. He said: "Hunter I distrust. I never saw him—but he is an enemy of mine"—

probably because of the slavery issue. Garfield described what may have been a further reason for antagonism between the two generals. He said that Hunter told him, based on a letter he had received from behind rebel lines from his ward, Mrs. Steuart, that McClellan "made overtures to [Jefferson] Davis for a command before he was appointed to a position in the Union army." To Hunter such a sign of disloyalty was, of course, unacceptable. No matter how he felt about McClellan, however, Hunter, was a good friend of Porter and met with the accused general at Willard's Hotel in Washington before the trial duty assignment. Another officer wrote that Hunter and the other court-martial officers were not likely to be influenced by politics in the Pope-Porter matter, but he also considered Hunter intellectually incapable of fairly comprehending evidence.[17]

Eventually, Porter's cashiering was set aside on grounds that the court-martial did not understand that Porter's disobedience was "only the simple necessary action which an intelligent soldier had no choice but to take." Porter was restored to the army in his permanent grade of colonel in 1886, but he never received back pay. Hunter was not criticized for his participation in the Porter affair, did nothing to assist Porter's long bitter campaign for reconsideration of the trial, and he was not living when the verdict was reversed.[18]

RETURN TO SOUTH CAROLINA

The end of the Porter trial left Hunter open for a new assignment. He had been considered for one that he would have enthusiastically welcomed. General McClellan was relieved by President Lincoln in November and Maj. Gen. Ambrose Burnside appointed in his place as commander of the Army of the Potomac. President Lincoln's same order assigned Hunter to replace Burnside leading the Ninth Army Corps. For reasons not explained, this assignment fell through, and Hunter was ordered back to Hilton Head—but without Garfield, who was later sent to be Maj. Gen. William S. Rosecrans's chief of staff in the Army of the Cumberland. Sometime in late December or early January, Hunter was summoned by General Halleck to receive instructions about affairs in the Department of the South. Also called to the meeting was Maj. Gen. John Gray Foster, a West Point–educated army officer who had been the chief engineer for fortifications in Charleston harbor before the war. Admiral Du Pont had been in Washington earlier seeking, among other things, an army commitment to provide about twenty-five thousand soldiers for an attack on James Island simultaneous with entry of his fleet into Charleston harbor. He was told that such an army force was unavailable, so he returned to Port Royal to perfect an almost totally navy operation.[19]

As it developed, General Foster, appointed commander of the new Eighteenth Army Corps consisting of forces in North Carolina, had under his direction a large detachment of troops from Virginia prepared to board ships at Yorktown and ready for use. The purpose for which it was formed—an attack on the important Confederate port of Wilmington—was delayed, so the force was now available to be used at Charleston. The army's effort, however, was not part of a full-scale, army-navy coordinated operation; each service by now was proceeding without depending on the other, except for incidental support. Halleck's briefing was given in the presence of President Lincoln and Secretary Stanton, the second time Hunter and Stanton had met. No record exists of the specifics of the briefing or what if anything Lincoln and Stanton might have added, but it is clear that the line of command for the army expeditionary force was not firmly fixed. That omission would almost immediately cause a problem in the Department of the South.

On 14 January, only four days after completing the Porter trial, Hunter left New York aboard the chartered government steamer *Arago* for the sixty-hour run to Port Royal. The passage was particularly stormy, and, even though the *Arago* had been designed for runs to Europe, it was not stable enough to keep all aboard from becoming sick on the passage. A *New York Daily Tribune* reporter aboard the ship described his view of the general: "He was over seventy years old [he was sixty], but tried to assume a younger appearance by wearing a full, dark-brown wig and giving his short moustache the same artificial color. He was a man of modest ability, but an ardent patriot, a true gentleman, and very pleasing in his intercourse with others."[20]

Hunter reported his arrival to General-in-Chief Halleck on 20 January, "after a very boisterous and stormy passage." As one of his first acts, he sent Brigadier General Brannan, who had commanded since Mitchel's death, to Washington for reassignment. Hunter reported 14,395 men in the Department of the South, the principal concentrations at Saint Helena Island, Hilton Head, and Port Royal Island (Beaufort). He also reported a buildup of naval vessels, particularly monitors, for the planned attack on Charleston and said that the health of the troops was good now that the yellow fever epidemic had subsided. As he had from the beginning of his last duty in South Carolina—notwithstanding Foster's troops on the way—he requested reinforcements. In particular, Hunter wanted the Sixth United States Cavalry, the regular army regiment of which he was the colonel, sent to him. The same day he published a general order to the officers and men of the department, intended, no doubt, to boost their spirits by praising their rather limited past accomplishments and promising new, significant action. Hunter tempered the praise and the promise, however, by directing his officers "instantly to put to death any officer or enlisted man who shall be found deserting his brave comrades who are doing their duty in front." He wanted records to be kept of the "name of the traitor slain" and, ex post facto, the justification for the execution.[21]

Because the department was now also the Tenth Army Corps, all of Hunter's staff was elevated one rank. Halpine, who accompanied the general from New York, was promoted to lieutenant colonel and remained assistant adjutant general. Among the aides were Col. James D. Fessenden, the senator's son; Capts. (and nephews) Samuel W. Stockton and Arthur M. Kinzie; and Lt. Charles E. Hay, the president's secretary's brother. The chief of staff was Brig. Gen. Truman Seymour, who was also chief of artillery and was commanding Port Royal Island from Beaufort. General Saxton was temporarily absent; he may have been seeing to the raising of the black regiments that Stanton had authorized in August. This effort was given a boost by the president's 1 January final emancipation proclamation, which provided that blacks "will be received into the armed service of the United States to garrison forts, positions, stations, and other places, and to man vessels of all sorts in said service." This was not full equality with white soldiers and sailors because black men continued to receive less pay (and no bounties), and the language did not appear to promise frontline combat service.[22]

When Admiral Du Pont ran into Hunter on shore two days after the general's arrival, he wrote that he hoped "he had come to do something else this time than to fool about Negro regiments." As will be seen, he accomplished very little but did not neglect the First South Carolina Regiment of Infantry (African Descent)—its first official name—then forming for the second time. In fact, Hunter visited the regiment's camp the day after he arrived at Hilton Head, and he promised the soldiers arms, blue trousers, and equipment.[23]

Hunter once again issued an order on his arrival at Hilton Head similar to one on his first assignment to the department in 1862. A newspaper correspondent described it and its result with humor:

> The most intense fluttering and excitement has been caused among this portion of our population by the fact Gen. HUNTER brought down an order from the Secretary of War that no more ladies be permitted to come to the Department, and that those here be sent North as rapidly as possible, that their presence may not interfere with active operations. On the announcement of this news such a buzzing and rustling was heard, and so many traps, devices and stratagems were immediately put in requisition to capture the Major-General and soothe his heart to the point of making him withhold the promulgation of the order.

Hunter's wife, Maria, had been left behind in Washington, so she was unaffected by the order that resulted in "no contraband crinoline . . . hereafter to be permitted to enter the harbor."[24]

NEW SENTENCE OF DEATH

The matter of black soldiers and what the Confederacy should do about them was not ended with the 21 August 1862 general order condemning Hunter and all white officers found with black troops. A new order at the end of December announced a Davis proclamation that was inspired by actions to arm blacks undertaken by Maj. Gen. Benjamin Butler in New Orleans. It said that all of Butler's officers—even those unassociated with black troops—were "not entitled to be considered as soldiers engaged in honorable warfare but as robbers and criminals deserving death, and that each of them be whenever captured reserved for execution." But Davis went beyond Butler's men, calling for "like orders to be executed in all cases with respect to commissioned officers of the United States when found serving in company with armed slaves." As for the slaves themselves, if "captured in arms," they were to be turned over to the states from which they came "to be dealt with according to the laws of such States," which meant certain re-enslavement and often death.[25]

Hunter did not react to this December elaboration on his own condemnation by Davis, but in April 1863 he sent Secretary Stanton another letter, not as long as his September draft, intended for Davis. The new one was possibly inspired by an early April Confederate policy, and its implementation, "that negroes captured will not be treated as prisoners of war." Halpine probably had much to do with its writing. Hunter's second letter was in some ways as severe as had been the first, although without mention of treason. He threatened to execute "every rebel officer and every rebel slaveholder in my possession" unless the August order were revoked. He also protested reported executions of captured blacks— not necessarily soldiers—by Confederate forces in the West and of the selling of others into slavery. For these crimes Hunter proposed execution of the highest-ranking rebels in custody, one for each killing or sale into bondage. He accused Davis of fighting for the "liberty to keep 4,000,000 of your fellow-beings in ignorance and degradation; liberty to separate parents and children, husband and wife, brother and sister; liberty to steal the products of their labor . . . ; liberty to seduce their wives and daughters, and to sell your own children into bondage; liberty to kill these children with impunity." Hunter compared Davis's liberty to that of Satan, the "liberty to do wrong." No doubt intending irony, he ended the letter, "I have the honor to be, very respectfully, your most obedient servant." This letter was likely also suppressed and never reached Davis. It was, however, published in the Northern press, was retained in Stanton's files, and was printed with War Department records after the war.[26]

Although the letter was Hunter's last comment on the question of rebel treatment of blacks and officers in command of them, the Confederate government did not rescind the orders and, on 1 May 1863, reinforced it with a joint congressional resolution saying, "every white person being a commissioned officer . . . who during the present war shall command negroes or mulattoes in arms against the Confederate States or who shall arm, train, organize or prepare negroes and mulattoes . . . shall if captured be put to death or be otherwise punished at the discretion of the court." The resolution went beyond Davis's order and provided that all blacks would be turned over to the states, whether they were former slaves or freemen. Rebel commanders did occasionally order or condone the murder of Union soldiers, but just the threat itself was an important deterrent to the enlistment of black troops and their officers and to the willingness of white soldiers to fight alongside blacks. Because Hunter consistently considered his command short of troops, his black regiments had special importance for offensive operations.[27]

The first offensive initiative of concern to Hunter was the long-planned, quasi–joint army and navy operation against Charleston. Foster's ten thousand troops to augment his forces arrived in the first days of February 1863. The navy was unable to begin the assault for several weeks, however, because all the new ironclad monitors intended to be the spearhead of the operation arrived late. Hunter was pleased that this time the army was ready before the navy, "the complaint having been too frequently heretofore that in joint operations the Navy has been retarded by having to wait for the land forces." Generals Hunter and Foster made a three-day trip to Fort Pulaski, returning to Hilton Head on 9 February. Foster decided not to wait for developments in South Carolina, and he departed the next morning to make a reconnaissance of the approaches to Charleston. His instructions to his subordinate, Brig. Gen. Henry M. Naglee, were to take command of "the detachment of the Eighteenth Army Corps in the department [of the South]." He wanted the troops disembarked on Saint Helena Island and his transports to be cleaned and provisioned for later use. His instruction included this important sentence: "As the detachment is only intended to cooperate with the troops in this department the command will be considered distinct." The meaning of this was that Foster did not recognize Hunter's authority over the new forces, which was to cause much difficulty.[28]

THE FOSTER-NAGLEE AFFAIR

On the day following Foster's departure on his inspection, after which he intended to go on to Washington, Hunter announced that he was taking command of the troops from North Carolina, which, he said, were now part of the Tenth Army Corps. The order made Naglee commander of Saint Helena Island, where Foster's troops had been disembarked, and requested reports (called returns) from Naglee as first division commander and from Brig. Gen. Orris S. Ferry, who headed Foster's second division. Naglee immediately protested on grounds that Foster's detachment had come to South Carolina for a limited purpose, the attack on Charleston. He said that Foster intended to return his troops to North Carolina when the task was done, "if not before," and that Foster's absence was only temporary because of the navy's delay. Furthermore, Foster had assured him "that he was sent by the Secretary of War and General Halleck to command the troops brought by him, and that the same assurance has been repeated by him since his conferences with General Hunter, and that during his stay I have been informed that no communication has been made by him to show the intention of General Hunter to assume command."[29]

Although Hunter was displeased with Naglee's position, he blamed the entire affair on Foster. He sent his order assuming command of the Eighteenth Corps troops to John Hay in the White House, telling the president's secretary that he thought Naglee's protest symbolic and not his own. Writing the same day to Halleck, he said he regretted "exceedingly that General Foster should have so far lost sense of his duty." Since he judged Foster's conduct—of which he had no direct evidence other than the order to Naglee—"disrespectful, insubordinate, and tending to excite mutiny among the troops ordered to re-inforce this department, in this matter I shall deem it my duty, should General Foster return here, immediately to arrest him." In a second letter the same day Hunter said, "It never entered my mind that he [Foster] could put upon his position (which I regarded as a guest) in my department, the interpretation now manifest in his orders to General Naglee." Furthermore, Hunter told Halleck that he outranked Foster, so he did not understand how anyone could doubt his authority.[30]

Just arrived in Washington, Foster received Naglee's letter protests to Hunter, and on 15 February he went to see Halleck, who had not yet heard from Hunter. Halleck sent copies of the Naglee correspondence to Lincoln and Stanton and was instructed what to tell Hunter. He wrote the same day to straighten out the "misunderstanding in this matter on both sides." He directed that the detachment was not to be part of the Tenth Army Corps and that it and the transport vessels were to remain part of the Eighteenth "so that the corps can at any time be returned entire (except casualties) to its proper department." Receiving Hunter's 11 November letters, Halleck wrote again on the sixteenth. He said that he, the secretary of war, and the president saw nothing in Hunter's submission to change the orders, and he emphasized that the Eighteenth Army Corps was subject to Hunter's orders while in the Department of the South and that General Foster agreed with this. Halleck told Hunter that the threatened arrest of Foster was disapproved and so was Naglee's protest. Hunter, however, was given a lecture: "It is to be regretted, general, that on the eve of important movements, when the most cordial co-operation of all the officers of the Government is imperatively required, anything should be permitted to occur which is calculated to disturb the harmony of the service. If the plans of the Government should fail to be carried out for want of this harmony, those who have engendered or fostered animosities and jealousies will incur a very serious responsibility."[31]

Foster started back south on 16 February by rail to Baltimore, intending to go by sea to Fort Monroe and on to South Carolina. Halleck sent Col. Edward D. Townsend, Adjutant General Thomas's principal assistant, with a letter for Foster and instructions from Stanton for the colonel to report from Hilton Head on the situation. Townsend caught up with Foster at Baltimore late that same evening. Foster was surprised that Halleck ordered the relief of Naglee, and he was concerned that Hunter "will probably regard this as a triumph over the respectful action of General Naglee, and this will, I fear, lead to interferences and mortifications inflicted on me when I return." Therefore, he said, he did not wish to go back to South Carolina and recommended that General Burnside—just relieved as the Army of the Potomac's next unsuccessful commander—be ordered to replace him as head of the detachment for the Charleston attack. Townsend reported that Foster was also worried that he would lose his North Carolina command as well, and Stanton telegraphed him at Fort Monroe that this was indeed the plan. Burnside was scheduled to replace him soon, and advanced notice of that might have been the reason Foster suggested that Burnside go to Hunter's command. That evening Foster telegraphed Halleck, "I think it will be best for me not to return to South Carolina." Halleck answered that Foster could do as he chose and that Hunter would be given the option of keeping Naglee or letting him go, as he might decide.[32]

Hunter did not immediately respond to Halleck's 15 and 16 February letters, and his conversations with Townsend went unrecorded. Yet he was not through exercising his authority. Because he thought that some of the officers on Foster's Eighteenth Army Corps staff, which accompanied the detachment, were making statements "tending to create disaffection, insubordination, and mutiny," he ordered the entire staff to "quit this department by the first steamer going North." He told Halleck that he was convinced that Naglee (whom he had decided to keep) and Ferry had taken no part in the objectionable activities. On 23 February Hunter finally got around to revoking that part of his earlier order putting the detachment in the Tenth Corps, and he wrote Halleck the next day about the general-in-chief's earlier letters. He justified all his actions, disclaimed any intent to alter the president's instructions, excluded himself from "those who have fostered animosities and jealousies," and reminded Halleck that he had once sent Halleck troops that he could not spare from Kansas for the Fort Donelson campaign.[33]

One would think that the problems were now solved, but Naglee was not appeased and did not believe, contrary to what Halpine told him, that Hunter "fully appreciated your many fine qualities as a brave, experienced, and efficient officer." Naglee objected immediately to an order splitting the detachment into two divisions, one to be headed by Naglee and the other by Ferry. The same day each general received separate orders from Chief of Staff Seymour. Ferry's command—which Hunter thought was in poor condition—was to be kept aboard ship as a reserve during the Charleston attack, "this pending some preliminary labor that will be probably accomplished by other troops." Naglee's troops were told that they would be landed on Sullivan's Island, north of Charleston harbor, and would be expected to take Fort Moultrie from the rear with some naval assistance. Ignoring the operational plans, Naglee wrote to Halpine, protesting that he had been deprived of his proper command and given charge of just half of it. Additionally, the loss of the staff made it impossible for him to manage the command. Naglee also wrote to Foster, his former commander, complaining that General Seymour was not keeping him informed: "I have no knowledge of the plan of attack." He also sent regards to "the disaffected," as he termed the staff sent away from South Carolina, and accused Hunter of not obeying the orders from Washington. Finally, he asked Foster to write to him in care of Admiral Du Pont, so that evidence of their plotting would not fall into Hunter's hands.[34]

It was not too long before Hunter was fed up with what he termed Naglee's "insubordinate protest[s]." On 5 March—the same day he heard that everything was ready to attack Charleston—he ordered the general's relief and sent him to New York, General Ferry taking over command of the two divisions on Saint Helena Island. Just two days earlier Hunter had offered a solution to the Naglee problem; he asked Halleck again to end the Eighteenth Army Corps identification for the troops and place all of them under his Tenth Corps structure. Halleck was very likely annoyed by Hunter's insistence, and he wrote Hunter a short, sharp note declining to change earlier instructions but approving Naglee's relief. As it developed, however, Foster's former troops came under Hunter's total control, were broken up, and most of them never returned to North Carolina.[35]

Naglee arrived in New York on the fifteenth, and he wrote to Foster expressing his frustration. He said, "I consider the conduct of Hunter in everything pertaining to your department as outrageously indecent, uncivil, illegal, and despotic in the extreme." He was also hoping that Foster would call on his "special friends" to help, but the matter was ended. No one won the unseemly squabble unworthy of three West Point professional officers; the reputations of none of them were enhanced.[36]

FIRST SOUTH CAROLINA REGIMENT

General Saxton's First South Carolina Regiment was slow getting started and was not organized until 31 January 1863. A detachment was sent off late that month on a limited operation, even though the troops were not officially mustered into the service of the United States. The expedition was a minor one to the St. Mary's River on the Georgia-Florida border, and the men performed satisfactorily. On this or a later expedition—it is not clear which—some of their officers, however, lost their way and were captured. According to Halpine, the officers "indiscreetly rode beyond our lines . . . in pursuit of game—but whether feathered or female this deponent sayeth not." Hunter said that one of them was taken to Charleston (Halpine thought it was to a Florida state prison) and "thrown into a common jail." Hunter said that he received a letter from the officer, saying that "he was to be sent back to Florida to be tried by the civil courts on a charge of exciting an insurrection of the negroes. I immediately notified the Confederate authorities that I would at once seize and place in confinement all citizens of any influence within my lines, and would immediately execute three of their number for every one of my officers injured." Hunter soon received another letter from the officer, who said he remained in Charleston, was being treated well, and was on the list to be exchanged.[37]

Hunter did not think that his black forces—which he did not include in his monthly returns of troops—could "consistently with the interests of the service (in the present state of feeling) be advantageously employed to act in concert with our other forces." In February he felt that they might be well employed on garrison duty at Key West and the Dry Tortugas forts. He said that blacks might be suitable because they were then commonly thought to be immune from the tropical diseases, such as yellow fever, which were not then understood and which took many men's lives. This employment of the First Regiment and the forming Second did not occur, possibly because the posts in southern Florida were soon thereafter transferred to the Department of the Gulf. Other work would soon be sought for them, and Hunter may also have been floating suggestions. One of them, reported in the press, was the use of five thousand black troops "to penetrate one of the most thickly-populated districts of the South with a view to rouse the slaves. . . . Although the scheme itself seems feasible, the story is generally discredited in the North."[38]

There was discontent in the ranks of white regiments about serving with black troops, but the problem went beyond the prejudices of enlisted soldiers. On 16 February, for example, Hunter took serious action against Brig. Gen. Thomas Greely Stevenson, a brigade commander in the detachment from the Eighteenth Army Corps and a volunteer officer from Boston. An order announced, "having stated publicly in the custom-house of Port Royal, Hilton Head Island, that he would rather be beaten than co-operate with a certain class of troops authorized by the Government, he is hereby placed in arrest, and ordered to report immediately in arrest, to the post commander, Hilton Head, where he will remain until the pleasure of the president on his case can be made known." Stevenson was soon restored to duty and to his brigade, but Hunter was convinced that the problem was the same in regard to the other generals from North Carolina. He complained about the "pro-slavery generals in whom I have not the least confidence," meaning Foster and Naglee, inferring that their views on blacks were the cause of their hostility toward him and claiming that actions of Washington encouraging these pro-slavery generals could cause failure of the attack on Charleston.[39]

Hunter did not stop with complaints about the attitudes of officers and men in his command but took other action to improve acceptance of his black regiments. Black troops also promised to help him make up manpower shortages, and voluntary enlistments were going slowly. Therefore, three days after the national conscription act was approved in Washington, he ordered the draft of all "able-bodied male negroes between the ages of eighteen to fifty" in the department but gave a third reason for his action in the order:

The major-general commanding believes that the discipline of military life will be the safest and quickest school in which these enfranchised bondsmen can be elevated to the level of our higher intelligence and cultivation, and that their enrollment in regular military organization, and the giving them in this matter a legitimate vent to their natural desire to prove themselves worthy of freedom, cannot fail to have the further good effect of rendering less likely mere servile insurrection, unrestrained by the comities and usages of civilized warfare.

He was repeating the prejudiced view of the Confederates—and probably most Northerners—that blacks had a naturally barbaric nature and needed control that Hunter thought army discipline could provide. He was not aware of his bias and believed that he was being progressive on the issue of race.[40]

It was early March before a better test of the black soldiers could be made. Saxton told Stanton that the First South Carolina and part of the Second were being sent to Jacksonville, Florida. Hunter asked Du Pont to alert his blockade commander off the Florida coast that Col. Thomas W. Higginson, commanding the "First South Carolina Brigade" was about to lead "an important mission." The expedition went well enough, and the soldiers behaved satisfactorily under fire, but the mission was minor. The units returned to South Carolina on the last day of the month, but Higginson thought it too soon. He said that the recall "was commonly attributed to proslavery advisors, acting on the rather impulsive nature of Major-General Hunter, with a view to cut short the career of colored troops." Much was made, nonetheless, of the satisfactory performance of the troops, and Lincoln, fully recognizing the importance of blacks in uniform who were fighting for their own freedom, wrote to Hunter:

> I am glad to see the accounts of your colored force at Jacksonville, Fla. I see the enemy are driving at them fiercely, as is to be expected. It is important to the enemy that such a force shall *not* take shape and grow and thrive in the South, and in precisely the same proportion it is important to us that it *shall*. Hence the utmost caution and vigilance is necessary on our part. The enemy will make extra efforts to destroy them, and we should do the same to preserve and increase them.[41]

ASSAULT ON CHARLESTON

While the blacks were being recruited, trained, and tested, planning for the Charleston naval attack was proceeding fitfully. Hunter reported that he was ready with about twelve thousand men available for a ground campaign against the city's defenses. He thought this number too few, believing as he had a year earlier that the defenders could bring sixty-five thousand men against him. All the same, he told Halleck that he needed no more troops for the Charleston operation. He saw his force as "sufficiently powerful to take permanent advantage of any successes gained by the Navy, as at New Orleans [where Adm. David G. Farragut had run his ships by the city's defenses], and will also, I trust, and shall strongly endeavor so to make it, be able to make a strong diversion in favor of the

Navy during the attack." Hunter was not able to overlook an opportunity to accuse General Foster of carelessness, which forced him to change the plan. He had intended to land his force on the lower end of Morris Island, located south of the harbor mouth, and the northern end of Folly Island, just across Light-House Inlet from Morris. He could not do this, he claimed, because Foster on his reconnaissance had alerted the enemy by carelessly landing with a party of fifteen on Folly. Hunter concluded that the result was that the defenders fortified Morris and made a landing there unfeasible. General Beauregard, then commanding Confederate forces at Charleston, later wrote that Hunter was wrong. He had about twenty thousand men in all of South Carolina, did not have sufficient force on Morris Island to contest a landing, and had not been alerted by Foster's indiscretion.[42]

Admiral Du Pont's doubts were increasing about whether the new ironclad ships were enough to reduce the fixed fortifications in Charleston harbor, particularly Fort Sumter and Fort Moultrie. He sent some of the vessels as a test of their effectiveness against Fort McAllister at the mouth of the Ogeechee River in Georgia. The experiment showed that the fleet was not yet ready, and indeed Du Pont was doubtful it would be. He had to be careful how he approached the assistant secretary of the navy, Gustavus V. Fox, the advocate of the weapon and one convinced of the invulnerability of the monitors. He wrote that "whatever degree of impenetrability they might have, there was no corresponding quality of destructiveness against forts." Hunter was called to see Du Pont aboard the *Wabash* on 13 March and was told that major improvements had to be made to the vessels, causing "a delay of some weeks." He was apparently told nothing of Du Pont's doubts. Hunter used the occasion of his report on the meeting to ask again for a regiment of cavalry and said that he needed two first-class brigadiers for the command. Halleck ignored the usual troop request and told Hunter that "your want of good and instructed brigadiers is one very generally felt in the service, and nearly every general commanding an army has made the same request." Halleck said that Hunter had "his share of the first class" but would be sent as many "of the second class as you may require." Army correspondence shows little concern about the long-delayed Charleston assault, probably because that service had a very small role in the proceedings.[43]

In early April Hunter made his deployments of the army units intended to support the navy's attack, but it does not seem that he had in mind any particular activity for them during the assault nor any agreement with Du Pont about how the army might follow up a naval success. He accompanied some of his regiments to the Edisto River aboard the steamer *Ben De Ford,* and on the third had half his intended expeditionary force landed on islands from Folly south. Du

Pont's plan was simple, and it did not include the army—at least in the assault phase. He proposed to sail his flagship and nine monitors across the Charleston bar and bombard the forts into submission. Beyond that there was apparently no further plan, although Hunter's forces could have occupied the surrendered city. The 7 April assault was decidedly unsuccessful. The monitors were unwieldy and could not fire with effect on Confederate positions; most of them were disabled by counterfire. After little more than an hour Du Pont ordered withdrawal, intending to return the next morning.[44]

Hunter watched the operation from the *Ben De Ford* and may have thought the long-awaited operation a success—at least he expected Du Pont to continue it on the eighth. That morning he sent the admiral a congratulatory message, but this may have been for public consumption and to encourage the navy to give direct support to the army on the coastal islands. On the other hand, Hunter's enthusiasm may have been genuine. John Hay, whom Lincoln had sent to South Carolina to witness what some believed would cause the fall of the secessionist city and the symbolically important Fort Sumter, arrived the day after the battle. He heard enthusiastic reports from army officers, possibly also from Hunter, who, always politically sensitive, appointed the president's secretary a volunteer aide. Hay carried orders for Du Pont from navy secretary Welles and Fox, both telling him of Lincoln's concern for the military situation on the Mississippi and ordering the admiral to take his ships there after Charleston. Fox added that he had, only with difficulty, prevented Lincoln—who did not think the attack could succeed—from ordering the navy and Hunter with his troops to New Orleans at once, abandoning the militarily less important Charleston objective. These instructions and results of the short bombardment on the seventh were enough to make up Du Pont's mind about his next step.[45]

Du Pont told Hunter, "I attempted to take the bull by the horns, but he was too much for us," and the monitors were "miserable failures where the forts are concerned." Therefore, he decided that he could not renew the attack. His officers and Hay agreed with him that the ships were unlikely to silence the forts, and, even if they passed them, the navy could be bottled up without land support. Hunter, notified of this decision, sent General Seymour, his chief of staff, and his engineer officer, Col. James C. Duane, to ask Du Pont to use the fleet to support a landing by Hunter's troops on Morris Island. Hunter believed that the army could do nothing to get a foothold on Morris Island and reduce Battery Wagner and Cummings Point defenses on its northern end without the navy's participation. His objective was to gain the whole island, which would allow Union siege artillery to be used against Sumter and even Charleston. Du Pont refused Hunter's request on grounds that he had other orders and that his ships were too battered for immediate employment.[46]

Hunter began to withdraw his forces from the temporarily occupied supporting positions on some of the coastal islands, and he sent Seymour to Washington to see the president, secretary of war, and Halleck to discuss the situation in the department and to request reinforcement. The need for more troops was made more apparent to Hunter because he received an urgent request from General Foster, who was besieged with a small force in Washington, North Carolina. Hunter had responded by sending a brigade withdrawn from the Charleston deployment to the adjoining state. Lincoln was alarmed by the situation in South Carolina, and he ordered Du Pont and Hunter to continue operations against Charleston. Hunter was told: "You will co-operate with your forces with Admiral Du Pont as you and he may deem best. It is the President's desire that these operations be continued." Lincoln sent a letter to both commanders on 1 April which was an attempt to clarify the conflicting instructions ordering the fleet to New Orleans. It said that the Mississippi operation was not an immediate priority and that "we still hope that by cordial and judicious co-operation you can take the batteries on Morris Island and Sullivan's Island and Fort Sumter." The president told the two at least to make a demonstration but not to risk present positions. Hunter's reaction was immediately to reverse the flow of his soldiers, but Du Pont could do nothing at Charleston until his ships completed repairs at Port Royal.[47]

One of Hunter's kinsmen, Lt. Col. David Hunter Strother, an author and artist nationally known as "Porte Crayon" and then on the staff of General Banks in Louisiana, recorded in a diary his impression of news received in late April of the Charleston attack. It may have been one that was widely held in the army. "I hope this will settle Hunter, who is a fool and DuPont, who lacks enterprise." In a few months and under different circumstances Strother's opinion of Hunter would change, and he scratched out his cousin's name in the diary entry.[48]

LAST MONTHS AT PORT ROYAL

Thus the Charleston situation stood for almost three more months, when operations were to be continued with great loss of life and equally ineffective results by new navy and army commanders. Hunter spent that time on alternatives to a new assault on Charleston, increasing and protecting black troops to substitute for the reinforcements he consistently requested and rooting out disloyalty to the policy of the government. As for the first of these, he told one of his field commanders, "The object is simply to hold Folly Island, without attracting too much attention to it, until projected operations can be recommenced." Hunter wrote directly to Lincoln to ask that he be given unlimited authority "to organize colored regiments and commission their officers, and that I may have authority to deal promptly and finally with all officers who oppose a vigorous prosecution of the war and any of its necessary measures." In the letter he attempted to put himself above "all the clique prejudices of the two professions, Army and Navy," and praised the president for having "taken control of affairs in your own strong, honest hands." He signed this with regards to Mrs. Lincoln and as a friend, but it is unknown how such flattery was received. With or without authority, Hunter acted against a Pennsylvania volunteer captain and dismissed the officer for disloyalty. Lincoln, who reviewed such actions personally, wrote to Hunter that the penalty was too severe, since "the sole evidence was his refusal to sanction a resolution (indorsing the emancipation proclamation I believe); and our friends assure me that this statement is doing the Union cause great harm." Nevertheless, Lincoln continued, "I think his dismissal is wrong, even though I might think the resolution itself right." He asked Hunter to restore the captain to duty if no more evidence beyond the statement could be found.[49]

Hunter did not restrict his requests to Lincoln but also wrote to Stanton. The letter ostensibly reported on the status of the black South Carolina regiments, yet it was also a thinly veiled request for more attention from Washington to department needs. Hunter said that he had three regiments organized and two more being raised, the last two from "surplus laborers" employed by the quartermaster, commissary, and other support activities as well as "those employed as servants or laborers by the speculators and traders at the various posts." He said that the units that so far had field service "have proved themselves brave, active, docile, and energetic . . . and never disgracing their uniform by pillage or cruelty." Hunter thought it important to note that "even our enemies . . . have been unable to allege against them a single violation of any of the rules of civilized warfare."

He said that the black soldiers had the "religious sentiment (call it fanaticism, such as like) which made the soldiers of Oliver Cromwell invincible." The soldiers "accept with patience the slights and sneers occasionally thrown upon them by thoughtless or malignant hands," looking forward to the chance to prove themselves. Hunter believed that the "prejudices of certain of our white soldiers . . . are softening or fading out as a result of his department's conscription order. The reason was that "vast numbers of non-commissioned officers and deserving privates of our white regiments" were being commissioned, and this was "increasing respect and interest in the organization and fortunes of the colored brigade." Hunter told Stanton that blacks in uniform were essential for Union victory but said that he could not send soldiers out to find more because he had too few troops for the posts then occupied and was on call to furnish support for the navy. "I have not yet been in a position to carry out my plans (already fully matured) of coastwise expeditions of mixed troops to penetrate regions where slaves are the densest, and therein to establish posts to which fugitives might flock." A few days later Hunter asked the secretary to help his shortage by forcing General Foster to return the troops sent to him when his positions in North Carolina were threatened. He took the occasion to put Foster in a bad light: "I have now to beg your interposition that this volunteered act of assistance on my part may not be turned to the detriment of the public service in this department by the failure of Major-General Foster to appreciate my motives and reciprocate the sentiment of public duty exhibited in sending the brigade to his relief." Stanton did not appreciate Hunter's generosity in this matter enough to order the troops returned.[50]

As a way of increasing his troops out of War Department channels, Hunter wrote to Governor John A. Andrew of Massachusetts, repeating much of the same report he had made to Stanton and asking the governor to ask the secretary of war to send the black regiments Andrew was raising to the Department of the South. These regiments of "intelligent colored men from the North" would help to strengthen his own "brigade of liberated slaves" for the coastal raid expeditions. Andrew heeded the request, and the first of his regiments, the Fifty-fourth Massachusetts Volunteers (Colored), arrived at Port Royal in June.[51]

With no obvious activity on the part of the navy to move again on Charleston, Hunter suggested a "joint demonstration on the Savannah River." He had in mind the use of two ironclads to run up the river and shell the Confederate floating battery *Georgia* to be found there. Hunter proposed to accompany the navy by following with "a large number of transports, with sufficient men shown on them to create the impression that a joint attack was about to be made." He justified this exercise as a way of alarming the rebels and possibly preventing them from reinforcing their "armies in Virginia or the West." Du Pont turned down the proposal on what seem to be sensible grounds. He thought that a demonstration could not be followed up, that a feint without a definite object "will be considered another repulse by the rebels," and that, if Union troops did not land, the same would be the North's opinion of the expedition. Whether or not Du Pont and Hunter exchanged other ideas and opinions, it was not long before the two men were estranged.[52]

Hunter used a letter to Lincoln as his way of showing his frustration with the navy and with the limiting instructions that Washington required he operate under. He began with a description of the first Charleston attack, stating that the army had been ready on the morning of 8 April to cross Light House Inlet and land on Morris Island. With navy gun support, Hunter said, he would have cleared the island and mounted his rifled guns at Cummings Point, from where "Fort Sumter would have been rendered untenable in two days' fire." He cited the lesson of Fort Pulaski "to show how certain would have been the fall of Fort Sumter." But, he said, Du Pont left the army to its own resources, allowing Hunter to do no more than hold his positions on Folly and other islands to the south while the now-aroused rebels strengthened their defenses nearer to the harbor. He complained about Lincoln's order "to co-operate with the Navy which now tie me down to share the admiral's inactivity." "Liberate me from this order," he continued, "and I will immediately place a column of 10,000 of the best drilled soldiers in the country . . . in the heart of Georgia," through counties with a high slave count. Hunter was convinced that the Confederacy was "a mere hollow shell," unable to defend Georgia from his planned march *from* the sea. He thought that the department's troops were anxious for such an offensive—except for "one brigadier-general [undoubtedly Stevenson] and one colonel commanding a brigade [probably Col. Henry R. Guss, also of Foster's late detachment]." He asked again for the cavalry and requested that pikes be issued "immediately; the weapons being the simplest and most effective that can be placed in the hands of the slaves who are liberated on the march into the interior." (Belief in the pike as best for use by black soldiers was shared among many officers—General Butler in New Orleans, for example—and, of course, by John Brown at Harper's Ferry.) He finished by saying that "I deem this matter of such importance that I send this letter by special steamer to Fort Monroe [and by a special messenger, his aide Captain Kinzie], and have instructed the captain of the vessel to wait for your reply." A response was not forthcoming; instead, the president and his advisors were discussing with another officer the issue of replacing Hunter in South Carolina.[53]

Hunter had only a few weeks before his planned relief from command of the department and the corps was known to him. He corresponded only once more from Hilton Head with the president, asking that Lincoln have Du Pont release some prisoners to him that he could use as hostages. Five of the nine prisoners the admiral held "are known to be the sons of some of the wealthyist [*sic*] and most influential Rebels in the Sea Islands." He wanted to be prepared if some of his officers were executed, as threatened by the Confederates, or if black soldiers were made slaves. On another matter related to black troops, he received a letter at Charleston from the Confederate Department of South Carolina, Georgia and Florida, complaining that it was Union practice for communications from rebel military authorities sent under flags of truce "to receive the flag by a detachment of negroes, commanded by officers belonging to regiments of negroes, which of course debars us from further communications."The writer said that he could not believe that Hunter was using soldiers of "obnoxious complexion" as an indirect way of refusing all further rebel flags of truce. Hunter, of course, answered that his government recognized no differences between its soldiers based on race or on the character of the regiments in which its officers served. As he put it, "The flag of the United States covers all its defenders with equal honor and protection, regardless of the accident of color." By the end of July, because of atrocities against black soldiers, Lincoln saw the need to threaten retaliation against rebel prisoners, his point being the same as Hunter's—that the Union gave full and equal rights and protection to all its troops. The president also promised execution for execution and "hard labor on the public works" for a Confederate prisoner whenever a black soldier was returned to slavery, a position not much different than the one Hunter had twice intended to declare to Jefferson Davis.[54]

Hunter concerned himself with administrative matters as well. He directed Col. James Montgomery, commanding the Second South Carolina Regiment (Colored), to obey the "laws and usages of civilized warfare" in his coastal operations. The caution may have had to do with the fact that Montgomery was Lane's deputy when the Jayhawkers were ravishing Missouri early in the war. His orders in the period established sanitary regulations for the troops and restricted visitors to the department. The latter was justified as required on grounds that "one known rebel spy [discovered by Hunter himself aboard *Arago* on the way to Hilton Head], several professional gamblers with the cheating implements of their trade, and others equally objectionable" were earlier landed as official and unofficial travelers on government vessels. Hunter ordered that such persons, and indeed "many hundreds of able-bodied men libel to the draft and not in the employ of the Government," were in the department. They were warned to depart or face conscription and assignment to Hunter's regiments.[55]

On 3 June orders were published relieving Hunter "temporarily from command of the Department of the South" and assigning Brigadier General Gillmore, the engineer who had planned and executed the successful siege of Fort Pulaski, to "the temporary command" of the department, but it not clear that Hunter was immediately notified. (Shortly afterward Du Pont was relieved as well, but his replacement died, leaving the admiral in place until another officer could be sent.) In late April Gillmore, on leave in New York, was approached about directing a second assault against Charleston. He thought that he could do the job in conjunction with the navy with only the resources available in South Carolina. He asked only that he be given full authority to execute his plans without interference from others, except as his plans involved cooperation with the navy. It must have been this condition that inspired Hunter's "temporary" relief; Gillmore would have his chance without Hunter's oversight.[56]

Gillmore did not leave New York for a few days after the order, having been detained on personal business. He wrote to Halleck that he was ready to leave for Port Royal (aboard the *Ben De Ford*) about the tenth. While Gillmore was en route, Hunter sent a last request to Halleck, again "urgently" requesting cavalry support. Gillmore relieved Hunter on 12 June, which upset Hunter, particularly since Gillmore seemed to have no plan beyond what Hunter would have done with naval support. He too intended to land on Morris Island, capture Battery Wagner and fortifications on Cummings Point, and "destroy Fort Sumter with breaching batteries of rifled guns," clearing the way for the navy to enter the harbor. Gillmore, however, understood that "no additional troops would be sent to South Carolina." Despite the new faces in command, much fighting, and heavy casualties, Charleston and Sumter remained in Confederate hands until February 1865, when the city was abandoned by its defenders, outflanked by Maj. Gen. William T. Sherman on his way through the state on his march from Savannah to North Carolina.[57]

NOTES

1. Special Orders No. 256, Adjutant General's Office, U.S. War Department, *The War of the Rebellion: A Compilation of the Official Records of the Union and Confederate Armies* (Washington, D.C.: Government Printing Office, 1901) (hereafter *ORA* and ser. 1, unless otherwise indicated), 19, pt. 1, 549–50; Julius White, "The Surrender of Harper's Ferry," in *Battles and Leaders of the Civil War,* ed. Robert Underwood Johnson and Clarence Clough Buel, 4 vols. (1887; reprint, Secaucus, N.J.: Castle, 1991), 2:612–15.

2. Report, 3 November 1862, *ORA,* 19, pt. 1, 798. Hunter may have been prejudiced against Miles, who commanded the Fifth Division at Bull Run. After that battle Hunter said that Miles was "believed to be a drunkard and a coward, and a great blower of his own trumpet" (Hunter's notes on battle, n.d., probably late 1862, Hunter MSS, Huntington Library, San Marino, Calif.

3. *New York Times,* 10 September 1862; diary entry, 17 September 1862, David Herbert Donald, ed., *Inside Lincoln's Cabinet: The Civil War Diaries of Salmon P. Chase* (Longmans, Green and Co., 1954), 147; letter to his wife, 20 September 1862, James Garfield, *The Wild Life of the Army: Civil War Letters of James Garfield,* ed. Frederick D. Williams (East Lansing: Michigan State University Press, 1964), 137.

4. Gideon Welles, *The Diary of Gideon Welles,* ed. Howard K. Beale, 3 vols. (New York: W. W. Norton and Co., 1960), 1:142–45; the "immortal decree of emancipation," 22 September 1862, in report, Provost Marshal General's Bureau, 17 March 1866, *ORA,* ser. 3, 5:656; proclamation, 1 January 1863, Abraham Lincoln, *Speeches and Writings, 1859–1865: Speeches, Letters, and Miscellaneous Writings, Presidential Messages and Proclamations* (New York: Library of America, 1989), 424–25; *New York Times,* 23 September 1862.

5. Letters, Davis to Lee and Lee to U.S. Army, 1 and 2 August 1862, *ORA,* ser. 2, 4:835, 328–29; General Orders No. 60, Adjutant and Inspector General's Office, Richmond, 21 August 1862, ibid. 14:599.

6. *Savannah Republican,* n.d., quoted in Charles Graham Halpine, *Baked Meats of the Funeral* (New York: Carleton, 1866), 190, 192–93.

7. Letter, Hunter to Davis, 20 September 1862, Halpine, *Baked Meats,* 193–201, William Hanchett, *Irish: Charles G. Halpine in Civil War America* (Syracuse: Syracuse University Press, 1970), 69.

8. Diary entry, 11 October 1862, Donald, *Inside Lincoln's Cabinet,* 172.

9. Ibid., 172–73.

10. Virginia Jeanes Laas, *Wartime Washington: The Civil War Letters of Elizabeth Blair Lee* (Urbana: University of Illinois Press, 1991), 194; James Garfield, *The Wild Life of the Army: Civil War Letters of James Garfield,* ed. Frederick D. Williams, (East Lansing: Michigan State University Press, 1964), 314. Steuart was promoted to colonel when his battalion grew to a regiment and was commanding a brigade when he was wounded (Ezra J. Warner, *Generals in Gray: Lives of the Confederate Commanders* [Baton Rouge: Louisiana State University Press, 1959], 290–91; Randolph Harrison McKim, *A Soldier's Recollections: Leaves from the Diary of a Young Confederate* [1910; reprint, Alexandria, Va.: Time-Life Books, 1984], 117, 122–23; Charles A. Dana, *Recollections of the Civil War* [1897; reprint, New York: Collier Books, 1963], 126; letter, Hunter to Halpine, 10 September 1863, Huntington Library). Frequent errors spelling Steuart's name caused him to be called "Maryland" Steuart. He is often confused with J. E. B. Stuart, a rebel cavalry general, who was also a dragoon officer at Leavenworth, although younger than Steuart.

11. Letters, Garfield to his wife, 7 and 9 November 1862, Smith, *Life and Letters of Garfield,* 1:254; Halpine was also alerted to return to South Carolina (Hanchett, *Irish,* 60).

12. Special Orders No. 216, Adjutant General's Office, 1 September 1862, General Orders No. 40, Department of the South, 17 September 1862, *ORA,* 14:380, 382; Don Carlos Buell, "Operations in Northern Alabama," in Johnson and Buel, *Battles and Leaders,* 2:701–8.

13. General Orders No. 123, 3 September 1862, letters, Mitchel to Halleck and Stanton, 20 September 1862, *ORA,* 14:380, 382–85. The *New York Times,* 24 September 1862, also thought the majority of Mitchel's soldiers were "bitterly prejudiced against the negroes."

14. Letter, Garfield to his wife, 21 November 1862, Garfield, *Wild Life in the Army,* 183; Special Orders No. 362, Adjutant General's Office, 25 November 1862, *ORA,* 12, pt. 2, supp., 821. To disparage Hunter, an enemy inaccurately wrote later that Hunter was appointed "because he was a Virginian with special hatred of his native state and therefore a fit tool for a tyrant like Stanton" (Henry Kyd Douglas, *I Rode with Stonewall, Being Chiefly the War Experiences of the Youngest Member of Jackson's Staff* [Chapel Hill: University of North Carolina Press, 1940], 183); Noah Brooks, *Washington, D.C., in Lincoln's Time,* ed. Herbert Mitgang (1898; reprint, Athens: University of Georgia Press, 1989), 24–25.

15. Richard R. Irwin, "The Case of Fitz John Porter," in Johnson and Buel, *Battles and Leaders,* 2:695–97; Court Martial Record, *ORA,* 12, pt. 2, supp., 821–1134; Roy Z. Chamlee, Jr., *Lincoln's Assassins: A Complete Account of Their Capture, Trial, and Punishment* (Jefferson, N.C.: McFarland and Co., 1990), 247.

16. Smith, *Life and Letters of Garfield,* 260. Garfield also observed that Hunter weighed 175 pounds and was five feet seven inches tall (Garfield, *Wild Life of the Army,* 187).

17. Letter, McClellan to Porter, 19 December 1862, Stephen W. Sears, ed., *The Civil War Papers of George B. McClellan: Selected Correspondence, 1860–1865* (New York: Ticknor and Fields, 1989), 532; letter, Garfield to his wife, 12 October 1862, Garfield, *Wild Life of the Army,* 314; Otto Eisenschiml, *The Celebrated Case of Fitz John Porter: An American Dryfus Affair* (Indianapolis: Bobbs-Merrill, 1950), 77–78; Charles Shields Wainwright, *A Diary of Battle: The Personal Journals of Colonel Charles S. Wainwright* (New York: Harcourt, Brace and World, 1962), 161, 260.

18. Quoting board of officers, 1879, Irwin, "Case of Fitz John Porter," 697.

19. Letter, Lincoln to Halleck, 5 November 1862, *ORA,* 19, pt. 2, 545; C. P. R. Rodgers, "Du Pont's Attack on Charleston," in Johnson and Buel, *Battles and Leaders,* 4:34–35; letter, Foster to General Thomas, 2 March 1863, *Correspondence, Orders, etc., between Major-General David Hunter, Major-General J. G. Foster, and Brigadier-General Henry M. Naglee, and Others, February and March, 1863* (Philadelphia: J. B. Lippincott, 1863).

20. Henry Villard, *Memoirs of Henry Villard,* 2 vols. (1902; reprint, New York: De Capo Press, 1969), 2:4.

21. Special Orders Nos. 16–17, 20 and 21 January 1863, Department of the South, Special Orders, Department of the South, vol. 28, Record Group 393,

U.S. Army Continental Commands, 1821–1920, National Archives (NA); letter, Hunter to Halleck, and General Orders No. 3, Department of the South, both 20 January 1863, *ORA,* 14:390–91.

22. General Orders No. 3, 20 January, *ORA,* 14:392; General Orders No. 1, Adjutant General's Office, 2 January 1863, the army implementing directive for the proclamation, ibid., ser. 3, 3:2–3.

23. John D. Hayes, ed., *Samuel Francis Du Pont: A Selection from His Civil War Letters,* 3 vols. (Ithaca: Cornell University Press, 1969), 2:373; *New York Times,* 28 January 1863; Thomas Wentworth Higginson, *Army Life in a Black Regiment* (1870; reprint, East Lansing: Michigan State University Press, 1960), 46. Higginson commanded the regiment that was mustered in on 31 January. It was redesignated the Thirty-third United States Colored Infantry a year later, on 8 February 1864.

24. *New York Times,* 28 January 1863.

25. General Orders No. 111, Adjutant and Inspector General's Office, 24 December 1862, announcing Davis's 23 December proclamation, *ORA,* ser. 2, 5:795–97.

26. Hanchett, *Irish,* 68–69; letter, Hunter to Stanton, 25 April, forwarding letter to Davis, 23 April 1863, *ORA,* 14:448–49; Letter, Secretary of War James A. Seddon to Lt. Gen. J. C. Pemberton, 8 April 1863, ibid., ser. 2, 5:867; *New York Times,* 2 June 1863.

27. Joint resolution, Confederate Congress, 1 May 1863, *ORA,* ser. 2, 5:940–41.

28. Letter, Hunter to Halleck, 13 February, and General Orders No. ——, Eighteenth Army Corps (Flagship *Farran*), 7 February 1863, *ORA,* 14:394–95.

29. Letters, Halpine to Naglee and Naglee to Halpine, 9 and 10 November, General Orders No. 13, Department of the South, 11 November, letters, Naglee to Foster and Halpine, 11 November 1863, ibid., 14:396–400.

30. Letter with General Order No. 13, 11 February, Department of the South, Hunter to Hay, 11 February 1863, documents no. 21660 and 21678, Lincoln Papers, Documents Division, Library of Congress (LOC), Washington, D.C.; letter, Hunter to Halleck, 11 November 1863, *ORA,* 14:396–98.

31. Telegram, Foster (at Fort Monroe) to Halleck, 13 February, letters, Halleck to Hunter, 15 and 16 February 1863, *ORA,* 14:400–402.

32. Letter, Halleck to Foster, telegrams, Foster to Halleck, Townsend to Stanton, Stanton to Townsend, Halleck to Foster, all 16 November, and telegrams, Townsend to Stanton, 17 November, Foster to Halleck and Halleck to Foster, Halleck to Townsend, 18 November 1863, ibid., 402–4.

33. General Orders No. 15, Department of the South, 23 February, letters, Hunter to Halleck, 23 and 24 February, ibid., 14:411–12; the officers who were

relieved asked for a court of inquiry (letter, eight Eighteenth Army Corps officers to Stanton, 2 March 1863, ibid., 14:417). Hunter sent Hay copies of his 19 and 24 February letters to Halleck, adding notes—a way, perhaps, of currying White House support (docs. 21840, 21938, Lincoln Papers, LOC).

34. Letter, Halpine to Naglee, 27 February, Special Orders No. 110, Department of the South, letters, Seymour to Ferry and Naglee, all 28 February, letter, Naglee to Halpine, 1 March, Naglee to Foster, 3 March 1863, ORA, 14:413–16, 419.

35. Letter, Hunter to Halleck, 3 March, Special Orders No. 127 and General Orders No. 16, Department of the South, 5 March, letters, Hunter to Halleck, 7 March, Halleck to Hunter, 13 March 1863, ibid., 14:417–18, 420, 425–27; Frank J. Welcher, *The Union Army, 1861–1865,* 2 vols. (Bloomington: Indiana University Press, 1989), 1:442–43.

36. Letter, Naglee to Foster, 16 March 1863, ORA, 14:428.

37. Halpine, *Baked Meats of the Funeral,* 203–4; Hunter's April 1873 report, vol. 9, U.S. Army Generals' Reports of Civil War Service, 1864–87, RG 94, Records of the Office of the Adjutant General, NA, 672–73.

38. Letters, Hunter to Halleck, 24 February and 7 March 1863, ORA, 14:410, 424; citing *New York Daily Tribune* reports, *Harper's Weekly,* 14 March 1863. The Second became the Thirty-fourth U.S. Colored Infantry in early 1864.

39. Special Orders No. 86, Department of the South, 16 February 1863, *Correspondence, Orders, etc.,* 46; letter, Hunter to Halleck, 23 March 1863, ORA, 14:431.

40. General Orders No. 17, Department of the South, 6 March 1863, ORA, 14:1020.

41. Reports, Saxton and Higginson, 1 and 2 February, letters, Saxton to Stanton, Hunter to Du Pont, both 6 March 1863, ibid., 14:194–98, 420, 423; Higginson, *Army Life in a Black Regiment,* 97; letter, Lincoln to Hunter, 1 April 1863, document no. 22740, Lincoln Papers, LOC.

42. Letter, Hunter to Halleck, 7 March 1863, ORA, 14:424–25; G. T. Beauregard, "The Defense of Charleston," in Johnson and Buel, *Battles and Leaders,* 4:12–13.

43. Rodgers, "Du Pont's Attack," 4:33–34; letters, Hunter to Halleck, 13 March, and Halleck to Hunter, 16 March 1863, ORA, 14:427–29.

44. Letter, Hunter to Halleck, 3 April 1863, ORA, 14:436–37; Rodgers, "Du Pont's Attack," 4:35–40; Beauregard, "Defense of Charleston," 4:11–12.

45. Letters, Welles and Fox to Du Pont, 2 April, Hunter to Du Pont, 8 April 1863, ORA, 14:436–37. The Mississippi plan was no secret, but the navy there thought little of it. Admiral David D. Porter wrote mockingly from New Cathage,

"I hear Hunter is in New Orleans with 50,000 men and 20,000 reporters" (letter, Porter to Fox, 14 May 1863, Gustavus Vasa Fox, *Confidential Correspondence of Gustavus V. Fox*, 2 vols. [New York: Naval History Society, 1920], 2:182); Taylor, *Life and Letters of John Hay*, 1:149–52. Hay was also on the scene to look in on his brother Charles, one of Hunter's aides, seriously ill with pneumonia at Hilton Head.

46. Two letters, Du Pont to Hunter, 8 April 1863, *ORA*, 14:437, 442; Taylor, *Life and Letters of John Hay*, 1:150–51; Rodgers, "Du Pont's Attack," 41–42.

47. Letters, Hunter to Lincoln and Stanton introducing Seymour, 10 April, documents no. 22912, 22914, Lincoln to Hunter and Du Pont, 14 April 1863, document no. 22978, Lincoln Papers, LOC; Special Orders No. 190, Department of the South, 12 April, telegrams, Lincoln to Du Pont and Halleck to Hunter, 13 April, letters, Hunter to Halleck, 15 and 16 April 1863, *ORA*, 14:440–42.

48. Entry, 22 April 1863, David Hunter Strother, *A Virginia Yankee in the Civil War: The Diaries of David Hunter Strother*, ed. Cecil D. Eby, Jr. (Chapel Hill: University of North Carolina Press, 1961), 174.

49. Letters, Seymour to Brigadier General Israel Vogdes, 22 April, Hunter to Lincoln, 25 April 1863, *ORA*, 14:446–48; letter, Lincoln to Hunter, 30 April 1863, document no. 23210, Lincoln Papers, LOC.

50. General Orders No. 24, Department of the South, 19 March 1863, allowed roundup of blacks for army service and letter, Hunter to Stanton, 4 May 1863, *ORA*, 14:429–30, 452; letter, Hunter to Stanton, 30 April 1863, doc. no. 52458, Stanton Papers, LOC.

51. Letter, Hunter to Andrew, 4 May 1863, *ORA*, ser. 3, 3:190–91; letters, Hunter to Andrew and Stanton, 3 June 1863, ibid., 14:462–63. The Fifth-fourth went on to make its reputation in the assault on Battery Wagner in July, and the Fifty-fifth Regiment was assigned later.

52. Letters, Du Pont to Hunter and Du Pont to Hunter (2 letters), 29 April and 4 May 1862, *ORA*, 14:454–55.

53. Letter, Hunter to Lincoln, 22 May 1863, document no. 23609, Lincoln Papers, LOC.

54. Letter, Hunter to Lincoln, 27 May 1863, document no. 23702, ibid.; letters, Brigadier General Thomas Jordan, chief-of-staff, Charleston, to Hunter, 3 June, Hunter to Jordan, 8 June 1863, *ORA*, 14:464–65; distributing to the army Lincoln's 30 July proclamation, General Orders No. 252, Adjutant General's Office, 31 July 1863, U.S. Department of War, Office of the Adjutant General, "The Negro in the Military Service of the United States, 1609–1889," 7 vols., RG 94, NA, 7:1097.

55. Letter, Hunter to Montgomery, 9 June, General Orders nos. 40–41, 22

and 26 May 1863, Department of the South, *ORA,* 14:466–67, 457–60. Mont-gomery did not heed the advice and on 11 June burned the undefended town of Darien, Georgia, sparing a church and three small buildings but promising to return to complete the work (report, Capt. W. G. Thomson, Twentieth Battalion, Georgia [Confederate] Cavalry, 23 June 1863, ibid., 318–19).

56. Special Orders No. 249, Adjutant General's Office, 3 June 1863, ibid., 464; letter, Gillmore to George W. Cullen, Halleck's staff chief, 23 May 1863, ibid., 459.

57. Letters, Gillmore to Halleck, 5 June, Hunter to Halleck, 10 June 1863, ibid, 465, 467–68; General Orders Nos. 46–47, Department of the South, 12 June 1863—the first, Hunter's announcement of his temporary relief and orders to Washington for "special service" and, the second, Gillmore's acceptance of command (ibid., 37, pt. 2, 3–4); Quincy A. Gillmore, "The Army before Charleston in 1863," in Johnson and Buel, *Battles and Leaders,* 4:54–55.

Hunter's first post, Fort Snelling, Michigan Territory (later Minnesota). Painting by Lt. Seth Eastman (Architect of the Capitol).

Painting of Fort Dearborn and the Kinzie home about 1830. Artist and date unknown (IChi–03052, Chicago Historical Society).

Comanches meeting dragoons, Indian Territory (later Oklahoma), 1834. Painting by George Catlin (National Museum of American Art, Smithsonian Institution, Gift of Mrs. Joseph Harrison, Jr.).

Volunteer guard at the White House, April 1861 (Library of Congress).

GEN. DAVID HUNTER

David Hunter in the uniform of a colonel of cavalry, late spring 1861. The number "1" on the hat is unexplained, but it may designate the First Dragoons (later First Cavalry), in which Hunter had served thirty years earlier (U.S. Army Military History Institute).

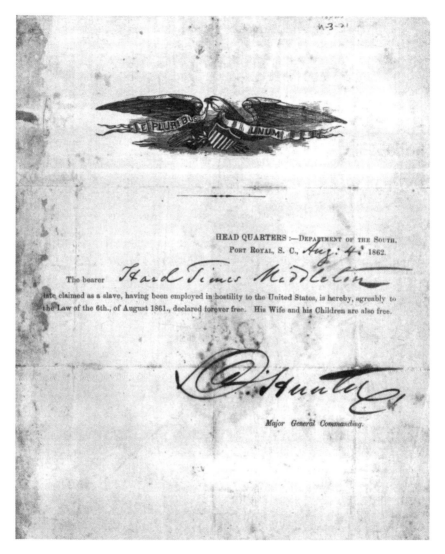

Certificate of freedom for a "contraband" former slave signed by Hunter (Lewis Leigh, Jr.).

Hunter's Department of the South headquarters at Hilton Head, S.C., circa 1863
(U.S. Army Military History Institute)

Gen. Fitz John Porter's court-martial, 1862. Hunter is at far left. Sketch by Henry Waud
(Library of Congress).

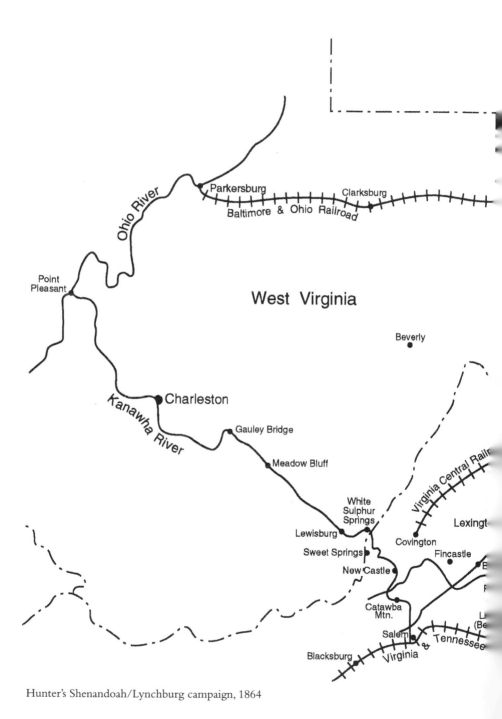

Hunter's Shenandoah/Lynchburg campaign, 1864

Pennsylvania

Chambersburg

● Gettysburg

Cumberland

Bath
(Berkeley
Springs)

Hagerstown
Williamport

Maryland

Hedgesville ●

Shepherdstown

Thurmont
● Middletown

Martinsburg

Harper's
Ferry

● Frederick
● Monocacy

Baltimore

Bunker
Hill

Charles Town

White's
Ferry

Winchester

Newton
(Stevans City)

Berryville

Leesburg

Moorefield

Rockville

Middletown

Washington

Strasburg

Shenandoah River

Woodstock

Potomac River

New Market

Blue Ridge Mountains

Virginia

Harrisonburg

River

Mount Crawford

Port Republic

Piedmont

Gordonsville

Waynesboro

Charlottesville

way
ele's
ern)

James River

Amherst

Richmond

Lynchburg

Petersburg ●

VMI superintendent's house, Hunter's headquarters in Lexington, 11–14 June 1864 (Edward A. Miller, Jr.).

VMI barracks before September 1866, when the statue of Washington was returned and reinstalled in front of the center archway. The cabins temporarily housed cadets (VMI Archives).

Ruins of Andrew Hunter's house, Charles Town, W. Va., 1864 (*Leslie's Illustrated Magazine*).

Col. David Hunter Strother ("Porte Crayon"), Hunter's chief of staff in the Shenandoah/Lynchburg campaign (U.S. Army Military History Institute).

Sketch of Hunter, near Harper's Ferry, 26 July 1864. By David Hunter Strother, "Porte Crayon" (The Library of Virginia).

Lt. Col. Charles Graham Halpine ("Private Miles O'Reilly"), Hunter's adjutant for most of the war (U.S. Army Military History Institute).

Lincoln conspirators' trial courtroom. Hunter is at the right end of the table (*Harper's Weekly*).

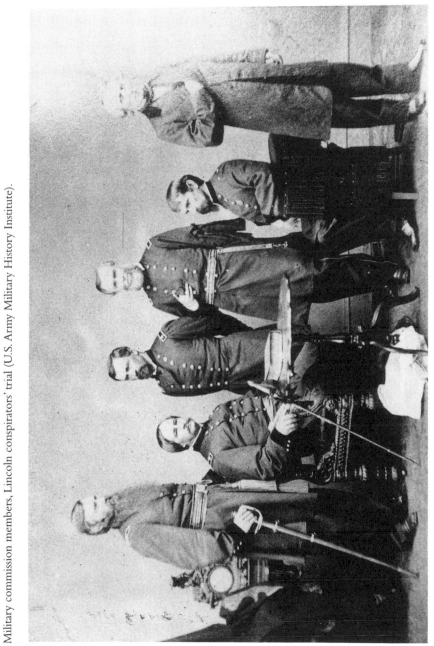

Military commission members, Lincoln conspirators' trial (U.S. Army Military History Institute).

The hanging of four of the conspirators, 7 July 1865 (Library of Congress).

Maj. Gen. David Hunter during the Civil War (U.S. Army Military History Institute).

Chapter 6

TEMPORARY ASSIGNMENTS
AND NEW OPPORTUNITIES

On the day of his relief and before leaving Port Royal, Hunter, believing his replacement was largely caused by Horace Greeley, editor of the *New York Daily Tribune,* wrote a sarcastic letter to the critic of the campaign against Charleston. He said:

> Since you have undertaken the campaign against Charleston, I sincerely hope you will be more successful than in your first advance on Richmond, in which you wasted much ink, and other men [Hunter among them] shed some blood. It is clear, from your paper, that you know nothing of my orders which bound me to a certain course of action, which orders I strictly followed and for obeying which I am now censured. Worse than any wound our enemies can inflict, are the stabs in the dark of personal friends. The country must be informed that you have charge of this second attack upon Charleston, so that on you may rest the praise or censure.[1]

The old soldier traveled to New York aboard the *Arago,* arriving on 17 June 1863, and went on directly to Washington to see the president. He apologized to Lincoln for not being in uniform, "saying it was the first time in my life I had ever been ashamed of it. I said to him that he had always been kind to me personally, and that I felt very grateful for it, but that he had allowed his subordinates to treat me with all kinds of disrespect and injustice." In a letter to Halpine—temporarily in New York without army assignment—Hunter described the three-hour meeting, outlining with the help of his letter book outrages such as McClellan's corrections of his conduct in Kansas, Halleck's responses over the Foster matter, and Lincoln-imposed restrictions on Hunter's plans to move into the interior from Port Royal. Hunter made an attempt to reconstruct the conversation in which Lincoln explained why Hunter had been relieved of his duties. The gist of it was that Greeley had said "he had found a man who would 'do the job'" and recommended that the president call for Gillmore. Hunter's temporary replacement was done only so that Gillmore could have freedom to do what he thought was needed to reduce Charleston, and moving Hunter north was a way to avoid an awkward situation over dates of rank and precedence among generals. The discussion continued about the war in general, and no doubt Hunter told the president, as he did Halpine, that "that vagabond Greeley" was probably happy because "he has put a copper head [peace Democrat] General in command of the Department of the South instead of a vile abolitionist."[2]

Following this and probably equally unrewarding meetings with Halleck and other army officials, Hunter went on to the family home at Princeton. Still angry over his removal from command on the eve of what he might have thought would be great triumphs, in late June he complained to Lincoln that it was "all but universally regarded as a censure on my conduct while in that command." He was convinced that all he did in the Department of the South was "in strict obedience to orders." Therefore, he asked Lincoln for permission to publish "such official documents and records as may be necessary to set me right in the eyes of my friends and in the justice of history." He closed with a request for the president to tell him soon if his publication plan was acceptable; otherwise, he said, "I shall regard your silence in reply to this note as giving me the liberty I ask and will act accordingly."[3]

The president's answer was immediate. Lincoln said: "I assure you, and you may feel authorized in stating, that the recent change of commanders in the Department of the South was made for no reasons which convey any imputation upon your known energy, efficiency, and patriotism; but for causes which seemed sufficient, while they were in no degree incompatible with the respect and esteem in which I have always held you as a man and an officer." On the other hand, Lincoln refused Hunter blanket permission to publish official information, because it could indicate the president assumed responsibility for whatever Hunter might write. Lincoln concluded that Hunter's "own sense of military propriety must be your guide and the regulations of the service your rule of conduct." Hunter made no response and did not publish the threatened defense of his conduct in command in South Carolina. Although officially silent on his removal, the general did not accept it with good grace. A fellow general wrote that Hunter "always chafed" about having been relieved of his command "and ascribed it to the machinations of his enemies."[4]

The Hunters did not remain in Princeton long, spending time also in New York and in Washington, where the couple was socially active, particularly Maria Hunter, who often went to the theater, among other places, with the Lincolns, John Hay, and others in power. Hunter actively sought new work in the army, but nothing was immediately available, even though the battle of Gettysburg in early July 1863 made and lost others' reputations. Lincoln was disappointed that Army of the Potomac commander George Meade had failed to follow up the victory and destroy Lee's army. Hunter was present in Lincoln's office on 16 July (ten days after Lee, relatively unmolested, crossed the Potomac River into Virginia), when the president and a number of generals discussed the military situation. While it is not clear what Hunter's contribution to the discussion of options might have been, it is known that Brig. Gen. James S. Wadsworth, who had commanded a division at Gettysburg, commented to Hunter: "General, there are a good many officers of the regular army who have not yet lost the West Point idea of Southern superiority. That sometimes accounts for an otherwise unaccountable slowness of attack." There can be little doubt that Hunter agreed with this observation.[5]

While in Washington, Hunter met with an unemployed relative, Colonel Strother, famous as "Porte Crayon," a contributor to *Harper's New Monthly Magazine* in the 1850s. The two men were not close and may have known each other only slightly prior to the war, but they were to begin a strong, lifelong friendship in the following spring and summer. They met for several hours at Willard's Hotel on two successive days, speaking of their friends and relatives in the Martinsburg, West Virginia, area near Strother's home, examining their future prospects in the army, and discussing the state of the war. Strother's diary does not detail what personal opportunities the cousins saw, but it does report Hunter's confidence in black troops and his belief that they would provide extensive service in the war. Strother, who had seen the soldiers fight well at Port Hudson on the Mississippi, believed that black men would not voluntarily join in fighting the war, a position that Hunter, with his South Carolina experience, shared. Both believed that conscription would be needed to fill the ranks in black regiments, and that proved to be so. Strother had written in June: "No acts of emancipation, no fanciful appeals of liberty, virtue, and independence will have any effect on them. To be made available, [the black man] must be taken hold of, controlled, and ordered. . . . Absolute power is necessary, so he must be drafted." Hunter probably shared this opinion, but he no longer had a role in raising black regiments and would never again command any of them. He thought more of the black man than did Strother and after the war promoted the franchise for him, a position Strother rejected. Strother told Hunter that he was negotiating with army generals and others for a place on active service. Meeting with Secretary Stanton in late July, he was sent as a staff officer to the new Department of West Virginia, a posting that would make good use of his knowledge of the country, in which new operations were planned. There the cousins would meet again.[6]

Visiting New York City after a two-week vacation at Newport, Rhode Island, Hunter wrote Stanton a private note expressing his concern about how he observed that the North was viewing the war. He concluded that the "hopeless state of the rebels" would induce them to make peace on conditions, "'The Union as it was, and the Constitution as it is.'" This would mean that slavery "will thus be fixed on us forever, and all our blood and treasure will have been expended in vain." He asked Stanton, "Cannot this be prevented by a general arming of the negroes and a general destruction of all the property of the slaveholders, thus making it in their interest to get rid of slavery?" Hunter proposed that he be permitted to take what men could be spared from New York City, and he would land them at Brunswick, Georgia, "march through the heart of Georgia, Alabama, and Mississippi to New Orleans, arming all the negroes and burning the house and other property of every slaveholder. A passage of this kind would create such a commotion among the negroes that they themselves could be left to do the work. I am a firm believer in the maxim that 'Slaveholders have no rights a negro is bound to respect.'" Stanton replied the next day that he had sent Hunter's proposal to the president, and, if Lincoln approved of it, orders would be issued for what sounded like a mission of vengeance and punishment such as John Brown might have sought.[7]

On the strength of Stanton's letter Hunter went to Washington, intending to find a house. (Maria, and Mrs. Steuart and her child, remained at Huntington [New York?] to avoid the capital's summer heat.) He also went to see Stanton again, who said "he most cordially approved of my plan, and asked me to see the President." Lincoln received the general "very kindly, not withstanding the hard talk I had with him the first time I came north." Hunter did not, however, get a firm commitment from Lincoln because cabinet members came into the room—"I found myself in the midst of a Cabinet meeting"—and so he took his leave.[8]

With time on his hands Hunter sought to explain what he thought were his own failures and turned toward the then popular practice of phrenology. The pseudoscience was based on a theory that the topography of one's skull could reveal mental faculties and character traits to a trained practitioner of the discipline. He was told that he was "'altogether too modest a man for this wicked world,' and allowed myself to be 'pushed aside by much inferior men.'" Thinking over this observation, Hunter concluded that he should not have listened to

General Benham about the James Island landing and should have insisted on Morris Island. Further, he thought he later "deferred entirely too much to Du Pont and Seymour." He wrote Halpine, "Should I ever have another command, I shall be as absolute as a Turk, and consult no body on the face of the earth, except perhaps it may be you." In seven months he was to have the opportunity to test this method of leadership.[9]

Meanwhile, in late September or early October the general and his wife went to St. Louis on what might have been an unofficial trip. They visited old friends, and the general evaluated the political situation in that area. He was disturbed that some leaders were not sufficiently devoted to getting rid of slavery as an important war aim. He said that there were men "who are anxious to conserve all so corrupt, putrid, rotten and abominable in our constitutions; and to deprive us of all we have gained by the loss of so much blood and treasure." Of the abolitionists he said: "Because they have such a black sheep in their flock as Jim. Lane it is no reason their cause is not a good one."[10]

Returning to Washington via Chicago and Philadelphia, visiting still other acquaintances and relatives, Hunter arrived in Washington on 13 October and began looking for a house to rent or purchase. He was successful and soon rented a dwelling at 288 I Street N and for some time boarded Col. Alexander James Perry, an assistant quartermaster on the army staff who was a first lieutenant at Leavenworth when the war began. On 14 October the general went to see Stanton, perhaps to get an update on job prospects. The secretary said that he was anxious to give Hunter a command, and he recognized that the general had been at a disadvantage in South Carolina because of Du Pont's reluctance to give the support requested by the army. Hunter took the opportunity of proposing yet another grand scheme in which he could lead the force to end the war. He suggested the enlistment of one hundred thousand men for six weeks or two months, "just to go on a little picknic [sic], landing on the James River, ten miles above City Point . . . , and marching directly on Richmond." Hunter thought that Richmond would soon fall and that the Army of the Potomac could replace his temporary army. There is no evidence that anyone took this suggestion seriously.[11]

EVALUATING GENERAL GRANT

From the summer of 1863 Hunter had no military duties significant enough to be recorded. Developing events in Tennessee, however, were to give him an eventual opportunity for another military command. Maj. Gen. William S. Rosecrans, commanding the Army of the Cumberland, was settled down at Murfreesboro, Tennessee, opposed by Gen. Braxton Bragg's Army of Tennessee.

Both armies had been relatively inactive for six months when Rosecrans began an advance on Chattanooga. That city was important because it sat astride one of the South's primary railroad lines connecting the East with the West. In Union hands it would open a way for campaigns against Georgia and Atlanta. During the important Chickamauga campaign, lasting to late September, Rosecrans and several of his commanders performed poorly. The inevitable investigation of this near disaster was to occupy Hunter at the turn of the year, but in the fall he had another duty, evaluating the man whom Lincoln had chosen to solve military problems west of the Allegheny Mountains.

Rosecrans having accepted a static defensive position at the end of a difficult supply line, it was time to look for new organization and leadership. The first change was combining all armies (except General Banks's on the Red River) west of the Alleghenies into a unified western command, the Military Division of the Mississippi. Selected by Lincoln to head it was U. S. Grant, who had completed his successful Vicksburg campaign. Grant, temporarily disabled since August by a serious accident, was ordered in mid-October to take command of the new organization. Stanton, who had never before met Grant, personally delivered him his orders at Louisville. That the secretary of war should go to such lengths indicates that he was unsure about the general and wished to make his own evaluation. It apparently was this concern, which may have been shared by Lincoln and Halleck, which caused Stanton to order Hunter to Grant's headquarters and to report his impressions of the new command—and its new commander.

Hunter, accompanied by Stockton, reached Louisville in early November, probably via Cincinnati and St. Louis. He seems also to have had some inspection responsibilities for hospital facilities in the West. At the Kentucky city he visited twenty hospitals, all of them supervised by Surgeon Charles Squire Wood, an old friend. Dr. Wood was staying with his family at the Galt House hotel, and Hunter wrote that he was comfortable to be near such close acquaintances. Hunter was disappointed that he could not get the War Department to recommission Halpine and allow the New Yorker to join him, and so he and Stockton went on without the former adjutant to Grant's Chattanooga headquarters.[12]

Grant had replaced Rosecrans with Maj. Gen. George Thomas, who was credited with saving the army at Chickamauga, and had gone himself to the critical city to oversee an attack on Bragg. Within a few days of Hunter's arrival at Chattanooga, in mid-November, Grant ordered the beginning of a battle that lasted three days. Grant, benefiting from unexpected accomplishments by troops under Thomas, thoroughly routed Bragg at Lookout Mountain–Missionary Ridge. Hunter explained to Stanton why he thought he had "a first-rate opportunity of judging the man." He said he was received warmly by Grant: "He gave me his bed, shared with me his room, gave me to ride his favorite war horse [Jack], read to me his dispatches received and sent, accompanied me on my reviews, and I accompanied him on all his occasions and during the three days of the battle. In fact, I saw him almost every moment, except when sleeping, of the three weeks I spent in Chattanooga."[13]

Hunter gave Stanton a long analysis of Grant, apologizing that his remarks "may appear trite and uncalled for, but having been ordered to inspect his command, I thought it not improper to add my testimony with regard to the commander." He added that he was convinced that, had Grant not been appointed and Rosecrans relieved, "we should have been driven from the Valley of the Tennessee, if not from the whole region." Hunter said of Grant:

> He is a hard worker, writes his own dispatches and orders, and does his own thinking. He is modest, quiet, never swears, and seldom drinks, as he only took two drinks during the three weeks I was with him. He listens quietly to the opinions of others and then judges promptly for himself; and he is very prompt to avail himself in the field of all the errors of his enemy. He is certainly a good judge of men, and has called around him valuable counselors.[14]

Hunter used the occasion of his report to add another request to make a long march through the center of the Confederacy. This time he was more specific than earlier:

> There is now crowded into the States of Alabama and Georgia near two millions of negroes, furnishing four hundred thousand fighting men, all ready, willing, and anxious to be drafted, and making much better soldiers than most of the men who require [bounties of] $600 and $700 to induce them to volunteer. Twenty thousand, fifteen thousand, or even ten thousand men, marched rapidly into these States, without baggage, without artillery, subsisting on the country, carrying arms and ammunition for the negroes, and officers enough for one hundred regiments, could go without serious opposition directly from Vicksburg to Charleston. "The Southern Heart" could thus be beautifully fired and in a very short time consumed.

He continued with his opinion that serious opposition would not be faced and that a general rebellion of the blacks would result. As for food, he planned to live on the corn found along the way. Further, he thought that, because blacks "would know every path, . . . we should be able to march just as well in the night as in the day." He did not mention again his proposal to torch the South.[15]

General Hunter ended this fanciful plea with a request that Stanton telegraph him at Louisville and give him the authority to proceed in charge of the expedition. Nothing came of it, of course, and it is difficult to imagine that Hunter, a military man, thought the suggested expedition possible, but he later repeated the request to launch it. An explanation may be that he was desperately seeking new employment in the war, in an active role commanding troops.

CHATTANOOGA INVESTIGATION

At the time he wrote his report to Stanton, Hunter was staying at the Galt House in Louisville, the city on the supply line to Chattanooga. Hunter was in the Kentucky city for several weeks, possibly awaiting orders to proceed with the hospital investigations at Knoxville and Memphis, or he may have had advanced notice of a new mission planned for him. He was anxious to return to Washington, where Mrs. Hunter and Mrs. Steuart were settled in the I Street house, because, he wrote, "We are expecting an addition to our family in the shape of another grand-child," a reference to Maria Steuart's pregnancy, a result of having visited her husband behind rebel lines. On 9 January General Hunter was detailed as president of a board of inquiry to look into the conduct of three generals at Chickamauga on 19 and 20 September. The officers were Maj. Gen. Alexander McDowell McCook, commanding the Twentieth Army Corps; Maj. Gen. Thomas Leonidas Crittenden, Twenty-first Corps; and Maj. Gen. James Scott Negley, Second Division, Fourteenth Corps. Hunter was not a completely uninterested party in the matter under investigation because he had run into Crittenden at Louisville on 8 November. Hunter recalled that the general had told him that he was relieved only because of the machinations of Charles A. Dana, the assistant secretary of war, a claim Hunter appeared to believe. Hunter obviously did not think this discussion disqualified him from presiding. All three generals were accused of causing the near disaster to Rosecrans's army by retreating contrary to or despite orders; allegations of cowardice and desertion were also made. After its organizing session at Louisville on 23 January, Hunter moved the trial to the Saint Cloud Hotel in Nashville, probably to be nearer to witnesses. The three cases were heard simultaneously to save time. Evidence on each officer's conduct was presented separately; some days evidence on all three was heard and, on others, that on one or two. Verdicts were returned on 23 February; Hunter and his court found insufficient grounds for further proceedings. The decision on McCook reads, "The evidence shows that General McCook did his whole duty faithfully on that day, with activity and intelligence." Likewise, Crittenden and Negley were excused from any responsibility "for the disaster" at Chickamauga. Despite the decision, however, none of the three were again given a command in the war. Negley attributed the inquiry to discrimination by West Pointers against civilian volunteer officers like himself and Crittenden. (McCook was a military academy graduate.)[16]

As the inquiry drew to an end, Hunter tried again to interest Stanton in a military expedition to cut the South in two from west to east. In late January he tried a different approach, pointing out that the government's policy had been "inequality to the negro." He said the black man had been chased from army camps, underpaid when given work, and sometimes delivered over to the rebels. It was time for a different policy that could produce "five or six hundred thousand well drilled men for the war." To sweeten the arrangements Hunter proposed distribution to the former slaves of lands they had worked in the South. Hunter may have added this as an offset to the forced service by black men which he favored, rather than a way to spur voluntary enlistments, which he had found unpopular in South Carolina. Hunter did not restrict his campaign to the expedition but, in early February, also requested that Stanton give him an army corps in the Army of the Potomac.[17]

General Hunter returned to Washington from Kentucky at the end of February or the beginning of March 1864. He went to see Secretary Stanton at once to find out the status of his 9 February telegraphed request to command an army corps in the Army of the Potomac. Hunter clearly thought his opportunities for new responsibilities were increased by Grant's promotion to lieutenant general and overall commander of all army forces, but he was not encouraged by Stanton. The secretary told him that Army of the Potomac commanding general George Meade objected to any suggestions about whom should have a corps and that Meade favored "his own particular set," from which Hunter was excluded. Stanton thought Hunter should see Lincoln and tell the president why a reorganization of the army was necessary. Finally, Hunter thought Meade's army "was as much under the command of McClellan as it ever had been and that it was only being used to bring about his election to the Presidency." The secretary of war could only offer Hunter command of the Baltimore district, but the general did not think that position promised the active service he sought.[18]

Hunter did see Lincoln—telling him also of his suspicions concerning McClellan—but the president made him no offers. He saw Stanton again a few days later and was offered command of the army on the Pacific coast, following a request for Hunter by California senator John Conness. The secretary said the offered command was an important responsibility because of the nation's then poor relations with France, which was active in Mexico—although how this was so is obscure. Hunter said, "I most respectfully begged to be excused"; he did not wish for a remote assignment that would keep him from the coming campaign in the East and the decisive theater of the war, Virginia.[19]

Hunter's status in the capital was such that he was invited by Lincoln with other generals to a White House dinner on 12 March. Grant was also asked. Indeed the event might have been to introduce the new commander to eastern army officers and administration officials. Grant knew few of them, apart from those with Mexican War experience, but he certainly had warm recent relations with Hunter. Grant, however, was not at the function because he had left for the West to turn over responsibility in that theater of war to Sherman, but Hunter spoke well of him, saying Grant was "a cool man: industrious, discreet, and enterprising." Stanton repeated the request that Hunter take the California assignment, but the general once again declined, and the two discussed who would get the Army of the Potomac corps, for which no one was yet named. Stanton told him that he had never had a chance to show what he could do with an army, and Hunter may have presumed his time would come, for he told Halpine to "keep yourself clear for action." Hunter wrote, "I am an old man, but I can tell you what [that] if they give me a command I intend to make it fly." He also reassured Halpine, who must have thought he was forgotten, with these warm words: "I am in wonder at your last letter. You talk of my not needing your services; you might as well talk of my not wanting my right arm, my right leg, my eyes, my tongue, or my ears. Has an extraordinary fit of modesty come over you, or are you somewhat crazed? I should judge the latter . . . but you know I have always insisted that you were flighty, and were it not for your best of wives there is no knowing what would become of you." Hunter was also concerned about Mrs. Halpine's health, and he reported to Halpine that his own household was upset because the expecting Mrs. Steuart was "quite ill, and I begin to fear she will never recover."[20]

Grant made many changes in the army's organization and command of its major units in the field. In early April he considered sending Hunter, who was then in Washington awaiting orders, to command at Memphis, but Halleck was opposed to the assignment. He told Grant that Hunter was unlikely to accept a post under Maj. Gen. James B. McPherson, commanding the Army of the Tennessee, who was junior to Hunter. If Hunter were to accept, Halleck thought "trouble would follow." Halleck, now in the newly created position of chief of staff under Grant, said that Hunter "is even worse than [Maj. Gen. John Alexander] McClernard in creating difficulties." Halleck was not entirely against Hunter in the suggested job, providing Grant kept him under his immediate command. He thought, however, that "before acting on General Hunter's case, it would be well for you to see his correspondence while in command of a department." Halleck was referring to the quarrel with Foster and Naglee and possibly the constant calls for reinforcement. Grant did not put Hunter's name forward for the post at Memphis, but he soon found another use for the unemployed general.[21]

RED RIVER INVESTIGATION

An unsolved matter that concerned Grant was the Red River campaign, which he had opposed at its onset and now had the authority to terminate, putting Banks's troops to better use in Alabama. Supported by gunboats and supply vessels, Banks had advanced well upriver but was ordered on 15 March to end the operation unless Shreveport could be taken in a month. At the end of that period Banks had withdrawn from the attack and was at Alexandria. Hunter was Grant's choice to replace Banks, who had been accused of certain improprieties, but it is said that Lincoln opposed the appointment or perhaps just its timing. Grant, who obviously admired Hunter's ability to observe military and other conditions in the field, decided to send the general to evaluate Banks's command, and he called Hunter to army field headquarters at Culpepper, Virginia, for instructions. Hunter's 17 April orders did not give the whole picture of his authority. They said simply that he "will proceed with dispatches and instructions from lieutenant-general commanding to Maj. Gen. N. P. Banks, . . . at New Orleans, or wherever it may be necessary to enable him to deliver the dispatches to General Banks in person. Upon delivery of his dispatches and the execution of his orders he will report in person to these headquarters." "Instructions" and "orders" were spelled out in Grant's letter the same day, directing Hunter to make it clear to Banks that he was to attack Mobile, Alabama, even if this meant abandoning all military posts in Texas except along the Rio Grande. He encouraged Hunter to see that Banks enlisted and employed more black troops. Hunter was told to stay with Banks until he left New Orleans, where Grant thought Hunter would find him, and arrived at a base from which he could assault Mobile. Finally, he told Hunter, "Write to me fully how you find matters immediately on your first interview with General Banks." At the same time, Grant told Banks that he was sending Hunter to help him, saying, "[he is] an officer of rank and experience."[22]

It took Hunter eight and a half days from Washington to reach Banks via Cairo, Illinois, and the Mississippi. He found the general still at Alexandria facing a serious problem that prevented his movement back to New Orleans. Water on the Red River was falling, and the navy's vessels were consequently stranded at the falls above Alexandria, with little hope of getting them farther downriver.

Hunter wired Grant on 28 April that he found the situation "complicated, perplexing, and precarious." It was his view that there was "no possibility" of getting the ships out. "My opinion is . . . to destroy the boats." He added his sense of frustration: "Why this expedition was ordered I cannot imagine. General Banks assures me it was undertaken against his opinion and earnest protest," as indeed it was. Within a few days it was obvious that the orders to Mobile could not be executed, so they were suspended. Banks and Hunter consulted on 29 April with Lt. Col. Joseph Bailey, attached as an engineer to the Nineteenth Army Corps. He briefed the generals about artificially raising the level of the Red River by temporary dams so that the navy's squadron could pass the shoals. Bailey said Hunter "remarked that although he had little confidence in its feasibility, he nevertheless thought it better to try the experiment." As it was, through hard work and Bailey's genius the operation was successful, the vessels passing Alexandria in mid-May.[23]

Hunter did not remain at Alexandria until Banks and the navy reached the Mississippi but traveled to New Orleans, instead, on 30 April, from which he sent Grant a more complete report on 2 May. He found Banks polite and kind but thought he should be replaced because he "has not certainly the confidence of his army." Hunter found the department to be "one great mass of corruption. Cotton and politics, instead of war, seem to have engrossed the army. The vital interests of the contest are set aside, and we are amused with sham State governments, which are a complete laughing-stock to the people, and the lives of our men are being sacrificed in the interests of cotton speculators." He recommended General McPherson for the command, concluding that "unless prompt action is taken immediately, we shall lose control of the Mississippi." Grant's reaction was to recommend that Hunter replace Banks. Although Banks was relieved, no action was taken to put Hunter in his place, because the department was broken up and many of its troops reassigned to other places.[24]

COMMAND IN THE VALLEY

While Hunter was thus engaged, other elements of Grant's grand strategy were developing a new opportunity for him. The new lieutenant general brought to the management of the Union army an ability to see clearly what had to be done to win the war. None of his predecessors showed such vision, and Lincoln to his own credit risked giving Grant full authority along with the responsibility. Grant's plan was to concentrate every resource against the two main armies opposing the North, Lee's in Virginia and Joseph E. Johnston's (Bragg's old command) in Georgia. Sherman was charged with the latter, and Grant made his headquarters near Meade's Army of the Potomac, which was responsible for pressing Lee. All Northern armies were to advance simultaneously in a coordinated movement at the beginning of May. Grant had a supplemental expedition planned for the Virginia theater of war. He ordered Maj. Gen. Franz Sigel, commanding the Department of West Virginia after Frémont's departure, to advance up the Shenandoah Valley to Staunton, gathering supplies that would have otherwise supported Lee. Staunton was an important center of communications between Lee's army and the riches of the valley essential to the Confederate war effort. The town of about four thousand people was on the Virginia Central Railroad, which ran from Richmond, through Gordonsville and Charlottesville, crossed the Blue Ridge Mountains at Rockfish Gap, and passed through Waynesboro before reaching Staunton. A branch of the Virginia Central continued on to Covington. Staunton also had some limited industry—a boot and shoe factory and a woolen mill—and was a military supply center for the upper valley.[25]

Sigel's military accomplishments from the days he was subordinate to Frémont and Hunter in Missouri were few, but his failures were many. He had been on leave for over a year when, in March 1864, he was assigned to command the department that included all of West Virginia, the Shenandoah Valley, and Maryland west of the Monocacy River. This was a significant command because it was responsible for protecting the vital east-west rail link running from Baltimore through Harper's Ferry and across West Virginia. This war theater, however, had recently been inactive. Sigel, a native of Baden, Germany, was an important politician whose appointment was specifically designed to appease large German populations in St. Louis, New York, and other places. That Sigel was only marginally qualified for a potentially important field command was not the overriding consideration.

As Sigel understood his mission, it was to move up the valley to distract Confederate attention from other operations well south in Virginia and West Virginia which were aimed at the destruction of the Virginia and Tennessee Railroad. He knew that about three thousand rebel troops could be expected to oppose the Union advance, which he began from Cedar Creek in early May. Commanding rebel forces was Maj. Gen. John C. Breckinridge, a former vice president under Buchanan and former U.S. senator, who drew forces from the upper valley to oppose Sigel, as he was expected to do. The two armies met at New Market on 15 May, each then able to deploy about five thousand men. In a battle lasting most of the day a Union attack on the deployed rebels was repulsed, and a Confederate charge broke the Union line, forcing Sigel to retreat with dispatch thirty-two miles north to Cedar Creek, near Strasburg. The center of the Confederate line for the defense and charge against the federal force was occupied by the corps of cadets of the Virginia Military Institute which had marched to the battle from the school's Lexington campus. The gallantry of the youthful cadets and their important contribution to Breckinridge's victory was to affect the future of VMI in three weeks' time, when the Yankee army reached Lexington under a new commander.[26]

The battle was tactically a small affair, but, had it gone the other way, the progress of the war in the East might have been altered significantly. Breckinridge's victory allowed most of the valley's wheat harvest to be gathered for Lee's use; it meant that Lee, heavily engaged against Grant, was not forced to draw off troops he could not spare, and it allowed the two Confederate brigades in the valley to join Lee in time for the next grinding battle at Cold Harbor. Brig. Gen. John D. Imboden, Breckinridge's second in command, wrote that, if Sigel had been victorious, Richmond would have been exposed to "immediate, and almost inevitable capture." He concluded that "there was no secondary battle of the war of more importance than that of New Market."[27]

Grant recognized how vital it was for Sigel to reach Staunton, and, not knowing of the battle on 15 May, urged him on. Halleck informed Grant, however, on 17 May that Sigel, instead of advancing on Staunton, was "in full retreat on Strasburg." As for Sigel, Halleck's patience was exhausted. He said: "If you expect anything from him you will be mistaken. He will do nothing but run. He never did anything else. The Secretary of War proposes to put General Hunter in his place." Grant, equally frustrated by the German's performance, replied, "By all means I would say appoint General Hunter, or anyone else, to the command in West Virginia." So Hunter was named, and he left Washington, along with "his horses" and accompanied by Halpine, who had been restored to his old rank of lieutenant colonel, and Lieutenant Stockton, aboard a special train on the Baltimore and Ohio Railroad. While in New York, Halpine had been writing for several newspapers and popularizing a character, "Private Miles O'Reilly," who in dialect told of army life with a political bent. Stockton, had been called from duty with another general and sent to join Hunter. The party arrived at Martinsburg via Harper's Ferry on 20 May. The following evening they were at Cedar Creek, just above Strasburg, after covering thirty-eight miles on horseback.[28]

Hunter had left behind in Washington what might have been a difficult domestic problem for him given his unforgiving nature. General Steuart was captured at Spotsylvania by the Army of the Potomac on 10 May 1864, and notice of his confinement at Fort Delaware near Wilmington must have taken some days to reach his wife at Hunter's house. Just two days after Hunter left for the valley "Mrs. Gen'l Stewart [*sic*]" took the oath of allegiance to the Union and requested permission to see her husband at Fort Delaware. Presumably, she was able to visit him shortly thereafter and possibly other times until his exchange in

November. How Hunter dealt with this perplexing matter when he returned to the capital in late September is not known. One imagines that his fondness for his almost-adopted daughter allowed him to continue to accept Maria Steuart's divided loyalties over the next few months, and she would remain resident with her daughters in the Hunter home until after the war.[29]

TAKING COMMAND

Sigel was on an inspection when Hunter reached Cedar Creek, but the new general was welcomed by the department chief of staff, Col. David Hunter Strother. Strother, the general's distant relative, was a native of the lower Shenandoah. His mother was a cousin of David Hunter and the general's sister—whom Strother called "Jersey Mary." The colonel's second wife was Mary Eliot Hunter of Martinsburg, a daughter of the David Hunter who was in the general's class at West Point. Strother was happy to see Hunter, not because of their complicated kinship, but because he was anxious to get rid of his old commander. He wrote in relation to New Market, "We can afford to lose such a battle to get rid of such a mistake as Major General Sigel." The two relatives met at the Hite house in which Sigel had his headquarters. "By this time I had recognized my kinsman, Major General David Hunter, and walked down the steps to meet him. He received me cordially and immediately took me aside to a secluded spot where he said, 'I have come to relieve General Sigel. You know it is customary with a general who has been unfortunate to relieve him whether he has committed a fault or not.' He then asked me to remain with him and to talk to him like a man and a kinsman and give him my views freely." The colonel briefed Hunter on the New Market battle and advised "an immediate move up the Valley to Staunton, there to meet [Brig. Gen. George] Crook and [Brig. Gen. William W.] Averell, with the combined force to occupy Charlottesville." Strother, who a year earlier did not have a good opinion of Hunter, was kept on as chief of staff and soon developed respect for his cousin's leadership, just as Hunter was impressed with the colonel's knowledge of the valley and ability to analyze tactical and strategic situations correctly.[30]

Sigel returned and was relieved at 7:00 p.m. The two generals had what Sigel described as a "friendly conversation." Hunter, Sigel said, "expressed his desire that I should remain in the department and accept either the command of the Infantry Division or of the Reserve Division, comprising all the troops at Harper's Ferry and the lines of the Baltimore and Ohio." As Hunter described the meeting, Sigel, "actuated by an earnest patriotism, was anxious to take a division of this army or to attend to any other duties." The next day Sigel accepted the second option and left for his headquarters at Martinsburg. It seems unlikely that

Hunter's offer was based on his own opinion of Sigel's worth as a general, as he had seen it demonstrated in Missouri. It was suggested that Sigel's political power in that election year was such that Lincoln and Stanton thought it necessary to keep him on duty rather than consigning him to the "awaiting orders" status customary for failed generals.[31]

Hunter did not have instructions for his operations when he left Washington. Halleck telegraphed Grant for this information, "I do not know what your orders to Sigel and Crook have been, but I presume they have looked mainly to the destruction of the rebel railroads and the protection of the Baltimore and Ohio Railroad." Grant answered immediately, explaining that he had more in mind for the West Virginia department's forces. Sigel was still under orders to move up the valley, with an emphasis on Staunton, for he said that the enemy was "relying for supplies greatly on such as are brought over the branch road" running east through the village. Crook, then at Gauley in the Kanawha Valley in West Virginia, was instructed to cut the Virginia and Tennessee Railroad and to continue east to Lynchburg. Alternatively, he might march to Fincastle in the Shenandoah Valley and then to Staunton. Halleck telegraphed his understanding of these orders to Hunter at 11:30 a.m. on 21 May, so they were at Hunter's headquarters when he arrived. He was given further orders to go beyond Staunton and proceed to Gordonsville or Charlottesville to meet the Army of the Potomac. After his retreat from New Market, Sigel had anticipated the next moves for the army. He directed Crook and his three thousand men to join him at Staunton, which he planned to move to once he had assembled more troops. Hunter improved on this instruction by ordering General Averell and his cavalry division, which had joined with Crook on 19 May, likewise to move on Staunton. He telegraphed the adjutant general at 9:30 p.m. of the day he took command that he was prepared to move east to join Grant after the linkup with his troops from the south at Staunton.[32]

Hunter's first days at Cedar Creek were busy indeed. He issued a flood of requests to Washington and orders to his department. His principal concern the day of his arrival was the poor state of the generals in the command, particularly the infantry division commander, Brig. Gen. Jeremiah C. Sullivan, who had little experience, and Maj. Gen. Julius Stahl, a Hungarian with a colorful past, commander of the cavalry. Perhaps it was because Hunter thought these officers a Sigel legacy that he wished to do without them; he wired Adjutant General Thomas: "If you can send me two energetic and efficient brigadiers it will add greatly to the availability of this command." In a letter to Halleck the next day Hunter elaborated on the problem and the possible solution. With respect to the cavalry, Hunter said it was "utterly demoralized from frequent defeat by inferior forces and retreats without fighting, and it most urgently needs a commander of grit, zeal, activity, and courage." As for the cavalry officer he had inherited, "It would be impossible to exaggerate the inefficiency of General Stahel." But Hunter's evidence of this appears flimsy, based solely on a request Stahel had made for infantry support that Halpine said was "to cover zi right flanke of his Cavalrie division" two hours before Hunter made the evaluation of his subordinate. To the adjutant general he wrote, "General Stahel . . . has but little experience as a cavalry officer in this country, nor am I aware that he has any experience elsewhere." Sullivan's faults beyond his lack of experience were not enumerated, and Hunter renewed the request to the adjutant general which he had wired the night before for "two additional brigadiers of experience, energy, and reliability."[33]

Hunter's staff, except for Chief of Staff Strother, Halpine, and Stockton, were inherited from Sigel and were drawn mostly from regiments in the command. Captain Kinzie, the Chicago nephew, was not assigned this time as another aide. He was then serving with his regiment, the Ninth Illinois Cavalry, in Tennessee, and was unavailable. Hunter thought that Stockton, an officer in the regular Fourth Cavalry, was "eminently fitted" for higher command. He requested that the lieutenant be appointed a brigadier general to command one of the cavalry brigades under Stahel or as Stahel's replacement. Halleck in two responses to the request for more brigadiers, said "energetic and efficient" officers of that rank were scarce, but, if Hunter could name some, "you shall have them." He also said that there were no spare brigadiers of volunteers. "You have three generals of cavalry in your department, Stahel, [Brig. Gen. Alfred N.] Duffié [a brigade commander], and Averell, certainly enough for your cavalry force. If any of them are worthless recommend them to be mustered out and I will indorse it." It meant that Stockton was not going to wear the stars of a brigadier. "No one," concluded Halleck, "can be appointed till some one else is mustered out." Consequently, Hunter had to be satisfied with the officers then assigned to lead in the coming campaign, and Stockton ended the war as a captain.[34]

Planning an advance in a few days, Hunter was busy with organization and instruction of his troops on the first full day that he was in command, 22 May. Halpine recorded that the general was "tense and bad-tempered, and remained so for days," which made the entire command anxious. It was clear that the troops were ill supplied and poorly disciplined, reasons enough for Hunter to feel pressure. His first order to the men was a call for sacrifice and a declaration that the country expected "every man to do his duty, and this done an ever kind Providence will surely grant us complete success." He ordered all tents and excess baggage sent back to Martinsburg, allowing but one wagon per regiment and its use restricted to "spare ammunition, camp kettles, tools, and mess pans." The individual soldier was told that he was limited to the clothes "on his back," plus an extra pair of socks and shoes. Each was to carry a hundred rounds of ammunition and bread, coffee, sugar, and salt to last eight days. The army was to subsist on the supplies taken from valley inhabitants, "cattle, sheep, and hogs, and if necessary horses and mules." Commanders were told to regulate strictly the conduct of their men on the march and the levies on the people—"No straggling or pillaging will be allowed."[35]

General Hunter directed Sigel in Martinsburg not to allow any civilians beyond that point on the ground that "large supplies [of] contraband of war reach the enemy through the agency of sutlers and unauthorized tradesmen." Probably for security reasons, he also ordered that no civilians were to be allowed within the command's lines, and those within them were not to be permitted to leave. As for discipline, Hunter made a number of examples. He dishonorably discharged a cavalry captain whose outpost was surprised and captured by a rebel party and placed a major under arrest for having similarly lost some of his men. A lieutenant from West Virginia, accused by his commanders of desertion at the New Market battle, was likewise "disgracefully dismissed from the military service of the United States." While these orders and punishments may have had some effect on the command, more important was the need to control random attacks on Union troops by rebel troops and irregulars.[36]

ANTIGUERRILLA MEASURES

Sigel had been plagued by such attacks on his supply trains since he began his advance almost a month earlier but had not satisfactorily countered them, except by providing large armed escorts. On 23 May Hunter's patience was tested when some unknown assailants fired on a wagon train passing through Newtown (now Stephens City) and wounded a sergeant. The next day he reacted strongly, as was his style, ordering a cavalry officer to proceed to the village and find the "house from which our train was fired upon last night, and *burn* the same with all its out-buildings, pertaining thereto." Hunter did not distinguish regularly enlisted partisan rangers—such as those commanded by Lt. Col. John S. Mosby and Maj. John H. McNeill—from lawless bushwackers and guerrillas but proposed, rather, to treat all of them as outlaws. Seen as romantic and dashing figures today, Halpine thought guerrillas were "about the filthiest, drunkennest, meanest, most ill-looking, ragged, mutinous, diseased, undisciplined, lousy, and utterly cowardly gang of horse and chicken-thieves, highway robbers, grand and petty larcenists, that the Lord . . . ever permitted to disgrace the noble calling of the soldier." It was a view shared with his general.[37]

The chief of artillery, Capt. Henry A. Du Pont, wrote that his commander "had reached the absolutely untenable conclusion that Mosby's command [the Forty-third Virginia Cavalry] was composed of the men of military age who lived in towns and villages along the Valley turnpike, although as a matter of fact there were very few of Mosby's men who were residents of those places." Whether Mosby's men were locals or not, Hunter ordered that "the inhabitants of the town and along the pike [be notified that,] if our trains or escorts are fired upon in that way again, that the commanding general will cause to be burned every rebel house within five miles of the place at which the firing occurs." Information about what a Baltimore newspaper called "a vigorous and wise policy with respect to guerillias [sic] and bushwackers" was further disseminated in a circular sent to about "30 of the prominent Secessionists resident in the Valley." The notice accused the rebel sympathizers of countenancing and abetting the bands that "infest the woods and mountains of this region." Since Hunter believed that their activities were not recognized by the rules of war, he warned the local people that "for every train fired upon, or soldier of the Union wounded or assassinated in any neighborhood in reach of my cavalry, the houses and other property of every Secession sympathizer residing within a circuit of five miles from the place of outrage shall be destroyed by fire." In addition, a fine of five times the value of public property destroyed or taken away was to be levied within a ten-mile circle, and the persons assessed were to be imprisoned until payment was made. Finally, when property of a loyal citizen was destroyed, the five-times-the-value levy would be applied.[38]

Colonel Strother, as chief of staff, was often called on to mediate questions about how Hunter's directives were to be applied. On 24 May, for example, he was sent toward Newtown to meet with some citizens of the hamlet who asked for an interview with the general. Meeting them at Middletown on the way north, Strother described to them Hunter's directive and told the men that they were bound to report guerrillas and their supporters if they wished to avoid the punishment the orders promised. Among other things the Newtown delegation told Strother that a Mrs. Wilson in their village allowed her house to be used as a rendezvous by guerrillas. He told Hunter about this when he got back to headquarters, and the general ordered the woman arrested for "feeding and harboring guerrillas." Mrs. Wilson's furniture and possessions were burned—but not her rented house—and she was marched six miles to the provost marshal. Hunter intended to deport her to Confederate lines, a punishment he later used more widely.[39]

Although houses of what Colonel Strother called "three Secessionists" were burned in Newtown, operations by Mosby in particular were not hampered, and the rebel was frequently reported to be threatening Hunter's lines of communication. On 30 May Newtown was the scene of another attack on Hunter's supply trains, Mosby burning twelve of fourteen wagons. Hunter immediately issued an order sending two hundred cavalrymen to the village "for the purpose of burning every house, store, and out-buildings in that place, except the church and the houses and out-buildings of those known to be loyal citizens of the United States." To this he added, "You will also burn the houses, &c., of all rebels between Newtown and Middletown," the latter town a few miles south of Newtown. When the patrol, commanded by Maj. Joseph K. Stearns of the First New York (Lincoln) Cavalry, arrived at Newtown the following day, townspeople—mostly women, children, old citizens, and perhaps some disabled former Confederate soldiers—begged him not to follow his orders. They argued, not in every case accurately, that their absent military-age males were not in Mosby's command but in distant rebel regiments. Further, they said, they had taken care of Union soldiers wounded in the raid. "Finally," Du Pont reported, "Stearns, who was a man of good sense and humanity, decided to spare the town notwithstanding his instructions and, upon rejoining his regiment at Strasburg on the third of June, personally reported the facts to General Hunter who, despite his wrath, evidently found that he had gone too far and let the whole matter drop." In another incident an officer sent off to burn a suspected bushwacker's house returned to say the wife was poor, had three children, had no place to go, and thus he had not followed his orders. Hunter reprimanded the officer but in the end "laughed and excused him." Such compassion did not prevent the burning of the house of a Strasburg farmer named Boyden "by Colonel [George W.] Wells [Thirty-fourth Connecticut Infantry] because it was said to be a rendezvous for bushwackers and hard by Fisher's Hill where five men of ours were recently murdered," Strother reported. The colonel also said he was sent by Hunter into Woodstock on 23 May "to ascertain who the parties were that attempted to confuse our scouts . . . as he wished to burn a few houses," but he does not mention if any were burned. These were apparently not the only reprisals as Hunter prepared to leave Cedar Creek and during the first few days after the army started up the valley, some of them for more distant offenses against the Union forces; for example, Lt. John R. Meigs found and burned the buildings of a man said to have assisted "in killing and capturing stragglers during Sigel's retreat." While these actions might be seen as vengeance by a short-tempered general, dealing with the serious military problem of guerrillas harassing communications called for strict measures. It can be argued that the ones Hunter chose were more severe than proper or justified, and he was to be criticized for the rest of his days, and after, for his harshness. The measures, however, did not restrict Mosby's later successes.[40]

MOVING SOUTH

The expedition got under way at 10:30 a.m. on 26 May; the command, now called the Army of the Shenandoah, had about eight-five hundred men of all arms. Hunter's orders were to move toward Charlottesville and Lynchburg, "living on the country," destroying canals and railroads that supported Lee's supply system. He was then to return down the valley or join Grant on the advance to Richmond. Leading units reached Woodstock, about fifteen miles from Cedar Creek, on the twenty-seventh, Confederate forces falling back without fighting. Hunter's headquarters was set up at the house of Isaac Painter at Pew Run, two miles north of Woodstock. At once difficulties arose about the conduct of Union troops as they encountered civilians. General Stahel, whose cavalry troops were the foragers for the army, was cautioned to leave certificates for all provisions taken, the debt to be repaid at some future date—but only to loyal citizens. He was also told to "allow no plundering or oppression of the inhabitants," doubtless after some incidents had been reported. Just a few days later Stahel was again cautioned about controlling "unauthorized pillaging," Halpine telling him that "men sent out on regular foraging parties break away from their officers and straggle into houses, carrying off dresses, ornaments, books, money, and doing wanton injury to furniture." "These practices are dangerous to the command," because, in a country "infested with guerrilla parties," wounded and sick soldiers might have to depend on the charity and kindness of the local population. The point was brought home to Hunter personally. Strother wrote on 29 May that, "passing through the town of Woodstock, the General halted and had the jail searched but found no one in it. He was evidently seeking an apology to burn something and proposed to set fire to the Hollinsworth Hotel, but I told him our wounded had lain there and had been well cared for while the place was occupied by the enemy."[41]

After three days in the Woodstock camp—the delay caused by a wait for a wagon train with supplies, especially shoes—the army set out once again, beginning the march at sunrise on 29 May. Each soldier was issued four days' rations, the food intended to last eight days and to be supplemented by requisitions on the population. Scouts reported that the enemy, commanded by Brig. Gen. John D. Imboden since Breckinridge's departure after New Market, appeared to be falling back on Harrisonburg. The Confederate force numbered only a thousand men, and it was obvious that it was insufficient to protect the valley from Hunter's advance. General Lee had no troops to spare from his Army of Northern Virginia, then heavily engaged against Grant's relentless advance, but he told Imboden to call out all reserves and for assistance from Brig. Gen. William E. Jones, who was commanding rebel forces—about three thousand troops—beyond Lynchburg in southwest Virginia and eastern Tennessee. With these hastily gathered forces he hoped to meet Hunter before the advancing Union army was joined by Generals Crook and Averell.[42]

Hunter's ire was raised again on 30 May, when the army reached the New Market battlefield and he saw a number of poorly buried Union soldiers. Halpine thought that the scene caused the general to be even less sensitive than he had been toward protecting civilians, but there is no evidence that this is so. Halpine argued that insensitivity became less important as the column moved south because fewer Unionists were being encountered, but, in fact, the lower valley was heavily populated by secessionists, while the southern counties often shared the pro-Union sentiments that had led to the formation of West Virginia. The problem of the sick countered whatever harsher retribution Hunter might have been inclined to order. Since wagon trains remained an unreliable link with Sigel and the North and because of the limited number of ambulances and wagons with the army, Hunter ordered that those unable to travel would not be evacuated and would not accompany their comrades on the march. The decision was announced in words designed to soften fears men had about being abandoned in the enemy's country. Conditions, the order read, "will render it necessary for the comfort and recovery of those who may fall too sick to be able to march, that they shall be left behind in care of the local inhabitants along the road." That these potential Good Samaritans were not all Unionists but were all uniformly subject to foraging parties supplying the army did not create many willing volunteers to provide unpaid care. Nor for that matter did another Hunter policy promise to improve the reception that abandoned sick and wounded would receive. He issued an order eliminating provision of receipts for requisitioned property. Exceptions were "those well-known and openly loyal men, and then only on the express approval of the general commanding, under his own signature." Presumably, no further receipts were given for the rest of the campaign.[43]

Cavalry scouts brought into New Market six prisoners who were had been carrying old flintlock hunting pieces when they were taken. General Hunter characteristically wanted to hang the men forthwith, but one of the general's aides, Stockton, troubled by this, asked Strother to intervene. The colonel questioned the captives and found that they were conscripted home guards, all of them over forty-five years of age, who had been sent to their homes to enlist their neighbors. He determined that the men, reaching home, had done little more that look after their farms and families and had taken no part in actions against the Union army. Strother's recommendation to Hunter was that the prisoners be given a loyalty oath and released. The general approved this, showing once again that, though he almost always called for severe, even excessive, immediate action against the nation's enemies, he sometimes could be swayed by the opinions of trusted staff members.[44]

The column remained at New Market for several days, the headquarters in the Reverend Addison Weber's home north of the battlefield where Sigel had been defeated two weeks before. The army did not continue south at once, possibly because it was now encumbered with wounded from the 15 May engagement who were now back in Union hands and needing care. Furthermore, not all of Hunter's staff thought there that should be any rush to advance to Staunton, Captain Du Pont, a regular officer, recommending further reconnaissance. Therefore, time was spent reburying the dead, scouting in all directions, receiving many refugees (mostly women and children), burning a gun stock factory, and building fires over the carcasses of the many dead horses that were encountered since Woodstock. Halpine found the "smell of roasted horseflesh very sickening," and Strother suggested that the odor be called "Bouquet de Chevals morgue." General Hunter was growing anxious, and Halpine said that he was "not in the most amiable humor." The adjutant did not record whether this mood was due to guerrilla activity, ill discipline in the Union ranks, or the delay in reaching Staunton, the first objective.[45]

The march continued from New Market on 2 June, only occasional rebel pickets being encountered. Late that afternoon Imboden was driven through the village of Harrisonburg "with some loss" by Hunter's cavalry. After a march of twenty-two miles the Union army camped that evening in the hills north of Harrisonburg and received news that the enemy was preparing to fight at Mount Crawford, entrenching behind the North River. Hearing that the rebel force was being reinforced, the federal leaders may have been concerned that General Crook had not yet appeared nor been heard from.[46]

Hunter spent the next day, 3 June, at his headquarters in the Gray home planning his next move. He could have continued down the valley turnpike until he reached the Confederate defense line but, on Colonel Strother's advice, planned a more elegant attack designed to outflank the enemy and defeat him. Strother, benefiting from his detailed knowledge of the valley, recommended that the army move east by a side road to Port Republic, cross the south fork of the Shenandoah River at that point, fight the battle, and capture Waynesboro with cavalry, thereby cutting off Lee's access to Staunton's supplies. The planned advance was scheduled for early the following morning, and the army prepared for it by replenishing its supplies by levies on Harrisonburg, which, according to Strother, "caused great consternation and disgust" in the town. "It seems hard but it is necessary as the army must feed," he continued. "The soldiers are plundering dreadfully from all accounts. This is not necessary and should not be permitted."

175

But Hunter apparently did not have sufficient means to enforce his anti-looting orders. Strother saw the danger of this lack of control: "There are some wounded Union soldiers here who have been well treated by the citizens." Plundering those citizens was poor payment and did nothing to encourage further charity to the soldiers left in the wake of the army.[47]

Halpine wrote in his diary on 3 June, "It is now certain that we shall begin to fight at about 10:00 a.m. tomorrow," but his forecast was inaccurate. Crossing the river was more complicated than it seemed.[48]

NOTES

1. Letter, Hunter to Greeley, 12 June 1863, Robert C. Schenck, "Major-General David Hunter," *Magazine of American History* 27 (February 1887): 149. A *Tribune* reporter, Henry Villard, was Hunter's guest aboard the *Ben De Ford* during the 7 April attack on Charleston; his report on the battle was printed on 14 April.

2. Letter, Hunter to Halpine, Hunter MSS, Huntington Library, San Marino, Calif.; Hunter's report of New York arrival, 17 June 1863, Letters Received, Adjutant General's Office, Record Group 94, Records of the Office of the Adjutant General, National Archives (hereafter AGO Letters Received, NA). The vessel carried six hundred passengers on the sixty-hour voyage (*New York Times,* 18 June 1863); Hunter's April 1873 report, U.S. Army Generals' Reports of Civil War Service, 1864–87, RG 94, NA, 9:688. Halpine resigned his commission, the effective date backdated to 1 July, and on 1 August took the civilian job of commissary general on the staff of New York governor Horatio Seymour but soon accepted a commission as a major—a reduction in the rank he held in South Carolina—and was appointed assistant adjutant general to General Dix in New York. Stockton was again a first lieutenant, his regular army rank.

3. Letter, Hunter to Lincoln, 25 June 1863, document no. 24398, Lincoln Papers, Documents Division, Library of Congress (LOC).

4. Letter, Lincoln to Hunter, 30 June 1863, document no. 24560, Lincoln Papers, LOC; James B. Ricketts, tribute to Hunter in *Seventeenth Annual Reunion of the Graduates of the United States Military Academy at West Point,* New York, 10 June 1886 (East Saginaw, Ill.: Evening News, 1886), 77.

5. Carl Sandburg, *Abraham Lincoln: The War Years,* 4 vols. (New York: Charles Schribner's Sons, 1939), 4:441; Hay's diary, 16 July 1863, William Roscoe Taylor, *The Life and Letters of John Hay,* 2 vols. (Boston: Houghton Mifflin Co., 1908), 1:194–95. Halleck sent Meade Lincoln's criticism of the latter's actions allowing

Lee's escape but did not replace him then (telegram, Halleck to Meade, 14 July 1863, in Henry J. Hunt, "The Third Day at Gettysburg," in *Battles and Leaders of the Civil War,* ed. Robert Underwood Johnson and Clarence Clough Buel, 4 vols. [1887; reprint, New York: Castle, 1990], 3:383). Vicksburg fell to Grant on 4 July, the day after the Gettysburg victory.

6. Entries, 10 June, 12 and 13 July 1863, David Hunter Strother, *A Virginia Yankee in the Civil War: The Diaries of David Hunter Strother,* ed. Cecil D. Eby, Jr. (Chapel Hill: University of North Carolina Press, 1961), 184–85, 191–92.

7. Hunter's reports, 7, 20, and 22 August 1863, AGO Letters Received, NA; Letter, Hunter to Stanton, 31 August 1863, U.S. War Department, *The War of the Rebellion: A Compilation of the Official Records of the Union and Confederate Armies* (Washington, D.C.: Government Printing Office, 1901) [hereafter *ORA* and ser. 1, unless otherwise indicated], 3, pt. 3, 740; letter, Hunter to Halpine, 10 September 1863, Hunter MSS, Huntington Library. Hunter also visited West Point.

8. Letter, Hunter to Halpine, 10 September 1863, Hunter MSS, Huntington Library.

9. Ibid.

10. Letter, Hunter to Halpine, 16 October 1863, ibid.

11. Ibid.

12. Letter, Hunter to Halpine, 9 November 1863, ibid.

13. Ulysses Simpson Grant, "Chattanooga," in Johnson and Buel, *Battles and Leaders,* 3:679–85; letter, Hunter to Stanton, 15 December 1863, document no. 53936, Stanton Papers, LOC. Another camp visitor, Julia Grant's Pennsylvania cousin, civilian William W. Smith, thought Hunter "a great Puritan," probably because of his temperate habits, and the two men joined Grant and Dr. E. D. Kittle, the medical director, at lunch brought to the field by headquarters cooks while waiting for Thomas's advance (Bruce Catton, *Grant Takes Command* [Boston: Little, Brown and Co., 1968], 67, 80).

14. Letter, Hunter to Stanton, 14 December 1863, Stanton Papers, LOC. He wrote to Halpine about Grant in almost the same words (letter, Hunter to Halpine, 18 December 1863, Hunter MSS, Huntington Library).

15. Letter, Hunter to Stanton, 15 December 1863, document no. 53936, Stanton Papers, LOC.

16. Special Orders No. 13, 9 January, Adjutant General's Office, "Record of the McCook Court of Inquiry," "Record of the Crittenden . . . ," "Record of the Negley . . . ," *ORA,* 30, pt. 1, 930–1044. On the panel with Hunter were Maj. Gen. George Cadwalader and Brig. Gen. James S. Wadsworth (Ezra J. Warner, *Generals in Blue: Lives of the Union Commanders* [Baton Rouge: Louisiana State University Press, 1964], 342); letter, Hunter to Halpine, 9 November 1863, Hunter

MSS, Huntington Library. Rosecrans was not investigated and got another command, even though Stanton said that McCook and "Crittenden both made good time away from the fight to Chattanooga, but Rosecrans beat them both" (Taylor, *Life and Letters of John Hay,* 1:200–201). Hunter thought Rosecrans "a catholic humbug, and if he had not been relieved, we should have been driven completely out of Tennessee," letter (Hunter to Halpine, 18 December 1863, Hunter MSS, Huntington Library).

17. Letter, Hunter to Stanton, 27 January 1864, document no. 54047, Stanton Papers, LOC; telegram, Hunter to Stanton, 7 February 1864, *ORA,* 32, pt. 2, 353.

18. Letter, Hunter to Halpine, 10 March 1864, Hunter MSS, Huntington Library.

19. Ibid. Halpine was hoping Hunter would accept California because he was told he might accompany the general as a brigadier and chief of staff (William Hanchett, *Irish: Charles G. Halpine in Civil War America* [Syracuse: Syracuse University Press, 1970], 100).

20. Earl Schenck Miers, ed., *Lincoln Day by Day: A Chronology,* 3 vols. (Washington, D.C.: Lincoln Sesquicentennial Commission, 1960), 3:246; 27 March 1864, diary entry, John Hay, *Lincoln and the Civil War in the Diaries and Letters of John Hay,* ed. Tyler Dennett (1939; reprint, Westport, Conn.: Negro Universities Press, 1972), 169. Hunter also dined at Chase's house on 8 March with twenty others and had the opportunity to cut Lane dead (letters, Hunter to Halpine, 10 and 17 March 1864, Hunter MSS, Huntington Library).

21. Telegrams, Grant to Halleck, Halleck to Grant, 9 and 11 April 1864, *ORA,* 32, pt. 3, 304, 322–23. Hunter reported on 29 March that he had no staff officers assigned to him, probably a result of Grant's orders to put the maximum number of troops in the field (AGO Letters Received, NA).

22. Richard B. Irwin, "The Red River Campaign," in Johnson and Buel, *Battles and Leaders,* 4:345, 350, 358 n; telegram, Grant to Halleck, 15 April, Special Orders No. 14, Headquarters, Armies of the United States, 17 April, letter, Grant to Hunter, 17 April 1864, *ORA,* 32, pt. 3, 160, 190–91, 397; telegram, Grant to Banks, 17 April 1864, roll 20, U. S. Grant Papers, LOC. When Hunter returned to Washington from Culpepper, he carried a personal letter from Grant to Grant's wife, showing the closeness of the two generals (letter, Grant to Julia D. Grant, 17 April 1864, John Y. Simon, ed., *The Papers of Ulysses S. Grant,* 20 vols. [Carbondale: Southern Illinois University Press, 1967–95], 10: 315–16).

23. Letters, Banks and Hunter to Grant, 29 and 30 April, Bailey's report, 17 May 1864, *ORA,* 32, pt. 1, 191, 403; pt. 3, 316; Irwin, "Red River Campaign," 4:358–60.

24. Letter, Hunter to Grant, 2 May, telegram, Grant to Halleck, 16 May 1864, *ORA,* 32, pt. 3, 390, 615.

25. Ulysses Simpson Grant, *Memoirs of Ulysses S. Grant,* 2 vols. (New York: Charles L. Webster and Co., 1885), 2:124–32.

26. Franz Sigel, "Sigel in the Shenandoah Valley in 1864," in Johnson and Buel, *Battles and Leaders,* 4:487–491. Accounts of the fight are many, but the most complete is William C. Davis, *The Battle of New Market* (1975; reprint, Baton Rouge: Louisiana State University Press, 1983).

27. Davis, *Battle of New Market,* 184–85; John D. Imboden, "The Battle of New Market," in Johnson and Buel, *Battles and Leaders,* 4:485. The VMI corps of cadets suffered 10 killed and 47 wounded, of the 225 who were engaged; the losses are commemorated by the corps every year on the anniversary of the battle. New Market is the only occasion when a military school fought in the United States as a unit.

28. Telegrams, Grant to Halleck, Halleck to Grant, Grant to Halleck, 17 and 19 May, General Orders No. 200, Adjutant General's Office, 19 May, several telegrams from Washington and Harper's Ferry from army and railroad officials, 20 May, reporting Hunter's progress, General Orders No. 27 and 28, Department of West Virginia, 21 May 1864, *ORA,* 37, pt. 1, 485, 492, 502–5, 508; Grant, *Memoirs,* 2:238; 19–21 May 1864, entries, Halpine's diary, Huntington Library.

29. Steuart's file, Complied Service Records of Confederate General and Staff Officers and Nonregimental Enlisted Men, M331, roll 236, RG 109, Records of Confederate Soldiers Who Served in the Civil War, NA. Steuart was assigned a brigade in Maj. Gen. George E. Pickett's division and surrendered at Appomatox with his command on 9 April 1865.

30. Strother, *Diaries,* 230–32. Halpine, in his Miles O'Reilly persona, wrote after the war, "There is no trace of cowardice in General Sigel, as there was certainly none of generalship" (Charles Graham Halpine, *Baked Meats of the Funeral* [New York: Carleton, 1866], 301). A private soldier gave this 20 May opinion of his new commanding general: "Dark complexion, black moustache, stern looking. We don't like his looks" (Charles H. Lynch, *The Civil War Diary, 1862–1865* [Hartford: privately printed, 1915], 62).

31. Sigel, "Sigel in Shenandoah," 4:491; Special Orders No. 102, Department of West Virginia, 22 May 1864, Special Orders, Department of West Virginia, vol. 20, Record Group 393, U.S. Army Continental Commands, 1821–1920, NA (hereafter subject, RG 393, NA); letter, Hunter to Stanton, 23 May 1864, *ORA,* 37, pt. 1, 524. Sigel resented Hunter, writing his wife "that Hunter cannot stand the 'foreigners'" (letter, 1 June [?] 1864, qtd. in Davis, *Battle of New Market,* 172); Du Pont, *The Campaign of 1864 in the Valley of Virginia and the Expedition to Lynchburg*

[New York: National American Society, 1925], 45. Strother wrote on 25 May 1864, "General Hunter is requested by the President to retain the Dutch in some position" (*Diaries*, 235); Cecil D. Eby, Jr., *"Porte Crayon": The Life of David Hunter Strother* (Chapel Hill: University of North Carolina Press, 1960), 137–38.

32. Telegrams, Halleck to Grant, Grant to Halleck, Sigel report, 19 May, telegrams, Grant to Halleck, 20 May, Halleck to Hunter, Hunter to adjutant general, 21 May 1864, *ORA*, 37, pt. 1, 493, 500, 507; Sigel, "Sigel in Shenandoah," 491.

33. Telegrams, Hunter to adjutant general, 21 May, Hunter to Halleck, 22 May 1864, *ORA*, 37, pt. 1, 508, 516–17; letter, Hunter to adjutant general, 22 May 1864, Letters Sent, Department of West Virginia, vol. 2, RG 393, NA; 22 May 1864, entry, Halpine Diary, Huntington Library. Hunter offered the cavalry command to Strother, who had a little experience, but the colonel declined (Strother, *Diaries*, 232–33).

34. Other staff members were: Maj. Levi C. Turner, judge advocate; 1st Lt. (soon Capt.) Henry A. Du Pont, chief of artillery; 1st Lt. John R. Meigs, engineer; Capt. A. V. Barringer, assistant quartermaster general; Capt. Franklin E. Town, chief signal officer; Lt. Col. William C. Starr, chief provost marshal; 1st Lt. J. H.V. Field, ordnance officer; Capt. George B. Elliott, chief of scouts; Capts. Philip G. Bier, Oliver Matthews, T. Melvin, and Will Rumsey, assistant adjutants general; Surgeon Thomas B. Reed, medical director; Capt. William Alexander, chief quartermaster; and Capt. S. Brownell, chief commissary officer (Halpine's Diary, Huntington Library). Kinzie was captured at Memphis in August and was exchanged and discharged a month later (Adjutant General's Office Certificate of Service, 25 March 1887, Pension record, Caroline G. Kinzie (wife), "Civil War and Later Survivors' Certificates," 1861–1934, Civil War and Later Pension Files, certificate no. 432940, RG 15, Records of the Veterans Administration, NA); Special Orders No. 183, Adjutant General's Office, 21 May, telegrams, Hunter to Halleck, 22 May, Halleck to Hunter, 23 May, and letter, adjutant general to Hunter, 23 May 1864, *ORA*, 37, pt. 1, 516–17, 525.

35. Hanchett, *Irish*, 108. A lieutenant colonel of one of the regiments wrote that two thousand men in the army had no shoes and a thousand were without arms (Thomas Francis Wildes, *Record of the One Hundred and Sixteenth Ohio Volunteer Infantry in the War of the Rebellion* [Sandusky: I. F. Mack and Bros., 1874], 89); General Orders No. 29, Department of West Virginia, 22 May 1864, *ORA*, 37, pt. 1, 517–18.

36. General Orders Nos. 30–32, 23, 24, and 25 May, Special Orders No. 103, Department of West Virginia, 23 May, letter, Halpine to Martinsburg, 22 May 1864, *ORA*, 37, pt. 1, 525, 527, 531–32, 537; Jeffery D. Wert, *Mosby's Rangers* (New York: Simon and Schuster, 1990), 163. The major's and captain's dishonor-

able discharges were reversed by the president in March and August 1865, and the major was restored to duty in his regiment.

37. Letter, P. G. Bier, assistant adjutant general, to Maj. Timothy Quinn, First New York (Lincoln) Cavalry, 24 May, telegrams, Brig. Gen. Max Weber, Harper's Ferry to Sigel, 24 May, Capt. A. V. Barringer, chief quartermaster, to Halpine, 26 May 1864; *ORA*, 37, pt. 1, 528, 534, 543; Letters Sent, Department of West Virginia, RG 393, NA. Halpine thought patrols looking for guerrillas "all bosh. Only breaks down the horses" (diary entry, 23 May 1864, Halpine's Diary, Huntington Library); Halpine, *Baked Meats*, 337.

38. Du Pont, *Campaign of 1864*, 49; Hanchett, *Irish*, 109; circular, Department of West Virginia, 24 May 1864, reprinted with correspondence, *American and Commercial Advertiser* (Baltimore), 2 June 1864.

39. Entry for 24 May 1864, Strother, *Diaries*, 235–36. Halpine similarly met with what he called "a delegation from FFVs [First Families of Virginia] to ask how they might be saved" from the consequences of the order to burn houses of guerrillas and their supporters (diary entry, 25 May 1864, Halpine Diary, Huntington Library).

40. Telegram, Sigel to Halpine, orders for Major Quinn, 30 May, report of Lt. Col. Augustus I. Root, Fifteenth New York Cavalry, 31 May 1864, *ORA*, 37, pt. 1, 557, 565. Mosby also sometimes executed his captives, hanging one the day after the 31 May raid on the trains (Wert, *Mosby's Rangers*, 164); Du Pont, *Campaign of 1864*, 50–51; William Harrison Beach, *First New York (Lincoln) Cavalry* (New York: Lincoln Cavalry Association, 1902), 355–58. Quoting his 24 May 1864 diary entry, Strother spoke to Hunter about Stearns "and satisfied the General that Stearns was right" (diary entry, 3 June, Strother, *Diaries*, 235–38, 341).

41. Circular (marching order), 25 May, letter, Grant to Halleck, 25 May, orders, Halpine to Stahel, 27 and 30 May, troop return for May 1864, *ORA*, 37, pt. 1, 535–38, 546, 555–56, 571. The usual army punishments were applied against looters; noncommissioned officers lost their stripes, and privates were forced to carry fence posts and other heavy objects (Hanchett, *Irish*, 112); diary entry, 26 May 1864, Halpine Diary, Huntington Library. A soldier wrote, "General Hunter had issued very stringent orders about foraging, and he had as many as 100 men at a time marching up and down in front of his headquarters for being caught at it" (George Case Setchell, "A Sergeant's View of the Battle of Piedmont," *Civil War Times Illustrated* 2 [May 1963]: 43; Strother, *Diaries*, 238).

42. Strother, *Diaries*, 238–39; Special Orders No. 107, Department of West Virginia, 28 May 1864, RG 393, NA; Marshall Brice Moore, *Conquest of a Valley* (Charlottesville: University of Virginia Press, 1965), 17; Imboden, "Battle of New Market," 4:485.

43. Hanchett, *Irish,* 113; General Orders Nos. 33–34, 31 May, 1 June 1864, *ORA,* 37, pt. 1, 560, 577. A soldier found it curious that the men were ordered on 31 May to burn no civilian property except fence posts (letter, Sergeant Walker, 8 June 1864, Wildes, *116th Ohio Infantry,* 92).

44. Strother, *Diaries,* 239–40; diary entry, 30 May 1864, Halpine Diary, Huntington Library.

45. Diary entries, 29 May–1 June 1864, Halpine Diary, Huntington Library; or "*Bouquet de Rottenhoss,*" Halpine, *Baked Meats,* 300.

46. Imboden, "Battle of New Market," 4:485; Strother, *Diaries,* 240–41; diary entry, 2 June 1864, Halpine Diary, Huntington Library.

47. Hunter's report, 8 June 1864, *ORA,* 37, pt. 1, 94; Strother, *Diaries,* 241; Hanchett, *Irish,* 114–15.

48. Diary entry, 3 June 1864, Halpine Diary, Huntington Library.

Chapter 7

VICTORY AND RETREAT

While Hunter was planning his flanking attack, Imboden's reinforcements were arriving at Confederate forward positions. Brig. Gen. William E. Jones himself rode in at sunrise on 4 June, most of his troops preceding him. A few hours later Brig. Gen. John C. Vaughn, with something less than a thousand Tennessee cavalry, also came up. In all, the rebel force numbered something between forty-five hundred and fifty-five hundred men, including the Augusta and Rockingham Counties' reserve forces and about a dozen cannon. Imboden did not remain commander of these forces; "on comparing dates of commission with Jones and Vaughn they were both found to be my seniors. Jones, holding the oldest commission, took command." An 1848 West Point graduate, he was known to be particularly irascible, not the sort to listen to others, a characteristic that may have contributed to the result of the coming battle.[1]

On that same Saturday morning Hunter sent his army toward Port Republic, the main body led by the First New York (Lincoln) Cavalry. His regiments included all those that had been defeated at New Market just over two weeks earlier. Only a few miscellaneous units had been added. Some pickets were encountered near Mount Jackson, but they did not slow the advance, as Hunter's two brigades of infantry turned east toward the intended river crossing. The pickets were certain to inform Jones of the direction of the Union attack, but he did little to establish a new defensive line until he was certain of Hunter's intentions. The rebels were somewhat distracted by the cavalry demonstrating before the Mount Crawford positions, an action that Chief of Staff Strother urged on his commander. Reaching the crossing site near Port Republic, the army settled down to wait until the pontoon bridge was erected, but the work went very slowly; the only competent engineer, Lieutenant Meigs, displaying youthful enthusiasm, personally directed the cavalry screen. Apparently, no one except Meigs had experience putting together the canvas boats that held up the roadbed. Some cavalrymen forded the river nearby and surprised a Confederate supply train, capturing thirteen wagons. According to Strother, they should have captured one hundred, "but the cavalry was cowardly." A large woolen mill making cloth for Confederate uniforms was burned, the flames entertaining Hunter's troops until the bridge was completed, and the force crossed over the river. This took until 6:00 p.m., so the army bivouacked only a mile south of Port Republic. It was too late to continue the march on Waynesboro.[2]

THE FIGHT AT PIEDMONT

Early the next morning, on 5 June, Hunter awoke Colonel Strother; both men expected a battle that day. Once again the cavalry led the advance on the Port Republic–Staunton road under poor weather conditions, mist, light drizzle, and fog. At 6:00 a.m., near Mount Meridian, a series of cavalry charges and countercharges forced the Confederate cavalry to withdraw. Seventy rebel prisoners were taken, among them Capt. Frank Imboden, the general's brother. Cavalry actions continued for several hours, the Union force moving slowly south through Meridian and Bonnie Doone, supported by skillfully handled artillery directed by Captain Du Pont. Imboden's cavalry had thus far borne the brunt of Hunter's advance, but he needed reinforcements to continue his delaying tactics. He realized that General Jones had had little time to prepare infantry positions, so he continued to fight on.[3]

Jones decided to entrench his two veteran infantry brigades at Piedmont, a small crossroads town six or seven miles south of Port Republic. Strother described the locale:

> The enemy's position was strong and well chosen. It was on a conclave of wooded hills commanding an open valley between and open, gentle slopes in front. On our right in advance of the village of Piedmont was a line of log and [fence] rail defenses very advantageously located on the edge of a forest and just behind the rise of a smooth, open hill so that troops moving over this hill could be mowed down by musketry from the works at short range and to prevent artillery from being used against them. The left flank of this palisade rested on a steep and impractical bluff sixty feet high and washed at its base by the Shenandoah [a branch called the Middle River]. Just behind this work was the village itself, a single street of wooden houses, and nearly a mile in the rear was another line of rail defenses also located on the border of a wood crossing the valley.[4]

Jones's position had a weakness, however, because Vaughn, with his mounted infantry on the Confederate right, did not fill a gap between his and Jones's forces. Imboden's cavalry, completing its morning delaying actions, deployed further right, his line bent to the south beyond New Hope about a mile and a half south of Piedmont. When Hunter was advised of Jones's deployment and intention to do battle at Piedmont, he said, "All right. We may as well fight them here as anywhere."[5]

Hunter's infantry had not been engaged all morning while it was waiting for the cavalry to clean out the territory before the rebels' main position. Hunter took advantage of this lull in the action to stiffen a regiment that had disgraced itself at New Market. He halted the unit and called it to attention so that he could make some remarks. Hunter never used profanity, and this might explain why his remarks were not more enthusiastically received—or remembered. A sergeant wrote (in 1898), "I cannot recall much that he said, except that he expected us to do our duty today, and wipe out the stain attached to the 18th Connecticut Volunteers since our last fight at New Market, under General Sigel, where we were badly whipped. We were all mad as hoppers when he got through, as we did not think it was any fault of ours that Sigel got licked. I think every man made up his mind then that if we did come up against the Rebs that day some of them would get hurt."[6]

The Union infantry advanced until it was in a line of woods that ran across the Port Republic road, less than a mile from Jones's position. The First Brigade of Sullivan's division, commanded by Col. Augustus Moor, deployed on the right and Col. Joseph Thoburn's Second Brigade to the left. Units of Stahel's cavalry not engaged in scouting, escorting trains, and patrolling took positions in the rear of the infantry. At about noon, in now clear, balmy weather, Moor's regiments (the Eighteenth Connecticut on the far right), "advancing with a yell," moved in the open toward Jones's lines on the hill, forcing rebel advanced pickets back on Jones's main defenses. The Union soldiers came under such heavy fire that they retreated hastily, followed by Confederate troops crying, "New Market! New Market!" The Union line held, and Moor's men reorganized in the woods. Meanwhile, Hunter and the rest of his headquarters personnel moved to the Shaver farmhouse in the center of the valley beyond the left flank, from which they could better observe the developing battle. The staff was under some artillery fire, and the officers, although none of them were wounded, were soon "all covered with dirt & leaves from exploding shells." Strother wrote: "We found here some skulkers plundering and two women crying bitterly. The soldiers were kicked and driven out and the women reassured. The General asked for the owner of the house and was informed that he was down in the cellar with the little children.

The General had him brought out and reviled him for his cowardice." Shaver, a Dunkard preacher, claimed to be a Union man, and he asked that his apple trees be protected, "this request at a time when a bloody battle was going on with death all around and the fate of an army uncertain disgusted us all."[7]

It took nearly an hour for Moor to reorganize his brigade, during which the cavalry kept pressure on Jones's left. Another Union charge was made with the same result as the first, and the forces moved forward and back across the open field. It was not clear who was winning the fight, and Hunter ordered his wagons turned toward the north as a precaution, in case he were defeated. Jones weakened his right flank to strengthen the pressure on Sullivan's First Brigade, a move, Hunter recognized, which would have to be challenged. He reinforced Moor with the cavalry brigade fighting as infantry and renewed his attack. Only one regiment of Thoburn's Second Brigade contributed to this action. The other two regiments had not yet been seriously engaged. The commander of one of them thought that his position on the Union left was potentially dangerous, and Hunter personally moved the unit farther back in the woods. In this position it was not visible to Jones, and it is likely that the rebel commander thought that he was actually engaging all of Hunter's infantry. Hunter decided that further reinforcement of his right would not be sufficient to turn the battle in his favor, so he sent urgent instructions to Thoburn. The brigade commander was ordered to send two regiments not yet in the fight around the Union left, south along a well-wooded ravine, aiming for Jones's weakened right flank, where the gap between the Confederate infantry and Vaughn's troops remained. Although the rebels detected this movement, Jones was not alarmed; he sent some green home guard reserves to cover the weak point and continued his attacks on the First Brigade and the units of Thoburn's Second Brigade remaining on his front.[8]

While these movements were evolving, Hunter received word that General Stahel, his cavalry commander, was wounded and, to further increase his anxiety, that a wagon train from his bases in the lower valley had not been told of the army's diversion and was moving down the valley pike directly to rebel-held Staunton. Stahel went back into the fight on foot, unable to ride because of a painful arm injury, and the wagon train was reached by cavalry before it was endangered. While the staff was concerned with these matters, the battle was about to go Hunter's way.[9]

Hunter's flanking move was the decisive maneuver of the battle. At 2:00 p.m. Jones launched his final assault on Moor's brigade but was beaten off by the infantry, the cavalrymen on foot, and the well-served Union artillery. Shortly afterward the Second Brigade's Fifty-fourth Pennsylvania and Thirty-fourth Massachusetts infantry regiments fell upon Jones's right flank and rear, and Moor's brigade followed up with yet another attack on the enemy's left. Under this pressure Jones, despite his personal participation in the fight, was unable to maintain his positions, and the battle became hand-to-hand. It was then that Jones was mortally wounded, and the Confederate infantry brigades broke and ran. Curiously, Generals Vaughn and Imboden did not go to Jones's assistance, perhaps because their orders were to screen against a wider Union envelopment of the Confederate right. It is possible, however, that they failed to move because they received no orders from Jones to do so, and their commander's reputation was that he did not encourage independent decisions by subordinates.[10]

Strother described the scene at Hunter's headquarters:

> The earth shook with the roar of guns and musketry, and the fresh,
> hearty cheers rose with the smoke and sounded like victory. Back rolled
> the cheers from the front. Stretcher men, ambulance drivers, wounded
> men, butchers, bummers, all took up the shout and back upon the hill
> crests. Negroes, teamsters, and camp followers re-echoed the joyful
> shout. I saw streams of graybacks and butternuts passing the woods at
> double-quick guarded by cavalry men with drawn sabres.

One of Hunter's orderlies told him that two rebel officers wished to see him. One introduced himself as Capt. Boyd Faulkner of Martinsburg, and he claimed kinship to the general. Not surprisingly, "the General was curt and hardly civil and ordered the sergeant to take them to the rear." Strother, however, Faulkner's cousin, shook the captain's hand.[11]

The fight was over by 3:00 p.m., some of the rebel infantry and reserves escaping by crossing the river on their left flank and others moving south. Strother urged a close pursuit of the shattered enemy, but near New Hope the cavalry ran into a defensive line "and then got a round of grape and canister in their faces which drove them back." Strother speculated that "the worthlessness of our cavalry was probably what induced the General to content himself with the affair as it stood." And he should have been well content because almost a thousand rebels were prisoners, among them sixty officers. Casualties on both sides were heavy, Hunter reporting five hundred killed and wounded and estimating that the enemy had lost six hundred. Hunter's army was intact; the Confederates, now commanded by Vaughn, were in full, disorderly retreat toward Waynesboro and Rockfish Gap to cover Charlottesville and Gordonsville, leaving the way to Staunton open. Hunter had every reason to be proud of his troops and of his own performance; he had gained the first Union victory in the upper Shenandoah Valley. He may well have thought that the triumph was important toward winning the war, and it might have been had his good fortune continued.[12]

Hunter ordered the army to camp on the battlefield. He moved his head-quarters to a house in the village of Piedmont, and, Strother reported: "We had a good supper and a triumphant evening. The bands played and the men sang and shouted. The army was intoxicated with joy. Verily they had wiped out the stain of New Market." The general's reaction to the day's events was not as restrained as usual. In the privacy of the cottage Halpine wrote that Hunter impulsively "first kissed Sam Stockton, then threw his arms around me & kissed me."[13]

Hunter and his staff bedded down on the floor, Halpine next to his general. In the morning the march to an undefended Staunton would begin. In that city the post commander, Col. Edwin G. Lee, receiving news of the rout at Piedmont, spent an anxious night and following morning doing what he could to evacuate the military supplies from the town. Failing to find transportation for much of the commissary and quartermaster supplies, he opened the warehouses to local citizens. This approved looting likely increased the confusion when Union forces reached Staunton.[14]

Grant's monthlong campaign against Lee and toward Richmond had provided the Union with no clear victories and enormous casualties. The last of the series of devastating battles had just been concluded at Cold Harbor, where, Grant said, "No advantage whatever was gained to compensate for the heavy loss we sustained." Lee would not meet Grant in the open, and the Confederates "seemed to have given up any idea of gaining any advantage of their antagonist in the open field. They had come to prefer breastworks in the front to the Army of the Potomac." It was time for Grant to abandon the head-to-head fighting that he had tried, each battle, whether a victory or a defeat, followed by an attempt to go around Lee's right flank. For all the sacrifice during the overland campaign, the Union army was no nearer Richmond than two years earlier, when McClellan, at considerably less cost, had reached the same positions from the Peninsula.[15]

Grant's offensive had failed to defeat Lee. It showed that attrition cut both ways and so far had acted to the disadvantage of the attackers. The lieutenant general had effectively used up the North's manpower resources, stripping Washington's defenses and exhausting the pool of draftees and the last call's state volunteers. It was time to modify strategy, and Hunter was to be a part of it. Grant heard of the Piedmont victory on 6 June, and he told Hunter how his maneuvers would fit into the plan. Maj. Gen. Philip H. Sheridan was ordered, with two cavalry divisions, to Charlottesville along the Virginia Central Railroad and the James River Canal, destroying these vital Confederate supply links as he went. Hunter was directed to join Sheridan on the rail line connecting

Charlottesville with Lynchburg or at the latter town itself, and he was told to use his own discretion about taking Lynchburg. If this plan succeeded, Lee's supplies from the west would be interdicted, and Hunter and Sheridan could join the Army of the Potomac. These and other movements had to be done carefully so that Lee did not oppose Sheridan too strongly and would not be prematurely driven behind Richmond's defenses, the security of which provided fortified positions from which he could spare troops to operate against Hunter.[16]

OCCUPATION OF STAUNTON

Hunter could not have received these instructions when he marched toward Staunton on the morning following the battle, but, apart from describing cooperation with the Sheridan expedition, they were not significantly different from earlier orders. He was not yet able to decide his next move because he had heard nothing from General Crook, who was marching toward Staunton with Averell's cavalry screening his infantry. Leaving Piedmont, Hunter's Union column stopped at the crossroads to Waynesboro, where Strother tried to convince his general to take that route and complete the victory by destroying Vaughn's and Imboden's forces. Hunter declined the suggestion, and the army moved into Staunton with bands playing, meeting no resistance. Headquarters was set up at the Virginia Hotel, and the staff took rooms at the American Hotel. There was further business that day. A delegation of local officials and leading citizens headed by the mayor asked Hunter to spare the town from the torch and were told that only military installations and property were to be destroyed and that all private property would be protected. Of course, they were cautioned, incidents by "ill-disciplined soldiery" could be expected, but unnecessary destruction was not army policy. Finally, Hunter ordered the inmates of the local prison—"thieves, spies, forgers, deserters, Irishmen, Union men, Yankee soldiers, Confederate officers, murderers, and rioters"—to be released, and he was particularly incensed that the jailor had held "a so-called Union soldier" in irons. Generally, conditions in Staunton were reasonably peaceful the first day, plundering held in check by the provost marshal. Yet Hunter was anxious and, as Halpine put it, "very cross," because he had not gotten any news about reinforcements.[17]

The following day the work of destroying Confederate military and transportation facilities and public property began. Hunter ordered the burning of the jail, the depot and other railroad installations, a woolen factory, government stables, a steam mill, wagon shops, and storehouses. Other structures such as the quartermaster's, the commissary, and ordnance buildings were spared, however, because they were private property. Their contents, described by Strother as "blankets, clothes, a thousand saddles, shoes, tobacco, etc., without end," were freely looted by a "mixed mob of Federal soldiers, Negroes, Secessionists, mulatto women, children, Jews, and camp followers and the riff raff of the town." The situation could not be controlled, and there is little evidence that Hunter considered good order in Staunton important then. He did move his headquarters from the town to an apple orchard outside it to avoid the smoke, and, despite the turmoil, it appears no civilian dwellings were burned. Indeed, Union soldiers worked to save those properties near the military-related facilities from the flames.[18]

Hunter's concerns were the location of Crook and Averell and what should be the next objective of his army. He sent cavalry toward Waynesboro to keep in touch with the fleeing enemy, and he seemed convinced that he should move directly on Charlottesville. The decision on this matter was postponed until Crook was located. Strother told Hunter that some black men had told him that Averell's cavalry was seen at Buffalo Gap, on the railroad about ten miles west of Staunton. Hunter decided to move there immediately, hoping to take by surprise Brig. Gen. John McCausland's small mounted force, the only remaining major Confederate unit in the valley. Hunter marched the army five or six miles toward Buffalo Gap, but scouts reported that the place was vacant. They also said McCausland was moving toward Waynesboro. Strother wrote, "Perceiving that we were marching away from the enemy, we faced about and returned to our encampment near Staunton the same day." When the force arrived back at the town, news was received that Crook was but ten miles away and was expected the following day.[19]

With Crook's arrival imminent, Hunter could plan his next move more fully, consulting his staff as he usually did. Strother favored an advance up the valley to Lexington and Buchanan, crossing the Blue Ridge Mountains at the Peaks of Otter and besieging Lynchburg via Liberty. He wrote after the war that "the country, we found, afforded abundant supplies for our troops, while the inhabitants were quiet, and in many instances, even favorable to us. We had also assurances that in South-western Virginia and North Carolina, we might hope for active assistance from the inhabitants." Were the Lynchburg plan to succeed, the railroad connecting Richmond and Lee's army with North Carolina would be interdicted, and the rebel army might even be forced from the Confederate capital. The weakness in the proposal was a shortage of ammunition which, unless alleviated, made serious fighting impossible. For the moment, however, no decision was made; Hunter perhaps preferred to wait and hear the views of Crook and Averell. Those generals arrived on Wednesday, 8 June, after a long march from positions near Lewisburg, to Callaghan, Warm Springs, Goshen Depot (destroying the Virginia Central Railroad from there), and Middlebrook to Staunton. Averell's cavalry screened Crook's infantry, encountering only scattered opposition from McCausland and Col. William L. Jackson, another rebel cavalry leader. The twelve thousand new troops increased Hunter's force to almost twenty thousand men. Moreover, the reinforcements, except for clothes and particularly shoes, were in good condition. Shortages were easily made up from the stores seized at Staunton. Halpine thought, "we can laugh at anything less than one of Lee's Army Corps to reinforce the valley troops," but a similar threat was to materialize.[20]

Hunter asked the two arriving generals to advise him about the further advances. Averell, who agreed with Strother's plan, was asked to draw up detailed operations orders to accomplish it in five days, but Crook recommended caution. He was concerned that Lee would not allow Lynchburg to fall and could be expected to oppose it strongly. Crook said that, unless a rapid advance was possible, the plan could not succeed, and he even offered to take his own command to Lynchburg by forced march. Hunter heard him out but was encouraged by a message from Grant which told him how important it would be for Hunter to "get possession of Lynchburg for a single day." The lieutenant general still preferred a march directly to Charlottesville for the linkup with Sheridan and a move from there down railroads and canals to Lynchburg. He did not, however, give Hunter an order but left the matter for his general in the valley to decide. Hunter kept the Charlottesville option open by sending another cavalry force to feel out the rebel positions on the Waynesboro road east of Staunton, but the maneuver was repulsed. The alarm it raised had the unintended effect of causing Lee to send Breckinridge, with his two brigades of New Market veterans, from the Cold Harbor battlefield toward Charlottesville and Lynchburg, but this should not have been dangerous, in that Sheridan could cut off this assistance.[21]

The ninth of June was spent re-equipping Crook and Averell, reorganizing the expanded expedition, communicating with headquarters, ordering supplies, and relieving Hunter's army of unproductive baggage. Strother informally named the combined force the Army of West Virginia, joining Hunter's Army of the Shenandoah and Crook's Army of the Kanawha. Sullivan remained in command of the First Infantry Division, and Crook was assigned the Second Infantry Division, both retaining intact the units they had commanded before Staunton. The First Cavalry Division was assigned to General Duffié, who replaced the injured General Stahel, and Averell's command was named the Second Cavalry Division. Captain Du Pont retained control of the artillery, but he did not take over Crook's two batteries. Stahel was sent back to Martinsburg and Harper's Ferry to raise new troops and gather munitions while he recovered from his wound. Hunter wrote to Halleck explaining what he expected of Stahel, generously adding, "It is but justice to Major-General Stahel to state that in the recent engagement he displayed excellent qualities of coolness and gallantry, and that for the final happy result the country is much indebted to his services." Hunter was not in a good mood, however, because the ad hoc headquarters in the orchard was rained on and papers blown about. Halpine wrote, "Hunter very angry &c."[22]

Hunter and Strother were concerned about the large number of prisoners, sick, wounded, and refugees in the army's lines. Strother said he had thought of a solution at dawn and had discussed it with his general then, Hunter's pallet being adjacent to his. Colonel Moor, a brigade commander who was colonel of the Twenty-eighth Ohio Infantry, wanted to return north with his regiment, their time of service having expired. The solution was to send the prisoners and refugees under a guard of the roughly eight hundred men due for discharge, the party under Moor to move via Buffalo Gap to Beverly (where it arrived on 14 June). Hunter gave Moor a report to wire to Secretary Stanton in Washington when he reached a telegraph line, and he issued orders for the march south to Lexington to begin the following day. Except for about two hundred wounded who could not be moved, Staunton would be abandoned.[23]

The army was divided into four columns, to join again at Lexington in two days' time. Averell's cavalry had the right flank, Crook the main valley road, Sullivan roads on his left, and Duffié along the base of the Blue Ridge Mountains. Hunter chose to accompany Sullivan's infantry. Other than some harassment of Averell by McCausland, who had only about fifteen hundred men, the march on 10 June to Midway (Steele's Tavern) was uneventful. Good news arrived that evening. A heavily escorted supply train of two hundred wagons with mail, supplies, and ammunition was on the way from General Sigel at Martinsburg and was expected to arrive the following day. Strother wrote, "The General is in high good humor," as the expedition appeared to be going smoothly.[24]

THREE DAYS AT LEXINGTON

The columns of Crook and Averell arrived at Lexington about midday on 11 June. McCausland was in positions behind the North (now Maury) River, a branch of the James. The bridge had been burned, and the Union forces were annoyed by musket fire and a few cannon shots from the opposite rocks and thickets on a bluff. When Hunter heard the guns he rode rapidly to the scene, Sullivan's division following. Hunter ordered Averell to cross the river north of Lexington at Rockbridge Springs, so as to outflank the defenders, and told Du Pont to fire on the Virginia Military Institute barracks, which dominated the heights opposite the federal force. Du Pont said he fired one round from each of the six guns of his regular battery at the towers of the barracks but ceased fire when he was told that the enemy was retreating. Hunter was incensed by the enemy's useless resistance. He wrote, "This unsoldierly and inhuman attempt of General McCausland to defend an indefensible position against an overwhelming force by screening himself behind the private dwellings of women and children, might have brought justifiable destruction upon the whole town, but as this was not rendered imperative by any military necessity, I preferred to spare private property and an unarmed population." McCausland, finally recognizing the hopeless military situation, evacuated the town by 3:00 p.m. The corps of cadets, which had returned to the institute only a few days earlier, fell back as well, not having been active in the town's defense. Crook blamed Averell's slow progress for McCausland's escape, and Hunter also believed Averell's tardiness and lack of boldness prevented capture or dispersal of the rebel force.[25]

Col. John M. Schoonmaker, of the Fourteenth Pennsylvania Cavalry, commanding Averell's First Brigade, led some of the first troops into Lexington, and he placed the VMI buildings under guard, but this did not prevent immediate looting of trunks left behind by cadets and of the library and scientific laboratories. Schoonmaker wrote forty-two years later that Hunter had relieved him of his command when he found out that the colonel had not burned the military institute's buildings. Schoonmaker said he was restored to command a day later with apologies from his general, possibly another example of Hunter's impetuousness. Hunter's critics have fully accepted Schoonmaker's account, one of them expanding the allegation to a report that a number of officers were placed under arrest for failing to obey orders to burn the school. This was done, the accuser writes, so Schoonmaker would be made "more wanton and reckless of the property rights of the enemy and the hostile inhabitants along the route. Hunter simply desired all his subordinates to take their cue from him and act in certain matters without explicit orders, for orders, especially when written, have an unpleasant way of springing up when least expected." The story does not ring true, however, because no evidence in the form of records or memoirs supports Schoonmaker's account or the conclusion Hunter's critic draws from it. In fact, Hunter did not immediately order the burning of VMI on the day he entered Lexington and did not do so until he had discussed the question with his staff and was convinced that the school was a legitimate military target. Other destruction in Lexington can be seen as excessive but not the burning of the military facility.[26]

Hunter and his staff made his headquarters that Saturday in the house of the VMI superintendent on the parade ground. Other officers were quartered in other faculty houses and in the town; guards were posted to prevent further looting by soldiers and citizens, and two companies of the 116th Ohio Infantry were camped at the home of former governor John Letcher, who had led Virginia out of the Union at the start of the war. In the evening, along with planning further moves of the Army of West Virginia, Hunter discussed with several officers of the command what should be done with VMI. Strother's view doubtless coincided with Hunter's. The colonel placed a great deal of the blame on the institute for having caused the rebellion. He saw it "as a most dangerous establishment where treason was systematically taught.... I believed the States Rights conspirators had with subtlety and forethought established and encouraged the school for the express purpose of educating the youth of the country into such opinions as would render them ready and efficient tools wherewith to overthrow the government of the country when the hour and opportunity arrived." More to the point, Strother and other officers found military reasons also compelling; the corps of cadets had fought as a unit against Union forces, the barracks were a state arsenal, and some thought that cadets had used the buildings to fire on Hunter's troops when they arrived at Lexington. So it was decided to burn the school the next morning, on 12 June, but Hunter added three other buildings associated with the institution to the list, a decision that called for the destruction of two faculty homes then occupied by families of the departed officer-professors. This additional damage was a cause of controversy then and later.[27]

Lieutenant Meigs, Hunter's engineering officer, was charged with the destruction, but it did not proceed without further looting of institute buildings. Hunter allowed the superintendent's house to be spared because a newborn infant was living there, but the rest was burned, beginning about 9:30 a.m. Meigs wrote in the record book of the Dialectic Literary Society of Cadets, "At this moment the Virginia Military Institute is a mass of flames." While this was being accomplished, Capt. Matthew Berry, a provost marshal officer, brought Hunter a copy of a manuscript found in a printing office, thought to have been written by the absent Letcher. Halpine wrote that it was a proclamation addressed to citizens of "Rockbridge [Lexington's county] and other Counties ... calling on them to 'arise and slay the foul Yankee invader;' and if unable to offer any organized resistance, then from behind every tree and stone in the valley, to kill us as they could. It was, in other words, a direct incitation to bushwack and murder." Hunter saw it the same way and, as he put it, "ordered [Letcher's] property to be burned under my order, published May 24, against persons practicing or abetting such unlawful and uncivilized warfare." Berry was sent to do the burning and was instructed to evacuate women and children and to refuse them permission to remove anything from the house. It is curious that, until he saw the proclamation, Hunter had protected Letcher's property, likely because he did not know about the man's uncompromising nature, which could alone have justified severe action against him. At the war's start the governor "favored trying captured Union soldiers from the breakaway counties [in western Virginia] for treason." Letcher furthermore favored trying Union officers in state courts for inciting slave insurrections, the same charge that Davis and the Confederate Congress had brought against Hunter—and which the state had used to hang John Brown.[28]

In total, Hunter's burnings at Lexington were five structures—Letcher's house, two sets of VMI faculty quarters, the barracks, and possibly the cadet hospital. In future years the destroyed structures took on more monumental dimensions, but the real damage was to the library and scientific equipment and specimens. VMI officials had tried to protect this valuable material from the destruction of the barracks, which was expected, by storing some items in the buildings of neighboring Washington College, but that institution was sacked by Union soldiers as well. (Of course, not all the pillage was by soldiers; a town resident wrote that much of it was done by blacks.) Hunter is also accused of ordering the burning of the college, but there is no evidence, apart from Schoonmaker's much later claim that he did so. A lieutenant colonel of an Ohio regiment thought that the plundering of the Washington College library would "always remain a deep reproach to General Hunter, gallant soldier though he was." Some officers did at the time object to destroying VMI. Col. Rutherford B. Hayes, a future president who was then commanding a brigade in Crook's division, wrote in his diary: "General Hunter burns the Virginia Military Institute. This does not suit many of us. General Crook, I know, disapproves. It is surely bad." In a letter home the same day he forecast that "General Hunter will be as odious as Butler and Pope to the Rebels and not gain our good opinion either." All the same, Hayes did not find the equally destructive looting so heinous, adding, "I got a pretty little cadet musket here which I will try to send the boys." Colonel Halpine wrote in his diary, "My heart revolts," when he heard about the decision to destroy "libraries, laboratories, chemical & astronomical apparatus, arms, ammunition, trunks, clothing, &c. &c., all the spoils of a glorious institution." "My judgement does not concur," he continued. "No seat of learning should be destroyed. If we subdue the rebellion, the place would be restored to the nation. If we fail, why this wanton waste? I can do nothing with General Hunter. I suppose he has his orders." Halpine modified this opinion after the war, believing then that the general was right after all. Captain Du Pont said, decades later, that he thought the burning was wrong and that he had himself, aided by Capt. William McKinley, another future president, helped to remove furniture from one of the faculty houses that was destroyed. In later years, through efforts of then Senator Du Pont, VMI was compensated by the federal government for "the damage and destruction of its library, scientific apparatus, and the quarters of its professors"—but not for the barracks. Consequently, the argument can be made that fifty or sixty years after the fact some of the actions of Hunter's army were officially labeled as not legitimate acts of war.[29]

In his report Hunter lists a number of cannon captured at Lexington. These guns had been loaded on barges but were not gotten away before the Union army occupied the town. Some of them, including two ornate, bronze twenty-four-pounders that had been brought to Virginia from France during the American Revolution, were sent north by Hunter. Also seized as a prize of war was a bronze statue of Washington, a copy of Jean-Antoine Houdon's work in the Virginia capitol. Strother said, "I felt indignant that this effigy should be left to adorn a country whose inhabitants were striving to destroy a government which he founded." The colonel recommended to Hunter that the statue be sent to Wheeling as a trophy for West Virginia, but Meigs, the engineer who was responsible for crating and shipping it, thought its proper destination was his (and Hunter's) alma mater, West Point. "Upon what principle [the taking was justified]," a soldier wrote at the time, "it was difficult to tell, as it neither could give aid and comfort to the enemy, nor be of any service to our arms." In the end, however, the work reached Wheeling, and after the war Strother, for a short period adjutant general of Virginia (and thus ex officio a member of VMI's Board of Visitors), saw to its return.[30]

As the burning in Lexington went on, Hunter, Averell, and some of the staff went up an adjacent hill to view the spectacle. The barracks burned slowly and, as it turned out, incompletely, but to Strother "the scene ... was grand." The arsenal in the barracks blew up at about 2:00 p.m., and, according to Strother, "the General seemed to enjoy this scene and turning to me expressed his great satisfaction in having me with him." Another officer viewing his general's reaction wrote that he "rubbed his hands and chuckled with delight, 'Doesn't that burn beautifully?'" Halpine was not so enthusiastic, writing in his diary, as he watched the main fire with the other officers, "How I wish it were over." He also wrote, "My God! how I felt on seeing Gov. Letcher's family sitting out on the lawn on their trunks & furniture, while their house was on fire beside them. The old fool deserves it all; but it is hard on the women. . . . I wish it were over."[31]

In spite of his apparent enthusiasm about events in Lexington, Hunter was growing concerned about the next steps in the campaign. Halpine found his temper "curt & captious": "One may be with him & never out of his sight for three days, & if he happens to call at any moment that one is not there, it is as bad as if one had systematically neglected his duties for a week." The problems the general faced were not all apparent, but there was still the urgency of reaching Lynchburg before Lee could react. Delay of at least an extra day was inevitable because Hunter hoped to renew his depleted ammunition supply when an ex pected wagon train arrived, and he ordered Duffié, from whom he had heard little for several days, to hasten to Lexington. Duffié, after a feint to distract Imboden at Waynesboro, had crossed the Blue Ridge and was moving on Amherst Court House, where he planned to cut the railroad between Charlottesville and Lynchburg. He started back when he received Hunter's order, arriving at the main force on Monday, 13 June. He reported capturing a number of rebel supply wagons, prisoners, and horses and had five miles of rail near Arrington torn up. It seems that Duffié's adventure went beyond his instructions—or at least beyond the understanding he had reached with Hunter when the army left Staunton. General Crook, who had little regard for the Frenchman, thought that his delay rejoining Hunter was due to misconduct. He wrote that Duffié "had been engaged in pilfering, that he had robbed some refugees of some Staunton City bonds, which, after the war, he was trying to dispose of. However, it was this that prevented us from arriving at Lynchburg at least one day earlier."[32]

Crook simplified the actual situation, since Hunter thought that he had to wait for the supplies rather than have them join him on the road. The train arrived at Lexington on 12 June, but it contained very little of the essential munitions—thirty loads of forage for the horses and much "superfluous clothing"—leading Hunter to tell Sigel not to send "one pound of any kind of stores" except ammunition in the future. As it developed, Hunter was about to cut his communications and was to be beyond reach of supplies or even mail for more than two weeks. That morning Hunter ordered Averell to proceed in advance of the main body to Buchanan, hoping to seize the bridge over the James River there before McCausland destroyed it. The army was to depart Lexington early the next morning for the same town.[33]

By 14 June the situation as Hunter understood it was that Breckinridge had arrived with his brigades at Rockfish Gap, had taken command of forces opposing the Union army in the valley, and was likely to be moving toward Lynchburg. This was not a serious threat because Hunter outnumbered the forces of Breckinridge and Imboden combined by about five to one. Duffié's prisoners said that Sheridan had been turned back short of Charlottesville and would not be joining Hunter for the advance on Lynchburg. This last information, while accurate, was not credited, Hunter interpreting the intelligence positively. He believed that Sheridan was still working his way toward a juncture of the two Union forces. Finally, Hunter was convinced that no significant numbers of Confederate troops were in the Lynchburg area. On the other hand, Hunter heard rumors that a large force was being dispatched toward the Shenandoah Valley from Richmond.[34]

THE MARCH ON LYNCHBURG

On the morning of 14 June, Hunter moved his main body, accompanied by the last wagon train sent by Sigel, to Buchanan. Averell had not been successful in preventing destruction of the James River bridge, but he had found a ford that would be suitable. McCausland's bridge burning was protested by inhabitants of the town because they feared that nearby homes and businesses would be endangered. Eleven of these structures were destroyed, but Averell's troops prevented further spread of the conflagration. The Union army sought out the several iron forges in the area and burned them all. The owner of the large iron works in Buchanan (it employed five hundred men) and others near Roanoke was Col. John T. Anderson. The Buchanan enterprise was a branch of the major Tredegar Iron Works at Richmond owned by John's younger brother, Brig. Gen. Joseph Reid Anderson. John Anderson's home, Mt. Joy, on a hill one and a half miles southwest of Buchanan, shared the fate of his business there. There is a question whether the destruction of Mt. Joy was ordered by Hunter or was the independent action of Capt. Thomas K. McCann, one of Hunter's quartermaster officers. McCann told Halpine that he had lived in Buchanan before the war and "claims he was persecuted for being a Union man. He avenges himself bitterly now on all his enemies."[35]

The diversion of the army to Buchanan was yet another delay on the march to Lynchburg. Delays were accumulating, and each of them was reducing Hunter's chances of success on his deep invasion of Lee's essential granary and the threats he posed to Richmond's lifelines to Tennessee and North Carolina. Sheridan's expedition had reached positions a few miles north of the Virginia Central between Gordonsville and Louisa on 10 June. His movement had earlier been detected, and Lee sent two divisions of cavalry to oppose him. The forces were engaged the following day and, on the twelfth, at Trevilian, on the railroad. Fighting was inconclusive, but Sheridan found himself blocked from proceeding along the line to Charlottesville, where he expected to join Hunter. Prisoners told Sheridan that Hunter was in the vicinity of Lynchburg, so, as Grant wrote, "there was no use of his going to Charlottesville with a view to meet him." The same day that Sheridan turned back, Lee ordered yet another counter to Hunter's advance. He directed Lt. Gen. Jubal A. Early, commanding Stonewall Jackson's old corps, consisting of about eight thousand infantry and some artillery, to the Shenandoah. Lee took a risk drawing these troops from his lines just as Grant crossed the James River and appeared before Petersburg. He may have felt somewhat secure being behind the defenses of Richmond—prematurely, according to Grant's plan. Early reached Charlottesville on the sixteenth, marching eighty miles in four days. Here he received word from Breckinridge, now in Lynchburg, that Hunter was moving on the town.[36]

Hunter, reportedly "in good spirits," left Buchanan on the fifteenth, crossing the Blue Ridge on the steep and winding Peaks of Otter road toward Liberty (now Bedford), Averell's cavalry reaching that town without difficulty that evening. Hunter made his headquarters short of Liberty in a comfortable brick house, Fancy Farm, in a grove of oaks and with a view of the Peaks of Otter. Rumors abounded about the military situation. Crook reported that Breckinridge was at Balcony Falls, which would have put him on Hunter's communications between Buchanan and Lexington, and some troops from Lee's Army of Northern Virginia were said to be at Lynchburg. Hunter said that he could get no reliable information. He wrote:

> Through rebel channels we had exaggerated rumors of disasters to our armies both under Sherman and Grant. Some reported that Sheridan had been defeated at Louisa Court-House, while others said he was already in Lynchburg. Negro refugees just from the town represented that it was occupied only by a few thousand armed invalids and militia, and that its inhabitants in the greatest panic were fleeing with their movable property by every available route. At the same time, from other sources worthy of respect, we were assured that all the rebel forces of West Virginia were concentrated there under Breckinridge, and that Ewell's [now under Early] corps of veteran troops, 20,000 strong, had already reinforced them. To determine the truth I determined to advance on Lynchburg immediately.[37]

On Thursday morning, 16 June, Duffié was sent to scout Lynchburg's approaches, less a strong detachment to check on the Balcony Falls rumor. Sullivan's infantry was to follow Averell's cavalry on the Bedford turnpike toward Lynchburg, and Crook was to march to the same place along the Virginia and Tennessee Railroad, destroying this vital link as he went. Baggage trains and spare artillery brought up the rear. Not much progress was made that day; Averell, halting just across the Great Otter River, reported stiffening resistance as he pushed McCausland ahead of him. The rest of the army camped short of the river, seven miles east of Liberty, headquarters in a large, unoccupied house "built on a stylish plan … and said to be haunted." From here Hunter ordered the wagon train that had joined him at Lexington back across the upper valley to Beverly, West Virginia, with 141 prisoners, 130 sick and wounded, and "the families of refugees white or colored" guarded by a regiment and a half of Ohio soldiers whose hundred-day enlistments had expired.[38]

THE FIGHT AT LYNCHBURG

Despite all the delays reaching Lynchburg, it was not yet too late for Hunter to attack and overwhelm the town's feeble defenses. Early was still at Charlottesville but was having difficulties finding enough railroad cars to move his troops to the point of conflict. He asked Breckinridge to send him locomotives from Lynchburg to help in the movement, giving that officer a hint that his orders went beyond the threat to the town: "My first objective will be to destroy Hunter, and the next it is not prudent to trust to telegraph." No train was ready until Friday morning and then only enough equipment to move half the corps. The roadbed and rolling stock were in such poor condition that Early, accompanying one of his divisions, did not reach Lynchburg until 1:00 p.m., 17 June; "the other trains were much later." Hunter personally roused his staff at 2:00 a.m. that morning, but the early start was negated because the bridge crossing the Great Otter was not ready for the artillery and baggage to cross. Consequently, when Averell drew up on the entrenched enemy five miles from Lynchburg at 4:00 p.m., he met more resistance than he might have found earlier. Furthermore, although Averell and Crook attacked and made some gains against the rebels, Hunter decided after some sharp engagements that it was "too late to follow-up this success, [and] we encamped upon the battle-field." He still did not know what he faced but thought Breckinridge had ten thousand to fifteen thousand troops, not including whatever men Lee might have sent. Hunter's estimate was wildly inaccurate; Breckinridge did not have more that five thousand effectives—mostly made up of his own infantry, dismounted cavalry and infantry who had escaped following the Piedmont defeat, Imboden's and McClausand's cavalry, invalids, and the VMI corps of cadets. Early's new troops were gradually added, but Hunter had "no positive information as the whether General Lee had dispatched any considerable force for the relief of Lynchburg" until the next day.[39]

Hunter was tense all day. While waiting for the bridge to be completed, the general was told by a staff officer about a local man named Leftwich who had spoken of the defeat of Union troops in the East and West. This so irritated Hunter that he ordered the man's house burned forthwith and Leftwich to be brought along as a prisoner. Strother wrote, "Halpine, Stockton, and myself rode away saying nothing, but we did not wish to look upon the scene." It was then reported that a courier was fired on from another dwelling (possibly belonging to a Mosley not related to the guerrilla leader), and Hunter ordered the building destroyed. "After burning Leftwich's he seemed to relent" and told Strother, "'I don't think I will burn it,' . . . and thus the matter ended." Tension must have been equally severe following the last fighting of the day, Crook's assaults, which ended about 7:00 p.m. Some of the staff wanted to continue the attack, but the generals concluded that it was best to wait for morning. Consequently, the generals— Hunter, Crook, and Averell—and their staffs occupied the house of former U.S. army paymaster Maj. George C. Hutter, who had resigned his commission at the start of the war. Halpine said that the former officer was "some kind of distant relative to General Hunter—as, by the way, in some degree of cousinship, more or less remote, were pretty nearly all the good families whose barns we had been emptying, and whose cattle we had been eating and driving off during the long march." He found it amusing "to hear Colonel David Hunter Strother ('Porte Crayon'), or the old General himself, inquiring anxiously after the health of 'Cousin Kitty,' 'Aunt Sallie,' 'Cousin Joe,' or 'Uncle Bob,' from some nice old Virginia lady with smoothed apron, silver spectacles, and in tears, or some pretty young rebel beauty in homespun, without hoops and in a towering passion," while soldiers looted their property. Indeed, Hutter had such a daughter, "the divine," ladies' man Halpine called her, who told the Yankee officers that she wished for peace but not subjugation by the Union. She said, "Oh, we have given up *everything* for the cause, save the barest necessities of life; and I cannot believe that God would allow a people to suffer so much as we have done, if not intending to reward us with final victory." Hutter's hospitality was apparently not lessened by his daughter's anger, Strother reporting that the generals and their staffs ate well and spent a comfortable night.[40]

During the night the Union men heard constant train traffic and even cheers and drums, leading to a conclusion that Lynchburg was being reinforced. It is possible that the noise was a rebel subterfuge, because few of Early's troops arrived that night. Hunter, still not certain what he faced, decided to look for weakness in the enemy line. In the morning he advanced his skirmishers in the center and directed continuous musket fire on the Confederate lines. General Sullivan, whose troops held that part of the line, thought that the enemy was much stronger than it had been the evening before, but it is likely that he was only facing improved defensive works. Because he thought his division was overmatched, he advised Hunter that a Union attack would result in disaster. Strother reported this opinion to his general, whom he found "dissatisfied and at the same time hesitated to order the advance." The morning was spent on a continuation of this steady firing but no movement by either side. The enemy made a sharp attack on Hunter's center at about 1:00 p.m., and for a time Sullivan's troops fell back. Hunter mounted his horse quickly, drew his sword, and personally rallied the men, sending in support from Crook's division. The situation was stabilized within the hour, as a result, according to Strother, of "the lionlike bearing of the commander."[41]

Fighting died down by about 3:00 p.m., and Hunter finally received solid information about rebel reinforcements. Some prisoners brought in by Sullivan's troops were North Carolinians from Early's corps, and they said that the Union force was facing twenty thousand or possibly thirty thousand new troops. The prisoners accurately told their captors that the Army of the Potomac had suffered a "temporary check at Petersburg, that Sheridan had been foiled in his attempt to open communications with us, and that General Lee had been enabled to detach a large force of veteran troops . . . to operate against us." Further, Averell on the right flank and Duffié on the left were reporting large and possibly superior enemy troop units building up on their fronts. All this convinced Hunter "that the enemy had concentrated a force of at least double the numerical strength of mine, but what added to the gravity of the situation was the fact that my troops had scarcely enough of ammunition to sustain another well contested battle." He, therefore, decided to retreat, Crook and Averell agreeing with the decision. Hunter ordered maintenance of a bold front by skirmishers for the remaining daylight hours, but he would withdraw from the battle when night fell. The difficult military maneuver of abandoning a battlefield surreptitiously while in contact with the foe was successfully accomplished; as one soldier wrote, "It was a very bad place to get an army from without alarming the enemy." The retreat ended the battle of Lynchburg—but not the campaign.[42]

Of course, Hunter was not outnumbered. His army was at least equal to and probably a third larger than his enemy's, but the shortage of munitions was real, since he could not depend on any further supplies reaching him from Sigel or Stahel in the lower valley. His communications down the valley were severed by Confederate guerrillas, reserves, home guards, and other small units that had reoccupied the valley towns—Lexington, Staunton, Harrisonburg—in his wake. Hunter and his staff returned to Major Hutter's and prepared to break contact with Early at dark. Hunter and his officers then fell back to the haunted house near Liberty which they had occupied on Thursday. Early, who had been planning to fall on Hunter in the morning, did not discover that Hunter had retreated until midnight, and he could not order the pursuit until daylight. The Army of West Virginia had gotten away clean, but Hunter did not know that yet.[43]

NOTES

1. John D. Imboden, "The Battle of New Market," in *Battles and Leaders of the Civil War,* ed. Robert Underwood Johnson and Clarence Clough Buel, 4 vols.

(1887–88; reprint, New York: Castle, 1991), 4:485; Jones had "eccentricities . . . almost as well-known to Virginians as those of Stonewall Jackson" (Edward A. Pollard, *Southern History of the Civil War,* 4 vols. [ca. 1865; reprint, New York: Blue and the Gray Press, ca. 1960], 4:33 n). Imboden said Jones was "of high temper, morose and fretful to such a degree that he was known by the soubriquet of 'Grumble Jones'" (J. D. Imboden, "Fire Sword and Halter," *The Annals of the War Written by Leading Participants, North and South* [Philadelphia: Time Publishing Co., 1925], 173).

2. Hunter's report to the adjutant general, 8 June 1864, U.S. Department of War, *The War of the Rebellion: A Compilation of the Official Records of the Union and Confederate Armies* (Washington, D.C.: Government Printing Office, 1880–1902), ser. 1 (hereafter *ORA* and ser. 1, unless otherwise indicated), 37, pt. 1, 94; David Hunter Strother, *A Virginia Yankee in the Civil War: The Diaries of David Hunter Strother,* ed. Cecil D. Eby, Jr. (Chapel Hill: University of North Carolina Press, 1961), 242; Marshall Moore Brice, *Conquest of a Valley* (Charlottesville: University of Virginia Press, 1965), 42.

3. Strother, *Diaries,* 242–43; *ORA,* 37, pt. 1, 94; Brice, *Conquest of a Valley,* 43–49.

4. Strother, *Diaries,* 243. Imboden did not like the position and made a "solemn and angry protest" to Jones, but he was ignored (Imboden, "Fire, Sword, and the Halter," 174).

5. Diary entry, 5 June 1864, Halpine's Diary, Huntington Library, San Marino, Calif.

6. Charles Graham Halpine, *Baked Meats of the Funeral* (New York: Carleton, 1866), 330; George Case Setchell, "A Sergeant's View of the Battle of Piedmont," *Civil War Times Illustrated* 2 (May 1963): 44. Strother thought the regiment's reaction was subdued, and the men "scarcely got up a decent cheer in response" (Strother, *Diaries,* 243, 251).

7. Diary entry, 5 June 1864, Halpine Diary, Huntington Library; Strother, *Diaries,* 244; Brice, *Conquest of a Valley,* 69–70; report, Col. William G. Ely, Twenty-eighth Connecticut, *ORA,* 37, pt. 1, 117.

8. Strother, *Diaries,* 244; Brice, *Conquest of a Valley,* 70–73.

9. Strother, *Diaries,* 244–45. Stahel was many years later given the Medal of Honor for his conduct in the battle.

10. Reports, Hunter, Col. Jacob M. Campbell, Fifty-fourth Pennsylvania Infantry, both 8 June 1864, *ORA,* 37, pt. 1, 95, 118–19; Brice, *Conquest of a Valley,* 73–74; Strother, *Diaries,* 244.

11. Strother, *Diaries,* 245; diary entry, 5 June 1864, Halpine's Diary, Huntington Library.

12. Ibid., 246; report, Hunter to adjutant general, 8 June 1864, *ORA,* 37, pt. 1, 95, message, Vaughn to Braxton Bragg, Richmond, 6 June 1864, 37, pt. 2, 151. Vaughn estimated that he had only three thousand troops, including Imboden's eight hundred cavalry.

13. Strother, *Diaries,* 246; diary entry, 5 June 1864, Halpine's Diary, Huntington Library; William Hanchett, *Irish: Charles G. Halpine in Civil War America* (Syracuse: University of Syracuse Press, 1970), 116.

14. Lee's report, 17 June 1864, *ORA,* 37, pt. 1, 153.

15. Ulysses Simpson Grant, *Memoirs of Ulysses S. Grant,* 2 vols. (New York: Charles L. Webster and Co., 1885), 2:276–77.

16. Martin T. McMahon, "Cold Harbor," in Johnson and Buel, *Battles and Leaders,* 4:220; letter, Grant to Hunter, 6 June 1864, *ORA,* 37, pt. 1, 598.

17. Strother, *Diaries,* 246–47; Brice, *Conquest of a Valley,* 99; diary entry, 6 June 1864, Halpine's Diary, Huntington Library.

18. Strother, *Diaries,* 248; Hanchett, *Irish,* 117. Five hundred wounded and sick rebel soldiers were found at Staunton (report, Hunter to adjutant general, 8 August 1864, *ORA,* 37, pt. 1, 96); Charles H. Lynch, *The Civil War Diary, 1862–1865* (Hartford, Conn.: Privately printed, 1915), 73.

19. Strother, *Diaries,* 248–49; Hunter's 8 June 1864, report, *ORA,* 37, pt. 1, 95.

20. Strother, *Diaries,* 249–50; Strother's August 1865 report to Hunter, appended to Hunter's April 1873 report, vol. 9, U.S. Army Generals' Reports of Civil War Service, 1864–87, Record Group 94, Records of the Office of the Adjutant General, National Archives (hereafter Hunter's 1873 Report, NA), 710; "Itinerary of general operations in the Department of West Virginia for May, June, and July, 1864," Hunter's 6 August, Crook's 7 July 1864, reports, *ORA,* 37, pt. 1, 4, 96, 120; diary entry, 8 June 1864, Halpine's Diary, Huntington Library.

21. Message, Grant to Hunter, 6 June, report, Averell to adjutant general, 1 July 1864, *ORA,* 37, pt. 1, 591, 146; Strother, *Diaries,* 250–51; Douglas Southall Freeman, *Lee's Lieutenants: A Study in Command,* 3 vols. (New York: Charles Schribner's Sons, 1944), 3:516; Brice, *Conquest of a Valley,* 106.

22. "Composition . . . of the Union Forces June 10–23," letter, Hunter to Halleck, 9 June 1864, *ORA,* 37, pt. 1, 103–4, 612; diary entry, 9 June 1864, Halpine's Diary, Huntington Library.

23. Strother, *Diaries,* 250; Special Orders No. 111, Department of West Virginia, 7 June 1864, Special Orders, Department of West Virginia, vol. 20, RG 393, U.S. Army Continental Commands, 1821–1920, NA (hereafter Orders, RG 393, NA); Hunter's 8 June report, message, Hunter to Stanton, 8 June, Stahel to adju-

tant general, 13 June 1864, *ORA,* 37, pt. 1, 94–95, 606 (also document no. 54212, Edwin M. Stanton Papers, Documents Division, Library of Congress [LOC]), 634.

24. Report, Hunter's 8 August report, orders of march, 9 and 10 June 1864, *ORA,* 37, pt. 1, 96, 614, 616; diary entry, 10 June 1864, Halpine Diary, Huntington Library; Strother, *Diaries,* 22; Thomas Francis Wildes, *Record of the One Hundred and Sixteenth Ohio Volunteer Infantry in the War of the Rebellion* (Sandusky: I. F. Mack and Bros., 1874), 102.

25. Hunter's 8 August 1864, report, *ORA,* 37, pt. 1, 96–97; VMI's superintendent, Col. Francis H. Smith, protested to McCausland against the hopeless defense that endangered the school and town (Jennings C. Wise, *The Military History of the Virginia Military Institute* [Lynchburg: J. P. Bell, 1915], 354); Henry Algerton Du Pont, *The Campaign of 1864 in the Valley of Virginia and the Expedition to Lynchburg* (New York: National American Society, 1925), 68. The number of cannon shots fired on Lexington is uncertain, but no one was hurt (William Couper, *One Hundred Years at V.M.I.,* 4 vols. [Richmond: Garrett and Massie, 1939], 3:32 n); George Crook, *General George Crook: His Autobiography,* ed. Martin F. Schmitt (1946; reprint, Norman: University of Oklahoma Press, 1986), 116–17; Strother, *Diaries,* 253. Some of Du Pont's cannonballs remain imbedded in the VMI barracks' walls.

26. Quoting Wise, *Military History of V.M.I.,* 368–69, reprinting Schoonmaker affidavit, 13 March 1914; letter, Schoonmaker to superintendent, VMI, 22 July 1922, Couper, *One Hundred Years,* 3:32–33.

27. Halpine, *Baked Meats,* 309; Strother, *Diaries,* 254–55. "I did all in my power to disuade him [Hunter]" from burning the school (Crook, *Autobiography,* 116); Charles H. Porter, "Operations of Generals Sigel and Hunter in the Shenandoah Valley, May and June, 1964," *Papers of the Military Historical Society of Massachusetts,* vol. 7 (Boston: by the Society, 1907), 79, attributes the cause of the burning order to cadets firing on Union forces from the institute.

28. Cecil D. Eby, Jr., "David Hunter: Villain of the Valley: The Sack of the Virginia Military Institute," *Iron Worker* 28 (Spring 1964): 7; Strother, *Diaries,* 255–56; quoting Meigs's note, original in VMI Archives, Couper, *One Hundred Years,* 3:40; Meigs, son of Montgomery C. Meigs, quartermaster general of the army in Washington, was killed on 3 October 1864, near Harrisonburg, perhaps by Confederate bushwackers dressed in Union uniforms (Matthew A. Capuano, *Rockingham County, Virginia(,) during the American Civil War, 1861–1865* [Harrisonburg: Chamber of Commerce, 1990], 7); Halpine, *Baked Meats,* 310; Hunter's 8 August 1864, report, *ORA,* 37, pt. 2, 97; quoting Edward Younger, ed. *The Governors of Virginia* (Charlottesville: University Press of Virginia, 1982), 15; F.

N. Boney, *John Letcher of Virginia: The Story of Virginia's Civil War Governor* (University: University of Alabama Press, 1965), 207.

29. Annual Report of Superintendent, VMI, 15 July 1864, in Couper, *One Hundred Years,* 3:36–40; Wildes, *116th Ohio Infantry,* 105; Cornelia (Peake) McDonald, *A Diary with Reminiscences of the War and Refugee Life in the Shenandoah Valley, 1860–1865* (Nashville: Cullom and Ghertner Co., 1935), 207; diary entry, letter, Hayes to his wife, both 12 June 1864, in Hayes, *Diary and Letters,* 4:473–74; diary entry, 11 June 1864, Halpine's Diary, Huntington Library; Halpine, *Baked Meats,* 312; Du Pont, *Campaign of 1864,* 68–69; Strother, *Diaries,* 256; transcript of Senate hearings on S. 544, 7 February 1914, in Wise, *Military History,* 464–84.

30. Hunter's 8 August 1864, report, *ORA,* 37, pt. 2, 97; Strother, *Diaries,* 356–57; diary entry, 12 June 1864, William Sever Lincoln, *Life with the 34th Massachusetts Infantry in the War of the Rebellion* (Worcester: Press of Noyes, Snow and Co., 1879), 306; Emmett MacCorkle, "George Washington: Prisoner of War," *Civil War Times Illustrated* 23 (March 1984): 30–35; Cecil D. Eby, Jr., *"Porte Crayon": The Life of David Hunter Strother* (Chapel Hill: University of North Carolina Press, 1960), 161. The cannons were returned separately.

31. Strother, *Diaries,* 256; William Harrison Beach, *First New York (Lincoln) Cavalry* (New York: Lincoln Cavalry Association, 1902), 371; diary entry, 12 June 1864, Halpine's Diary, Huntington Library.

32. Diary entry, 12 June 1864, Halpine's Diary, Huntington Library; letter, Hunter's 8 August report, Hunter to Duffié, 11 June 1864, *ORA,* 37, pt. 1, 97, 625; Strother, *Diaries,* 258; Crook, *Autobiography,* 116.

33. Orders, Strother to Averell, letter, Halpine to Sigel, 12 June, Special Orders No. 114, Department of West Virginia, 13 June 1864, *ORA,* 37, pt. 2, 627–28, 631.

34. Hunter's 8 August 1864 report, ibid., 98; Strother, *Diaries,* 258.

35. Hunter's 8 August 1864 report, *ORA,* 37, pt. 1, 98; Strother, *Diaries,* 259; Halpine, *Baked Meats,* 322; McDonald, *A Diary,* 336; diary entry, 14 June 1864, Halpine Diary, Huntington Library.

36. Grant, *Memoirs,* 2:302; Jubal A. Early, "Early's March to Washington," in Johnson and Buel, *Battles and Leaders,* 4:492.

37. Diary entry, 15 June 1864, Halpine Diary, Huntington Library; Strother, *Diaries,* 261; Hunter's 8 August 1864 report, *ORA,* 37, pt. 1, 98.

38. Hunter's 8 August report, Special Orders No. 115, Department of West Virginia, 15 June 1864, *ORA,* 37, pt. 1, 99, 634, and Orders, RG 393, NA; quoting Strother, *Diaries,* 262–63.

39. Early, "Early's March," 4:494–95; Hunter's 8 August report, telegram, Early to Breckinridge, 16 June 1864, *ORA*, 37, pt. 1, 99, 762–63; Wise, *Military History*, 373–74; Strother, *Diaries*, 263–64.

40. Strother, *Diaries*, 263–64; Halpine, *Baked Meats*, 344–46. Hutter, a Pennsylvania native, was commissioned an additional paymaster during the Mexican War, a paymaster in 1849, and resigned in April 1861. He was likely married to a Virginian.

41. Strother, *Diaries*, 264–66; Halpine, *Baked Meats*, 347; Early does not mention the attack in his account ("Early's March," 4:493; Hunter's 8 August 1864 report, *ORA*, 37, pt. 1, 99–100.

42. Strother, *Diaries*, 266; Strother's 1865 report in Hunter's 1873 Report, NA, 714; Hunter's 8 August 1864, report, *ORA*, 37, pt. 1, 100; Hanchett, *Irish*, 121; William B. Stack, "The Great Skedaddle," *Atlantic Monthly* 162 (July 1938): 86.

43. Hunter's 8 August 1864, report, *ORA*, 37, pt. 1, 100; Early, "Early's March," 4:493; Strother, *Diaries*, 266–67.

Chapter 8

FINAL CAMPAIGN

Hunter's retreat from Lynchburg was far from a rout. He was convinced that he had accomplished all that Grant's orders had required of him, and, although he did not follow up with an assault on Confederate positions at that town, he considered his subsequent movements a continuation of the successful expedition. Criticism of his actions would come later, but for another week or ten days no one in the North heard from him, information and the status and location of his command being restricted to reports in the Confederate press. It is perhaps this obviously biased slant on his activities which blackened Hunter's name, but the movement of the enemy army which he elected not to challenge at Lynchburg certainly contributed to the damage his reputation as a general suffered.

Early's instructions were that, following a defeat of Hunter at Lynchburg, he was to decide if his command was in sufficiently good condition to move down the valley, driving the remnants of Hunter's army before it. He was to continue that movement until he crossed the Potomac River, entered Maryland, and threatened Washington, D.C. Just as Hunter's advance on Lynchburg had drawn off a good part of Lee's infantry—Early's corps—Lee hoped that a threat to the Yankee capital would ease Grant's pressure on his lines south of the James River. Hunter's retreat meant that Early did not have to pay the price of disposing of Hunter by battle and that the advance down the valley might be possible. Still, Hunter commanded an unbloodied army, and much would depend on the direction in which the Union general marched his forces.[1]

Early was not yet able to execute his follow-up orders because his first objective, destruction of Hunter's army, had not been accomplished. On Sunday, 19 June, Hunter moved with deliberation and without panic through Liberty, sending Duffié's cavalry to secure the pass over the Blue Ridge Mountains at Buford Gap and assigning Averell's horseman as the rear guard. Early thought he could still bring the enemy to battle, and he sent infantry and cavalry to make contact. The Confederate column met Averell's troops at Liberty at about 4:00 p.m., and a sharp fight followed, Averell's men retreating through the town to join the main body. Hunter was eating dinner when the firing began, and he ordered members of his staff to mount their horses and organize the army to meet Early. The infantry and artillery were drawn up a mile west of the town to meet the attack, but Early's men did not continue the advance. The Union force resumed the march west at midnight under a full moon and in good weather, entering Buford Gap at dawn.[2]

The column was accompanied by a growing body of slaves, who had decided to leave all behind and join their fortunes with those of Hunter's army. An officer remarked, "The ever faithful colored people now began flocking to our army by the hundreds." A sergeant explained more fully: "The negroes have had no chance to escape until now. We have an army of them on our hands, nearly all of them carrying great bundles of clothing hastily packed. Old men and women, children and babies all going for freedom. Some of them took their masters buggys and loaded them with young nigs and rode along quite stilish," but hard times for them and the soldiers were coming.[3]

Clearly, Hunter did not wish to meet Early in battle, believing that he was outnumbered and because he considered his munitions supply too low. He did not, however, have much intelligence about his enemy's position and intentions, and the Union troops were several times seized by rumors that an attack was imminent. On the twentieth the march continued to Bonsack's Station, on the Virginia and Tennessee Railroad, the army burning its bridges, water tanks, and depot buildings as it moved; Hunter himself sometimes joined in the destruction. By late afternoon plans were made for resting the troops, but a 2:00 p.m. attack on Averell's rear guard and a report from Crook that he was being pressed by the enemy changed the situation. Hunter ordered the trains, protected by Duffié, to move to Salem, and Averell notified Hunter that the army "must prepare to fight immediately and this is the crisis of our fate, as this battle will save or ruin us." As it developed, the demonstration by the enemy was minor, so the move to Salem that night was uncontested. Early did not challenge Hunter, because Union artillery protected the mountain pass, but he moved over that barrier the following morning when it was no longer being defended.[4]

Early's last attack on Hunter was a minor affair. About 9:00 a.m. a demonstration was made against Hunter's rear guard, and the Union troops, who had slept little that morning, were spurred into activity. The train carrying supplies and spare artillery was hurried out of Salem westward on the road to New Castle. According to Strother, it was accompanied by "a disorganized rabble of mounted men, Negroes, skulkers, and fricoteurs [camp followers]" but not a properly organized guard. McCausland's cavalry raiders got into the train, spiked the guns of two batteries, disabled the carriages, and got away with the horses. The rebels were easily driven off, but eight of the disabled guns could not be moved and had to be abandoned. The affair was regarded as a significant defeat of Hunter and was so reported in the rebel press, possibly because the rebels needed a victory for morale purposes. Indeed, it is still written about as an action of importance, but official Richmond was not deceived; General Lee, writing to President Davis that Hunter had escaped Early, said, "I fear he has not been much punished, except by the demoralization of his troops and the loss of some artillery."[5]

A DAMAGED REPUTATION

Indeed, Hunter's army was becoming demoralized by the constant alarms, lack of rations, and uncertain future of the force. Such demoralization was shown by a growing breakdown in discipline, particularly with respect to the pillage and destruction of the territory through which the army marched. Early remarked on this aspect of the retreat:

> The scenes on Hunter's route from Lynchburg had been truly heart-rendering. Houses had been burned, and helpless women and children left without shelter. The country had been stripped of provisions and many families left without a morsel to eat. Furniture and bedding had been cut to pieces, and old men and women robbed of all the clothing they had except that on their backs. Ladies trunks had been rifled and their dresses torn to pieces in mere wantonness. Even the negro girls had lost their little finery.

Questions remain about whether depredations by Hunter's troops were as widespread as Early's accusations claim and whether damage done was according to the commander's policy or by lawless soldiers and camp followers. Moreover, Early's condemnation goes on to describe the burnings and plundering at Lexington, about which he may have been influenced by later Hunter actions. It seems unlikely that Hunter's troops performed as many reprehensible deeds as were ascribed to them during the march from Buchanan to Lynchburg and from there to Salem. The army was living off the land and without question robbed citizens of their food, and lawless elements among the soldiers no doubt thoroughly looted civilian property, even wantonly. A Connecticut soldier described the suffering on the march from Lynchburg: "Gen. Hunter is a great one for burning property, but everything he destroyed is rebel property, and should have

been destroyed." The letter betrays what may have been a common rationaliza-
tion for acts of vandalism among Hunter's soldiers as hardships increased. What
cannot be verified—at least until destructions of several weeks later are counted—
is that Hunter was a house burner as a matter of policy and practice.[6]

A soldier wrote in his diary on 17 June, when the army was before Lynchburg:
"General Hunter, for reasons best known to himself, has ordered the burning of
many fine old Virginia mansions with all their contents. Many fine appearing
ladies weep while their homes are burning." He had heard that the destruction
was retaliatory, because Union troops had been fired on from those residences,
but he does not specify that he is speaking about happenings at Lynchburg. Another observer, a Confederate officer, went beyond these uncertain comments:
"It was a scene of desolation. Ransacked houses, crying women, clothes from the
bed chambers and wardrobes of ladies, carried on bayonets, and dragged on the
road, the garments of little children, and here and there a burning house marked
the track of Hunter's retreat." And, finally, a Southerner writing nineteen years
after the retreat claimed that "a broad, black path marked his [Hunter's] trail," not
necessarily only on the retreat, and he goes on to say that from a peak in the Blue
Ridge Mountains 118 burning houses could be counted. Colonel Halpine insisted that Hunter ordered burning of just five private homes during the entire
valley campaign, a few in Newtown, Letcher's at Lexington, Anderson's at
Buchanan, and Leftwich's near Lynchburg. No source names citizens other than
these burned out before Hunter arrived back in the lower valley after the retreat,
but it seems certain that residences were burned under the May antiguerrilla
order, accidentally, and by marauding soldiers and camp followers. Although none
of the other house burning incidents are identified, Hunter may have acted im-
petuously when under pressure or when irritated. Crook said that during the
retreat women often asked Hunter to protect their property, and "his inevitable
answer would be: 'Go away! Go away, or I will burn your house!'" Crook does
not say, however, that any houses were indeed burned. It is difficult, therefore, to
explain Hunter's reputation for cruelty and unnecessary destruction.[7]

Halpine, writing immediately after the war, thought it was because reports
of "our miscreancies" came exclusively from rebel newspapers during the period
when Hunter's communications with the North were cut off. It seems more
likely that Hunter was a convenient villain during postwar Southern romanti-
cism of the conflict and a need to justify the enormous sacrifices made for the
Confederate cause. Some wished to remember the war as a struggle for Southern
genteel civilization against an uncultured and barbaric North that fought without mercy. It was useful, therefore, to emphasize suffering of the weak and help-
less, particularly delicate Southern women. Hunter was a convenient target in

this effort because his Virginia heritage could paint him as a traitor as well. The same label was placed on some of his troops—those in West Virginia regiments—who "like their leader were renegades from the traditions and instincts of their forefathers, and hence very little to be trusted." In some ways Hunter was more reviled than Sherman, Virginian Winfield Scott, and Sheridan, even though the Shenandoah Valley exploits of the latter were to be much more devastating than were Hunter's.[8]

THE LONG MARCH

Contributing to the defamation of Hunter's character was the retreat from Lynchburg, because it allowed cowardice to be added to the sins of cruelty, abolitionism, and arming blacks. After the 21 June probing of his rear guard outside Salem and McCausland's raid on the train, Hunter was no longer disturbed by Early, who decided that the pursuit had gone on long enough. His enemy was entering a mountainous area that made successful attack difficult, and, Early told Lee, the enemy was moving too fast—twenty miles a day—for him to catch up. Early's troops were not in good condition. "A great part of my command had had nothing to eat for the last two days, except a little bacon which was obtained at Liberty. It had marched sixty miles over very rough roads." Consequently, Early decided to rest a day and then move his command toward the Potomac, marching down the valley in the opposite direction along the track that Hunter had taken.[9]

Hunter had no idea that Early had abandoned his pursuit, and, when he found out he was no longer being followed by the rebels, it was still another ten days before he learned that they had turned down the valley. He did not consider returning to the Potomac northward through the Shenandoah Valley because he thought his army would be too vulnerable. Furthermore, Hunter knew that large supplies of rations were available in West Virginia, while the valley promised little. In the afternoon of 21 June the Union troops crossed the Catawba Mountain, descending into the valley of the same name, the route along a steep, zigzag road. Averell, along with all the cavalry, was sent on toward New Castle, twelve miles across further mountainous terrain, to clear the road for the rest of the troops. He was instructed to defend the route until the army appeared the next day. If Averell failed, the plan was to retire south from Catawba on the road to Blacksburg and the New River on the road to Western Tennessee. On the morning of 22 June an attack was still expected; Strother wrote:

> Our position will be a gloomy one if the reports we hear are confirmed.
> Worn out with fatigue, without supplies in a country producing little

and already wasted by war, the troops are beginning to show symptoms of demoralization, and short of ammunition we will hardly save our army if the enemy is as far ahead as it appears and occupies the positions reported. The General must have had an anxious time last night.[10]

Anxiety continued all day, but the army crossed Craig's Mountain, descended to Craig's (now Craig) Creek, and straggled into New Castle in the evening, foraging freely along the way. Strother thought that the "day's march was the crisis of our retreat," as rumors of the enemy were received from several directions. A council of war considered the army's options were it to be cut off, Crook recommending a move to the south to hit the Virginia and Tennessee Railroad, following it west to Tennessee, and destroying lead and salt mines in Wythe and Smyth Counties en route. Strother's recommendation was to destroy all baggage, to slip between the suspected enemy positions at Salem and Covington and move by forced marches to Fincastle, Buchanan, and over the Blue Ridge to Charlottesville, arriving finally at Harper's Ferry. Crook thought the plan "rash and impractical," but Hunter decided to continue as planned to Sweet Springs and possibly White Sulphur Springs, keeping a wary eye on what might appear from Covington.[11]

The twenty-third of June was very hot, and the army moved twenty hard miles over mountains toward Sweet Springs, arriving in the afternoon. The soldiers, as was by now their normal procedure, were soon "plundering generally or rather seeking plunder as there was little to be found here." Remarking on the meager spoils, a soldier said that the troops had no "real use for the articles of female apparel, such as bonnets and dresses; nor of household furnishings, such as pillowcases, sheets, &c" which they found. Hunter received word that the wagon train he had sent back from Liberty had been attacked by guerrillas. Its commander had abandoned the plan to go to Charleston via Lewisburg and had turned north to Beverly. As might be expected, Hunter was infuriated that guerrillas should be operating in the area, "and he threatened to burn right and left," a threat that he did not, however, carry out. After a comfortable night in the hotel at the Springs, staff discussions were once more held about the army's next move, and it was finally decided that the enemy was not pursuing with a large force. Hunter now believed that Early had returned to Lee's army opposite Grant, but this did not simplify the choice of direction for the Union column. Strother thought the better route was north to Warm Springs, Franklin, and Moorefield, West Virginia, to the Baltimore and Ohio Railroad at New Creek and Cumberland. Averell saw a danger in the proposal, because supplies would be scarce, and the rebels might attack through a number of gaps from the Shenandoah Valley. Crook's alternative was Lewisburg to Charleston, where water transportation along the Kanawha and Ohio Rivers back to the Baltimore and Ohio Railroad connecting with northern Virginia could be secured. It made more sense, Hunter agreed, because supplies were available at Meadow Bluff, Gauley, and Charleston.[12]

Hunter's staff had some concern about what might be expected in the lower Shenandoah Valley once the rebels found out that Hunter's force was well out of the way. Strother wrote, "It was foreseen that Early would, in all probability, make a counter-raid against the Baltimore & Ohio Rail Road, overthrow Gen'l Sigel's force and do much mischief," but the situation did not seem urgent. No one thought that Early would take a major force north to confront the Union armies before Washington. At the same time, Grant was also unaware of Early's destination and was facing a stalemate on the line before Richmond and Petersburg. Initial assaults on the latter were unsuccessful because of the failure by Union generals to follow up on opportunities, and for a time Grant had no further plan to defeat Lee. On 19 June Halleck sent Grant his views of the Hunter expedition, from which nothing had been heard for some time. He told the lieutenant general that he doubted that General Stahel would be able to reach Hunter with ammunition and reinforcements and that Hunter might be in some peril. Halleck said, "If the enemy's force, as is reported, is superior to Hunter's, his only escape will be into West Virginia, or by crossing the James and reaching you [Grant] on the south side [of Richmond]." He did not know that Hunter had reached the same conclusion, although Hunter did not consider the escape around Richmond, which Halleck thought extremely risky, except perhaps for cavalry. Grant answered two days later, "The only word I would send to General Hunter would be verbal, and simply to let him know where we are, and tell him to save his army in the way he thinks best, either by getting back into his own department or by joining us." He too thought a wide sweep to the south might be practical, but neither Grant nor Halleck had any way to communicate with Hunter, so suggestions about his options were moot.[13]

The column, Crook's division leading, started for the Greenbrier White Sulphur Springs at 2:00 p.m. on 24 June, the late start due to the time spent discussing the army's destination. The resort was reached that night after traveling through ideal bushwacker country, wooded with narrow gorges, but no enemy was encountered. The large resort hotel was abandoned and stripped, having been used as a Confederate hospital. The next morning Hunter took breakfast with his staff on the hotel's lawn, and the troops were soon on the road for Lewisburg and Meadow Bluff. The route had been well ravaged by competing armies and guerrilla bands, and, although Hunter's hungry troops looted extensively as usual, not much was left for burning, accidental or otherwise—most houses, bridges, and other structures having previously been destroyed. Hunter "ascertained that the officer left in command at [Meadow Bluff] with 400 men had become alarmed at some demonstration by guerrillas, and had, with baggage and supplies, fallen back to Gauley Bridge." This meant that the near-starving army had to go farther west before rations would be found. Halpine recalled the hundreds of stragglers from the army each day: "Our column trailed its weary length like a wounded, all but dying serpent."[14]

Hunter decided to go on ahead with a small escort, the infantry and trains to follow, and from 25 to 27 June he left the main body behind, a practice that Halpine thought unnecessarily risky. The retreating army arrived at Loup Creek near Gauley Bridge on Monday, 27 June. Hunter ordered it to remain there for two days with now ample rations, to give stragglers time to catch up. Finally, contact was made with Washington, where there was surprise that he turned up undefeated. Hunter reported to the adjutant general that his command was in excellent health and had lost few men on the "extremely successful" expedition that inflicted "great injury upon the enemy, and [was] victorious in every engagement." He explained that his retreat was due to the ammunition shortage and a belief that the enemy was superior in numbers to the Union force as well as easily reinforced from Richmond. "I have," he said, "two fine divisions of infantry and one of cavalry, all in good heart." He requested permission to hasten to the capital to plan how the Army of the Shenandoah should be employed. Crook wanted to repeat the valley expedition in the fall to prevent the rebels from gathering valuable crops. This seems to have been Hunter's plan as well, but he had not heard of Early's plan and progress. He thought that the rebel general was back in Richmond.[15]

THE RETURN NORTH

Hunter rested three days at Gauley. He was "quite sick. Has had a bad chill. No wonder!" Halpine recorded. Feeling better on 30 June, the general decided to go on with his staff to Charleston ahead of the main body to expedite the organization of river transportation from that town. He left General Crook in command, and, riding in an ambulance, passed with his escort over devastated old battlegrounds from earlier in the war, entering friendly territory for the first time in two months of campaigning. Hunter and his staff went the last ten miles into Charleston aboard a stern-wheel steamer, *General Crook,* on the Kanawha River, and landed at the town after dark, 30 June, in the rain. Strother wrote in his diary of his great relief that the campaign was over—but, of course, it was not.

Now the army, useless to the Union at Charleston, had to be moved again to face an enemy. Its bases at Martinsburg and Harper's Ferry were far distant and would soon be under threat of Confederate forces.[16]

Early, having left off pursuit of Hunter on 21 June, rested the next day and was at Buchanan on the twenty-third. He seemed particularly outraged to view the destruction at Lexington of the military institute and to learn that Mrs. Letcher had been given little time to evacuate her house before it was burned. Early would soon get his revenge for what he called these "deeds of a malignant and cowardly fanatic," as will be seen. Proceeding to Staunton, he left that town on the twenty-eighth with twenty thousand infantry, two thousand cavalry, and rations for seven days, the supplies reaching him from Waynesboro. General Lee told President Davis that his own troops were not hard-pressed by Grant, who seemed to have gone on the defensive. Lee did not know where Hunter was and told Davis that he was ordering Early down the valley from Staunton so as to draw Hunter after him. This would allow the Confederate commander to defeat Union forces in the lower valley and to deal with Hunter next. He concluded, "If circumstances favor, I should also recommend his crossing the Potomac."[17]

Early reached New Market on the thirtieth and was in Winchester by 2 July. Washington, D.C., was unaware of his strength or objectives, although scattered reports were received about what were considered raiding parties. The rebel general's situation was somewhat perilous, however, because his troops were out of supplies, which could not be expected to be sent to him from the south. Early's choice was made simple because his only source of provisions was the federal army, and he divided his forces in two, sending half to Martinsburg and the rest to Harper's Ferry. Sigel, commanding at Martinsburg, was not concerned on 2 July, but, when he was attacked the next day, he retreated from the town and depots with only token resistance, solving Early's supply problem.[18]

While Hunter was unaware of Early's movement against his department's bases commanded by his subordinates, Grant and Halleck also did not understand the military situation along the Potomac. In a series of telegrams sent on 3 July, Halleck told Grant that he had heard nothing from Hunter and did not know his destination. He thought Hunter was proceeding to Beverly, Moorefield, or Romney in West Virginia, but not because he had any information. Halleck added that he wanted to tell Hunter that the rumor was that Early had moved beyond Staunton. Grant was not convinced of this and asked Army of the Potomac commander, Maj. Gen. George Meade, if Early was somewhere in the defenses of Richmond/Petersburg; Meade replied that he had no such evidence. By late afternoon Stanton was informed of Grant's conclusion, that Early was indeed in the Shenandoah but that no position had been identified.[19]

Given this confusion among the army's leaders, Hunter's relative inaction moving his army to its bases in West Virginia is understandable. Hunter remained at Charleston until 3 July,

> reorganizing and refitting the troops, and gathering up the steamers to transport the army to Parkersburg [where the Baltimore and Ohio Railroad could be joined]. Feeling assured that the enemy would take advantage of the absence of these troops to make some demonstration in the Valley, every nerve was strained to hasten their movement. But the obstacles were for a time insurmountable. After their recent fatigues neither men nor animals were in any condition for a further march, and the excessive heat of the weather would have rendered such an attempt ruinous to the army. . . .Yet, on account of the long drought, the Ohio River was reported to be so low as to be impassable for all but the smallest boats; nevertheless, all the light-draught boats that could be found were seized and the troops embarked.[20]

Hunter and the staff boarded the steamer *Jonas Powell,* passed into the Ohio River at Point Pleasant, and reached Parkersburg the following day, 4 July, at about 6:00 p.m., taking rooms at the Spencer House. Here information was received that Sigel had been driven out of Martinsburg and that demonstrations were being made along the important Baltimore and Ohio, but it is not clear that Hunter and his staff interpreted the news as evidence of more than minor enemy probing. By 5 July Harper's Ferry also having been abandoned to Early, the real situation was recognized, and Stanton telegraphed Hunter in what appears to have been aggravation:

> The rebels have for two days back been operating against Martinsburg, Harper's Ferry, and other points on the line of the Baltimore railroad. These points being in your department you are expected to take promptly such measures as may be proper to meet the emergency. This Department has for some time been without any information as to where your forces are and how employed. You will please report to the Adjutant-General the position of your forces, and acknowledge the receipt of this telegram.

Hunter's answer was short; he said he was pushing on to Martinsburg as soon as his straggling troops were gathered in Parkersburg. Halleck, who probably wrote Stanton's message, also sent orders emphasizing that Hunter was in command of all forces opposing the enemy's threat to Maryland and the rail-road.[21]

Hunter was, of course, more active than Stanton knew reorganizing his regiments and sending them on to the scene of the threat. He was, Halpine judged, like "a chafed tiger," knowing he would be blamed for letting Early by and not arriving in time to defend the Potomac. His temper, often easily aroused, was triggered by an editorial that Strother characterized as "traducing the General and the expedition from which we have just returned." It appeared in the *Parkersburg Gazette* on 7 July, and Hunter ordered the editor, James E. Wharton, arrested and imprisoned, his paper destroyed, and his office closed. Hunter later explained to West Virginia Governor Arthur I. Boreman why he thought it necessary to take these actions. It was not, he said, because of criticism of his conduct, which Hunter considered "merely a matter of taste." The offense was, he continued, printing the words: "General Hunter with his command has passed through our city (Parkersburg) on their way east." Hunter said this was "contraband news and utterly untrue" because only one-third of the army had reached the town, and much of it remained there. The second offense was more serious—Wharton's words: "We were sorry to see so much suffering among them. Men are completely worn out, and many in the division had died of starvation. . . . The suffering of the soldiers in their movement from Lynchburg to Charleston was terrible, and they half require rest and surgical care"—gave "aid and comfort to the enemy." The general argued that "the business of a soldier is one in which 'suffering' forms an inevitable part." He said that his men were in better shape than were troops "resting in their camps. The worst enemy to health are [*sic*] not privations and fatigue; the licentiousness of an idle camp or an ill-regulated town will swell the hospital returns far quicker and more seriously than all our men suffered in their march from near Lynchburg to near Gauley Bridge." That the editor's view of his troops' condition was accurate bothered Hunter not at all, but the soldiers seem to have resented the general's claims that they were in fine shape. One wrote in his diary:

> Hunter disgraced himself in our eyes at [Camp] Pyatt [Piatt at Charleston] when he reported to the war department at Washington that his retreat from Lynchburg was successful. He said some had fared rather hard owing to the want of supplies in the enemies country, but were all doing well and were well satisfied and in high spirits and would be ready for another grand tour in a few days. . . . This was too much for flesh and blood to bear. Hundreds and thousands were entirely used up. None of us were in fit condition to go immediately into the field and he knew it as well as we did.

Another told of a song inspired by the ordeal:

> General Hunter, on the Lynchburg raid,
> D-d near starved the First Brigade.[22]

Editor Wharton was released a few days later, apparently because he showed sufficient contrition, but Hunter wanted the message to be sent to other newspapers in Wheeling and elsewhere. His reason was that, because his army contained many West Virginia troops, "it would seem an act both of justice and charity to disabuse their friends and families of the harrowing pictures of distress which have been put forth."[23]

Another newspaper, the *Wheeling Daily Register,* on 9 July found yet another way to irritate the general. The journal reported some of Hunter's burnings, but the real issue was a condemnation of the purloining of the statue of Washington from the Virginia Military Institute. On that very day Strother had at Hunter's direction written to Governor Boreman, turning over the statue—which had been destined for West Point—to West Virginia. Hunter may have seen an advantage in making this gift to the state and was angered that the gesture was ridiculed. The *Register's* perhaps unexpectedly bitter condemnation of Hunter's action caused him to order the officer commanding the military post at Wheeling, Capt. Ewald Over, in the words of the *Wheeling Daily Intelligencer,* "to arrest the responsible editors of the *Wheeling Register* and put them in military prison, and suppress for the present the further publication of the newspaper." Over arrested the newspaper's owners, Lewis Baker and O. S. Long, and, despite their letters to Hunter asking reasons for their detention and for an end to it, they were held until mid-September by the district commander.[24]

General Sullivan's infantry division left Parkersburg Wednesday morning, 6 July, and Hunter followed with his staff the next evening, bound for Cumberland, reaching the town at 10:00 a.m. Friday the eighth. The trip was not without excitement, the general's party being awakened at 2:00 a.m. by the sound of musket fire. Captain Stockton shouted, "Bushwackers!" causing "general consternation. . . . Everyone else was lying on the floor and the General looking out the window." As it turned out, the firing was intended as a salute to Hunter by the guard at Clarksburg. Hunter set up his headquarters at the St. Nicolas Hotel and spent the day hurrying his troops to the east. Early, after demonstrating against the Union forces from Martinsburg and Harper's Ferry which were at Maryland Heights, crossed the river on the fifth, and most of the Confederate troops were in or near Frederick on the ninth. Early's approach caused panic in Washington, particularly as refugees fleeing Maryland appeared in the capital. The situation seemed particularly critical when, for two or three days, the city had no mail service and telegraph lines and rail connections to the west were suspended.[25]

ATTACK ON WASHINGTON, D.C.

Grant, once he understood Early's intention, acted to defend the capital, whose own troops had largely been stripped to feed his high-casualty actions against Lee. He and Halleck took the opportunity to relieve Sigel and Stahel, both for failure to use their troops against the rebel raiders, and the first primarily for making one too many "successful retreats," abandoning "stores, artillery and trains" to the enemy. Both were ordered to report to Hunter, who sent Sigel immediately to Washington, but he kept Stahel, sending him on a twenty-day disability leave. Strother had hoped that the poor performance of the officers would "finish the Dutch element in this department." When it had at least partially done so, he wrote with satisfaction, "Thus ends this political speculation of the President, in disgust, mortification, and injury to all concerned." Grant did more than shuffle commanders, however; he also ordered new troops to Washington, Maj. Gen. Horatio G. Wright's Sixth Army Corps from the Army of the Potomac and, later, elements of the Nineteenth Army Corps arriving in the East from the Red River campaign in Louisiana. Few of these new troops were on hand to meet Early south of Frederick, at the railroad and turnpike crossings of the Monocacy River, where Maj. Gen. Lew Wallace had gathered militia and other raw troops to meet twice as many rebel veterans.[26]

The battle of Monocacy was fought on Saturday, 9 July, and Wallace's outmatched troops were defeated, but they delayed Early by a day. Two days later Early's exhausted soldiers appeared before Fort Stevens in the District of Columbia, but the defenders were able to prevent an assault. The Confederate commander decided on Tuesday morning that he was facing impossible odds—Hunter was assembling troops in the rear, reinforcements sent by Grant were arriving in Baltimore and Washington, Pennsylvania was raising militia regiments, and the large federal force at Maryland Heights was a potential threat. Late on 12 July, Early withdrew from before the capital city, leaving behind looted houses and the burned ruins of "Falkland," the home of Postmaster General Montgomery Blair near Silver Spring. Early believed in retaliation but denied that he had ordered Blair's house destroyed or the burning of Maryland governor A. W. Bradford's residence near Baltimore by a rebel cavalry detachment. Still, these actions looked very much like vengeance for the loss of Letcher's house and VMI. Early reported that he withdrew westward on the thirteenth and "crossed the Potomac at White's Ford, above Leesburg, in Loudoun County, on the morning of the fourteenth, bringing off the prisoners captured at Monocacy, and our captured beef and horses, and everything else in safety." He was chased by General Wright with troops from the Sixth and Nineteenth corps but was unmolested and not followed into Virginia, resting at Leesburg on the fourteenth and fifteenth.[27]

Hunter remained at Cumberland, far from the actions near Washington, until 14 July. The evening before Halleck wired that Wright, with twelve thousand men, was following Early, and the chief of staff suggested that Hunter join in the pursuit. He also asked Brig. Gen. Albion P. Howe—Sigel's replacement—who had reoccupied Harper's Ferry, if he had heard from Wright and directed him to take his orders from General Sullivan, who was thought to be at Martinsburg. Later in the day, however, Hunter lost track of Sullivan, who departed Martinsburg for an unknown place. Finally, in apparent frustration Hunter wired a quartermaster officer at Martinsburg: "Where is General Wright? Where is the enemy?" Sending Duffié's just-arrived cavalry ahead, Hunter left by rail for the east to take over direction of the principal forces in his department. On reaching Martinsburg in the morning of 14 July, he found the town and surroundings desolate, not yet recovered from resupplying Early's army a few days earlier. Hunter and the staff left on horseback for Harper's Ferry, to join up with Howe and to obey orders to get between Early and the nation's capital.[28]

While Hunter was making his way to his troops in the field, Wright was bombarding Halleck with reports of his own slow and cautious progress in going after Early. By late evening on 14 July he was concentrated at Poolesville, Maryland, not far from where Early had crossed into Virginia at least twenty-four hours ahead of the pursuit. In a 6 p.m. message Wright told Halleck the situation:

> I have not been able to get any intelligence from General Hunter's command, and have, therefore, for further operations only two divisions of my corps [the Sixth], numbering perhaps 10,000, and some 500 possibly of the Nineteenth Corps, which, unless I overrate the enemy's strength, is wholly insufficient to justify the following up of the enemy on the other side of the Potomac. I presume this will not be the policy of the War Department, and shall, therefore, wait instructions.[29]

QUARRELING WITH WASHINGTON

Hunter already felt pressure that he had not done as much as he could to take charge of the defenses of Washington and that he had failed to keep the War Department fully informed of the status of his troops since he left Staunton over a month before. At 1:30 A.M. on 15 July, upon his arrival at Harper's Ferry, he received a telegram from Halleck forwarding decisions made by Lincoln, Stanton, and Grant, orders that increased his sense that he was being made an example. Halleck said Hunter had "not answered dispatches, [and] we are left in the dark in regard to your force and movements." In what can be interpreted to be the result of this supposed failing, Hunter was informed that Wright was appointed by Lincoln to be "in supreme command of the forces operating" against Early. Hunter was given a choice of continuing to command, although subordinate to Wright, the troops he had brought from West Virginia and the garrisons he had left behind on the late Lynchburg expedition or to retain command of the Department of West Virginia, turning his troop command responsibilities over to General Crook. The message closed with a final admonition: "It is highly important that you take all possible means to keep the War Department advised of the condition of affairs in your department. For the last two weeks little or nothing of a reliable character has been heard from you."[30]

Lincoln biographer Carl Sandburg saw Halleck's wire as "either pathetically stupid or intentionally malicious," giving the impression, as it did, that Hunter was losing his command because he was "slow and dumb." Strother did not see it this way. His reaction to the new order was mild, but he no doubt added to Hunter's natural resentment of it by his views about the Early invasion and the likelihood that his general was being blamed for the failures of others. He thought the rebels' clean escape "with all their spoils . . . the most disgraceful affair of the war. . . . The enemy has made his raid and is gone scot-free without a fight. The damage is small, but the disgrace unspeakable." Hunter wired Stanton the next day to express his "sincere regret that the President should have seen fit . . . to have so far censured my conduct as to place before me the alternatives, either of turning over my command of troops in the field to one of my own brigadiers, or volunteering to serve under a junior of my own rank." As for his tardy reporting, Hunter said that he had been "too busy in the task of pressing forward my command to give time for any labor that did not appear of public benefit." He added that he had personally had to perform the jobs of chief of ordnance, commissary, and quartermaster because of illness and incompetence among his staff. He went on to describe other difficulties—low water in the rivers, railroad interruptions, and so on—not forgetting to remind the secretary that he had no responsibility for Sigel's failure to defend Martinsburg. Hunter concluded with a request that he be replaced by another officer, one "more enjoying the confidence of the President."[31]

Hunter did not neglect his duties while awaiting his relief. From his Harper's Ferry headquarters he ordered Sullivan, with almost nine thousand infantry and cavalry, to join Wright; told Washington that he expected Crook to arrive any time with a brigade, another thirty-four hundred men to follow; and resolved that Averell would operate from Martinsburg against Early's cavalry when he arrived there from Parkersburg. He also told Washington that there was no chance of his troops or Wright's overtaking the enemy. Hunter's actions appear to have been in keeping with Grant's desires about how to counter Early. Grant told Halleck to direct Hunter to chase the rebels up the valley, even as far as Gordonsville and Charlottesville. When it could be definitely established that Early was out of Maryland, Hunter "should have upon his heels veterans, militia men, men on horseback, and everything that could be got to follow to eat out Virginia clear and clean so far as they go, so that crows flying over it for the balance of this season will have to carry their provender with them." At the same time, the lieutenant general was defending Hunter from criticism he was hearing from Washington, much of it likely to have originated with Halleck, who had little tolerance for Hunter's dislike for proper military channels and, perhaps, Hunter's excesses. At Stanton's direction Assistant Secretary of War Charles A. Dana wrote to Grant about one of these excesses, telling him that "certain rumors about Hunter . . . had reached the War Department," such as "that Hunter had been engaged in an active campaign against the newspapers of West Virginia." Grant's answer was that, if Hunter had engaged in such warfare, "he has probably done right." He said that he was "sorry to see such a disposition to condemn a brave old soldier . . . without a hearing." Hunter had conducted a successful campaign "in a country where we had no friends" but the enemy had many. "I fail to see yet that General Hunter has not acted with great promptness and great success. Even the enemy give him great credit for courage, and congratulate themselves that he will give them a chance of getting even with him."[32]

Hunter did not know about Grant's defense of him, and, still chaffing over Halleck's telegram, wired Lincoln from Harper's Ferry on 17 July, asking to be relieved. "Your order, conveyed through General Halleck, has entirely destroyed my usefulness. When an officer is selected as the scapegoat to cover up the blunders of others, the best interests of the country require that he should at once be relieved of the command." Lincoln answered an hour and a half after receiving Hunter's message, saying that the order was "only nominally mine" but had been written by others (Stanton and Halleck) without a thought of making a scapegoat. Grant wanted Wright to command the force against Early because he had the majority of the troops, but Hunter "had the rank." Therefore, the odd command structure was a device to work around the problem. Lincoln concluded with, "General Grant wishes you to remain in command of the department and I do not wish to order it otherwise."[33]

Strother interpreted Lincoln's telegram as a promise that the unusual command relationships were temporary, although such a suggestion is not in the message. In any event, Hunter was satisfied with Lincoln's apology, and he concerned himself with conditions and events in his department. His first order of business was to recommend to Stanton that Crook be immediately promoted to major general, as many of his former commanders recommended and because Hunter considered him "one of the best soldiers I have ever seen." Stanton replied the same day that he would be delighted to grant the request but that there was no vacancy in the army, so Crook would have to be content at present with a brevet promotion, the full appointment to come later. Hunter also received directions from Halleck which were mostly a paraphrase of Grant's "crows" correspondence but which contained further orders and cautions that Halleck said were Grant's. One seemed to be a rebuke of Hunter's conduct after Lynchburg: "If compelled to fall back you will retreat in front of the enemy toward the main crossings of the Potomac, so as to cover Washington, and not be squeezed to one side, so as to make it necessary to fall back into West Virginia to save your army." Hunter did not immediately see these words as pejorative but would six months later.[34]

A TIME OF EXCESS

His concern about conditions in the department were no doubt exacerbated by the exchanges Hunter was having with Washington and the belief that he was being blamed for exposing the capital to Early's attack. This pressure may explain why the general entered a particularly dark period, ordering many actions that were certainly beyond normal military practice. He was also sixty-one years old, no doubt tired from the long campaign and the hundreds of miles he had traveled by wagon and on horseback. That Maria Hunter joined him at Harper's Ferry does not seem to have tempered his disposition. Events that took place by his orders were the basis for much of the cruel and heartless reputation for which Hunter has largely been remembered. He had no better understanding of the military situation along the Potomac than did Halleck, Wright, and other generals; none of them were able to determine Early's position and movements. In fact, the Confederate leader had left Leesburg and was at Berryville in the valley on 17 July, ten miles from Winchester.

Hunter clearly believed that he was forced to operate among a hostile and aggressive population and that it was therefore necessary to show strong authority and no tolerance of any actions or opinions that might be termed anti-Union or pro-Confederate. Some of the ways his policy was implemented include suppression of the press, as mentioned, the continued application of the order authorizing seizure and burning of civilian property near sites of guerrilla activities, reparation payments for damages sustained by loyal Unionists, deportation from their homes behind federal lines to rebel territory of citizens thought to be disloyal, and—most remembered—destruction of the homes of prominent lower Shenandoah Valley citizens associated with Confederate or rebel Virginia governments. It is curious that Hunter ordered these burnings when the 17 July order from Halleck, claiming to be from Grant, specifically told Hunter to clean out the valley. "I do not mean that houses should be burned, but . . . the people [should be] notified to move out." Hunter apparently did not consider this caution to apply to the conduct of every affair of the Department of West Virginia.

Apparently in retaliation for Early's burning of Governor Bradford's house, on 17 July he issued orders sending Capt. Franklin G. Martindale with a detachment of the First New York (Lincoln) Cavalry to Charles Town, West Virginia, to "burn the dwelling-house and outbuildings of Andrew Hunter, not permitting anything to be taken therefrom except the family." Hunter, who some say was named after the general's father and who was a distant cousin, had been a Virginia state senator since secession and had been associated with the prosecution of John Brown at Harper's Ferry. His home was destroyed and he himself imprisoned. The same order called for burning "Boydsville," the home of Charles James Faulkner, father of the Confederate officer captured at Piedmont—another Hunter relative—but, to Hunter's dismay, the act was not carried out. Hunter explained that Mrs. Faulkner confused the matter by bringing up questionable ownership, as indicated in a will, and Lincoln personally exempted her property from retaliatory burning. A day later the homes of Edmund Jennings Lee, a distant relative of General Lee, and Alexander Robinson Boteler, a former Confederate congressman, were leveled. Boteler, a politician who had strongly supported the Union before Virginia's secession, was related to Hunter by marriage. Boteler probably met his wife, born Helen Macomb Stockton, while a student at Princeton College in the early 1830s. Hunter, however, "spared no rebels 'for relation's sake,'" a young officer observed. These Jefferson County, West Virginia, destructions would be the reason given for retaliation by Early before the end of the month. They were not thought to be proper actions by officers of the First New York Cavalry, the unit called upon to carry them out, but the offices made no formal protest. Hunter did receive a protest in the form of a letter from the evicted Mrs. Henrietta Lee, who accused Hunter of wronging a harmless woman with small children while her husband was "absent, in exile" (he was a rebel officer). She asked if the burning was because her husband was related to Robert E. Lee, "the noblest of Christian warriors, the greatest of Generals. . . . Heaven's blessings be upon his head forever"—not words to raise Hunter's sympathy. Mrs.

Lee continued with such phrases as "weak women and innocent children, agonized hearts of widows, defenceless [*sic*] villages and refined and beautiful homes." The words would be useful in later years, as the letter's editor said, to "have given General Hunter a place in the annals of infamy only equaled by the contempt felt for his military accomplishments."[35]

Andrew Hunter was Strother's uncle and Boteler and Lee his friends before the war, but he was not responsible for their treatment. He was ambivalent about the usefulness of house burning and wrote that three times he had dissuaded Hunter from burning all of Charles Town, the seat of Jefferson County, where the houses were located. "I am sorry to see this warfare begun and would be glad to stop it, but I don't pity the individuals at all." He wrote that mutual devastation was likely "to depopulate the border counties which contain my kindred on both sides of the question," but there was not much he could do. Another official, John W. Garrett, president of the Baltimore and Ohio, whose line ran through and was protected by Hunter's command, went to see Hunter the day after Strother protected Charles Town for the third time. The reason for the visit was to request protection for a track restoration crew near Harper's Ferry, but Hunter volunteered house burning comments. He described the order to destroy Andrew Hunter's and Faulkner's houses and said "that it is his intention if he finds guerrillas at Charles Town to burn that town; and as Clarke County [West Virginia] only polled two votes against the [Virginia] ordinance of secession, he will burn every house in the county." Garrett was alarmed by this and wired Stanton that Hunter's policies only forced retaliation and would "add to the losses and suffering of our border." He thought that moderation would be a better course.[36]

On the day Andrew Hunter's house was burned Hunter ordered that the citizens of Frederick, Maryland, a town briefly occupied by Early, be screened to determine which citizens had pointed out "the property of Union men and otherwise manifest[ed] their sympathy with the enemy." These men were to be sent at once to Harper's Ferry with their families, the men to be sent on to a military prison at Wheeling and the women and children to be taken beyond Union lines into Confederate-held territory. The property of the rebel supporters was to be seized, their houses to be converted to public purposes, and their furniture to be sold at auction, the proceeds from which would be used to reimburse loyal citizens who had suffered losses from Early's occupation. Hunter's order went beyond punishing those identified as aiding the rebel army: he also wished the Frederick town commander to round up "all male secessionists" and send them to Harper's Ferry; their families, however, were not to be deported.[37]

Hunter followed up with another order to Frederick, directing that the editors of the *Republican Citizen* be moved south "beyond the military lines of the United States Forces, within twenty-four hours."Were they to return before war's end, they were to be "punished as spies and traitors." Hunter also named in orders Charles Cole, editor of the *Maryland Union,* and twenty-two others who, along with their families, were to be arrested and transported to the South. He told the provost marshal at Hagerstown to gather up all quartermaster department employees "known to be in sympathy with the rebellion" and send them to Harper's Ferry. The order went further, calling for notification of "all open and avowed sympathizers with the rebellion, as well as those who have by word or act aided or assisted the rebel army, residents of Hagerstown, and vicinity, to remove with their families, beyond our lines, & within the limits of the so called Southern Confederacy, within forty-eight hours."[38]

Other towns in the Department of West Virginia apparently received similar directions. How many suspected rebel sympathizers and supporters were moved and from what towns is not fully recorded, but Lincoln made an inquiry about citizens of Cumberland, Maryland. Hunter told the president that he had evidence that some people of the town "were known as secession sympathizers, and . . . had sons in the rebel army, had within the present month communicated with them through our lines, and had sent clothing, money, and important military information to said rebels in arms, and had also received and concealed said rebel soldiers in their houses in Cumberland." Hunter thought that sending "such offending families outside our lines" was necessary for the security of his department. In the case of Mr. William O. Sprigg and family—probably the deportees whom Lincoln had asked about—he admitted he had no evidence that the avowed rebel was in touch with the South, but "I yet thought that considerations of public safety required his removal, also as the presumption was that clandestine correspondence is carried on in all such cases where practical." Hunter's explanation did not settle the question, and it was to arise again a few days later.[39]

In a variation on forced deportations of civilians, Hunter directed General Averell at Martinsburg to keep a number of citizens of Hedgesville, a nearby town, in custody. They were to be released only on the condition "that they pay to Mr. Coakus, of North Mountain Station, double the amount of property destroyed for him during the recent rebel raid. If the money is not paid at once their houses will be burned, and their families will be sent across our lines south." Hunter was to be asked again about this matter, and it became the formal reason given for his removal from his command.[40]

On 19 July Crook discovered Early at Berryville, engaged him, and was defeated, losing 422 men, after which Early occupied Winchester. The following day Averell's cavalry had a sharp fight with the rebel horse north of Winchester. Early, expecting to be pursued by Wright, fell farther back up the valley to Strasburg.

Wright, who had no part in these fights, did not move aggressively, which Grant blamed on "the constant and contrary orders he had been receiving from Washington." On 22 July, apparently convinced that the threat to the capital had diminished, the War Department ordered Wright's troops returned to the defenses of Washington for transport to Grant's forces opposing Lee. Wright's move left Crook in field command of the troops in the valley under Hunter's department supervision. Yet Hunter wired Lincoln that, without Wright's force—and perhaps other reinforcements—he was not strong enough to resist Early if he were to attack. Hunter, however, thought that Early was returning to the Richmond area, his scouts having reported, erroneously, that Strasburg was clear of rebels. At this critical time Grant's immediate communications with Washington were cut off by the failure of the cable across Chesapeake Bay which he depended on.[41]

ANOTHER CONFEDERATE INVASION

Early correctly read the changing nature of his opposition and decided to attack, moving north down the Valley Pike toward Crook's and Averell's forces at Winchester. He met Crook and soundly defeated him at Kernstown, a few miles south of Winchester, on 24 July. Crook lost almost twelve hundred men in the rout, most of them captured, and he hastily retreated to Bunker Hill, ten miles north of Winchester. Strother reported, "Martinsburg is in wild stampede, everything is being sent off and the trains on the B&O stopped running." Next day Early and Crook's detachments covering the way east to Washington skirmished at Martinsburg and Williamsport, Crook successfully retreating with his wagon trains into Maryland. The rebels, who were resupplied from abandoned Union stores, set about destroying the railroad near Martinsburg and threatened to cross the Potomac near Williamsport.[42]

Hunter had the responsibility for opposing Early, and, despite the peculiar command arrangement, he gave Crook general directions and had similar authority over Wright, who had not gotten away from Washington and was hastening westward through Rockville, Maryland. Under Halleck's overall supervision the Union army was not aggressively opposing Early. It was deploying to protect rather than to attack. Hunter told Crook to concentrate at Middletown on the Catoctin River near Frederick, believing that Early was still at Winchester. Because of the uncertainty of the military situation, Hunter told Lincoln that he thought it was more important to screen "Washn & Balto" than to prevent Early from gathering crops, which Hunter understood to be Early's objective. Since he was convinced that Early had a limited mission and because not much enemy activity was reported from 26 July to early 29 July, Hunter spent some time on departmental matters. Strother recorded with some satisfaction, "The General is making numerous preemptory dismissals of officers for various misdemeanors and misconduct." One officer on Hunter's list was Maj. Henry Peale, of the Eighteenth Connecticut Infantry, who was recommended for dismissal on grounds that he made "exagerated [*sic*] & false statements in regard to the suffering and losses of the Army of West Virginia in the late military operation." To retain such an officer would, Hunter held, encourage "a very demoralizing tendency." At least two other field officers—Col. L. P. Pierce, Twelfth Pennsylvania Cavalry, and Lt. Col. Alonzo W. Adams, First New York (Lincoln) Cavalry—were also found to have various qualities of incompetence as officers. Hunter took the precaution of asking Lincoln not to reverse actions against officers guilty of "drunkeness [*sic*][,] cowardice and General incapacity and worthlessness." He said he was forced to act because "immediate action [was] essential to the organization and efficiency of my command."[43]

Writing to Halpine, then in New York, Hunter explained the need to dismiss officers found wanting. "Our Cavalry and some of our Infantry behaved in a disgraceful manner in the recent fight of Crook's near Winchester. The officers in many instances leading off their men to the rear, stampeding the trains, and starting all sorts of lying reports with regard to disaster, defeat &c. &c. . . . I have dismissed some thirty officers for cowardice, drunkenness, basely deserting their commands, and spreading lying reports." The bright spot, he said, was the infantry returned from the Lynchburg raid, which showed bravery and steadiness and prevented total disaster.[44]

The rebel crossing was made on the twenty-ninth, Early making demonstrations against Harper's Ferry and once again causing panic in Washington, Gettysburg, Harrisburg, and among citizens of Maryland and West Virginia. Hunter's information late in the day was that Early had pushed Averell through Hagerstown, Maryland, and was forcing the Union cavalry back on Chambersburg, Pennsylvania. The next day Chambersburg was occupied by fifteen hundred Confederate cavalrymen commanded by General McCausland, with this order from Early: "That in retaliation of the depredations committed by Major-General Hunter, of the U.S. forces during his recent raid, it is ordered that the citizens of Chambersburg pay to the Confederate States by Gen McCausland the sum of 100,000 in gold; or in lieu thereof of 500,000 in greenbacks or national currency, otherwise the town would be laid in ashes within three hours." One of McCausland's subordinates wrote years afterward that Early had intended the money, if paid, to be used to reimburse Edmund Lee, Boetcher, and Letcher (he did not mention Andrew Hunter) for the losses of their properties. Since such a large sum of money could not be found, the village was destroyed, leaving about three hundred families homeless. McCausland withdrew to the southwest and, after skirmishes with Averell and Brig. Gen. Benjamin F. Kelley, rejoined Early south of the Potomac several days later, much the worse for wear.[45]

Early gave several further reasons for this raid. One was that he had heard of the destruction of the Andrew Hunter and Boetcher houses when he reached Martinsburg on the twenty-sixth. He also gave a broader explanation for the retaliation: "I had often seen delicate ladies, who had been plundered, insulted and rendered desolate by the acts of our most atrocious enemies, and while they did not call for it, yet in their anguished expressions of their features while narrating their misfortunes, there was a mute appeal to every manly sentiment of my bosom for retaliation which I could no longer withstand." The raid on Chambersburg was not the end of incendiary actions and counteractions, although it was the last one connected with General Hunter. Two weeks later Lincoln sought to end the practice of "house burning and other destruction of private property," but it continued.[46]

Grant, who had been out of touch some of the time, was, also simultaneously with Early's advance, trying to get the better of Lee before Petersburg. Some of the potential pressure on the rebels was relieved by the two army corps diverted to Washington, and Grant sought to prevent Lee from concluding that he could spare troops to reinforce his western armies. But Grant was not satisfied with fixing Lee's troops. He also sought to overcome the thin defenses of Petersburg by setting off an enormous mine under Confederate lines, rushing the city, and outflanking Richmond. The mine was exploded on 30 July, but the execution of the follow-up was, Grant said, "a stupendous failure," due to the incompetence and inefficiency of subordinate commanders. Chambersburg's burning on the same day as the mine attack failure directed Grant's personal attention to the Shenandoah and caused him to send additional reinforcements north in order to apply more vigorous military measures against the rebels in that much fought-over area of operations.[47]

As Grant analyzed the problem, defensive failures at the mouth of the valley had been due somewhat to weak commanders, but he placed the principal blame on interference from Washington. "It seemed to be the policy of General Halleck and Secretary Stanton to keep any force sent there, in pursuit of the invading army, moving right and left so as to keep between the enemy and our capital; and, generally speaking, they pursued this policy until all knowledge of the whereabouts of the enemy was lost." On 1 August he told Halleck that he was sending General Sheridan, and his seasoned cavalry divisions, with instructions to take over field command and to "put himself south of the enemy and follow him to the death. Wherever the enemy goes let our troops go also." Lincoln was pleased that Grant was about to take charge of the confused situation and advised the lieutenant general that nothing would be done "unless you watch it every day, and hour, and force it." Grant, receiving this message, set out at once for Hunter's headquarters.[48]

Lincoln asked Hunter at 9:40 a.m. on the thirtieth, the short message outlining his apprehension over Early's movements, "What news this morning?" By late morning Halleck was telling Hunter that Early's entire force was over the Potomac in Maryland and was moving into Pennsylvania. Early's feints and deceptive moves had convinced official Washington that McCausland's raiding party headed for Chambersburg was much more than it was. Hunter believed Halleck's analysis because he had no better information than did the chief of staff, and he wired his understanding of what it meant. Wright's divisions had come up to Harper's Ferry, largely spent by excessive summer heat and the rapid march from Washington. Hunter deployed them with Crook's troops four miles north of the ferry at Hallstown, but, believing Early's main force was north of the river, thought his own deployments wrong; he was uncertain about what to do. He told Halleck:

My information is so unreliable and contradictory that I am at a loss to know in which direction to pursue the enemy. If I go towards the fords over which he has passed to cut off his retreat by the Valley, he turns to the right, pushes toward Baltimore and Washington, and escapes by the lower fords of the Potomac. If I push on toward Frederick and Gettysburg, I give him a chance to return down the Valley unmolested. Please, with your superior chance for information with regard to the whole position of affairs, direct me what is best to be done.[49]

By noon it was decided. War Department officials (and Hunter) were so badly deceived that they planned to withdraw from the positions near Harper's Ferry and move to the Middletown area to prevent a right turn toward the capital by Early. The realistic Strother said: "I have never felt so disgusted. We permit our army of thirty thousand to be stampeded by the silliest rumors and are now marching away from the enemy to take a position to save Washington which is not menaced and to be reinforced against an enemy which had no existence." The colonel's views did not prevail, and the army made its move the fifteen miles or so farther into Maryland, the staff making its new headquarters at the City Hotel in Frederick. The move wore out the troops. As Hunter put it: "The heat is so intense and the dust so deep that our infantry is suffering dreadfully. Six fell dead yesterday in one of our smallest brigades, and others are suffering in proportion." All the same, Halleck and Stanton, who were directing their general in the field from offices far away from these realities, were ready with other advice, finding that the rebels were "now closer to Baltimore, York and Harrisburg than you at Harpers Ferry or if in his rear at Williamsport or Sharpsburg." Therefore, Hunter was told to march still farther north up the valley east of South Mountain so as to cover passes through the Catoctin Mountains through which Early might strike eastward.[50]

By noon on 31 July it was apparent that only a small rebel cavalry detachment was in Maryland and Pennsylvania and that Early was someplace near Martinsburg or Bunker Hill. McCausland, completing his work at Chambersburg, was thought to be threatening Bath (now Berkeley Springs), Strother's home. The colonel was frustrated by being "bound up with a large army in a cowardly retrograde protecting Washington against its own cowardness, [while] a few thousand scoundrels are burning my property and insulting my family." He also was critical of Hunter, who, like War Department officials, was responding to every rumor, many of them tales brought to him by local citizens. For example, rebels were said to be at Gettysburg, and Early was reported to be on his way to Rockville to invade the capital. The rumors caused alarm, and troops were sent each time to counter them. Strother had good reason to feel "utterly disgusted" and so frustrated that he decided to leave the service. Halpine had already departed, although not for the same reason.[51]

By 1 August Hunter's troops were posted in a thirty-mile arc from the Potomac to Emmitsburg, Maryland, near the Pennsylvania border, and Nineteenth Corps reinforcements had arrived at Harper's Ferry. The military situation stabilized along this line, Early making no moves for several days. To be closer to the main railroad line from Washington to the West and the pikes from Washington and Baltimore, Hunter decided to move the headquarters from Frederick to the Monocacy battlefield. Grant, understandably alarmed about command structure and hesitant leadership in the Department of West Virginia, was soon on his way to take personal charge of resolving the uncertainty. Bypassing Washington and thus ignoring Stanton and, especially, Halleck, Grant and his aides arrived by train at Hunter's headquarters at Monocacy at 7:00 p.m., 5 August. Grant had a cursory view of the army camped in the vicinity and of the hundreds of Baltimore and Ohio cars and locomotives that Hunter had collected at that point as a precaution. The lieutenant general asked Hunter where the enemy was. "He replied that he did not know. He said the fact was, that he was so embarrassed with orders from Washington moving him first right and then left that he had lost all trace of the enemy." Hunter was ordered to move all the army south toward Harper's Ferry and to move up the Shenandoah Valley, for Grant was convinced that, because of its importance to the Confederacy, the lost enemy would soon appear to challenge the move. Only an hour after reaching Monocacy, Grant wired Halleck about the movement directive and that the army's orders were to maintain contact with the enemy "wherever he may go," not let him get between the army and Washington, and to clean out all food along the march, sparing buildings.[52]

Grant and Hunter continued their discussions that evening. Grant told his general that Sheridan was to be the new field commander of all troops in three departments—Susquehanna, West Virginia, and Washington—and would arrive in a few days from Washington with the first three brigades of his seasoned cavalry. Hunter was to remain in command of the Department of West Virginia and could set up his headquarters in Cumberland, Baltimore, or elsewhere. (He picked Cumberland.) Strother felt that this left "department commanders in the positions of simple provost marshals," and so did Hunter. Hunter, also convinced that his quarrel with Halleck would make future service in the department difficult, asked for relief. Grant recorded that Hunter "did not want, in any way, to embarrass the cause; thus showing a patriotism that was none too common in the army. There were not many major-generals who would voluntarily have asked to have the command of a department taken from them on the supposition that for some particular reason, or for any reason, the services would be better performed. I told him, 'very well then.'"[53]

Grant left the next day after informing Halleck that Sheridan had the field command and that Hunter's instructions had been turned over to the new commander. Hunter told Strother that "he feels relieved greatly for the responsibility of a command which was muddled with at Washington." The question of Hunter's department position was not decided for a few days, however, when Hunter resigned more formally over a continuing controversy.[54]

NOTES

1. Jubal A. Early, "Early's March to Washington in 1864," in *Battles and Leaders of the Civil War,* ed. Robert Underwood Johnson and Clarence Clough Buel, 4 vols. (New York: Castle, 1989), 4:492–93.

2. Ibid., 4:493; Captain Du Pont, writing years later, said he found Hunter confused on the morning of the nineteenth and unable to recognize the need to move westward rapidly (Henry Algerton Du Pont, *The Campaign of 1864 in the Valley of Virginia and the Campaign to Lynchburg* [New York: National American Society, 1925], 83–85); David Hunter Strother, *A Virginia Yankee in the Civil War: The Diaries of David Hunter Strother,* ed. Cecil D. Eby,

Jr. (Chapel Hill: University of North Carolina Press, 1961), 266–67; report, Hunter to adjutant general, 8 August 1864, U.S. War Department, *The War of the Rebellion: A Compilation of the Official Records of the Union and Confederate Armies* (Washington, D.C.: Government Printing Office, 1880–1902), ser. 1 (hereafter *ORA* and ser. 1, unless otherwise indicated), 37, pt. 1, 100–101; William B. Stark, "The Great Skedaddle," *Atlantic Monthly* 162 (July 1938): 87.

3. Thomas Francis Wildes, *Record of the One Hundred and Sixteenth Ohio Volunteer Infantry in the War of the Rebellion* (Sandusky: I. F. Mack and Co., 1874), 112; Stark, "The Skeddadle," 87.

4. Early, "Early's March," 4:493; Hunter's 8 August 1864 report, *ORA,* 37, pt. 1, 101; Strother, *Diaries,* 267–68.

5. Hunter's report, 8 August, letter, Lee to Davis, 23 June 1864, *ORA,* 37, pt. 1, 101, 683; Strother, *Diaries,* 268–69; William Hanchett, *Irish: Charles G. Halpine in Civil War America* (Syracuse: Syracuse University Press, 1970), 122; Stark, "The Skedaddle," 88; Robert E. Denney, *The Civil War Years: A Day-by-Day Chronicle of the Life of a Nation* (New York: Sterling Publishing Co., 1992), 427–28.

6. Jubal A. Early, *A Memoir of the Last Year of the War for Independence in the Confederate States of America* (Lynchburg: Charles W. Button, 1867), 48 n. Early's wartime report differs from his postwar remarks: "The enemy did a great deal of damage to citizens in Bedford and Campbell [counties], but not so much in Roanoke" (Early to Lee, 22 June 1864, *ORA,* 37, pt. 1, 160); letter by F.E.H., n.d., to *New Haven Journal and Courier,* reprinted in *New York Times,* 13 July 1864.

7. Charles H. Lynch, *The Civil War Diary, 1862–1865* (Hartford, Conn.: Privately printed for the author, 1915), 78; Henry Kyd Douglas, *I Rode with Stonewall, Being Chiefly the War Experiences of the Youngest Member of Jackson's Staff* (Chapel Hill: University of North Carolina Press, 1940), 290; John W. Daniel, "Unveiling of Valentine's Recumbent Figure of Lee at Lexington, Va., June 28th, 1883," *Southern Historical Society Papers* 11 (1883): 367; Charles Graham Halpine, *Baked Meats of the Funeral* (New York: Carleton, 1866), 311, 360; Hanchett, *Irish,* 128; George Crook, *General George Crook, His Autobiography,* ed. Martin F. Schmitt (1946; reprint, Norman: University of Oklahoma Press, 1986), 120.

8. Halpine, *Baked Meats,* 318; Hanchett, *Irish,* 126. The writer quoted thought it fortunate that most of Hunter's men were "the higher type of the soldier from Pennsylvania, Ohio and New York" (Charles M. Blackford, "The Campaign and Battle of Lynchburg," *Southern Historical Society Papers* 30 [1902]: 281).

9. Hunter was "swift to evade battle and retreat" (Daniel, "Figure of

Lee," *Southern Historical Society Papers* 30 [1902]: 367); letter, Early to Lee, 22 June 1864, *ORA,* 37, pt. 1, 160; Early, "Early's March," 4:493.

10. Strother, *Diaries,* 269.

11. Ibid., 270–71.

12. Ibid., 271–72; William Sever Lincoln, *Life with the 34th Massachusetts Infantry in the War of the Rebellion* (Worchester: Press of Noyes, Snow and Co., 1979), 328; Hunter's report, 8 August 1864, *ORA,* 37, pt. 1, 101–2.

13. Strother's August 1865 report in Hunter's 1873 Report, vol. 9, U.S. Army Reports of Civil War Service, 1864–87, Record Group 94, Records of the Office of the Adjutant General, National Archives (hereafter Hunter's 1873 Report, NA), 719; Strother, *Diaries,* 273; letters, Halleck to Grant, 19 June, Grant to Halleck, 21 June 1864, *ORA,* 37, pt. 1, 650–51.

14. Strother, *Diaries,* 273; Special Orders No. 117, Department of West Virginia (at Sweet Springs), 24 June 1864, Special Orders, Department of West Virginia, vol. 20, RG 393, U.S. Army Continental Commands, 1821–1920, NA; Stark, "The Skedaddle," 90–91; Hunter's report, 8 August 1864, *ORA,* 37, pt. 1, 102. Halpine wrote little in this time because he was ill and so demoralized that he made up his mind to leave the army "the moment I get back to civilization" (diary entries, 23–25 June 1864, Halpine's Diary, Huntington Library, San Marino, Calif.); Halpine, *Baked Meats,* 367.

15. Diary entries, 25–27 June, Halpine's Diary, Huntington Library; Strother, *Diaries,* 274–75. Hunter's losses were 103 killed, 564 wounded, and 273 missing ("Composition and losses of the Union Forces June 10–23," Hunter's report, 8 August telegram, Hunter to adjutant general, 28 June 1864, *ORA,* 37, pt. 1, 102–6, 683–84). Brigade commander Hayes wrote, "While we have suffered a great deal from the want of food and sleep, we have lost very few men, and are generally in the best of health" (Rutherford B. Hayes, *Diaries and Letters,* ed. Charles Richard Williams, 5 vols. [Columbus: Ohio State Archaeological and Historical Society, 1922], 477–78).

16. Diary entries, 28–30 June 1864, Halpine's Diary, Huntington Library; Strother, *Diaries,* 275.

17. Early, *A Memoir,* 48 n; Early, "Early's March," 4:493; letter, Lee to Davis, 26 June 1864, *ORA,* 37, pt. 1, 466–67.

18. Early, "Early's March," 4:494; telegrams, Sigel to adjutant general, 2 July, John W. Garrett, president, Baltimore and Ohio Railroad, to Stanton, 3 July 1864, *ORA,* 37, pt. 1, 175, pt. 2, 17–18.

19. Telegrams, Halleck to Grant, Grant to Meade, Meade to Grant, Charles A. Dana, assistant secretary of war, then at Grant's headquarters at City Point, to Stanton, 3 July 1864, *ORA,* 37, pt. 2, 15–16.

20. Hunter's report, 8 August 1864, ibid., 37, pt. 1, 102.

21. Strother, *Diaries,* 277; Strother's 1865 report in Hunter's 1873 Report, NA, 722–23; telegrams, Stanton to Hunter, Hunter to Stanton, Halleck to Hunter, 5 July 1864, *ORA,* 37, pt. 2, 62.

22. Hanchett, *Irish,* 126; Strother, *Diaries,* 278; Halpine, *Baked Meats,* 352; letter, Hunter to Boreman, 13 July 1864, *ORA,* 37, pt. 2, 291–92; Stark, "The Skedaddle," 94; Wildes, *116th Ohio Infantry,* 123.

23. Letter, Headquarters, Department of West Virginia, Cumberland, 13 July 1864, ordered release of Wharton's printing office and other property, "he being discharged from custody" (letter no. 166, letter, Hunter to Boreman, 13 July 1864, letter no. 165, Letters Received, Department of West Virginia, RG 393, NA); *ORA,* 37, pt. 2, 291–92.

24. Strother, *Diaries,* 278; Emmett MacCorkle, "George Washington: Prisoner of War," *Civil War Times Illustrated* 33 (March 1984): 33–34; *Wheeling Daily Intelligencer,* 11 July 1864.

25. Strother, *Diaries,* 278; Noah Brooks, *Washington, D.C., in Lincoln's Time,* ed. Herbert Mitgang (1895; reprint, Athens: University of Georgia Press, 1989), 159.

26. Special Orders No. 230, Adjutant General's Office, telegram, Grant to Halleck, 7 July 1864, *ORA,* 37, pt. 2, 104, 40, pt. 3, 59; Special Orders Nos. 126–27, Department of West Virginia, 15 and 16 July 1864, Record Group 393, NA; Grant, *Memoirs,* 2:304–6; Strother, *Diaries,* 277, 279.

27. Grant, *Memoirs,* 2:305–6. Early claimed that Lincoln, Grant, and General Butler were responsible for retaliation for what happened to the Blair house—destruction of "the house [on the Rappahannock River] of the widow of the brother of the Hon. James A. Seddon, the Confederate Secretary of War" (Early, *Memoir,* 62 n); report for 8–14 July, Early to Lee, 14 July 1864, *ORA,* 37, pt. 1, 347–49; Early, "Early's March," 4:497–99.

28. Strother, *Diaries,* 279; telegrams, Halleck to Hunter, Hunter to Howe, to commanding officer at Martinsburg, to Capt. Thomas K. McCann, all 13 July 1864, *ORA,* 37, pt. 2, 291, 293.

29. Telegrams, Wright to Halleck (3 messages), to Hunter, to Howe, 14 July 1864, *ORA,* 37, pt. 1, 314–16.

30. Telegram, Halleck to Hunter, 14 July 1864 (midnight), ibid., 315–16; diary entry, 14 July 1864, Halpine's Diary, Huntington Library.

31. Carl Sandburg, *Abraham Lincoln: The War Years,* 4 vols. (New York: Charles Schribner's Sons, 1939), 3:143; Strother, *Diaries,* 279. Strother thought that "since his arrival at Harper's Ferry, Gen'l Hunter had no control or responsibility" for operations against Early (Strother's 1865 report, Hunter's 1873 Report, NA, 727); telegram, Hunter to Stanton, 15 July 1864, *ORA,* 37, pt. 1, 339–41. Wright, it

will be remembered, served as a brigadier under Hunter in South Carolina.

32. Telegrams, Grant to Halleck, 14 July, Hunter to adjutant general (2), to Cook, to Wright, 15 July, Grant to Dana, 15 July 1864, *ORA,* 37, pt. 1, 300–310, 338, 341, pt. 2, 332–33; Strother, *Diaries,* 280. Another transgression was Hunter "had horsewhipped a soldier with his own hands" (telegram, Dana to Grant, 15 July 1864). This could have placed him "subject to trial; but nine chances out of ten he has only acted on the spur of the moment, under great provocation" (telegram, Grant to Dana, 15 July 1864, Charles A. Dana [Ida M. Tarbell], *Recollections of the Civil War* [1897; reprint, New York: Collier Books, 1963], 206). Halpine (*Baked Meats,* 352) reprints the message to Dana, omitting the horsewhipping matter, as does Hunter in his 1873 Report, NA, 695–96. Nothing is known of the incident.

33. Telegram, Hunter to Lincoln, 17 July 1864, document no. 34534, Abraham Lincoln Papers, Documents Division, Library of Congress (LOC); telegrams, Hunter to Lincoln, Lincoln to Hunter, 17 July 1864, *ORA,* 37, pt. 1, 365.

34. Strother, *Diaries,* 280; Hunter to Stanton, Stanton to Hunter, Halleck to Hunter, 17 July 1864, *ORA,* 37, pt. 1, 365–66.

35. Special Orders No. 128, Department of West Virginia, 17 July 1864, *ORA,* 37, pt. 1, 367; letter, Hunter to Edmunds Pendleton, a lawyer, 18 July 1864, Letters Sent, Department of West Virginia, vol. 2, RG 393, NA. Andrew Hunter was released in early August (Strother, *Diaries,* 285); Lincoln telegram, 17 July 1864, Roy P. Basler, ed., *The Collected Works of Abraham Lincoln,* 9 vols. (New Brunswick, N.J.: Rutgers University Press, 1953), 7:445; Douglas, *I Rode with Stonewall,* 297–99; John McCausland, "The Burning of Chambersburg, Penn.," *Southern Historical Society Papers* 31 (1903): 267; Early, *Memoir,* 401; William Harrison Beach, *First New York (Lincoln) Cavalry* (New York: Lincoln Cavalry Association, 1902), 353, 393; Henrietta E. Lee, "Mrs. Henrietta E. Lee's Letter to General Hunter on the Burning of her House," *Southern Historical Society Papers* 8 (May 1880): 215–16.

36. Strother, *Diaries,* 280–81; telegram, Garrett to Stanton, 18 July 1864, *ORA,* 37, pt. 2, 374–75.

37. Letter, Hunter to Maj. J. J. Yellott, 18 July 1864, Department of West Virginia Letters Received, RG 393, NA.

38. Letters, Hunter to Yelloff, 23 July, Lt. E. C. Watkins, 25 July 1864, ibid. Another letter to Yelloff, 3 August 1864, added six more families to be deported from Frederick (Special Orders No. 141, Department of West Virginia [at Frederick], 1 August 1864, Special Orders, vol. 20, RG 393, NA). Special Orders No. 134, 23 July 1864, directed the release of eight citizens of Berkeley County from the Martinsburg guardhouse.

39. Strother, *Diaries,* 282; Douglas, *I Rode with Stonewall,* 299; telegram, Hunter to Lincoln, 19 July 1864, document no. 34594, Lincoln Papers, LOC.

40. Letter, Hunter to Averell, 19 July 1864, Department of West Virginia Letters Sent, RG 393, NA.

41. Grant, *Memoirs,* 2:315–16, Strother, *Diaries,* 281; telegram, Hunter to Lincoln, 23 July 1864, document no. 34713, Lincoln Papers, LOC.

42. Strother, *Diaries,* 282.

43. Letters (3), Hunter to Adjutant General Thomas, 8 August 1864, Department of West Virginia Letters Sent, vol. 2, RG 393, NA—but these names and others were identified to the War Department earlier (telegrams, Hunter to Lincoln, 27 and 29 July 1864, docs. no. 34805, 34845, Lincoln Papers, LOC; Strother, *Diaries,* 283). Adams was promoted to colonel, 27 July, and later to brevet brigadier general, and likely no officers were dismissed on Hunter's recommendation.

44. Letter, Hunter to Halleck, 30 July 1864, Hunter MSS, Huntington Library, San Marino, Calif.

45. Strother, *Memoirs,* 284; Report, Maj. Gen. Darius N. Couch, Department of the Susquehanna, 8 August 1864, *ORA,* 37, pt. 1, 331–35; letter, Brig. Gen. Bradley T. Johnson to Lieutenant Beach, 7 May 1895, Beach, *First New York Cavalry,* 409; Grant, *Memoirs,* 2:316. Chambersburg had no military value and was destroyed purely for revenge, showing the changing nature of the war (Charles Royster, *The Destructive War: William Tecumseh Sherman, Stonewall Jackson, and the Americans* [New York: Alfred A. Knopf, 1991], 39).

46. Early, *Memoir,* 67 n. John McCausland, a graduate of the school, added the burning of VMI to the list of reasons ("Burning of Chambersburg," *Southern Historical Society Papers* 31 [1903]: 266).

47. Grant, *Memoirs,* 2:315–16.

48. Telegrams, Grant to Halleck, 1 August, Lincoln to Grant, 3 August 1864, ibid., 2:350–51.

49. Telegrams, Lincoln to Hunter, Halleck to Hunter, Hunter to Halleck, 30 July 1864, *ORA,* 37, pt. 2, 511–12.

50. Strother, *Diaries,* 284; telegrams, Halleck to Hunter, 31 July, Hunter to Halleck, 6:30 a.m., 1 August 1864, *ORA,* 37, pt. 2, 531, 564.

51. Telegrams, Hunter to Halleck (three messages), Halleck to Hunter, 31 July 1864, *ORA,* 37, pt. 2, 531–32; Strother, *Diaries,* 284–85. Strother's property, a hotel, survived the war; Halpine went off on a sixty-day leave to get care for his "impaired eyesight," but he resigned for personal reasons and did not return to the army (Special Orders No. 126, Department of West Virginia, 15 July 1864, vol. 20, RG 393, NA).

52. Grant, *Memoirs,* 2:319–20; Telegrams, Grant to Halleck (2), 5 August 1864, *ORA,* 43, pt. 1, 681, 697–98; Strother, *Diaries,* 286.

53. Grant, *Memoirs,* 2:320–21; Strother, *Diaries,* 286.

54. Telegram, Grant to Halleck, 11:30 p.m., 5 August 1864, reel 20, Ulysses S. Grant Papers, LOC, and *ORA,* 41, pt. 1, 695; Strother, *Diaries,* 286.

Chapter 9

WAR'S END—AND AFTER

Before Grant's visit to his Monocacy headquarters, Hunter was in correspondence with Washington, D.C., because of his initiatives sending Maryland citizens who were accused of disloyalty to the Union south behind rebel lines. The policy did not find favor in Washington, and Lincoln directed Stanton to send Hunter this order:"The Secretary of War will suspend any order of General Hunter mentioned within until further orders, and direct him to send to the Department a brief report on what is known against each person to be dealt with." Hunter answered the same day, not with a list of deportees and their offenses but, instead, with a general justification of the practice:

> The persons that have been ordered south and sent beyond the lines of this department have been indicated to me by the loyal citizens of good standing as dangerous persons, sympathizers with the rebellion, who have by all means in their power aided and abetted the rebel cause, communicating habitually with the enemy across our lines, giving military information, denouncing loyal citizens on the advent of rebel raiders, and otherwise giving moral and material aid to the rebel cause. It is impossible for me to conduct military operations advantageously in this department if these spies and traitors are permitted to go at large and continue their disloyal practices in the midst of my army.[1]

A few days later Colonel Strother recorded that Early was complaining about the dispatch of an unidentified newspaper editor (from Frederick?) into his lines at Hunter's orders. Strother said Early's point was that, if the newsman "has offended our laws, we should try him and punish him. That this sending of people south untried is contemptible and shows weakness in our Government." Strother, who that very day got Hunter's promise to endorse his chief of staff's resignation favorably, said that Early was right and that the deportations showed "a lack of power and principle." While Strother thought his general was wrong on this issue, he approved of another Hunter action.[2]

The action was that Hunter, upset with lack of Washington support for his deportations, once again offered his resignation. He did not send it to Stanton, Grant, or Halleck, however, but to Lincoln, another example of his neglect of military channels. His telegram read:

> In sending the rebel citizens & their families beyond our lines I was obeying the order of Lieut Gen Grant communicated through Gen Hallick [sic] your Chief of Staff with several thousand wealthy rebel spies in our midst constantly sending information & supplies to the Enemy & pointing out union men to their vengeance it is impossible to conduct affairs of my Department successfully. I most humbly beg that I may be relieved of command of the Department of West Virginia.

He did not wait for an answer but the next day requested twenty days' leave "to visit friends," a request approved the same day. Strother and Stockton also were given twenty-day leaves and, one assumes, accompanied their general to Washington.[3]

Whether because of his requests to Grant and Lincoln for relief or because the Department of West Virginia had been stripped of any significant mission, Hunter's resignation was accepted effective at the end of his leave, 30 August. Three days later Sherman occupied Atlanta, a triumph that was at once seen as critical for Lincoln's reelection against McClellan, running as a Democrat. At the time Hunter wrote to Halpine in answer to a request the colonel had made regarding a Dr. Dougherty of Cumberland, one of Hunter's supposedly disloyal detainees. Hunter said that he asked the War Department to release the man, and he added an observation on the changed political atmosphere in the capital. "Uncle Abe appears full of fun, and I infer that he at least feels well with regard to the result in Nov." To the general's satisfaction the Republican president was reelected. Hunter was also pleased with results in his home state of New Jersey that "no longer belong[ed] to the Camden & Amboy R.R. Co. and I am not ashamed to confess I was born there." After the election Hunter found Washington dull but told Halpine that a "little storm" was expected when Congress reconvened. He expected, no doubt, further debate on Radical Republican plans for reconstructing the South.[4]

General Crook, who succeeded to the position heading the Department of

West Virginia, remained simultaneously one of Sheridan's subordinate troop commanders, which proved that the department had no further use. Sheridan began his valley campaigns cautiously. Over the next several months he moved south to Staunton and Waynesboro, destroyed the harvest in the Shenandoah Valley, and ultimately thoroughly defeated Early. Although Sheridan was, like Hunter, accused by the Confederates of atrocities in the form of impoverishing women and children in his path, he did not burn many dwellings nor reinstate the practice of removing disloyal citizens from behind Union lines and depositing them in rebel territory. It was well-known that General Halleck opposed destruction of residences or other civilian property. For example, he told Sherman, who had just successfully completed his siege of Atlanta, the practice "is barbarous; but I approve the taking or destroying whatever may serve as supplies to us or to the enemy's armies." President Lincoln was also convinced that Hunter's policy should not become widespread, telling Grant, "The Secretary of War and I concur that you had better confer with General Lee and stipulate for a mutual discontinuance of house burning and other destruction of private property." No similar joint repudiation of deportation was found necessary, although Lincoln was told by a Hagerstown judge that seven citizens of the town were arrested by Early as hostages in retaliation for Hunter's Frederick banishments.[5]

Colonel Strother's resignation was, like Hunter's, accepted at the end of his leave. The chief of staff, however, received a special honor, mention beyond the perfunctory in special orders. The commendation read that Strother, "having tendered his resignation because of three (3) years hard service in the field, had rendered him unable to endure the fatigue and exposure of a campaign and that a younger and more active officer already commissioned may take his place, is hereby honorably discharged."[6]

Hunter left what was to be his final command probably believing that he would be given another opportunity to lead troops against the rebellion, but his relationship with the War Department was strained, and Grant at the front could not be conveniently lobbied on the matter. Some were glad to see him go; Admiral Du Pont wrote to a friend expressing his pleasure over "another traitor to me being brought to grief." The admiral was still smarting over his own relief at Port Royal, which he blamed in part on the general's complaints about the navy not showing sufficient vigor in the 1863 campaign against Charleston. The admiral's satisfaction is evident in these words: "Hunter, relieved the third time for military incapacity—the contriver of a wretched raid, which brought on us two humiliating invasions."[7]

The general, now sixty-two years of age, might have thought himself too old for active service, but he was still vigorous and had shown his stamina on the long, hard campaign in the Shenandoah Valley. He wanted another assignment but was not likely to be considered for one by Halleck or Stanton, both of whom had a low opinion of his recent performance and ability as a field commander. Hunter does not appear to have done more in August than recover from his ordeals in the Shenandoah Valley, but in the next month he telegraphed Grant, just returned from a visit to Sheridan in the valley, "May I come to see you at City Point?" Grant answered immediately, "Certainly you can," and it can be assumed that Hunter asked the lieutenant general to find him an active position in the army. Grant, who had always had a high opinion of Hunter, and who consistently defended him in the face of official dissatisfaction with his accomplishments and his quarrelsome and impetuous nature, likely explained to Hunter the impediments to finding him a post.[8]

One of these was that Hunter was one of the most senior generals in the army, so vacancies at a suitable level were not available. More important, however, was the opinion of many in official and unofficial Washington that he was responsible for the frights the capital had suffered from Early's expeditions and Hunter's inability to locate the rebel force and defeat it in battle. Hunter blamed whatever failures might be attributed to him to misunderstandings and to General Halleck. In correspondence with Grant he said that the chief of staff's instructions were no help and had had "a very depressing tendency" on him. (War Department records identify the example that Hunter sent to Grant as Halleck's 17 July "crows carrying provender" telegram, which seems a poor choice, as it contains no obvious criticism.) Hunter reviewed the Lynchburg campaign, reminding Grant that, when he had relieved Sigel, "I found his command very much disorganized and demoralized, from his recent defeat at New Market, and the three generals with it, Sigel, Stahel, and Sullivan, not worth one cent; in fact very much in my way." Nonetheless, Hunter "dashed on" to Lynchburg because he saw that Grant was then hard-pressed by Lee and needed a diversion. Failure to take the city Hunter attributed to "the stupidity and conceit of that fellow Averell, . . . of whom I unfortunately had at the time a very high opinion, and trusted him when I should not have done." Hunter's opinion of Averell began to go bad at Lexington, when the brigadier failed to cut off McCausland's retreat from the village, but there had to have been other reasons. (Averell himself was convinced that Hunter was displeased with him and his cavalry for the loss of the cannon on the march from Lynchburg.) During the retreat General Crook thought, "Gen Hunter had no confidence in the rest of the command, and I shared this opinion with him."[9]

Placing blame on subordinates reflects as much upon the commanding general as it does on those accused of failure, particularly when no action was taken to correct inadequacies. Hunter's case rested largely on finding fault with Halleck, because Hunter said that "I was not informed that I had anything to do with the defense of Washington, and supposed that General Halleck had made ample provision for this purpose." Preventing Early from getting between Hunter's army and Washington "was a perfect impossibility." Looking for Grant's approval of his conduct and exoneration for any problems associated with it, Hunter asked, "I hope, general, you will do me the justice to say I have done my whole duty, and I hope you will give me a command of some kind." Showing considerable humility, he added: "If I am not deemed worthy of a corps, give me a division, a brigade, or a regiment. I have tried to do my whole duty, and if I have failed, I am much mortified."[10]

General Grant later faintly praised Hunter's conduct of the campaign up to the retreat from Lynchburg. He thought that Hunter had had no choice except to retreat through West Virginia but also that, had Hunter gone straight to Charlottesville from Staunton, instead of to Lexington, "he would have been in a position to have covered the Shenandoah Valley against the enemy, should the force he met have seemed to endanger it. If it did not, he would have been within easy distance of the James River Canal, on the main line of communication between Lynchburg and the force sent for its defense." Having said this, Grant concluded: "I have never taken exception to the operations of General Hunter, and I am not so disposed to find fault with him, for I have no doubt that he acted within what he conceived to be the spirit of his instructions and the interests of the service. The promptitude of his movements and his gallantry should entitle him to the commendation of his country." Grant did not directly reply to Hunter's call for exoneration, and he never defended his general's performance from 4 July 1864, the day that Hunter arrived at Parkersburg and was in touch with—and responsible for—the situation along the Potomac.[11]

Not only did Hunter seek justification for his actions and performance from General Grant; shortly after the war he introduced a new factor into the matter and asked the defeated General Lee for his opinion. Halpine wrote in 1866 that "rebel archives showed that Early's corps of thirty thousand picked men, thrown upon us finally by Lee, had been collected and were [sic] designed as a reinforcement for General Johnson [Joseph E. Johnston], who was then facing our Sherman before Atlanta." The colonel concluded that Hunter's movement on Lynchburg "might very materially, and to our detriment, have altered the results in that region, had Lee's primary intention been carried out." Strother, writing about the same time, went so far as to claim that his general was responsible for the fall of Atlanta, because the strike at Lynchburg had diverted Lee. Because of Hunter's movements, "Atlanta, unrelieved, fell before the conquering armies of Sherman."

Hunter, who shared this thinking, wrote to Lee asking if the raid on Lynchburg had prevented Lee from reinforcing Johnston with forty thousand troops, and did the former Confederate commander not think Hunter's line of retreat was the most feasible available. Lee told Hunter that he did not have forty thousand men in his entire Army of Northern Virginia at the time but did not otherwise comment on plans for Johnston's support. As for the second question, Lee replied, "I would say that I am not advised as to the motives which induced you to adopt the line of retreat which you took, and am not, perhaps, competent to judge of the question, but I certainly expected you to retreat by way of the Shenandoah Valley, and was gratified at the time that you preferred the route through the mountains to the Ohio—leaving the Valley open for General Early's advance into Maryland." Thus, Hunter got no more satisfaction from his former opponent than he did from General Grant.[12]

The Hunters's domestic arrangements following the general's return to Washington were much the same as they had been before he took over Sigel's department in May. Maria Hunter had visited her husband in Harper's Ferry, but, given the uncertainty of the military situation, it is unlikely that she stayed very long. The couple and Mrs. Steuart and her two daughters lived in a house at 288 I Street N, owned by a Mrs. Johnson, after the return from South Carolina in 1863. They gave some thought to moving elsewhere, but, Hunter said, "Mrs. Johnson was so sadly disappointed and miserable, when we changed our mind about the house, that we are now inclined to enter into the old arrangement with her." There was another boarder (and perhaps had been others), the cavalryman acquaintance from Fort Leavenworth days, Colonel Perry, still on the War Department staff. Hunter inquired in October if Perry wanted to renew the old arrangement for the coming winter; if so, his share would be two hundred dollars a year. Hunter and his wife would pay four hundred dollars. Mrs. Johnson thought that she could manage on this income, "keeping the parlours as they are, which will be much more cheerful, and having no one else in the house." Hunter asked Perry, who was not then in Washington, to telegraph him at once with his decision, "and Mrs. Johnson will have your rooms ready for you on your arrival." Colonel Perry agreed to the arrangements and boarded at the house with the Hunters for the rest of 1864 and into 1865.[13]

At the end of 1864 an operation was mounted against Fort Fisher at the mouth of Cape Fear. The installation protected the important blockade runner port at Wilmington, North Carolina, one of the last left to the Confederacy. General Benjamin Butler, in whose command the fort lay, decided to lead the army component of the combined army-navy expedition himself, but an assault on Christmas day was not followed up and was, Grant said, "a gross and culpable failure." The muddled attack meant the end of Butler's military service, and Hunter, perhaps inspired by news of the general's relief, asked Grant: "Will you not ask Mr. Stanton to give me a command against Wilmington? I will take Fort Fisher or leave my bones in the sands." He was too late, however, because Grant had appointed Brig. Gen. Alfred H. Terry to head the next attempt on the fort. Terry was successful on 15 January.[14]

The Fort Fisher command was the last that Hunter attempted to secure for himself, perhaps bowing to the reality that Stanton was not likely to see him appointed to any such position in the army. Although no command was found for him, he was still useful for incidental duties that called for an officer of rank. One of these responsibilities had been to preside over investigations or courts-martial of senior officers, a practice with which Hunter had had some experience when he was awaiting orders between assignments in the past. Another of these temporary duties arose in February 1865, when Hunter was ordered to Paducah to preside over the court-martial of Brig. Gen. Eleazer A. Paine, a friend of Lincoln, whose last assignment was command of the District of Paducah from July to early September 1864. He had been ordered there by Lincoln with the job "to collect assessments on rebel sympathizers." Those were turbulent times in Kentucky because of local elections in early August, the first to be contested since Lincoln's election in 1860. The elections were seen as a bellwether for the coming 1864 presidential contest, in which Lincoln then appeared to be an underdog. Paine was clearly overeager in the performance of his duties; Governor Thomas F. Bramlette complained to the president that the general had too zealously enforced martial law before the local elections (which the Republicans lost). The governor was more concerned, however, that the citizens of western Kentucky were "subjects of insults, oppression, and plunder by officers who have been placed to defend and protect them."[15]

Paine attempted to resign his commission on the grounds of ill health shortly after his relief from duty, but his superior asked that the request not be granted. He told Stanton that he had begun an investigation at Paducah "concerning alleged outrages committed in the S.W. part of the Military District under the authority of and by the order of Brig. Gen'l E. A. Paine." Settlement of the matter took a few months, and two charges were made. The first charge and specification was that Paine had used "contemptuous and disrespectful words against Governor Thomas E. Bramlette" on 20 August. The second charge had twenty-seven specifications. The first was that Paine "did publicly speak of and denounce his superior officer Major General H. W. Halleck, as a 'God-damned coward,' and as a 'damned rascal,' or words to that effect" at Paducah in the last days of July. The other twenty-six specifications listed lootings, robberies, and extortions by Paine's troops and even some crimes by the general himself, including imposing unauthorized fines and theft of clothes, bed linens, and other goods for the benefit of Paine's son, who was one of his aides. All these incidents were said to have occurred in late August 1864 in Union County.[16]

A court-martial was ordered on 1 February, and Hunter was named president of the court. He traveled west, arriving in Cairo on 9 February 1865, and was in Paducah on the thirteenth, from which he complained to the War Department that the inquiry proceedings were delayed, as Paine had not yet arrived from his home in Illinois. The trial began on 17 February and took some days to complete. Paine, who might have expected to be dismissed from the army, was not, however, found guilty of the large number of offenses charged. The only offense sustained was the first specification of the second charge, that Paine had denounced Halleck. Even this was not accepted completely, the court finding that Paine's use of the words "and as a damned rascal" had not been proven. The sentence was not much, only that Paine "be reprimanded by the President of the United States in General Orders." Hunter reported the job completed on 6 March, and he was soon back in Washington, reporting himself awaiting orders on 31 March.[17]

LINCOLN'S FUNERAL

The war was winding down, Lee evacuating Richmond and Petersburg on the night of 2 April, Grant's relentless pressure finally paying off. Lee surrendered the Army of Northern Virginia on 9 April, but not all the fighting ended. General Johnston was still active in North Carolina, and other generals and their troops continued the fight elsewhere, but the capitulations of Richmond and Lee a week apart meant to most in the North that the war was over. The euphoria of victory lasted only a short time. The shooting of President Lincoln on 14 April and his death the following day sobered the nation. While the president lay wounded in a private house across the street from the theater where his assassin had struck, influential Illinois citizens in Washington were organizing to return the body of the clearly mortally wounded man to Springfield. Among these Illinoisans were Governor Richard T. Oglesby, former governor and now U.S. Senator Richard Yates, General Grant, and other generals from the state. It is possible, indeed likely, that Hunter was one of these planners. He may have been in the delegation that visited Mrs. Lincoln for approval of the Springfield move, and he surely was one of the officers who accompanied Lincoln's body from the place he died to the White House on the rainy night of the fifteenth. Hunter could also have been present in the guest bedroom of the president's house for the autopsy.[18]

Hunter was designated by Stanton as one of eight general officers to attend the lying in state at the White House and the Capitol. The other officers appear to have been selected because each represented a branch of the army staff; Hunter's distinction was that he and the president were friends. The others were: Maj. Gen. Montgomery C. Meigs, quartermaster general; Bvt. Brig. Gen. Charles Thomas, assistant quartermaster general; Brig. Gen. George D. Ramsey, ordnance department; Brig. Gen. Amos B. Eaton, commissary general of subsistence; Bvt. Brig. Gen. Daniel C. McCallum, superintendent of military railroads; Bvt. Maj. Gen. John G. Barnard, lieutenant colonel of engineers; and Brig. Gen. Albion P. Howe, chief of artillery. These officers, other junior officers, and noncommissioned officers were assigned as guard of honor when the president's body was in the East Room at the White House on 16 April and after it was moved to the Capitol rotunda two days later. At least one of the generals was to be continually in view of the remains while they were on public display.[19]

The East Room looked decidedly different than it had four years previously, when Hunter had commanded the White House guard of irregulars and his men had used the chamber as a barracks. Lincoln's fifteen-foot-tall catafalque dominated the black-draped room. An arched canopy of black cloth with four pillars and a lining of white silk was over the casket. The corpse was viewed by thousands of people over the day and a half before it was moved. A historian, perhaps basing his words on a contemporary account, wrote, "At the edge of the coffin, dark, reticent David Hunter rested a white-gauntleted hand as if in deep thought, pausing in his vigil over the man he had accompanied from Springfield." Funeral services were held in the White House, and the body was taken to the Capitol on 19 April in a long procession of dignitaries, honorary pallbearers, military units, and citizen groups. Another vigil was mounted in the rotunda, and on 21 April, six days after his death, Lincoln's body was taken to a special train that was to return him to Springfield.[20]

Secretary Stanton took charge of the funeral arrangements, and he appointed most of the same officers who had maintained the Washington watch to escort the body to Illinois. General Meigs was dropped because Grant required him to go to the scene of the continuing hostilities in North Carolina; Bvt. Brig. Gen. James A. Ekin, another quartermaster officer, took his place. A captain, three lieutenants, and twenty-five sergeants made up the train guard. Stanton thought his duties as secretary of war prevented his accompanying the remains, so he appointed Asst. Adj. Gen. Edward D. Townsend to represent him "and to give all necessary orders in the name of the Secretary as if he were present, and such orders will be obeyed and respected accordingly." Whether Hunter, the senior officer in the group, was annoyed that he was once again serving under a junior (and a colonel at that) is not known. Stanton may have intended to show by this his lack of confidence in Hunter, not even trusting him to command an honor guard and ceremonial party.[21]

The special train—an engine and seven cars—departed Washington at 8:00 a.m., Friday, 21 April. Three hundred persons were aboard, some of them intending to go but a short distance and some of them planning to travel the seventeen hundred miles that retraced much of Lincoln's journey to his inauguration four years and two months before. Only six of these men had made the first trip—son Robert; Lincoln's friend Ward Lamon; presidential secretaries John G. Nicolay and John Hay; David Davis, whom Lincoln had appointed an associate justice of the Supreme Court; and David Hunter—but of these only the young Lincoln and Lamon were still aboard at Springfield, the others returning to duties in Washington and elsewhere.

The length of the trip and the vast public outpouring of grief associated with the funeral provoked commentary. In New York it was said that the body of Lincoln was being displayed in the interest of the Republican Party and particularly its radical wing, which was orchestrating the crowds. The accusation was baseless; Lincoln's now recognized greatness inspired hundreds of thousands of citizens along the way to watch the funeral train pass or to view the body in several cities. The whole nation responded to its loss, and the atmosphere of grief accompanied by a common desire to see the guilty punished for the great crime were to have a profound impact on events to follow.[22]

THE MILITARY COMMISSION

Jefferson Davis and much of the Confederate government fled Richmond when the city was turned over to the Union, but, at the time of Lincoln's funeral, the rebel chief of state was still at large, making his way south. In addition, Lincoln's assassin, John Wilkes Booth, although identified immediately, had not yet been apprehended. Some of Booth's accomplices in the murder and perpetrators of planned attempts on the lives of the vice president and cabinet officers had been arrested, but the apparent widespread conspiracy was troublesome. Stanton had taken over the investigation and supervision of the pursuit of the suspects, and his vigor was responsible for some early conclusions about the nature of the plot. Some of these theories were wrong, but the heinousness of the crime seemed to call for unusual measures in its investigation and expiation.

From the beginning of the investigation Jefferson Davis was considered a participant in the conspiracy to kill Lincoln, but the immediate connection to the Confederacy was found in accused assassin Booth's visits to Canada to meet with agents of the Richmond government. Several hundred persons were questioned, and a large number of them were confined pending further questioning or charges. The process of gathering evidence was assigned by Stanton to a special judge advocate, Bvt. Col. Henry L. Burnett. His search was indeed complete, going so far as to arrest and place in "close confinement" the person responsible for renting out private boxes at Ford's Theater, the shooting site; confiscating undergarments of actors and actresses; detaining the theater's wardrobe keeper; and even seizing musical instruments at Ford's. No detail was too small.[23]

No consideration was given to the option of trying the conspirators in a civilian court. Probably at Stanton's urging, the matter was referred to Attorney General James Speed, who was asked his opinion about the legality of a military trial. This was Stanton's preferred option, because it promised more rapid justice; he hoped the accused could be tried, convicted, and hung before Lincoln's body reached its grave in Springfield. This schedule could not be met because Booth evaded capture until 26 April, and the attorney general's opinion was delayed. Speed's considerations were not simply the case at hand but had a broader application. Earlier in the war citizens had been tried in military courts in the West. One of these cases, that of Lambdin P. Milligan of Indiana, was then before the Supreme Court for resolution, the defendant claiming that military courts had no jurisdiction when civilian courts were functioning. Speed likely consulted on this matter with Colonel Burnett, who was the successful prosecutor in Milligan's trial. The attorney general's unwritten opinion held that military proceedings were justified because Washington was a fortified camp, still threatened by enemy action, as not all Confederate troops had surrendered. He may have also assumed that new guerrilla warfare, such as earlier attacks on New England towns from Canada-based rebels, was likely if not inevitable. President Johnson, accepting the argument, issued a proclamation announcing the attorney general's opinion and directing that a military commission be established and nine officers appointed to it.[24]

While the investigation and preparation for a trial were being conducted, the funeral train with Hunter and the other officers of the escort aboard made its way to Illinois. The route was Washington, Baltimore, Harrisburg, Philadelphia, New York, Albany, Buffalo, Cleveland, Columbus, Indianapolis, and Chicago, arriving at the last place on Sunday, 30 April. The body was brought to Cook County Courthouse in the city the next day for ceremonies, and it was from here that Hunter was ordered by War Department telegram to return immediately to Washington. He was told that he would be appointed by Stanton as the senior officer on the military commission that was to meet within a few days.[25]

Hunter was not the only officer in the funeral party named to the commis-

sion; Generals Howe and Ekin were also appointed, and they probably accompanied Hunter to the capital. While the officers were away on the journey to Illinois, the case against the apprehended conspirators had been perfected, but assassin Booth would be spared a trial because he had been cornered in a barn in
Virginia and killed on 26 April. One other person thought culpable in the
president's murder was still at large. President Johnson's 2 May proclamation explained official thinking: the plot against Lincoln and his cabinet and its partial
execution "were incited, concerted, and procured by and between Jefferson Davis,
late of Richmond, Va., . . . and other rebels and traitors against the Government of
the United States, harbored in Canada." Davis was not, however, formally charged
and was not captured until 10 May, the day after the military commission was to
convene.[26]

Meanwhile, a charge and specification against seven men and a woman were
drafted. All were charged with "maliciously, unlawfully, and traitorously, and in
aid of the armed rebellion against the United States of America, . . . combining,
confederating, and conspiring, together with one . . . John Wilkes Booth, Jefferson
Davis [and seven men, mostly Confederate procurement officers resident in
Montreal and other places in Canada, and the son of the indicted woman], and
others unknown, to kill and murder, within the Military Department of Washington, and within the fortified and intrenched lines thereof, Abraham Lincoln,
late . . . President of the United States of America and Commander-in-Chief of
the Army and Navy thereof; [as well as Johnson, Seward, and Grant]," and the
actual murder of Lincoln, the assault on Seward, and plans to murder Grant and
Johnson. The indictment thus had the justification for the military commission,
and the detailed specification emphasized that the conspiracy was primarily a
traitorous act intended to aid the rebellion and the murder and other actions
designed to strip the nation at war of its military leadership.[27]

Most of the many citizens gathered up in Washington, and that large proportion confined in the Old Capitol Prison were released by the beginning of May.
The eight held for trial were kept first in ironclad ships on the Anacostia River,
and, as the trial date approached, were moved to the Arsenal Penitentiary, at what
is now Fort Leslie McNair in southeast Washington. From 23 April the jailors
were told, "The Secretary of War requests that the prisoners, . . . for better security against conversation, shall have a canvas bag put over the head of each and
tied about the neck, with a hole for proper breathing and eating, but not seeing."
The bags were padded with one-inch-thick cotton batting and had to be worn
twenty-four hours a day. In addition, the accused were heavily ironed, each secured by handcuffs with a stiff bar between and leg shackles. There is some dispute whether Mrs. Mary Surratt, the only woman among them, was similarly

restrained, as was claimed at the time. In 1873 Hunter addressed this issue, claiming that he read the same in newspapers in 1865 and had "immediately addressed 'a note' to the officers in charge to learn if the report was true." He was assured, he said, that it was false, but the question remains why he waited so long to comment publicly on the matter. As a historian of the period wrote, the prisoners "were outcasts and the War Department was free to do as it wished with them."[28]

Military commission members were named in orders on 6 May, which were amended on 9 May. Hunter, the senior officer, was designated president; Lewis Wallace and August V. Kantz were the other major generals. Brig. Gens. Robert S. Foster and Thomas M. Harris, Howe and Ekin, Bvt. Col. C. H. Tompkins, and Lt. Col. David R. Clendenin rounded out the panel. Prosecuting attorney was Brig. Gen. Joseph Holt, then the army's judge advocate general and a former postmaster general and briefly secretary of war in the Buchanan administration; he was assisted by John A. Bingham, a former U.S. representative from Ohio. Colonel Burnett was the special judge advocate charged with deciding points of law—calling on his Milligan case experience—during the trial. It should not be surprising that the trial was seen as a cover-up and commission members as prejudiced because the entire proceedings were hurried and irregular. A defense attorney thought it likely that commission members had concluded in advance that all the accused were guilty and that the purpose of the proceedings was to decide punishment.[29]

The commission convened for the first time at 9:00 a.m., Monday, 8 May, at the Arsenal, the third floor of the old penitentiary having been prepared for it. As he would be every morning, Hunter was met at his residence by a mounted escort of a sergeant and eight men provided by the special provost marshal, Maj. Gen. John F. Hartranft, who commanded a brigade of volunteers and some veteran reserve corps troops on the special assignment. The courtroom was twenty by forty-five feet, its eleven-foot-high ceiling supported by three pillars down the center. Only four small barred windows ventilated the room, a hardship on all due to the particularly hot and humid weather. Along the twenty-foot east end a dock a foot high by four feet wide with a railing at the front had been constructed. It was connected through a door with the cells, and this convenient security feature was likely the reason the venue was selected. The commission sat behind a long, green-covered table near the west end and parallel to the north wall. Across from the commission was a witness stand and behind it a table for counsel and official reporters. Except for a man from the *National Intelligencer,* no press or public were to be admitted. Hunter, however, decided that the proceedings need not remain secret, and passes signed by himself personally allowed other journalists and interested (and important) citizens to attend. Commission members arranged themselves by rank as was customary in army trial procedure: Hunter was in the center, with Wallace, Ekin, and Colonel Tomkins on his right and Kautz, Foster, Harris, Howe, and Clendenin on his left. The room was freshly whitewashed and the floor newly carpeted with coconut matting.[30]

Business of the commission on the first day was short. The defendants, ironed but without hoods, were given copies of the charge and specification, the first time they had seen them. No prisoner had been allowed counsel before, but they were now asked if they wished to retain such representation. All declared that intention, and so the court was adjourned until 10 May, allowing a day and a half for the search. Reconvening on that Wednesday, Reverdy Johnson presented himself as counsel without compensation for Mrs. Surratt, an announcement that caused an immediate objection by one member of the court. Johnson, a former attorney general of the United States, one of the foremost attorneys in the nation and now a U.S. senator from Maryland, had crossed Hunter's path earlier. He had defended Gen. Fitz John Porter before another court-martial that Hunter headed, and a historian claims that Johnson "published a pamphlet belittling Hunter's military qualifications, stating that he had been removed from command twice for mistaken policy." Johnson, although a staunch Unionist who consistently opposed secession, often represented individual rebels, and, of course, he came from a suspect state in which divided loyalties were common. Some indeed thought him a rank—if secret—secessionist and said that he was concealing Confederate sympathies.[31]

One of these was commission member General Harris, a Virginia native who had served through the war with West Virginia troops. He objected to Johnson as a defense counsel "on the ground that he did not recognize the moral obligation of an oath designed as a test of loyalty to the Government of the United States, referring to a printed letter, dated Baltimore, October 7, 1864," which dealt with a dispute about a Maryland election. In that matter Johnson had argued that a Maryland oath requirement was beyond the authority of the constitutional convention that imposed it, a technical question. Hunter raised the challenge to Johnson without identifying which commission member raised it. When Johnson asked who was his accuser, Hunter answered, "It is General Harris; and if he had not made it, I should have made it myself." Johnson's defense was that he had taken oaths to practice before the Supreme Court, twice as a senator and also as attorney general, and had been a loyal citizen all his life. Something he said in this explanation angered Hunter. "Mr. Johnson has made an intimation in regard to holding members of this court responsible for their action." He ordered the court cleared, saying, as he pounded the table, "I was going to say that I hoped the day had passed when freeman [*sic*] from the North were to be bullied and insulted by the humbug chivalry, and that, for my part, I hold myself personally responsible for everything I do here." After the recess the commission confirmed Johnson's right to defend Mrs. Surratt, but he recognized that his usefulness was damaged. Johnson allowed junior counsel to attend most future proceedings and to read his final written argument.[32]

Johnson, however, was not finished for the day; he challenged the jurisdiction of the commission on grounds similar to Milligan's pending appeal. Considering the motion in closed session, the commission rejected it without comment in a few minutes. Since haste was as much as anything the reason Stanton had selected a military rather than a civilian court, the defense was notified that "the argument of any motion will, unless otherwise ordered by the Court, be limited to five minutes by one Judge Advocate, and counsel on behalf of the prisoners." Objections to this procedure would be noted. These matters took up the first trial day, and, accompanied by his escort, Hunter returned home.[33]

The trial dragged on for several weeks, but nothing of particular note was heard. A former Confederate who was called to testify thought that he saw why the military commission was trying the case. It was obvious to him and to many others that the aim was to "connect the Confederate army, in some way, with the assassination. In fact this . . . seemed to be the main object of the investigation, although at this day no reputable man would risk his reputation for intelligence by saying there was ever the slightest ground for such a charge." He enumerated the type of irrelevant evidence heard, concluding, "It reads like the heading of a dime novel and detective story." A more recent student of the trial, Phillip Van Doren Stern, in his 1954 introduction to a reissued trial transcript, wrote: "Hard facts, dubious speculation, sheer fantasy, and downright perjury are quoted as if all were of equal value. It is hard to imagine any court taking such stuff seriously, but this was a special military commission acting under unusual circumstances." It should be added that the commission members' participation in the proceedings was limited to voting on challenges—and, of course, finding the verdicts. Hunter and his colleagues were not judges, but were, under the usual procedures regulating general courts-martial, the jury, depending on their law officer, Burnett, for legal guidance. All of them were certainly determined to punish the perpetrators of Lincoln's assassination and those whom Burnett's investigation had rounded up. It is not fair to say, as one historian did, "The lounging officers of the commission obediently aligned themselves with the prosecution." There was hardly a defense to offset the blizzard of relevant and irrelevant testimony from scores of witnesses. But, for all of this, no indictment of the now imprisoned Jefferson

Davis or of any former Confederate military or civilian official was ever re-turned.[34]

Hunter, as one might expect of him, was impatient with delays caused by irrelevant testimony, among other things, during the trial, and it may have been that he was not up to the mark physically to withstand the heat, humidity, and poor courtroom conditions. It must have been unbearable for the officers in their dress uniforms, because the jackets were heavy wool worn in winter and summer. An observer wrote, "The appearance and demeanor of the court . . . were neither solemn nor impressive," and the officers "sat about in various negligent attitudes." Further distraction was caused by the "many ladies [who] were present; . . . their irrepressible whispering was a continual nuisance." The last testimony was no doubt gratefully heard on 28 May, and the commission reached verdicts two days later, the severity of them probably determined by the strength of prosecutor Bingham's summation. Four of the accused were sentenced to hang, and four received prison terms. One of those sentenced to death was Mary Surratt, but Hunter, Kautz, Foster, Ekin, and Tompkins, a majority of the commission, signed a plea (written by Ekin) to President Johnson, asking the president to commute her sentence to life imprisonment. Colonel Holt took the verdict and the amendment to the War Department for review, and on 5 July Johnson approved the verdict and sentences. Controversy still exists about whether the request for leniency for Mrs. Surratt was given to the president or, if it had been, whether Johnson seriously considered it. Hunter wrote several years later that he was confident that the president reviewed the clemency petition, but the general provided no evidence that he did. Speculation had it that Holt had seen that this last-page addition did not reach the White House, and there the matter rests today. Although there were strong rumors in Washington that Mrs. Surratt would be let off with prison, Hunter does not seem to have questioned at the time Johnson's failure to grant her partial amnesty. The convicted conspirators were notified of the sentences at noon on 6 July, and the four condemned were executed twenty-four hours later. Those sentenced to be confined at an Albany, New York, penitentiary were (as a result of a 15 July presidential order) taken instead to Fort Jefferson in the Dry Tortugas beyond Key West, where conditions were extremely harsh. These events were the last chapter in the Lincoln assassination, and Hunter's military commission was dissolved effective 15 July.[35]

AWAITING ORDERS AND RETIREMENT

Hunter, now just sixty-two years old, his special duty completed, was again awaiting orders without much chance of receiving them as the wartime army dissolved. He considered at once returning to the paymaster corps but not at his old rank of major. He was, in addition to his general's commission in the U.S. Volunteers, a colonel in the regular army, the Sixth U.S. Cavalry, but he was no doubt too old for field service. Col. Thomas P. Andrews, who had been paymaster general since 1862, retired at the end of 1864; he, like Hunter, had entered the army in 1822. The pay department's next in line by seniority was a 1825 West Point graduate, Col. Benjamin W. Brice, but his appointment as head of the office was not yet approved when Hunter sought the job. It cannot be determined when Hunter began his campaign; the first recorded activity on his behalf was a July 1865 recommendation from Isaac W. Arnold, the former Illinois congressman, an early Hunter supporter who was now auditor general of the treasury. Arnold made the claim that President Lincoln had been in favor of Hunter's appointment to the post. General Grant asked Stanton a few months later to appoint Hunter on the ground that Colonel Brice had not been approved for appointment. Nothing came of this, however, and a year after his first attempt Hunter got backing from Illinois Senator Richard Yates and a number of other prominent Illinoisans, again with no result.[36]

David and Maria Hunter did not consider moving to Illinois; most relatives there had moved elsewhere, but surely Maria Steuart and her two daughters were a better reason to remain in the capital. After Appomattox General Steuart settled on a farm, "Mt. Steuart," at South River, Anne Arundel County, Maryland, and his wife and children were therefore close to Mrs. Steuart's uncle and aunt, her adopted father and mother. The Hunters might have gone to the general's ancestral home in Princeton, but, although they visited the town, living there did not have the same attraction as did Washington. The couple moved to H Street a few houses closer to downtown in 1866, to the 200 block of I Street a year later, and finally settled in 1869 at 1726 I Street NW. Colonel Perry did not follow them; instead, he moved into his own place near the Hunters in 1867 or perhaps earlier.[37]

It is likely that after the war Mrs. Steuart spent less time with the Hunters, and the old couple were very sorry to see her leave for Europe to join her husband, who was already there. In August 1865 Mrs. Hunter, accompanied by Sam Stockton, now out of the regular army, went with the lady to Boston, where she took passage aboard the *China*. Hunter wrote: "We part with her with the greatest regret. She has always been so amiable and *ultra* royal that she has become very dear to us." The separation was not permanent, however, because Mrs. Steuart returned to the Hunter household as a regular, if not semipermanent, visitor over the years. In January 1868 Hunter wrote Halpine a whimsical letter, telling him that Halpine had captured all the women of the house with "that bewitching Irish way of yours." This explained, he said, why Mrs. Hunter kept after him to write to the New York resident, and "little Lady Steuart" followed up with, "I declare Uncle it is perfectly abominable the way you treat Halpine!" Hunter said that he looked forward to seeing Mrs. Margaret Halpine and daughter Syble in Washington, where they would join Mrs. Steuart, her children, and a niece and nephew from Philadelphia, children of brother Lewis Boudinot Hunter.[38]

Although Hunter's military service was nearly complete, he continued to receive letters resulting from that service. One of these exchanges might have been costly to him but was probably just the product of an overzealous quartermaster auditor. In July 1864, when commanding the Department of West Virginia from Parkersburg, just days after his arrival there from the Lynchburg retreat, Hunter sought to repair the cavalry in his army, a branch that had always been poor and which was then nearly unhorsed. He ordered that one thousand horses be purchased locally at a ceiling price of $160 each animal and less than a week later ordered another thousand. Hunter's price paid exceeded the price authorized for animals by the cavalry bureau. In addition, Hunter authorized procurement of mares, again contrary to army policy, because his agents were having trouble finding enough horses. What brought all this to the army's attention were a number of claims from civilian horse dealers, whose bills were disapproved for exceeding government limits. Hunter was asked about the matter, and he explained:

> When the horses were purchased, Washington was beleaguered, and the national credit was greatly suffering. It was all important that these horses should be furnished *immediately,* and the prompt furnishing of a part of them enabled Gen. Averell on my most urgent and oft repeated orders, to attack and defeat a position of the enemy's cavalry, and thus, I believe, causing his rapid retreat from our territory. . . . I should have had no hesitation in ordering the horses purchased at one thousand dollars each.

This may have been the end of the question, but the records do not say whether the horse dealers were paid the full amounts they claimed were due.[39]

In September 1865 Hunter received new honors, which were not, however, much of a distinction. He was appointed by the president, effective 13 March 1865, brigadier general and major general in the U.S. Army by brevet "for faithful service during the war." Since he already held these ranks in the volunteer service, they could not have meant much to him, but he accepted the brevets by letter in October. Yet the honors may not have been a sure thing, because the records show that Hunter was not initially recommended for brevet major general by Gen. William T. Sherman's board, which ruled on such awards, but he received the nomination by the end of June 1865.[40]

The list of brevet promotions—which were all honorary and did not bring pay or authority—runs for 178 pages, most of the awards dated the same, 13 March 1865, because of a Senate committee technicality. Wags called the date "that bloody day" when so many promotions were earned. A historian who has studied the practice of awarding brevets notes that many officers who were never at the front received multiple promotions, and many of the higher ranks were given those in staff positions in Washington and other headquarters. The brevets presented on the "bloody day" and at other times were a problem in the postwar army, because regular officers serving in lower permanent ranks sometimes used their brevets to gain precedence. The practice was ended late in the century because of the abuses and confusion it caused, some illustrating how the brevet system worked by explaining that a mule might be called a brevet horse.[41]

Hunter was mustered out of the volunteer service as a major general on 15 January 1866 and continued on awaiting orders status in his permanent rank of colonel, Sixth U.S. Cavalry, until the end of July. He received orders that said, "Having served over 40 years; [General Hunter] was on his own application, and by direction of the President, retired from active service." The retirement was found to be in error because it was approved under a law (scc. 15 of the act approved on 3 August 1861) which specified that the forty years must be con-secutive service. Hunter did not qualify because of the gap from 1836 to 1841, when he was a civilian at Chicago. Fortunately, however, another law (sec. 12 of the act approved on 17 July 1862) permitted the retirement of officers over the age of sixty-two who had served forty-five years in uniform. The sixty-four-year-old Hunter qualified on the basis of age, but he was short two years of active service, even if his cadet years were counted. The point seems to have been overlooked or ignored, and Hunter's retirement received no further challenge. Officers retired then received the pay of their highest grade with four rations per day, a total of $7,011 a year for a major general.[42]

Although he was retired, Hunter was called on from time to time for special duties; that he lived in Washington made it convenient for the army and for himself. He was appointed a member of the Special Claims Commission of the War Department and was on the board to examine cavalry officers for appoint-ment and promotion, from just after retirement to June 1868, but these duties were not notable. His last special duty must have pleased him greatly; in 1869 he was named by President Grant as one of seven members of the board of visitors of his alma mater, the military academy at West Point. The members—a judge, a former member of Congress, two university presidents, Hunter, and two other former volunteer officers—assembled at the school on 1 June and, along with academy officials, spent a week examining members of the first class. The board found "a marked deficiency among the cadets as a whole" in their ability to express themselves clearly. This was important because West Point at the time had only oral examinations, a practice that the board recommended be changed, in the interest of fairness, to written tests. Other findings were that the curriculum was short on physical geography, military and civil history, and the "care of horses in health and disease," subjects that—except for horse care—are sometimes found wanting in public institutions today. Among other objectives the board recommended raising the standards of admission to the academy. Also considered was ethics training, which "had long been regarded by the cadets as a study particularly distasteful." Although some consideration was given to discontinuing the subject altogether, elimination of "moral science" was not recommended, but a change in professors was: chaplains, who were then Protestant clergymen, should not be allowed to continue to teach the subject.[43]

Hunter was loyal to his former officers, particularly to Halpine and Strother. As a supporter of radical reconstruction as put forward by a branch of the Republican Party, he did not always agree with them politically, but differences did not diminish their mutual regard. In 1865 Halpine wrote that, while he had voted for General McClellan in 1864, Hunter, of course, had supported Lincoln's reelection. Furthermore, Halpine said, Hunter "is to-day in favor of extending the right of suffrage to every negro in the South [but not the North?], and disfranchising every white man in the least degree prominent on the rebel side—two points with neither of which the writer can agree." When Halpine was nominated by the state Democratic Party for registrar of the city and county of New York, Hunter supported his candidacy—as did Horace Greeley (who put Halpine in nomination), Generals Meade, John A. Dix, Daniel Sickles, and Averell, and Admiral Farragut. Halpine's bid was successful, and he was installed on 1 January 1867. He lived only a year and a half more, however, and Hunter attended his elaborate funeral in New York City. Many prominent New Yorkers were there—including Greeley, the mayor of the city, political bosses William M. Tweed and Peter B. Sweeny, newspaper publisher James Gordon Bennett—and the body was escorted by the Sixty-ninth New York Infantry, the militia regiment with which Halpine had gone to war and which had been in Hunter's brigade for a short time.[44]

Hunter was able to assist Strother as well. Following the war the former chief of staff had entered the Restored Government of Virginia under Governor Francis H. Pierpont (then Pierpoint) as secretary of state and adjutant general. Strother also owned a hotel at Berkeley Springs which required his attention and by 1877 was seeking more substantial employment in the consular service of the United States. Although Hunter had access to President Grant, the 1876 election of Rutherford B. Hayes, one of Hunter's wartime subordinates, gave him a new opportunity to further Strother's ambitions. He called on Hayes, and the new president sent this note to his secretary of state: "I conceive [sic] with General Hunter in thinking favorably of Gen. Strother. Please confer with him about the case of Gen. S." This and assistance from others secured for Strother the post he wanted, and he was sent to Mexico City as consul general in 1879.[45]

Hunter must have given much thought in his later years about his accomplishments during the war, but the most forward thinking of them had to be his abortive freeing of the slaves in his Department of the South and, most important, his early advocacy of employment of blacks in the military service. That his enlistments of former slaves had not been supported when he undertook the initiative was a constant regret. In 1870 he wrote to an unknown fellow general, "If our prayers with regard to negro troops had been answered from Washington early in the war we could have saved tens of thousands of lives and thousands of millions in treasure."[46]

In their last years the Hunters seem to have been active and without significant illness. In February 1886, when the old general was in his eighty-third year, he returned to the house at 1726 I Street NW, in Washington, after completing some business in the nearby downtown. He was complaining of chest pains and died twenty minutes later. An army surgeon summoned to the address reported his demise on the day of his death, citing an undetermined cause. The surgeon later attributed death to angina pectoris and wrote—perhaps to secure some advantage for the seventy-seven-year-old widow—that the heart disease was "due to causes incidental to a lifetime spent in the military service of the United States." Hunter's passing was not particularly commemorated in Washington, his adopted home, probably because his wartime service was not well remembered but also because his brand of radical Republicanism was out of style, and Democrat Grover Cleveland now occupied the White House.[47]

Following her husband's burial at Princeton, Maria Hunter continued to live in the house in Washington. She applied for a widow's pension and on 23 March 1886 was awarded an income of thirty dollars monthly, the amount provided for by law for survivors of a colonel or major general. A bill was introduced in Congress without, it is said, the knowledge or consent of Mrs. Hunter to increase her pension to fifty dollars a month. The legislation passed both houses and was forwarded to President Cleveland for approval. He chose, however, to veto it, saying, "I have no doubt his [Hunter's] widow will receive ample justice through the instrumentality organized for the purpose of dispensing the nation's grateful acknowledgement of military service in its defense." Furthermore, he pointed out that, when the bill was passed, Maria Hunter's application was still before the pension bureau. Finally, Cleveland did not think that twenty dollars more than the law allowed was justified, particularly as it was "not alleged or claimed that this widow needs an increase of her pension."[48]

The veto was not the end of the matter, because Republicans submitted more bills to benefit Maria Hunter. South Carolina Congressman Robert Smalls, the former slave who had spirited the Confederate ship *Planter* from Charleston in 1862, entered in the *Congressional Record* a long discourse on the injustice of Cleveland's action. He said that Hunter's contributions to the black citizens of the nation were large and deserved to be remembered by rewarding his widow. Smalls considered Hunter "the Moses who led us out of bondage." Listing Hunter's accomplishments and particularly his support of blacks, Smalls said that the veto by the Democratic president and the failure of the Democratic House to override it provided a lesson about the Democratic Party: "It exposes the hypocrisy of its assurances of friendship for the colored man by striking a blow at the nation's brave defenders and the colored man's best friend."[49]

These words and subsequent proposed legislation had no effect, and Maria Hunter remained pensioned at the thirty dollars monthly rate, collecting it until 4 December 1886. On 20 August 1890 she was dropped from the rolls for failure to claim pension money due for three years. Likely, she had died about a year following the general's death, her passing not noted, because neither she nor David Hunter left behind any children to keep their memories.[50]

EPILOGUE

Hunter's death was not much noticed, because he had outlived most of his former antagonists and friends. Few of his Civil War contemporaries had followed the same career pattern nor begun army service so early in the nineteenth century. Tributes to David Hunter were few, but he was remembered at his alma mater, the military academy at West Point, where a reunion of graduates of that institution was coincidentally held in the year of Hunter's death. A retired major general wrote of him: "No officer merits greater prominence in the future history of the late civil war, and his recent death is mourned by those, who enjoyed his personal friendship, and fully recognized his genial, noble qualities, blended with undaunted courage, ardor, vigor and devotion to the Union." No doubt this tribute is overdrawn, but it does contain much that is accurate.[51]

It is common now, when he is recognized at all, to accuse Hunter of being guided during the war by self-serving and dishonest motives and to view some of the actions he took as a general officer as unworthy and unjustified. Part of this is the result of a belief that he turned against his Virginia heritage, but, curiously, Ulysses S. Grant, whose father had twenty-six Virginia and Kentucky cousins and only eleven in his native Ohio, is not so accused. Hunter's view of the national scene and of issues guiding the nation's leaders were no doubt influenced, as much as they could have been, by his West Point education. Here he was brought into contact with youths from all over the country—it seems unlikely that slavery was a significant divider that early in the republic's life. He was still further molded by his service on the frontier, but nothing is recorded about how he viewed Indians, who were often wards of the army or sometimes free plains dwellers. Hunter could not have been unaffected by his wife's and the Kinzie family's acceptance of Great Lakes and upper Mississippi tribes, which they regarded paternalistically. The Kinzies were unusual for having earned the respect of Indians by tolerating their native ways and their actions taken to protect the natives' interests against marauding whites. Hunter probably accepted these attitudes as his own.

Discharged from the army in 1836, Captain Hunter made his political connections in the small town of Chicago, where he had instant status because of his army service and Maria's family contacts. His reputation naturally extended to other parts of Illinois and to the neighboring Wisconsin Territory. That Hunter failed in business cannot be put down to personal incompetence but was, rather, the result of a national depression. Returning to the army was the available option and would permit him to provide for himself and his wife in difficult times.

By accepting recommissioning as a paymaster in 1841, Hunter rejoined the army a grade higher than he had left it, effectively catching up with and even passing his academy classmates. The paymaster corps, however, was not troop service, nor was it high visibility, even at army or department headquarters. Furthermore, paymaster was considered a quasimilitary position, and paymasters took no part in military activities on army posts. Because they were often on the road paying troops, paymasters, but not their families, must also have been strangers to much garrison life. Post returns of troops, the monthly report of strength—on which every assigned and attached officer, whether on duty, on leave, or on detached service, was listed by name—excluded paymasters until 1860. Isolation of paymasters from the mainstream of officer career paths—for example, they could not be promoted beyond major—and their physical isolation from post life and command of troops, meant that, unlike other officers, they were not necessarily becoming better equipped for the military profession. Hunter was never seen as an intellectual, nor does it seem that he read many professional books, but some of the knowledge needed by senior soldiers could not have entirely escaped him. Certainly, he would be better able to command large bodies of troops than officers who had left the army and were called back into uniform many years later.

The war with Mexico disrupted frontier army life and drew most of the army to the theater of war. Hunter's participation as paymaster on Wool's march to join Zachery Taylor and his subsequent duty paying troops until the last of them left Mexico were not particularly noteworthy. Unrecorded is whether Hunter realized the national controversy that would be generated by questions of free or slave states being formed from conquered territories. Because Hunter's postwar assignments were initially at Detroit and New York, he may have formed opinions about the Free-Soil question based on the most prominent local views. Ordered to Fort Leavenworth at the very time that Kansas was suffering from the excesses that earned it the "bleeding" label, Hunter's political sensitivities appear to have been firmly formed. He recognized the evil of slavery and became one of the few officers in the army who advocated ending it. In this view he was much ahead of most Whig and Republican political figures, who were not dedicated to the abolition of slavery but, rather, to making sure it did not spread further.

Hunter's first contact with Abraham Lincoln was in 1860, before Lincoln was elected president, a timing that shows that Hunter aligned himself with a candidate without an overwhelming edge in the contest. It cannot be confidently said, therefore, that, by supporting Lincoln, Hunter expected his army career to be enhanced; in fact, he was putting it at risk, hardly a self-serving act. Lincoln's approach to the perplexing problem of slavery was not to confront the South on the question. Hunter, however, opposed such moderation. Concluding even before the election that the nation would be divided, Hunter thought it was essential that the Union be preserved, and he was convinced that advocates of secession were dangerous traitors.

That he had this view put Hunter at odds with most of his brother officers, because, logically, it led to a deeper conflict than moderation would justify. The dominant U.S. military tradition at the time was to distinguish between a government and its army and the people in the belligerent state. The concept was "civilized warfare," in which there was no need to demonize the opponent or to punish him severely. Hunter, from the first, thought it necessary to use maximum force to make errant states return to the Union, and he was gratified that Virginia seized the Harper's Ferry arsenal, because, he reasoned, the act would cause the North to pursue the war more vigorously.[52]

In 1861 and 1862, however, at least until major campaigns began, the official Union position was to be conciliatory to the departed Southern states and people, based partly on a commonly held opinion that the South contained a large majority of loyal citizens led astray by selfish leaders. Conciliation, therefore, was thought to be sound and workable. Hunter, of course, did not believe in the efficacy of moderation and, from his first assignment as a major general, sought to punish the South for its apostasy by arming freed slaves and sending them from Kansas to ravage the South. The notion of moderation did not seem to promise reunion to him. While nothing came of this proposal, Hunter was soon in South Carolina, where military necessity—the shortage of troops—led him to free and arm slaves. The declaration of freedom would, he thought, demoralize the South, force the rebels to distrust the slaves, and might have diverted Confederate troops from military duties to slave control. In arming the black man, Hunter tested his notion that former slaves wanted to fight to defend their newfound freedom, but in this he was mistaken. Few blacks eagerly enlisted, and Hunter resorted to press gangs and, eventually, conscription to fill the ranks.

A recent student of the changing concept of war during the rebellion has suggested that Hunter's motivations behind his actions combining emancipation and military service were political and not driven by military necessity, but the call can go either way. Hunter undoubtedly believed he was vastly outnumbered in South Carolina and needed supplementary troops to man isolated posts so as to free white troops for combat. It is more likely that Hunter's ambitions were military, although he could have had in mind how his actions would be perceived by Radical Republicans in Congress. He was soldier enough, however, to realize that his military future depended on Lincoln, Stanton, and the army's hierarchy and hardly at all on other politicians.[53]

It cannot be concluded that Hunter's actions in the Department of the South helped move Lincoln from his conciliatory policy designed to keep border states loyal, but their recognition by Lincoln surely kept emancipation and arming blacks in public view. It is difficult to separate the two issues, and they soon became one in the public's mind, just as they had always appeared to Hunter. Hunter, like Lincoln, did not think that emancipation should be a war objective, but from the start it was to him a means for victory over the secessionists. He believed that slavery was the primary cause of the conflict and did not share the president's concern about the border states. Lincoln's position was political, Hunter's military, and the general believed that the wavering states were controllable only by force. There was no need for compromise, particularly as Union strength was marshaled. He was from the beginning an advocate of making uncompromising war, not as punishment for the South but to suppress the rebellion.[54]

Hunter's opinion of hard war may have been tempered by the harsh actions of James Lane in Missouri early in the conflict, but his quarrel with the Jayhawk leader was centered more on matters of rank and command. Lane's depredations may have given Hunter pause in his hard war application. He sometimes sought to go the third step, by calling for armed blacks to punish the Southern people themselves for the war as a way to pressure rebel leaders. Hunter's advocacy more often went no farther than seeking to reduce the South's ability to wage war by destroying its means to support the conflict. In this he was not far from mainstream military thinking of the time.

Hunter's application of the theory that war demanded more than proclamations, emancipation, and arming of former slaves was not possible until his unexpected May 1864 assignment to command of the Department of West Virginia. Hunter was determined to use his little army effectively, believing that he had to prove himself. While Hunter may have exchanged opinions on how war should be conducted with Grant in Tennessee and possibly later and more briefly in Virginia, his orders to replace General Sigel in the Shenandoah Valley were accompanied by no instructions or direct advice from the lieutenant general, Grant's chief of staff, or the secretary of war. He had Sigel's failed objective—a march to Staunton and beyond—to accomplish, but how he was to do it was left up to him.

Hunter had the same problems executing his objective as did Grant and other generals with theirs. The biggest difficulty was supplying his forces on the march in hostile or disputed territory. In the Shenandoah the situation was more critical than in other theaters of war, because of small but effective bands of guerrilla forces, which Hunter and his staff considered, with some cause, to be fighting outside the rules of warfare. Guerrillas made it impossible for Hunter to depend on supply from depots in the North, and, the more distant he was from these bases, the more critical was the need for food and fodder for the army. Hunter knew from the start that he would have to live off the country, in this case the rich and little-damaged valley that was the breadbasket of the Southern war effort in Virginia. He did not favor looting as a tactic of war and directed his subordinates to control foraging to what the army needed and no more. In this Hunter was expressing conventional military wisdom; every professional officer knows lawlessness among troops destroys military discipline and unit cohesion. Control was ineffective, however, and, as elsewhere, soldiers freely warred against civilians. This warfare was restricted, however, to looting; there was little rape and murder. It is not surprising that Hunter and his generals recognized, as did commanders on other fronts, that the soldiers' initiative—which clearly could not be regulated—might be an important weapon against the rebellion. From the beginning Hunter destroyed rebel property, but, other than clearly military resources, it was almost exclusively in retaliation for guerrilla acts he thought required strong reactions. Later, of course, his burnings, deportations, and suppression of unsupporting newspapers were sometimes vengeful, but more often he justified them by citing military necessities. In ordering these actions, he was not unique among Union generals commanding in the field, but Hunter was disproportionally condemned.[55]

Hunter's legacy lacks known details of the depth and variety of his opinions and motivations, such as Charles Royster has revealed about another reviled general, William T. Sherman. Sherman, however, took warfare to degrees of severity and efficient execution exceeding Hunter's limits. Hunter's view of war was not as thoughtful, and he did not so ably construct a coherent explanation of his conduct in his various commands. Sherman's beliefs, however, led him far beyond Hunter in carrying out the new, hard methods of warfare. Hunter did not feel, as Sherman did, that any means was moral if it helped to end the war. Hunter controlled the level of violence he imposed on the citizens of rebel territory; Sherman, the more modern soldier, did not.[56]

Hunter's later excesses were committed in loyal West Virginia and Maryland, although against accused rebel supporters. The actions were close to and visible in Washington, so Hunter did not avoid instant critical attention. Valley atrocities, combined with the ultimate offense of arming blacks—supposedly intended to encourage the murder of Southerners—completed the list of accusations made about Hunter. Consequently, Hunter was remembered for the case the South made against him, not for his lifetime achievements in the uniform of his country. The reputation for cruelty and disloyalty to Virginia, the state in which he and his parents had never resided, tainted all of his public actions. He has not had a biographer in the past, so his story has never been told. This book may help to restore balance and a recognition of David Hunter's accomplishments, which go beyond an old soldier's real and imagined faults.

NOTES

1. Telegrams, Stanton to Hunter, Hunter to Stanton, 3 August 1864, U.S. War Department, *The War of the Rebellion: A Compilation of the Official Records of the Union and Confederate Armies* (Washington, D.C.: Government Printing Office, 1901) (hereafter *ORA* and ser. 1, unless otherwise indicated), ser. 2, 47:527, 37, pt. 2, 583–84. Hunter suspended his earlier deportation order (letter, Hunter [at Monocacy] to Major Yellott at Frederick, 3 August 1864, Letters Sent, Department of West Virginia, vol. 2, Record Group 393, U.S. Army Continental Commands, 1821–1920, National Archives).

2. David Hunter Strother, *A Virginia Yankee in the Civil War: The Diaries of*

David Hunter Strother, ed. Cecil D. Eby, Jr. (Chapel Hill: University of North Carolina Press, 1961), 287.

3.Telegram, Hunter to Lincoln, 7 August 1864, document no. 35121, Abraham Lincoln Papers, Documents Division, Library of Congress (LOC); letter, Hunter to adjutant general, Middle Military Division, Harper's Ferry, 8 August 1864, David Hunter file, Generals' Papers, box 26, RG 94, Records of the Adjutant General's Office, 1780–1917, NA; Special Orders No. 2, Headquarters, Middle Military Division, 3 August 1864, *ORA,* 51, pt. 2, 726; Special Orders No. 147, Department of West Virginia, 8 August 1864, Special Orders, Department of West Virginia, vol. 20, RG 393, NA. The same order appointed Stahel to the command of the department during Hunter's leave. The Middle Military Division was a new organization created following Sheridan's assumption of field command.

4. General Orders No. 248, Adjutant General's Office, 30 August 1864, *ORA,* 43, pt. 1, 962; letters, Hunter to Halpine, 9 September and 17 November 1864, Hunter MSS, Huntington Library, San Marino, Calif. At the time of the November letter Mrs. Hunter and possibly Mrs. Steuart and children were visiting Princeton. In the second letter Hunter sent the always strapped Halpine a five hundred dollar loan.

5. Letter, Halleck to Sherman, 28 September, letter, Judge D. Weisel to Lincoln, 10 August 1864, *ORA,* 43, pt. 1, 39; pt. 2, 503; ser. 2, 7:576–78; Wesley Merritt, "Sheridan in the Shenandoah Valley," in *Battles and Leaders of the Civil War,* ed. Robert Underwood Johnson and Clarence Clough Buel, 4 vols. (1887–88; reprint, New York: Castle, 1989), 4:500–521; Edward A. Pollard, *Southern History of the War,* 4 vols. (1865; reprint, New York: Blue and Gray Press, 1952), 4:105; telegram, Lincoln to Grant, 14 August 1864, Abraham Lincoln, *Speeches and Writings, 1859–1865* (New York: Library of America, 1989), 619.

6. Special Orders No. 167, Department of West Virginia, 10 September 1864, Special Orders, Department of West Virginia, vol. 20, RG 393, NA.

7. Letter, Du Pont to William Whetton, 15 August 1864, John D. Hayes, ed., *Samuel Francis Du Pont: A Selection From His Civil War Letters,* 3 vols. (Ithaca: Cornell University Press, 1969), 3:367.

8. Letters, Hunter to adjutant general, reporting himself "waiting orders" in Washington, D.C., 30 August and 30 September 1864, Generals' Papers, box 26, RG 94, NA; telegrams, Hunter to Grant, Grant to Hunter, 23 September 1864, *ORA,* 48, pt. 2, 153.

9. Letter, Hunter to Grant, 6 December 1864, *ORA,* 37, pt. 2, 366–67; diary entry, 2 July 1864 (at Charleston), Halpine's Diary, Huntington Library; George Crook, *General George Crook: His Autobiography,* ed. Martin F. Schmitt (1946; re-

print, Norman: University of Oklahoma Press, 1986), 118. Averell's memoir does not mention a conflict with Hunter (William W. Averell, *Ten Years in the Saddle: The Memoir of William Woods Averell,* ed. Edward K. Eckert and Nicholas J. Amato [San Rafael: Persidio Press, 1978]).

10. Letter, Hunter to Grant, 6 December 1865, *ORA,* 37, pt. 2, 366–67.

11. Grant's report to the secretary of war, 22 July 1865, Grant, *Memoirs,* 2:592.

12. Charles G. Halpine, *Baked Meats of the Funeral* (New York: Carleton, 1866), 383; Strother letter, August 1865, included in Hunter's report, April 1873, vol. 9, U.S. Army Generals' Report of Civil War Service, 1864–87, RG 94, NA, 738–39; quoting Lee letter, n.d., Douglas Southall Freeman, *R. E. Lee: A Biography* (New York: Charles Schribner's Sons, 1935), 4:240–41. Early's corps numbered little more than eight thousand muskets.

13. Letter, Hunter to Perry, 11 October 1864, box 1, folder 49, Schaefer Civil War Collection, Princeton University Library, New Jersey.

14. Telegram, Grant to Lincoln, 28 December 1864, Grant, *Memoirs,* 2:490–96; telegram, Hunter to Grant, 6 January 1864, *ORA,* 46, pt. 2, 53. Butler was relieved on the fifth.

15. Letter, Bramlette to Lincoln, 3 September, relief order, 6 September, General Orders No. 325, Adjutant General's Office, 30 September 1864, *ORA,* ser. 3, 4:688–89, 39, pt. 2, 349, 544.

16. Letter, Bvt. Maj. Gen. Stephen G. Burbridge, commanding Military District of Kentucky, to Stanton, 15 September 1864, General Court Martial Orders No. 167, Adjutant General's Office, 15 October 1865, roll 40, M1064, Letters Received by the Commission Branch of the Adjutant General's Office, 1863–70, M698, RG94, NA. The investigation of Paine by Brig. Gen. Speed S. Fry, sent to the judge advocate general in Washington for action in October, runs more than seven hundred pages of affidavits and exhibits, including evidence of murder and other crimes not later charged (file 1394 B 1864, Letters Received by the Adjutant General's Office, RG94, NA [hereafter AGO Letters Received, NA]).

17. Special Orders No. 51, 1 February, No. 64, 9 February 1865, General Court Martial Orders No. 167, letters, Hunter to adjutant general, 9, 13, and 28 February; 6 and 31 March 1865, AGO Letters Received, NA. Paine resigned his commission in the spring of 1865, not waiting for Stanton's approval of the sentence in October.

18. Victor Searcher, *A Farewell to Lincoln* (New York: Abingdon Press, 1965), 52–53.

19. Letter orders to each general, 18 April 1865, *ORA,* 46, pt. 3, 822. These letters undoubtedly confirmed earlier verbal orders.

20. Quoting Searcher, *Farewell to Lincoln,* 71; Noah Brooks, *Washington, D.C.,*

in Lincoln's Time, ed. Herbert Mitgang (1895; reprint, Athens: University of Georgia Press, 1989), 232–35.

21. General Orders No. 72, Adjutant General's Office, letter, Stanton to Townsend, both 20 April 1865, *ORA,* 46, pt. 3, 807–8, 845–46.

22. Carl Sandburg, *Abraham Lincoln: The War Years,* 4 vols. (New York: Harcourt, Brace and Co., 1939), 4:400.

23. William Hanchett, *The Lincoln Murder Conspiracies* (Urbana: University of Illinois Press, 1983), 61; letters, Burnett to Col. J. A. Foster, Brig. Gen. C. C. Augur, 23, 26, and 29 April 1865, roll 1, M599, Investigation and Trial Papers Relating to the Assassination of President Lincoln, RG 158, Records of the Judge Advocate General, NA (hereafter Trial Papers, RG 158, NA).

24. Johnson proclamation, 1 May 1865, roll 8, Trial Papers, RG 158, NA; *Ex parte Milligan* was decided in 1866 for the defendant, the court finding that Indianapolis, unlike Washington, was remote from the war (Margaret Leech, *Reveille in Washington, 1860–1865* [New York: Harper and Bros., 1941], 411).

25. Hunter's April 1873 report to the adjutant general, vol. 9, roll 5, U.S. Army Generals' Reports of Civil War Service, 1864–87, RG 94, NA, 697. The train that brought Lincoln to Washington in 1861 did not go through Chicago, but the demands of citizens of the state explain the detour. The burial at Springfield was on 4 May.

26. Proclamation, 2 May 1865, *A Compilation of the Messages and Papers of the Presidents,* vol. 3 (New York: Bureau of National Literature, 1897), 3505–6; Hanchett, *Lincoln Conspiracies,* 64; Charles A. Dana, *Recollections of the Civil War* (1897; reprint, New York: Collier Books, 1963), 245.

27. Charge and specification, General Court Martial Orders No. 356, Adjutant General's Office, 5 July 1865, *ORA,* 46, pt. 3, 696–98.

28. David Miller Dewitt, *The Assassination of President Lincoln, and Its Expiation* (1909; reprint, Freeport: Books for Libraries Press, 1970), 280 n; Leech, *Reveille in Washington,* 410.

29. Special Orders No. 211, 216, Adjutant General's Office, 6 and 9 May 1865, roll 8, Trial Papers, RG 158, NA; Searcher, *Farewell to Lincoln,* 191, 285 n; Hanchett, *Lincoln Conspiracies,* 67–68. Bingham was defeated for reelection to the Thirty-eighth Congress and was appointed a major in the judge advocate corps in 1864. Later a solicitor in the court of claims, he was made a special judge advocate for the trial.

30. Roy Z. Chamlee, Jr., *Lincoln's Assassins: A Complete Account of Their Capture, Trial, and Punishment* (Jefferson, N.C.: McFarland and Co., 1990), 225, 368; Dewitt, *Assassination,* 101–4; Leech, *Reveille in Washington,* 411; Brooks, *Washington in Lincoln's Time,* 236–37; diagram of courtroom, T. B. Peterson (comp.?), *The*

Trial of the Assassins and Conspirators at Washington City, D.C., May and June, 1865 (Philadelphia: T. B. Peterson and Bros., 1868), following 112.

31. Trial Papers, roll 8, RG 158, NA. The pamphlet cannot be located. Chamlee, *Lincoln's Assassins,* 247; Dewitt, *Assassination,* 106. Johnson was also a pallbearer representing the Senate for the movement of Lincoln's body from the president's house to the Capitol. Other defense lawyers were not controversial.

32. *The Assassination of President Lincoln and the Trial of the Conspirators,* comp. Benn Pittman, facsimile ed. (1865; reprint, New York: Funk and Wagnalls, 1954), 22; Bernard C. Steiner, *Life of Reverdy Johnson* (New York: Russell and Russell, 1970), 115; Peterson, *Trial of the Assassins,* 22–23; Dewitt, *Assassination,* 106. The exchange may have sealed the fate of Mrs. Surratt (Hanchett, *Lincoln Conspiracies,* 67).

33. *Assassination and Trial,* 21; Trial Papers, roll 8, RG 158, NA.

34. Henry Kyd Douglas, *I Rode with Stonewall, Being Chiefly the War Experiences of the Youngest Member of Jackson's Staff* (Chapel Hill: University of North Carolina Press, 1940), 343; Stern's intro., *Assassination and Trial,* xxix; Leech, *Reveille in Washington,* 414. It is unfair to accuse Hunter of excluding evidence in favor of the defense, as does Ezra J. Wagner in *Generals in Blue: Lives of the Union Commanders* (Baton Rouge: Louisiana State University Press, 1864), 244.

35. General Court Martial Orders No. 356, 5 July 1865, *ORA,* 46, pt. 3, 696–700; Chamlee, *Lincoln's Assassins,* 244, 387, 441; quoting Brooks, *Washington in Lincoln's Time,* 240–41; Thomas Reed Turner, *Beware the People Weeping: Public Opinion and the Assassination of President Lincoln* (Baton Rouge: Louisiana State University Press, 1982), 177; Hanchett, *Lincoln Conspiracies,* 69, 98–99, 112–13; Leech, *Reveille in Washington,* 444; Peterson, *Trial of the Assassins,* 204.

36. Letters, Arnold and Grant to Stanton, July, 13 November 1865, Yates and others to Johnson, 12 July 1866, Letters Received by the Appointment, Commission, and Personal Branch, M1395, RG 94, NA.

37. Steuart's and his father's estates in Baltimore were lost in tax sales during the war (Steuart obituary, *Baltimore Sun,* 23 November 1903); William H. Boyd, *Boyd's Directory of Washington and Georgetown* (Washington, D.C.: William H. Boyd, 1867–69), 327 (1867), 289, (1869).

38. Letters, Hunter to Halpine, 30 June 1865, 6 January 1868, Hunter MSS, Huntington Library. Stockton inherited the family estate, "Morven," at Princeton and much other property (Thomas Coates Stockton, *The Stockton Family of New Jersey and Other Stocktons* [Washington, D.C.: Carnahan Press, 1911], 129). The Steuarts' trip to Europe may have been to accompany or visit old General Steuart, who relocated there after the war (*Baltimore Sun,* 23 November 1903). Halpine named his sixth child—born on 29 June 1864, the day Hunter's army reached

Charleston on the retreat—Charles William Camac Hunter Halpine. The name Hunter also appears among several generations of Stocktons and Kinzies.

39. Special Orders No. 122, extract Special Orders No. 125, 7 and 13 July, telegram, 9 July 1864, letter, Hunter to Stanton, 4 December 1867, box 876, Consolidated Correspondence Files, 1794–1915, RG 92, Records of the Office of the Quartermaster General, NA.

40. Appointment as brevet major general, 29 September, Hunter's oath of office for brevets, 6 October 1865, Letters Received by the Appointment, Commission, and Personal Branch, M1395; list of officers not recommended, file no. A419 CB 1866, Letters Received by Commission Branch, M698, all RG 94, NA.

41. Francis A. Lord, *They Fought for the Union* (New York: Bonanza Books, 1960), 343. For a concise explanation of the complex brevet matter, see Roger D. Hunt and Jack R. Brown, *Brevet Brigadier Generals in Blue* (Gaithersburg, Md.: Olde Soldier Books, 1990), v–xx.

42. General Orders No. 58, Adjutant General's Office, 6 August 1866, Letters Received by the Appointment, Commission, and Personal Branch, RG 94, NA; Holdup Stevens Hamersly, ed. and comp., *Complete Army Register of the United States: For One Hundred Years (1779-1879)* (Washington: T.H.S. Hamersly, 1880), 193.

43. Orders, Adjutant General's Office, 9 August 1866, Letters Received by the Appointment, Commission, and Personal Branch, RG 94, NA.; Report of the Board of Visitors, United States Military Academy, 19 June 1869, *Report of the Secretary of War,* 1869, House Exec. Doc. No. 1, part 1, 41st Cong., 2d sess., 20 November 1869, 477–94. The board received eight cents a mile for travel expenses and room and board, but no pay.

44. Charles G. Halpine, *Baked Meats of the Funeral* (New York: Carleton, 1866), 332; William Hanchett, *Irish: Charles G. Halpine in Civil War America* (Syracuse: Syracuse University Press, 1970), 1, 128, 158–59. Halpine was breveted brigadier general for "meritorious service during the war," effective 13 March 1865 (Hunt and Brown, *Brevet Brigadier Generals,* 253).

45. Letter, Hayes to William M. Evarts, 1 August 1877, Rutherford B. Hayes Papers, LOC; Cecil D. Eby, Jr., *"Porte Crayon": The Life of David Hunter Strother* (Chapel Hill: University of North Carolina Press, 1960), 196–97. Strother's brevet as brigadier general for "faithful and meritorious service during the war" was effective 23 August 1865. Strother returned from Mexico in 1885 and died at Charles Town, W.Va., in March 1888 (Hunt and Brown, *Brevet Brigadier Generals,* 597).

46. Hunter letter, to "Dear Gen.," 13 April 1870, Military Order of the Loyal

Legion of the United States (Mass.) Collection, U.S. Army Military History Institute, Carlisle Barracks, Pa.

47. *Washington Post, New York Times,* 3 February 1886; *Army and Navy Journal,* 8 February 1886; Adjutant General's Office Letter 591, signed by Asst. Surg. Robert M. O'Reilly, 2 February letters, O'Reilly to adjutant general, 19 March and 29 June 1886, AGO Letters Received, NA.

48. Maria Hunter's Pension Record, Civil War and Later Pension Files, RG 15, Records of the Veterans Administration, NA; Cleveland veto message, 23 June 1886, Letters Received AGO, NA, and *Compilation of Messages,* 10:5031–32.

49. "Maria Hunter," *Congressional Record,* 49th Cong., 1st sess., app., 319–20.

50. U.S. House of Representatives, Committee on Invalid Pensions, *Maria Hunter,* report 3214, 4066, 49th Cong., 1st sess., 13 July 1886, 15 February 1887; U.S. Senate, Committee on Pensions, no title, report 1778, 49th Cong., 1st sess., 2 February 1887; Maria Hunter Pension Record, NA.

51. James B. Ricketts, in *Seventeenth Annual Reunion of the Association of Graduates of the United States Military Academy at West Point, New York* (10 June 1886) (East Saginaw, Mich.: Evening News, 1886), 78.

52. Edward Hamilton Phillips, *The Shenandoah Valley in 1864: An Episode in the History of Warfare,* The Citadel Monograph Series no. 5 (Charleston: The Citadel, 1965), 1–3.

53. Christopher Mark Grimsley, "A Directed Severity: The Evolution of Federal Policy toward Southern Civilians and Property, 1861–1865" (Ph.D. diss., Ohio State University, 1992).

54. William Hanchett, *The Lincoln Murder Conspiracies* (Urbana: University of Illinois Press, 1983), 14. Grimsley ("Directed Severity," 273–74) views Lincoln's Emancipation Proclamation as not surprising, because by then border states were secure, Southern Unionists had been proven ineffectual, and more Northeners considered slavery a worse evil than they had thought before.

55. Skelton, *American Profession of Arms,* 22–25; Gerald F. Linderman, *Embattled Courage: The Experience of Combat in the American Civil War* (New York: Free Press, 1987), 180, 185, 201.

56. Charles Royster, *The Destructive War: William Tecumseh Sherman, Stonewall Jackson, and the Americans* (New York: Alfred A. Knopf, 1991), 352–55; Phillips, *Shenandoah Valley,* 3.

BIBLIOGRAPHY

BOOKS AND ARTICLES

Abel, Annie Heloise. *The American Indian in the Civil War, 1862–1865*. 1919. Reprint. Lincoln: University of Nebraska Press, 1992.

Agnew, Raymond Bradford. *Fort Gibson: Terminal on the Trail of Tears*. Norman: University of Oklahoma Press, 1980.

Andreas, Alfred Theodore. *History of Chicago*. 3 vols. 1884–85. Reprint. New York: Arno Press, 1975.

The Annals of the War Written by Leading Participants North and South. Philadelphia: Times Publishing Company, 1879.

Arrington, Leonard J. *Brigham Young: American Moses*. New York: Alfred E. Knopf, 1985.

Atwater, Caleb. *Remarks Made on a Tour to Prairie du Chien, Thence to Washington, in 1829*. 1831. Reprint. New York: Arno Press, 1975.

Averell, William W. *Ten Years in the Saddle: The Memoir of William Woods Averell*. Ed. Edward K. Ekert and Nicholas J. Amato. San Rafael: Presidio Press, 1978.

Balestier, Joseph N. *The Annals of Chicago*. Chicago: Fergus Publishing Company, 1876.

Bandel, Eugene. *Frontier Life in the Army, 1854–1861*. Glendale, Ill.: Arthur H. Clark Company, 1932.

Barry, Louise. *The Beginnings of the West: Annals of the Kansas Gateway to the American West, 1540–1854*. Topeka: Kansas State Historical Society, 1972.

Basler, Roy P., ed. *The Collected Works of Abraham Lincoln*. 9 vols. New Brunswick: Rutgers University Press, 1953.

Bayard, Samuel John. *A Sketch from the Life of Com[modore]. Robert F. Stockton*. New York: Derby and Jackson, 1856.

Beach, William Harrison. *First New York (Lincoln) Cavalry*. New York: Lincoln Cavalry Association, 1902.

Beers, Henry Putnam. *The Western Military Frontier, 1815–1846.* 1935. Reprint. Philadelphia: Porcupine Press, 1975.

Benton, Colbee Chamberlain. *A Visitor to Chicago in Indian Days: "Journal to the 'Faroff West.'"* Ed. Paul M. Angle and James R. Getz. Chicago: Claxton Club, 1957.

Billington, Ray Allen. *The Far Western Frontier, 1830–1860.* New York: Harper and Row, 1956.

Blackford, Charles M. "The Campaign and Battle of Lynchburg." *Southern Historical Society Papers* 30 (1902): 279–314.

Blue, Frederick J. *Salmon P. Chase: A Life in Politics.* Kent: Kent State University Press, 1987.

Boney, F. N. *John Letcher of Virginia: The Story of Virginia's Civil War Governor.* University: University of Alabama Press, 1965.

Boyd, Willliam H. *Boyd's Directory of Washington and Georgetown.* Washington, D.C.: William H. Boyd, 1865–69, 1887.

Boorstin, Daniel J. *The Americans: The National Experience.* New York: Random House, 1965.

Brice, Marshall Moore. *Conquest of a Valley.* Charlottesville: University of Virginia Press, 1965.

Brooks, Noah. *Washington, D.C., in Lincoln's Time.* Ed. Herbert Mitgang. 1895. Reprint. Athens: University of Georgia Press, 1989.

Browning, Orville Hickman. *The Diary of Orville H. Browning.* 2 vols. Springfield: Trustees of the Illinois State Historical Library, 1925–33.

Buley, R. Carlyle. *The Old Northwest: Pioneer Period, 1815–1840.* 2 vols. 1950. Reprint. Bloomington: Indiana University Press, 1962.

Burton, E. Milby. *The Siege of Charleston, 1861–1865.* Columbia: University of South Carolina Press, 1970.

Carse, Robert. *Department of the South, Hilton Head in the Civil War.* Columbia: University of South Carolina Press, 1961.

Castel, Albert. *A Frontier State at War: Kansas, 1861–1865.* 1958. Reprint. Westport, Conn.: Greenwood Press, 1979.

Catlin, George. *Letters and Notes on the North American Indians.* Ed. Michael MacDonald Mooney. 1841. Reprint. New York: Clarkson N. Potter, 1975.

Catton, Bruce. *Grant Takes Command.* Boston: Little, Brown and Company, 1968.

Chamlee, Roy Z. *Lincoln's Assassins: A Complete Account of Their Capture, Trial, and Punishment.* Jefferson, N.C.: McFarland and Company, 1990.

Coffman, Edward M. *The Old Army: A Portrait of the Regular Army in Peacetime, 1784–1898.* New York: Oxford University Press, 1986.

Colt, Mararetta Barton. *Defend the Valley: A Shenandoah Family in the Civil War.* New York: Orion Books, 1994.

A Compilation of the Messages and Papers of the Presidents. Vols. 8 and 10. New York: Bureau of National Literature, 1897.

Cooke, Philip St. George. *Scenes and Adventures in the Army.* Philadelphia: Lindsay and Blakison, 1859.

Correspondence, Orders, etc., between Major-General David Hunter, Major-General J. G. Foster, and Brigadier-General Henry M. Naglee, and Others, February and March, 1863. Philadelphia: J. E. Lippincott, 1863.

Couper, William. *One Hundred Years at V.M.I.* 4 vols. Richmond: Garrett and Massie, 1939.

Craighill, Edley. "Lynchburg, Virginia, in the War between the States." *Iron Worker* 24 (Spring 1960): 1–13.

Crogan, George. *Army Life on the Western Frontier: Selections from the Official Reports Made between 1826 and 1845 by Colonel George Croghan.* Norman: University of Oklahoma Press, 1958.

Cronon, William. *Nature's Metropolis: Chicago and the Great West.* New York: W. W. Norton, 1991.

Crook, George. *General George Crook: His Autobiography.* Ed. Martin F. Schmitt. 1946. Reprint. Norman: University of Oklahoma Press, 1986.

Cullum, George W. *Biographical Register of the Officers and Graduates of the U.S. Military Academy from 1802 to 1867.* Vol. 1. New York: James Miller, Publisher, 1879.

Curry, Seymour. *The Story of Old Fort Dearborn.* Chicago: A. C. McClung and Company, 1912.

Dana, Charles A. *Recollections of the Civil War.* Written by Ida M. Tarbell. 1897. Reprint. New York: Collier Books, 1963.

Daniel, John W. "Unveiling of Valentine's Recumbent Figure of Lee at Lexington, Va., June 28th, 1883." *Southern Historical Society Papers* 11 (1883): 337–88.

Davis, William C. *Jefferson Davis: The Man and His Hour.* New York: HarperCollins, 1991.

———. *Battle at Bull Run: A History of the First Major Campaign of the Civil War.* Garden City, N.Y.: Doubleday and Company, 1977.

———. *The Battle of New Market.* Baton Rouge: Louisiana State University Press, 1875.

Dewitt, David Miller. *The Assassination of President Lincoln, and Its Expiation.* 1909. Reprint. Freeport: Books for Libraries Press, 1970.

Donald, David Herbert, ed. *Inside Lincoln's Cabinet: The Civil War Diaries of Salmon P. Chase.* New York: Longmans, Green and Company, 1954.

Douglas, Henry Kyd. *I Rode with Stonewall, Being Chiefly the War Experiences of the Youngest Member of Jackson's Staff.* Chapel Hill: University of North Carolina Press, 1940.

Du Pont, Henry Algerton. *The Campaign of 1864 in the Valley of Virginia and the Expedition to Lynchburg.* New York: National American Society, 1925.

————. *Rear-Admiral Samuel Francis Du Pont, United States Navy: A Biography.* New York: National American Society, 1926.

Dyer, Brainerd. *Zachery Taylor.* New York: Barnes and Noble, 1946.

Early, Jubal A. *A Memoir of the Last Year of the War for Independence in the Confederate States of America.* Lynchburg: Charles W. Button, 1867.

Eby, Cecil D., Jr. "David Hunter: Villain of the Valley. The Sack of the Virginia Military Institute." *Iron Worker* 28 (Spring 1964): 1–9.

————. *"Porte Crayon": The Life of David Hunter Strother.* Chapel Hill: University of North Carolina Press, 1960.

Eisenhower, John S. D. *So Far from God: The U.S. War with Mexico, 1846–1848.* New York: Anchor Books, 1989.

Eisenschiml, Otto. *The Celebrated Case of Fitz John Porter: An American Dreyfus Affair.* Indianapolis: Bobbs-Merrill, 1950.

Fergus' Directory of the City of Chicago, 1839. Comp. Robert Fergus. Chicago: Fergus Publishing Company, 1876.

Ferris, Robert G., ed. *Soldier and Brave: Historic Places Associated with Indian Affairs in the Trans-Mississippi West.* Washington, D.C.: National Park Service, 1971.

Fox, Gustavus Vasa. *Confidential Correspondence of Gustavus V. Fox.* 2 vols. New York: Naval History Society, 1920.

Freeman, Douglas Southall. *Lee's Lieutenants: A Study in Command.* 3 vols. New York: Charles Schribner's Sons, 1944.

————. *R. E. Lee: A Biography.* 4 vols. New York: Charles Schribner's Sons, 1935.

Gardner, Hamilton. "The March of the First Dragoons from Jefferson Barracks to Fort Gibson in 1833–1834." *Chronicles of Oklahoma* 31 (Spring 1953): 22–36.

Garfield, James. *The Wild Life of the Army: Civil War Letters of James Garfield.* Ed. Frederick D. Williams. East Lansing: Michigan State University Press, 1964.

General Register of the United States Navy and Marine Corps. Washington, D.C.: Thomas H. S. Hamersly, 1882.

[Giddings, Luther]. *Sketches of the Campaign in Northern Mexico: In Eighteen Hundred Forty-six and Seven.* New York: G. P. Putnam and Company, 1853.

Grant, Ulysses Simpson. *Memoirs of Ulysses S. Grant.* 2 vols. New York: Charles L. Webster and Company, 1885.

Halpine, Charles Graham [Private Miles O'Reilly]. *Baked Meats of the Funeral.* New York: Carleton, Publisher, 1866.

Hamersly, Holdup Stevens. Ed. and comp. *Complete Army Register of the Unites States: For One Hundred Years (1779-1879).* Washington: Thomas H.S. Hamersly, 1880.

Hanchett, William. *Irish: Charles G. Halpine in Civil War America.* Syracuse: Syracuse University Press, 1970.

———. *The Lincoln Murder Conspiracies.* Urbana: University of Illinois Press, 1983.

Hansen, Marcus Lee. *Old Fort Snelling, 1819–1858.* Iowa City: State Historical Society of Iowa, 1918.

Hay, John. *Lincoln and the Civil War in the Diaries and Letters of John Hay.* 2 vols. 1939. Reprint. Westport, Conn.: Negro Universities Press, 1972.

Hayes, John D., ed. *Samuel Francis Du Pont: A Selection from His Civil War Letters.* 3 vols. Ithaca: Cornell University Press, 1969.

Hayes, Rutherford Birchard. *Diary and Letters.* Ed. Charles Richard Williams. 6 vols. Columbus: Ohio State Archaeological and Historical Society, 1922.

Heitman, Francis B. *Historical Register and Dictionary of the United States Army, from Its Organization, September 29, 1789, to March 2, 1903.* 2 vols. 1903. Reprint. Urbana: University of Illinois Press, 1965.

———. *Historical Register of Officers of the Continental Army during the War of the Revolution, April, 1777, to December, 1783.* Rev. ed. Washington, D.C.: Rare Book Shop Publishing Company, 1914.

Herr, John H., and Edward S. Wallace. *The Story of the U.S. Cavalry, 1775–1942.* Boston: Little, Brown and Company, 1953.

Higginson, Thomas Wentworth. *Army Life in a Black Regiment.* 1870. Reprint. East Lansing: Michigan State University Press, 1960.

Hildreth, James. *Dragoon Campaigns to the Rocky Mountains.* New York: Wiley and Long, 1836.

Hitchcock, Ethan Allen. *Fifty Years in Camp and Field: Diary of Major-General Ethan Allen Hitchcock.* 1909. Reprint. Freeport: Books for Libraries Press, 1971.

Holland, Rupert Sargant, ed. *Letters and Diary of Laura M. Towne Written from the Sea Islands of South Carolina.* 1912. Reprint. New York: Negro Universities Press, 1969.

Hunt, Aurora. *Major General James Henry Carleton, 1814–1873, Western Frontier Dragoon.* Glendale: Arthur H. Clark Company, 1958.

Hunt, Elvid. *History of Fort Leavenworth, 1827–1927.* Leavenworth: United Service Schools Press, 1926.

Hunt, Roger D., and Jack R. Brown. *Brevet Brigadier Generals in Blue.* Gaithersburg, Md.: Olde Soldier Books, 1990.

Hunter, David. *Report of the Military Services of Gen. David Hunter during the War of the Rebellion, Made to the War Department, 1873.* 1873. Reprint. New York: Van Nostrand, 1892.

Huntington, Sanuel P. *The Soldier and the State: The Theory and Politics of Civil-Military Relations.* Cambridge: Belknap Press, 1957.

Johnson, Robert Underwood, and Clarence Clough Buel, eds. *Battles and Leaders of the Civil War.* 4 vols. 1887. Reprint. Secaucus, N.J.: Castle, 1989.

Judge, Joseph. *Season of Fire: The Confederate Strike on Washington.* Berryville, Va.: Rockbridge Publishing Company, 1994.

Kimball, William J. "The 'Outrageous Bungling at Piedmont.'" *Civil War Times Illustrated* 5 (January 1967): 40–56.

Kinzie, Juliette. *Wan-Bun: The "Early Day" in the Northwest.* 1856. Reprint. Urbana: University of Illinois Press, 1992.

Laas, Virginia Jeans. *Wartime Washington: The Civil War Letters of Elizabeth Blair Lee.* Urbana: University of Illinois Press, 1991.

Lamon, Ward Hill. *Recollections of Abraham Lincoln, 1847–1865.* Ed. Dorothy Lamon Teillard. Washington, D.C.: By the editor, 1911.

Latrobe, Charles Joseph. *The Rambler in North America.* 2 vols. New York: Harper and Brothers, 1835.

Lavender, David. *Bent's Fort.* Garden City, N.Y.: Doubleday and Company, 1954.

Lee, Henrietta, E. "Mrs. Henrietta E. Lee's Letter to General David Hunter on the Burning of Her House." *Southern Historical Society Papers* 8 (May 1880): 215–16.

Leech, Margaret. *Reveille in Washington, 1860–1865.* New York: Harper and Brothers, 1941.

Lincoln, Abraham. *Abraham Lincoln: Speeches and Writings, 1859–1865: Speeeches, Letters, and Miscellaneous Writings, Presidential Messages, and Proclamations.* New York: Library of America, 1989.

Lincoln, William Sever. *Life with the 34th Massachusetts Infantry in the War of the Rebellion.* Worcester: Press of Noyes, Snow and Company, 1879.

Linderman, Gerald F. *Embattled Courage: The Experience of Combat in the American Civil War.* New York: Free Press, 1987.

Lord, Francis. *They Fought for the Union.* New York: Bonanza Books, 1960.

Longacre, Edward G. "A Profile of Major General Davis Hunter." *Civil War Times Illustrated* 16 (January 1978): 4–9, 36–43.

Lynch, Charles H. *The Civil War Diary, 1862–1865.* Hartford: Privately printed for the author, 1915.

McCausland, John. "The Burning of Chambersburg, Penn." *Southern Historical Society Papers* 31 (1903): 266–70.

MacCorkle, Emmett. "George Washington: Prisoner of War." *Civil War Times Illustrated* 23 (March 1948): 30–35.

McDonald, Cornelia (Peake). *A Diary with Reminiscences of the War and Life in the Shenandoah Valley, 1860–1865.* Nashville: Cullom and Gherther, 1935.

McElroy, John. *The Struggle for Missouri.* Washington, D.C.: National Tribune Company, 1909.

McKim, Randolph Harrison. *A Soldier's Recollections: Leaves from the Diary of a Young Confederate, with an Oration on the Motives and Aims of the Soldiers of the South.* 1910. Reprint. Alexandria, Va.: Time-Life Books, 1984.

Malone, Dumas, ed. *Dictionary of American Biography.* Vols. 1, 7, and 9. New York: Charles Schribner's Sons, 1927.

Matloff, Maurice, ed. *American Military History.* Army Historical Series. Washington, D.C.: Government Printing Office, 1969.

Meneely, A. Howard. *The War Department, 1861: A Study in Mobilization and Administration.* New York: Columbia University Press, 1928.

Merk, Frederick. *History of the Westward Movement.* New York: Alfred A. Knopf, 1978.

The Mexican War and Its Heroes: Being a Complete History of the Mexican War. Philadelphia: Lippincott, Grambo and Company, 1848.

Miers, Earl Schenck. *Lincoln Day by Day: A Chronology.* 3 vols. Washington, D.C.: Lincoln Sesquintennial Commission, 1960.

Miller, Edward A., Jr. *Gullah Statesman: Robert Smalls from Slavery to Congress, 1839–1915.* Columbia: University of South Carolina Press, 1994.

Miller, John C. *Origins of the American Revolution.* Boston: Little, Brown and Company, 1943.

Monaghan, Jay. *Civil War on the Western Border.* New York: Bonanza Books, 1955.

Monroe, Haskill M., Jr., and James T. McIntosh, eds. *The Papers of Jefferson Davis.* 8 vols. Baton Rouge: Louisiana State University Press, 1991–95.

Moore, J. Scott. "General Hunter's Raid." *Southern Historical Society Papers* 27 (1899): 179–91. Reprinted from Richmond *Dispatch,* 4 June 1899.

Ness, George T., Jr. *The Regular Army on the Eve of the Civil War.* Baltimore: Toomey Press, 1990.

Nicolay, Helen. *Lincoln's Secretary: A Biography of John G. Nicolay.* New York: Longmans, Green and Company, 1949.

Norris, J. E. *History of the Lower Shenandoah Valley.* 1890. Reprint. Perryville: Virginia Book Company, 1972.

National Cyclopaedia of American Biography. Vol. 12. New York: James T. White and Company, 1904.

Pearson, Elizabeth Ware, ed. *Letters from Port Royal, 1862–1868.* 1906. Reprint. New York: Arno Press, 1969.

Pelzer, Louis. *Henry Dodge.* Iowa City: State Historical Society of Iowa, 1911.

———. *Marches of the Dragoons in the Mississippi Valley between the Years 1833 and 1850.* Iowa City: State Historical Society of Iowa, 1917.

Perrine, Fred S., ed. "Journal of Hugh Evans, Covering the First and Second Campaigns of the United States Dragoon Regiment in 1834 and 1835." *Chronicles of Oklahoma* 3 (September 1925): 175–215.

Peterson, T. B. (comp.?). *The Trial of the Assassins and Conspirators at Washington City, D.C., May and June, 1865, for the Murder of President Abraham Lincoln*. Philadelphia: T. B. Peterson and Brothers, 1868.

Phillips, Edward Hamilton. *The Shenandoah Valley in 1864: An Episode in the History of Warfare*. Citadel Monograph Series. Charleston: The Citadel, 1965.

Pittman, Benn. *The Assassination of President Lincoln, and the Trial of the Conspirators*. Facsimile of 1865 ed. New York: Funk and Wagnalls, 1954.

Pond, George E. *The Shenandoah Valley in 1864*. New York: Charles Schribner's Sons, 1883.

Porter, Charles, H. "Operations of Generals Sigel and Hunter in the Shenandoah Valley, May and June, 1864." *Papers of the Military Historical Society of Massachusetts*, 6:59–82. Boston: By the Society, 1907.

Prucha, Francis Paul. *Broadax and Bayonet: The Role of the United States Army in the Development of the Northwest, 1815–1860*. Madison: State Historical Society of Wisconsin, 1953.

———. *The Sword of the Republic: The United States Army on the Frontier, 1783–1846*. Toronto: Macmillan, 1969.

Quaife, Milo Milton. *Chicago and the Old Northwest, 1767–1835*. Chicago: University of Chicago Press, 1913.

Register of Graduates of the United States Military Academy. West Point: West Point Alumni Foundation, 1970.

Richards, Kent D. *Isaac I. Stevens: Young Man in a Hurry*. Provo, Utah: Brigham Young University Press, 1979.

Roberts, Robert B. *Encyclopedia of Historic Forts: The Military, Pioneer, and Trading Posts of the United States*. New York: Macmillan, 1988.

Rose, Willie Lee Nicols. *Rehearsal for Reconstruction: The Port Royal Experiment*. Indianapolis: Bobbs-Merrill, 1964.

Royster, Charles. *The Destructive War: William Tecumseh Sherman, Stonewall Jackson, and the Americans*. New York: Alfred A. Knopf, 1991.

Salter, William, ed. "Letters of Henry Dodge to Gen. George W. Jones." *Annals of Iowa*, 3d ser., 3 (October 1897): 220–23.

Sandburg, Carl. *Abraham Lincoln: The War Years*. 4 vols. New York: Charles Schribner's Sons, 1939.

Schenck, Robert C. "Major-General David Hunter." *Magazine of American History* 27 (February 1887): 138–52.

Searcher, Victor. *The Farewell to Lincoln*. New York: Abingdon Press, 1965.

———. *Lincoln's Journey to Greatness: A Factual Account of the Twelve-Day Inaugural Trip*. Philadelphia: John C. Winston Company, 1960.

Sears, Stephen W., ed. *The Civil War Papers of George B. McClellan: Selected Correspondence, 1860–1865*. New York: Ticknor and Fields, 1989.

Showell, Margaret Letcher. "Ex–Governor Letcher's Home." *Southern Historical Society Papers* 18 (1890): 393–97. From *Baltimore Sun,* 11 July 1890.

Simpson, Brooks D. *Let Us Have Peace: Ulysses S. Grant and the Politics of War and Reconstruction, 1861–1868.* Chapel Hill: University of North Carolina Press, 1991.

Steiner, Bernard C. *Life of Reverdy Johnson.* New York: Russell and Russell, 1970.

Setchell, George Cass. "A Sergeant's View of the Battle of Piedmont." *Civil War Times Illustrated* 2 (May 1963): 42–47.

Seventeenth Annual Reunion of the Association of Graduates of the United States Military Academy at West Point, New York, June 10, 1886. East Saginaw, Ill.: Evening News, 1886.

Simon, John Y., ed. *The Papers of Ulysses S. Grant.* 20 vols. Carbondale: Southern Illinois University Press, 1967–95.

Skelton, William B. *An American Profession of Arms: The Army Officers Corps, 1784–1861.* Lawrence: University of Kansas Press, 1992.

Smith, Theodore Clarke. *The Life and Letters of James Abram Garfield.* 2 vols. New Haven: Yale University Press, 1925.

Stark, William B. "The Great Skedaddle." *Atlantic Monthly* 162 (July 1938): 86–94.

Stephenson, Wendall Holmes. *The Political Career of James H. Lane.* Vol. 3 of Publications of the Kansas State Historical Association. Topeka: Kansas State Printing Plant, 1930.

Stevens, Hazard. *The Life of Isaac Ingalls Stevens, by His Son.* 2 vols. Boston: Houghton, Mifflin and Company, 1900.

Stockton, Thomas Coates. *The Stockton Family of New Jersey and Other Stocktons.* Washington, D.C.: Carnahan Press, 1911.

Stoddard, William Osborn. *Lincoln's Third Secretary: The Memoirs of William O. Stoddard.* Ed. William O. Stoddard Jr. New York: Exposition Press, 1955.

Stone, Charles P. "Washington in March and April, 1861." *Magazine of American History* 14 (July 1885): 1–24.

Strother, David Hunter. *A Virginia Yankee in the Civil War: The Diaries of David Hunter Strother.* Ed. Cecil D. Eby Jr. Chapel Hill: University of North Carolina Press, 1961.

Taylor, William Roscoe. *The Life and Letters of John Hay.* 2 vols. Boston: Houghton, Mifflin and Company, 1908.

Thomas, Benjamin P., and Harold M. Hyman. *Stanton: The Life and Times of Lincoln's Secretary of War.* New York: Alfred A. Knopf, 1962.

Thompson, Parker C. *The United States Chaplaincy: From Its European Antecedents to 1791.* Vol 1. Washington, D.C.: Office of the Chief of Chaplains, U.S. Army, 1978.

Townsend, Edward Davis. *Anecdotes of the Civil War in the United States.* New York: D. Appleton and Company, 1884.

Turner, Thomas Reed. *Beware the People Weeping: Public Opinion and the Assassination of President Lincoln.* Baton Rouge: Louisiana State University Press, 1982.

Upton, Emory. *The Military Policy of the United States.* Washington, D.C.: Government Printing Office, 1911.

Van Every, Dale. *The Final Challenge: The American Frontier, 1804–1845.* New York: Mentor Books, 1964.

Villard, Henry. *Memoirs of Henry Villard.* 2 vols. 1902. Reprint. New York: De Capo Press, 1969.

Wakelyn, Jon L. *Biographical Directory of the Confederacy.* Westport, Conn.: Greenwood Press, 1977.

Walker, Gary C. *Yankee Soldiers in Virginia Valleys: Hunter's Raid.* Roanoke, Va.: A&W Enterprises, 1989.

Wainwright, Charles Shields. *A Diary of Battle: The Personal Journals of Colonel Charles S. Wainwright.* Ed. Allen Nevins. New York: Harcourt, Brace and World, 1962.

Warner, Ezra J. *Generals in Blue: Lives of the Union Commanders.* Baton Rouge: Louisiana State University Press, 1964.

———. *Generals in Gray: Lives of the Confederate Commanders.* Baton Rouge: Louisiana State University Press, 1959.

Welles, Gideon. *Diary of Gideon Welles.* Ed. Howard K. Beale. 3 vols. New York: W. W. Norton, 1960.

Wentworth, John. *Early Chicago.* Vols. 7–8 of Fergus' History Series. Chicago: Fergus Publishing Company, 1876.

———. *Early Chicago: Fort Dearborn.* Chicago: Fergus Publishing Company, 1881.

Wert, Jeffery D. *Mosby's Rangers.* New York: Simon and Schuster, 1990.

Westwood, Howard C. "Generals David Hunter and Rufus Saxton and Black Soldiers." *South Carolina Historical Magazine* 86 (1985): 165–81.

Wildes, Thomas Francis. *Record of the One Hundred and Sixteenth Ohio Volunteer Infantry in the War of the Rebellion.* Sandusky: I. F. Mack and Brothers, 1874.

Williams, T. Harry. *Lincoln and the Radicals.* Madison: University of Wisconsin Press, 1941.

Wise, Jennings Cropper. *The Military History of the Virginia Military Institute from 1839 to 1865.* Lynchburg: J. P. Bell Company, 1915.

Wise, John Sergeant. *The End of an Era.* Ed. Curtis Carroll. New York: Thomas Yosloff, 1965.

Younger, Edward, ed. *The Governors of Virginia.* Charlottesville: University Press of Virginia, 1982.

GOVERNMENT PUBLICATIONS

U.S. Congress. *American State Papers, Documents, Legislative and Executive, of the Congress of the United States.* Vols. 5–6. Washington, D.C.: Government Printing Office, 1860.

U.S. House of Representatives. *South Carolina Volunteers.* Executive Document No. 143, 37th Cong., 2d sess., 1962.

U.S. War Department. *Annual Reports of the Secretary of War,* 1822–69, generally published as House or Senate documents.

————. *The War of the Rebellion: A Compilation of the Official Records of the Union and Confederate Armies.* 127 vols. Washington, D.C.: Govenment Printing Office, 1880–1902.

UNPUBLISHED MATERIAL

Gamble, Richard Dalzell. "Garrison Life at Frontier Army Posts, 1830–1860." Ph.D. diss., University of Oklahoma, 1956.

Grimsley, Christopher Mark. "A Directed Severity: The Evolution of Federal Policy towards Southern Civilians and Property, 1861–1865." Ph.D. diss., Ohio State University, 1992.

Hendricks, George Linton. "Union Army Occupation of the Eastern Seaboard, 1861–1865." Ph.D. diss., Columbia University, 1954.

Huntington Library, San Marino, Calif., David Hunter Manuscripts, Charles G. Halpine Pocket Diary.

Princeton University Libraries, Princeton, N.J., General Manuscripts (Misc.), Special Collections.

U.S. Army Military History Institute, Carlisle Barracks, Pa., Misc. Collections; Military Order of the Loyal Legion of the United States, Massachusetts Commandery, Eugene A. Carr Papers.

U.S. Library of Congress, Washington, D.C., Documents Division. Papers of Salmon P. Chase, Rutherford B. Hayes, Abraham Lincoln, Edwin M. Stanton, Lyman Trumbull.

U.S. National Archives, Washington, D.C., Department of War, Record Group 12, Records of the Office of the Quartermaster General, U.S. Army, Consolidated Correspondence Files, 1794–1856.

————. Department of War, RG 93, Revolutionary War Records, 1775–83: Compiled Service Records of Soldiers Who Served in the American Army during the Revolutionary War.

————. Department of War, RG 94, Records of the Office of the Adjutant General, 1780–1917: Letters Received by the Office of the Adjutant General,1812–88; Compiled Service Records of Volunteer Soldiers Who Served during the Civil War; Generals' Papers; U.S. Army Generals' Reports of Civil War Service, 1864–87; Letters Received by the Appointment, Commission, and Personal Branch; Letters Received by the Commission Branch, 1863–70; The Negro in the Military Service of the United States, 1609–1889; Post Returns of Troops from United States Military Posts, 1800–1916, Forts Armstrong, Brady, Crawford, Dearborn, Gibson, Howard, Leavenworth, Smith, and Winnebago and Jefferson Barracks; Returns for Regular Army Cavalry Regiments, 1833–1916, Regiment of Dragoons, and for Regular Army Infantry Regiments, 5th U.S. Infantry Regiment, June 1821–1 December 1916; United States Military Academy Application Papers, 1805–66; Consolidated Weekly Grade Reports, 1819–23; Merit Rolls, 1818–66; Register of Cadets, 1803–65; and Reports of the Conduct of Cadets, 1820–25.

————. Department of War, RG 99, Records of the Office of the Paymaster General: Letters Received; List of Paymasters' Stations, 1799–1864; Personal History of Paymasters, 1848–89; Press Copies of Letters Sent, 1808–48; Register of Paymasters, U.S. Army, 1815–68.

————. Department of War, RG 109, Records of Confederate Soldiers Who Served During the Civil War.

————. Department of War, RG 153, Records of the Office of the Judge Advocate General: Court-Martial Case Files, 1809–94; Investigation and Trial Papers Relating to the Assassination of President Lincoln; Registers of the Proceedings of the U.S. Army General Courts-Martial, 1809–90.

————. Department of War, RG 159, Records of the Office of the Inspector General, 1814–42: Miscellaneous inspection reports.

————. Department of War, RG 393, Records of U.S. Army Continental Commands: General and Special Orders, Department of the South; Letters Received and Letters Sent, Department of West Virginia; Special Orders, Department of West Virginia.

————. Veterans Administration, RG 15, Civil War and Later Survivor Certificates, Civil War and Later Pension Files.

NEWSPAPERS AND PERIODICALS

American and Commercial Advertiser (Baltimore)

Army and Navy Journal: Gazette of the Regular and Volunteer Forces (Washington, D.C.)

Baltimore American

Baltimore Sun

Charleston Mercury

Congressional Globe

Congressional Record

Daily Intelligencer (Wheeling)

Daily National Intelligencer (Washington, D.C.)

Daily Register (Wheeling)

Harper's Weekly

New South (Port Royal)

New York Times

New York World

Richmond Examiner

Washington Post

Washington Evening Star

Index